Peer-to-Peer Programming on Groove

James Edwards

Addison-Wesley

Boston • San Francisco • New York • Toronto • Montreal
London • Munich • Paris • Madrid
Capetown • Sydney • Tokyo • Singapore • Mexico City

The publisher offers discounts on this book when ordered in quantity for special sales.

For more information, please contact:

Pearson Education Corporate Sales Division
201 W. 103rd Street
Indianapolis, IN 46290
(800) 428-5331
corpsales@pearsoned.com

Visit AW on the Web: www.awl.com/cseng/

ISBN 0-672-32332-x

05 04 03 02 4 3 2 1

First printing, January 2002

Executive Editor
Rochelle J. Kronzek

Development Editor
Tiffany Taylor

Managing Editor
Matt Purcell

Project Editor
Christina Smith

Copy Editor
Cheri Clark

Indexer
Sandra Henselmeier

Proofreader
Plan-It Publishing

Technical Editor
Mark Grecco

Team Coordinator
Pamalee Nelson

Interior Designer
Gary Adair

Cover Designer
Alan Clements

Page Layout
Octal Publishing, Inc.

Contents at a Glance

Foreword **xii**

Introduction **1**

1 Why Peer-to-Peer? **5**

2 What Is Groove? **17**

3 Exploring the Groove Application **35**

4 Understanding Groove Architecture **67**

5 Essential XML **87**

6 Essential OSD **113**

7 Creating a Groove Development Environment **135**

8 Customizing Groove **151**

9 Building a Basic Groove Tool **175**

10 Publishing a Basic Groove Tool **243**

11 Easier Groove: The Tool Creator and Tool Publisher **255**

12 Easier Groove: Modifying the Basic Groove Tool with Tool Creator and Tool Publisher **269**

13 Data Integration and Groove Bots **321**

14 Advanced Topics **345**

15 The Future of Peer-to-Peer **369**

A Groove Template Component Reference **383**

B Glossary **397**

C Complete Trivia Quiz Code **401**

Index **439**

Table of Contents

Introduction 1

1 Why Peer-to-Peer? 5

A Short History 6
Dynamic IP Addresses and NAT 7
Client/Server Applications 8
Peer-to-Peer Versus Client/Server Applications 10
A Tour of the Peer-to-Peer Landscape 12
Distributed Processing 12
Distributed Storage Services 13
Distributed Network Services 14
Decentralized Collaboration 15
Summary 16

2 What Is Groove? 17

In the Beginning. 18
Stealth Mode 19
Ease of Use 19
What It Is 19
Tools 21
Mix, Match, and Customize 30
Example: Great Schools Now, Inc. 30
Example: American Wooden Widgets 32
How to Think 33

3 Exploring the Groove Application 35

Installing Groove 36
Creating an Account 36
About Identities 37
Multiple Devices 38
Creating a Shared Space 40
Adding Tools 42
Deleting a Shared Space 42
Inviting Others 42
Issuing an Invitation 43
Receiving Invitations 45
Shared Space Members 46

Groove Tools 47
Calendar Tool 48
Contact Manager 50
Discussion Tool 52
Files Tool 54
Outline Tool 56
Pictures Tool 58
Notepad Tool 60
Sketchpad Tool 61
Web Browser 63
Summary 65

4 Understanding Groove Architecture 67

The Model-View-Controller Structure 68
The Groove Structure 69
The Shared Space 70
Groove Platform Services 72
Account and Identity Services 72
UI Services 73
Component Services 74
Shared Space Services 75
Dynamics Services 76
Communications Subsystem 77
Storage and XML Services 79
Security Manager 80
Web Services 84
Customer Services Subsystem 85
Summary 85

5 Essential XML 87

XML History 88
Standard Generalized Markup Language (SGML) 88
HTML 89
XML 89
What XML Is 90
An XML Document 90
Prolog 91
DTD 91
Namespaces 102
XML Schema 104
Background 104
Building a Schema 105
Groove's Use of XML 109
Groove Schemas 110
Summary 111

6 **Essential OSD** **113**
The History of OSD 114
Microsoft's OSD Specification 115
Groove's Use of OSD 117
The Groove Manifest 120
Writing an OSD File 121
The Groove Manifest 130
The Model Changes 131
`ComponentURLProviders` 131
Groove Assembly Files 132
Thinking in OSD 132
Summary 134

7 **Creating a Groove Development Environment** **135**
The DevZone 136
The GDK 136
Development Account 137
Supplemental Applications 138
Specialized Groove Tools 138
The Groove Database Navigator Tool 139
The Tool Creator and Groove Tool Publisher Tools 141
Registry Files 141
`EnableScriptDebugging.reg` 141
`EnableCellBorders.reg` 142
`EnableMyTemplates.reg` 142
The Plan 142
Groove Tool Development 143
Tool Template Development 143
Publishing Your Tool 149
Summary 150

8 **Customizing Groove** **151**
Groove Skins 152
Getting Ready 152
Modifying the Images 153
Image Editing 154
Understanding the Changes 154
Changing `TransceiverWindowBackground.jpg` 155
Changing the Look of Buttons 156
Sounds 162
Publishing a Skin 163
Creating the Descriptor File 164
Creating the Injector File 167
Testing Injection 168

The Transceiver Template 169
Summary 173

9 **Building a Basic Groove Tool** 175

Tool Templates 176
View Container Components 177
UI Components 178
Engine Component 179
Glue Code Components 179
Creating a Tool Template Skeleton 180
The `ToolTemplate` Element 180
`ComponentGroup` Elements 181
The Layout 183
The Button 184
The Engine Component 185
The Glue Code 186
The Completed Skeleton 189
`TriviaQuiz1` 192
Creating the Layout 194
The `TitleLabel` Component 195
The `QuestionLabel` Component 196
The `AnswerLabel` Components 196
The `Elapsed Time` Components 197
The `NextQuestionButton` Component 198
The Glue Code 199
The Finished Tool 211
`TriviaQuiz2` 212
The `PropertyList` 213
Setting the Question and Answer Labels 214
Changing Labels 215
Elapsed Time 216
Handling Multiple Guesses 219
The Revised Tool 220
`TriviaQuiz3` 225
Initialization Code 225
The `OnPropertyChanged` Function 227
Synchronizing Screens 229
A Few Tweaks 232
Summary 241

10 **Publishing a Basic Groove Tool** 243

Preparation 244
Writing the Files 245
Creating a Tool Descriptor 245

Creating Your OSD ...246
Creating the .GRV ...251
Testing and Troubleshooting ...253
Summary ...254

11 Easier Groove: The Tool Creator and Tool Publisher 255
Tool Creator ...256
Installation ...256
Tool Creation ...257
Tool Modification ...260
Overlay a Tool ...261
View Source ...261
Tool Publisher ...261
Installation ...262
Preparation ...262
Publishing a Tool ...262
Summary ...267

12 Easier Groove: Modifying the Basic Groove Tool with Tool Creator and Tool Publisher 269
The Welcome Screen ...270
Adding a Layout ...272
Adding a Graphic ...273
Adding a Title Element ...274
Adding Two Buttons ...275
The Add Questions Screen ...275
Adding Components ...279
Adding the `DataViewer` ...281
Viewing the Layout ...287
Changing Screens ...287
Code for Entering Questions ...290
The Play Trivia Screen ...298
Publishing `TriviaQuiz` ...317
Taking It to the Web ...320
Summary ...320

13 Data Integration and Groove Bots 321
Data Integration and Groove ...322
Connectors ...323
Bots ...334
Groove Enterprise Integration Server ...340
Data Integration, Bots, and `TriviaQuiz` ...341
Using a Bot with `TriviaQuiz` ...343
Summary ...343

14 Advanced Topics 345

More About OSD 346
Managing the Component Tree Structure 347
Versioning 350
Major and Minor Versions 351
Roles and Permissions 352
Tool-Level Access Control 353
Adding Help 356
Subforms 362
Using Subforms 366
Summary 368

15 The Future of Peer-to-Peer 369

The Killer App 370
Peer-to-Peer Challenges 370
Potential Growth Areas for Peer-to-Peer 371
Matchmaking 372
Knowledge Portals 372
Supply Chain Coordination 373
Distributing Clinical Information 374
Online Bill Payment 374
Document Management 375
Real-Time Searching 376
Real-Time Collaborative Publishing 376
Personalization 376
The Microsoft/Groove Partnership 377
Features of the Killer App 379
Is There a Killer App? 380

A Groove Template Component Reference 383

`ViewContainer` 384
`HTMLTableLayout` 384
`MultiCellLayout` 385
`XYLayout` 386
`Splitter` 387
`SingleCellViewContainer` 387
`ScriptHost` 388
`GrooveEdit` 388
`GrooveComboBox` 388
`GrooveStatic` 389
`ActiveXWrapper` 389
`GrooveButton` 390
`GrooveImage` 390

Foreword

I remember the first time my brother, Ray, told me about a new concept he had for a software product. It was 1997. We were enjoying a summer family event at my brother's home along Massachusetts' North Shore, when he suggested we take a walk along the beach. As he started to outline the concept of Groove, I recall my initial sense of excitement. It was a feeling very similar to the time in 1987 when Ray initially invited me to join the team that conceived and developed Lotus Notes.

I also recall the initial metaphor Ray used to differentiate his concept of Groove from Lotus Notes. "It's the difference," Ray said, "between a jam session and an orchestra." As a drummer, I immediately grasped the meaning. When a few musicians get together to "jam," the small, tight group naturally coordinates itself, establishing its own tempo and rhythms, improvising outcomes, and tolerating both consonance and dissonance, dynamically building on each other's creations. The outcome is so fluid and effective that rehearsal is indistinguishable from performance. Conversely, when the number of collaborators is large, as in an orchestra, coordination requires a conductor and rigid discipline. And although the music that results is of high quality, the potential creative variance is far less than is possible through the inspired passion of a few individuals.

Groove is software for small groups of individuals to come together to get things done. Because of Ray's insight into the increasingly decentralized nature of today's businesses, Groove is especially effective at facilitating not only intra-company collaboration, but also inter-company coordination with partners, suppliers, and customers. As John Ellis of *Fast Company* magazine wrote recently, "How do you get at the creativity and energy that exist within the people at the edge of every large enterprise? Electrify it. Groove makes it possible to light up the edge."

What I've described so far is Groove the application. Groove also is a rich development platform for creating business applications. It offers developers a new business opportunity—an opportunity to create people-to-people solutions that address the needs of today's highly decentralized businesses. Significantly, it allows developers to utilize their existing skills in JavaScript, VBScript, Visual Basic, Visual C++, and C#. The Groove communications platform is component-based (using the COM specification) and features an XML object store, as well as a rich set of built-in services (security, storage, peer connection, synchronization) that simplify the developer's job. These services make it easier for developers to integrate Groove with the Web and business-process systems they've already built.

For more than a year now, our GDK has been freely available from our Web site (`www.groove.net/developers`). We've been providing training classes at our headquarters in Beverly, Massachusetts, and developers have been scouring the DevZone on our Web site (`www.groove.net/devzone`). But what they've lacked is the product I always gravitate to first when investigating a new technology: a good reference book. Thanks to Sams Publishing and author Jim Edwards, the growing community of Groove developers now has this resource. Jim's book provides readers a solid overview of Groove, and a sample of what's possible with Groove the application, and Groove the platform. This project wouldn't have been completed without the tireless work of our technical editors at Groove Networks. I work very closely with this team, so I know firsthand the sacrifices they made to ensure that Jim's book is complete and accurate. That's actually not as easy as it sounds, because one of the benefits of our highly componentized architecture is that significant updates now arrive in a matter of months, not years.

This made completion of this book a challenge for Jim and our technical review team. But they persevered and always brought a "reader first" approach and attitude to this project.

After you've completed this book, we would love to hear from you. Please send your feedback, ideas, and programming tips to `devzone@groove.net`. We would especially love to see the new tools and applications you create. Groove requires a slightly different mindset from the norm, but after you grasp it, you have the power to deliver a new class of people-to-people applications that will differentiate you from your competitors.

Once again, I would like to thank Sams Publishing and Jim Edwards for believing in the value of Groove. And to all of you who are about to make a commitment of time and energy to Groove, I offer two simple words: Let's jam!

Jack Ozzie
Vice President, Developer Services
Groove Networks

About the Author

Jim Edwards, as a member of the Personal Solutions Group while Groove was under development**,** used a combination of Macromedia Director, Flash, ActiveX, XML, and JavaScript to develop custom applications on Groove's peer-to-peer application platform, and pioneered Macromedia Shockwave and Flash integration into Groove applications. After having spent the past 15 years creating multimedia titles for Millipore, the Federal Aviation Administration, Digital Equipment Corporation, Parametric Technology, and McGraw-Hill, Jim now writes and provides multimedia and programming services for educational software developers.

Acknowledgments

I would especially like to thank Mark Greco at Groove Networks for challenging my thinking. Without his hard work, and the work of those he enlisted, this book would never have been as technically sound.

I would also like to thank Richard Eckel at Groove and Shelley Kronzek at Sams for providing me with the opportunity to write this book.

The very professional editorial support from Tiffany Taylor and Christina Smith made things as easy as possible for me.

Finally, I'd like to thank my wife, Ali, for helping me keep this effort in perspective.

Introduction

The Internet Web site `webopedia.internet.com` defines peer-to-peer architecture as "A type of network in which each workstation has equivalent capabilities and responsibilities. This differs from client/server architectures, in which some computers are dedicated to serving the others." But peer-to-peer is much more than a technology; it represents a radical change in how we will soon use our computers. It is, all at once, a revolution, an evolution, and a revision.

It is a revolution because it turns today's current client/server architecture on its ear. Suddenly, we're all producers of information as well as mere consumers.

Peer-to-peer computing is also a cultural revolution. Peer-to-peer technology will fundamentally change the way small groups work and interact over the Internet. By making it easy to find and download music over the Web, Napster not only has shown how fragile intellectual property rights of digital material are, but has probably affected the business model of the major media players, too.

It is an evolution because the current state of software engineering makes possible distributed processing and storage across personal computers, as well as the first attempts to provide an operating system for the Internet.

It is a revision because, in the early days of the Internet, peer-to-peer is how all computers were interconnected. The rise of the Web, with millions of people surfing, engaging in e-commerce, and downloading streaming video, made client/server architecture a really good idea.

About Groove

Groove is an application that uses the Internet to make direct connections between members of a group. That group can consist of friends, family, co-workers, or any collection of people who want to communicate, solve problems, or work on a common task. Some of the functions of Groove let you talk, chat, send instant messages, draw pictures, share photos and files, play games, and browse the Web with other members of your group. With Groove, you communicate within secure, shared virtual spaces, in real-time, or in different places at different times. In addition, Groove is a platform that allows you to create, deploy, and run your own peer-to-peer applications.

At the time of this writing, Groove runs only on PCs running the Windows operating system. These are the minimum requirements for installing and running Groove:

- A 233MHz Pentium processor or equivalent
- 64MB of RAM
- 40MB of available hard disk storage

- A 56kbps modem (DSL or cable modem preferred)
- Microsoft Internet Explorer 4.0 or greater (IE 5.0 or greater recommended)
- A sound card, speakers, and microphone, for using the voice features

Updated minimum requirements are posted at `www.groove.net/downloads/groove`.

Who Should Read This Book

This book is intended for those who want to develop peer-to-peer applications in Groove. The skills required to develop Groove applications include an understanding of the peer-to-peer paradigm, a working knowledge of eXtensible Markup Language (XML), familiarity with Open Software Description (OSD), and the ability to understand programming in JavaScript. Only the programming skill will be assumed—this book will help the reader develop the remaining skills. Information on these skills will be presented before Groove tool development is presented. The material is slanted toward intermediate programmers and advanced beginners but should be useful for advanced programmers with little prior knowledge of the peer-to-peer space.

How the Book Is Structured

The following 15 chapters give advanced beginner or intermediate programmers all the necessary background needed to understand the peer-to-peer paradigm, the Groove application, Groove architecture, XML, and OSD, as well as the ability to program and deploy an application on the Groove peer-to-peer platform:

- Chapter 1, "Why Peer-to-Peer?" explores the historical roots of peer-to-peer applications and discusses why peer-to-peer will be even more important in the future. Peer-to-peer applications are contrasted with client/server applications, highlighting strengths and weaknesses for various tasks.
- Chapter 2, "What Is Groove?" touches on the history of Groove—why and how it was developed. It describes the product and presents a case study of its use to solve an actual business problem. The chapter concludes showing why Groove is particularly useful to intermediate programmers or advanced beginners wanting to program in the peer-to-peer space.
- Chapter 3, "Exploring the Groove Application," exposes you to the Groove application. Detailed instructions for installing the application from the CD and a tour of Groove features let readers have the opportunity to experience peer-to-peer interaction. You will see and use some Groove tools similar to the ones you will soon be building.

- In Chapter 4, "Understanding Groove Architecture," you learn the concept of a shared space and the function of the Groove transceiver. The underlying services that take care of security, persistence, and dissemination of data are explored so that you'll understand what services Groove provides. Component services are particularly covered so that you'll know how versioning and automatic dissemination of Groove tools—including tools you may build—takes place.
- Chapter 5, "Essential XML," presents the basics of XML as they relate to Groove operation and tool development.
- Chapter 6, "Essential OSD," explores the concept of Open Software Description. OSD provides an XML-based vocabulary for describing software packages and their interdependencies. With OSD, Groove provides the means for extending and updating the Groove application, including tools like the ones you will develop. Writing OSD is an essential step of tool development in Groove.
- Chapter 7, "Creating a Groove Development Environment," assists you in configuring your machines to easily develop Groove tools without affecting their capability to use Groove. You will verify that you have the applications you need to program Groove tools. All necessary applications are either included in system software or freely downloadable from the Net. Next, you'll learn how to reconfigure Groove to be able to safely build tools. Finally, we will walk you through the installation of the Groove Development Kit (GDK) and explore its contents.
- Chapter 8, "Customizing Groove," gives you the opportunity to create your own Groove skin. Creating a skin provides an easy entry into many of the concepts needed to develop Groove tools.
- In Chapter 9, "Building a Basic Groove Tool," a short discussion of the steps and elements needed to develop a Groove tool is followed by a step-by-step tutorial. The tutorial begins the creation of a peer-to-peer trivia game tool, and addresses User Interface (UI), persistence, and dissemination issues. This part requires hand-coding of the XML for both understanding and experience.
- After an exploration of the tool descriptor, OSD, and `.GRV` files, Chapter 10, "Publishing a Basic Groove Tool," is a step-by-step tutorial on publishing the tool created in the preceding chapter.
- Chapter 11, "Easier Groove: The Tool Creator and Tool Publisher," introduces two tools supplied by Groove to make creating and publishing tools easier. You use these tools to finish the trivia game application.
- Chapter 12, "Easier Groove: Modifying the Basic Groove Tool with Tool Creator and Tool Publisher," is a tutorial that uses Tool Creator and Tool Publisher to modify and extend the trivia game tool and to republish it.

- Chapter 13, “Data Integration and Groove Bots,” is a study of data integration in Groove through connectors and Groove bots. Data integration extends the reach of Groove tools by allowing them to connect with external information and applications resources. The chapter also covers some of the features and capabilities of bots and the Groove Enterprise Integration Server.
- Chapter 14, “Advanced Topics,” continues the ongoing discussion of OSD, particularly redirection and directory structure strategies, and introduces some of the advanced features found in Groove. We explore Groove versioning and its implications for writing tools, and then talk about how to add roles and permissions to your tools, and how to provide overview and context help. We finish by talking about subforms and how they can be used.
- In Chapter 15, “The Future of Peer-to-Peer,” we make some guesses about how peer-to-peer applications will develop in the years to come, and examine the opportunities that will arise for peer-to-peer application programmers.

If you’re ready, let’s get started!

Why Peer-to-Peer?

CHAPTER

1

IN THIS CHAPTER

In this chapter, we will explore the historical roots of peer-to-peer applications and discuss why peer-to-peer will be even more important in the future. We will study the differences between peer-to-peer applications and client/server applications, and we will highlight the strengths and weaknesses of each with respect to various tasks.

A Short History

In the late summer of 2000, headlines began to appear in major newspapers about the overloading of college networks. College students were downloading music files from each other using a program called Napster, a program that allowed those files to be transferred over the Internet—not from a server, but between two personal computers.

On May 17, 1999, researchers from the University of California at Berkeley released the SETI@home Project. This effort uses the processing power of thousands of idle personal computers connected to the Internet to analyze small chunks of data from outer space to aid in the Search for Extraterrestrial Intelligence (SETI).

The two programs Napster and SETI@home, and a handful of others, are responsible for today's huge interest in peer-to-peer computing.

These two projects make peer-to-peer seem like a technological revolution, and it is; but the roots of peer-to-peer go back to the very beginnings of networking and, more recently, to the Web. To understand what has changed in today's peer-to-peer landscape, we need to review the history of peer-to-peer and the Internet.

In September 1969, ARPAnet was born as a network of four nodes—UCLA, Stanford Research Institute (SRI), the University of California at Santa Barbara, and the University of Utah at Salt Lake City—using an Interface Message Processor designed by Honeywell.

That first design qualifies as a peer-to-peer network for the following reasons:

- Those early computers were connected to each other with no intervening hierarchy.
- They were assumed to have equal status with each other as both producers and consumers of information.
- They were assumed to have common capabilities.
- Even though TCP/IP protocols would not be developed until 1982, those early computers had permanent network addresses.

For the next 21 years, most computers on ARPAnet and later the Internet were connected peer-to-peer. Then, in 1990, Tim Berners-Lee, of the European Laboratory for Particle Physics (CERN), began using a NeXt computer to write programs for what would become the world's first Web server and for a client machine.

The CERN browsers had text interfaces that were somewhat difficult to use, so Marc Andreesen's work at the University of Illinois' Center for Supercomputer Applications (NCSA) was really exciting. He and others developed the NCSA Mosaic point-and-click graphical browser, and NCSA released free versions for the Macintosh and Windows-based computers. In December 1993, Andreesen left NCSA, and by April 1994, he and SGI founder Jim Clark had established the company that would become Netscape Communications. The combination of Tim Berners-Lee's work and Marc Andreesen's interface caused the Web to explode.

The numbers that demonstrate that explosion are staggering:

- In 1990, the year of the debut of URLs, HTTP, and HTML, there were about 300,000 hosts on the Internet. By 1993, the year of the graphical browser, the number of hosts had grown to 2 million. There were about 600 WWW sites.
- Two years later, there were 6.5 million hosts, and more than 100,000 WWW sites.

The effects of that explosion were that several earlier systems responsible for maintaining addresses and directories on the Internet were severely strained.

Remember that TCP/IP was introduced in 1982. TCP/IP identified each device on the network with a unique identifier. The domain name server (DNS) system, which links human-readable names (for example, `www.groove.net`) with IP addresses, came into being in 1984. The inventors of these systems could not have imagined the need for hundreds of millions of addresses for users, tens of million addresses for hosts, and more than a million addresses for Web sites.

During this time, two trends developed that eased that strain but, at the same time, complicated the Web enormously.

Dynamic IP Addresses and NAT

The first of these trends was the advent of the Internet service provider (ISP). ISPs were permanently connected to the Net and connected others through dial-up accounts. Because dial-ups were by nature transitory connections, a system was developed to provide temporary, dynamic IP addresses. Dynamic IP addresses meant that fewer total addresses would be used, but it also meant that those addresses did not uniquely point to a given device as the older addresses had. On one connection, a user might be at address `109.876.543.21`. On another conncetions, the user's address might be `109.876.543.96`.

The second trend resulted from the need to protect networks from unauthorized access. In January 1993, Paul Francis and Tony Eng published a paper in *Computer Communication Review* that proposed Network Address Translation (NAT). NAT lets one device, usually a router, act as an intermediary between the Internet and the computers on an internal network. NAT means that a single, unique IP address can represent an entire group of computers.

NAT automatically creates a firewall between an internal network and the Internet. NAT allows only connections that originate inside the internal network; therefore, a computer on the internal network can connect with the Internet to browse, and even download, but a computer on an external network cannot connect to one on the internal network. Like dynamic IP addresses, NAT means that many computers attached to the Internet today have no permanent IP addresses. As a result of these trends, peer-to-peer today is quite different from the peer-to-peer of history.

Client/Server Applications

Another factor affecting both the current need for peer-to-peer applications and the complexity of implementing them is the development of client/server applications.

Tim Berners-Lee's first two web programs were a server and a client (in this case, a browser). In those days, it was assumed that desktop computers would always trail their mainframe counterparts in storage and processing power. That assumption argued for a large repository of information residing on a mainframe. The server would provide information piecemeal to numerous less-capable clients. The server would be the publisher and provider of information, and the client would be the consumer.

Today, that technology is pervasive on the Web. Active Server Pages and Java Server Pages are ubiquitous. Many companies are building server applications that solve common business data-intensive tasks, sending the results back to remote, "thin" clients.

Figure 1.1 shows a simple client/server system.

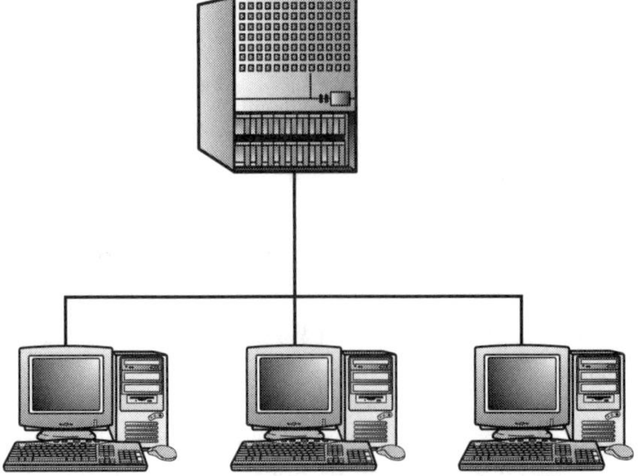

FIGURE 1.1
Client/server architecture.

In a client/server system, one server is connected to one or more client machines. The server usually contains a database and some application software that manipulates the database and presents the results to the client for display. These systems are particularly suited to a "broadcast" model in which many, many clients are presented with essentially the same information.

Peer-to-peer systems are built on entirely different logic and assumptions. Peer-to-peer applications are written with the assumption that, although all computers in the system may not have exactly the same capabilities, they will be both consumers and providers of information. There is no hierarchical structure. In addition, peer-to-peer systems do not assume that the user is always connected. Users might have a dial-up connection, or might choose to work offline while in transit to another geographical area. Peer-to-peer systems have to account for intermittent connections.

Figure 1.2 shows a simple peer-to-peer system.

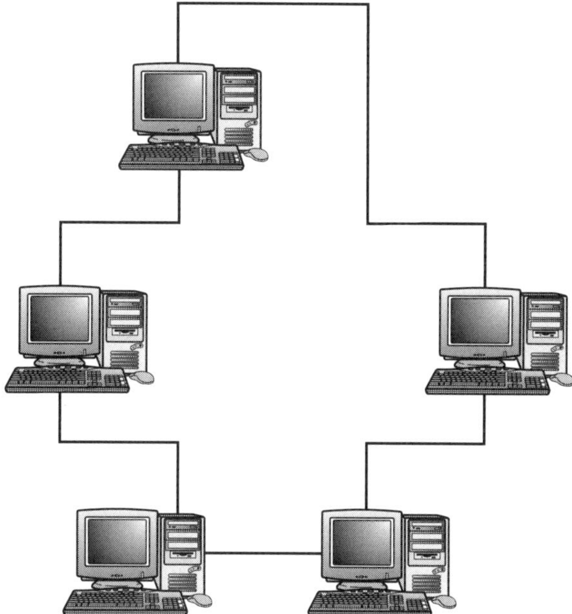

FIGURE 1.2
Peer-to-peer architecture.

Other variations of peer-to-peer architecture include a server. This type of hybrid system is used by Napster to provide directories of the addresses of Napster users and the songs they have available for download. As you will see later, Groove also uses a hybrid system to accommodate offline activity and to provide a directory of users. Figure 1.3 shows a simple hybrid system.

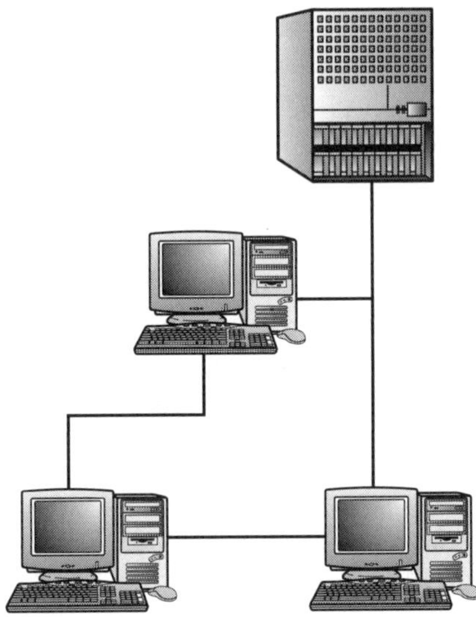

FIGURE 1.3
Hybrid peer-to-peer architecture.

Peer-to-Peer Versus Client/Server Applications

Not only are there technological differences between client/server and peer-to-peer applications, but there are significant differences in how they are used as well:

- Client/server applications tend to be associated with programs that apply rules to recurrent problems—for example, "If the inventory falls below 2,796 widgets, issue a purchase order to American Widget for an additional 3,000."
- Client/server systems are very centralized and usually limit client flexibility and autonomy.
- Client/server systems are susceptible to outages and interruptions of productivity because the failure of a server also causes failure of all the dependent clients.
- Client/server systems primarily use the resources of the server for both storage and processing.

Client/server solutions are particularly good for broadcast-type activities, such as video streaming or Web page serving. They are also a good choice for rule-based systems in which flexibility and autonomy are discouraged.

Conversely, peer-to-peer applications tend to deal with less structured problems—for example, "Find out who has the latest Eminem single, and if I don't already have it, download it":

- Peer-to-peer applications are particularly useful for empowering decentralized, ad hoc groups to deal with exceptions to the rules. You will see this demonstrated later when we look at a hypothetical business use for Groove.
- Peer-to-peer applications are very decentralized. They also tolerate, and even encourage, flexibility and autonomy.
- Peer-to-peer applications tolerate the absence of peers. Productivity does not cease because one member is absent.
- Peer-to-peer systems can be designed to use the resources of the peers for storage and processing. For example, Napster users have access to huge amounts of storage, accessing the hard drives of millions of PCs.

Peer-to-peer systems are particularly good for person-to-person communications, for small group collaborations, for systems that expect intermittent activity, and for tasks without rules, or in which the rules are not well understood.

Peer-to-peer applications also have the potential to access incredible resources for both processing and storage. Clay Shirky, a partner at The Accelerator Group, has estimated that "the world's Net-connected PCs presently host an aggregate ten billion megahertz of processing power and ten thousand terabytes of storage." Read the sidebar "SETI@home" to see how some of these resources are already being used.

SETI@home

SETI stands for the Search for Extraterrestrial Intelligence. David Gedye, along with Craig Kasnoff, conceived the idea for SETI@home in 1996. SETI@home uses a screensaver that can use the Internet to retrieve a chunk of data from the University of California at Berkeley Space Sciences Laboratory over the Internet, analyze that data, and then report the results. When the user needs the computer, the screensaver goes away. The next time it comes on, the screensaver program continues its analysis.

SETI get its raw information from the Arecibo radio telescope in Puerto Rico, which produces 35GB of data per day. That data is sent to Berkeley, where it is divided into 256KB chunks. Extra information describing the chunk is added so that the information sent to a SETI@home PC totals 340KB. This contains about 107 seconds of scan data.

The individual PC acts on the raw data by analyzing specific frequencies. The SETI@home screensaver acts, scanning the frequencies and checking the signal strength. If the signal strength goes up, the information could be significant.

continues

Because the rotation of the earth makes the sources of the signals seem to pan across the telescope, it typically takes about 12 seconds for a target to cross the focus of the antenna, so an extraterrestrial signal should get louder and then softer over a 12-second period.

The program is analyzing various combinations of frequency, Doppler shifting, and pulsing. Because of all the possible combinations and permutations involved, slightly more than 275 billion operations are performed by the "idle" PC on the 107 seconds of data.

The program then begins to look for regularly spaced pulses that vary in power over time. Working its way through the 10KHz range in the data, it looks for three regularly spaced pulses. These are stored to be sent back to Berkeley.

Another test then tries to identify repeating pulses that are too weak to be detected by the method just described. The program checks all of its frequencies for any signals that repeat at any interval. If such signals are found, they are also logged.

Depending on how the telescope was moving when the work unit was recorded, the PC will contribute between 2.4 trillion and 3.8 trillion mathematical operations to the study. This could take between 10 and 50 hours of PC computation time while your PC is "idle."

If you would like to join this exciting peer-to-peer project, point your browser to `http://setiathome.ssl.berkeley.edu/download.html`.

A Tour of the Peer-to-Peer Landscape

Clay Shirky compares the term *peer-to-peer* to the term *horseless carriage*. To a certain extent, peer-to-peer describes what it isn't, and what it isn't is a centralized hierarchical system. It is a distributed system that uses resources at the "edge" of the Internet—that is, in close proximity to the end users. Current development in this distributed system concentrates on four key areas: distributed processing, distributed storage services, distributed network services, and decentralized collaboration. Within this framework we can explore the value that various companies and projects bring to this distributed space.

Distributed Processing

SETI@home is an example of distributed processing. It is the best known because it is one of the oldest, but many other projects are in their beginnings.

Intel Philanthropic Peer-to-Peer Project

The Intel Philanthropic Peer-to-Peer Project, or iPPPP, might well become the world's largest and most important distributed computation project. It will screen 250 million molecules to determine their possible effectiveness as cancer-fighting drugs.

The project represents a partnership among Intel, who has been using peer-to-peer computational models to develop processor designs for more than a decade, United Devices, and Oxford University's Centre for Computational Drug Discovery.

Using a model similar to SETI@home's, iPPPP will use a drug-discovery program called THINK to create three-dimensional computer models of molecules of possible cancer-fighting drugs. After the models are built, THINK will evaluate how each molecule interacts with a target protein. Promising candidates will be logged and archived for further investigation.

United Devices' network operates by breaking down large data objects into smaller ones, shipping these smaller ones off to PCs for processing, and then collecting the processed results to a central server for reassembly.

The partners are hoping to use the spare computing cycles of 6 million Internet-connected PCs to supply the 24 million hours of computational time needed to complete the project.

Other distributed processing companies include Entropia, DataSynapse, and Parabon.

Distributed Storage Services

When you connect to a popular Web site with your browser, a Web cache server at your ISP intercepts the request and determines whether the page you requested is stored (cached) on your machine. If it is, it serves your browser that page, eliminating the congestion and latency associated with downloading the information from a remote or slow Web site. This makes sense for the ISP because the user gets the information faster and the ISP conserves bandwidth, which is more expensive per megabyte than local storage. The concept of trading bandwidth costs for local storage costs is the factor driving distributed storage services.

Distributed storage services refer to an outsourced storage service that distributes data in a geographically meaningful way. These distributed servers are often linked to one another on a peer-to-peer basis.

If an insurance company with many offices worldwide maintained an outsourced distributed storage system, customer records could be pulled as easily from Singapore as from Manhattan, New York, or from Manhattan, Kansas. The company would realize savings in the costs of transmitting the data and in the productivity increases associated with less latency.

Scale Eight

Scale Eight wants to become the world leader of storage services to the Internet. The proliferation of multimedia files on the Internet and complex data objects creates an opportunity to store and deliver this content to end users efficiently and cost-effectively.

Scale Eight wants to solve that problem by coupling a distributed storage network with off-the-shelf storage devices to offer Internet-based storage services at prices considerably less than a custom-built wide area network (WAN) storage solution. By installing a device called a MediaPort in the customer's local area network (LAN), customers can access files from Scale Eight's data centers and can cache frequently requested files locally.

Other players in this sector include Storage Networks, EDS, and Zambeel.

Distributed Network Services

Caching and other distributed storage give rise to the distributed network services sector. These services include load balancing/traffic management systems.

Most Web sites have multiple servers with varying capacities. Load balancers/traffic managers can determine how effectively each of theses servers is being utilized and divert traffic to the underutilized resources. If the load balancer/traffic manager has the capability to determine the source of the request, it can direct the request to the most appropriate server.

This approach does work well for server farms, but it does not address the new realities of distributed storage. Distributed network services work by localizing traffic. If an end user can get the information he or she needs without leaving the LAN, costs are lowered and performance is increased.

One example of a distributed network services company is OpenCola.

OpenCola

OpenCola is working on getting networks to search themselves in order to share data assets more effectively. If an end user is looking for a file on the Internet, for example, OpenCola's product Swarmcast looks to see whether that file is available on the LAN. If it is available on several machines, Swarmcast draws small portions of the file from several of the end user's peers and resplices them into the requested file. Latency is improved because the file is available locally, and transmission costs are reduced because local bandwidth is cheaper than the Internet to local area network connection.

McAfee ASaP

Another example of distributed network services is McAfee ASaP. VirusScan ASaP uses a peer-to-peer distribution model called Rumor. Rumor sends software patches between systems on a network and updates users' computers with protection from the latest viruses. Because updates are managed in the background, users can continue to work on their computers without interruption.

One computer on a network connects with McAfee's Web site and downloads the patches. When a second computer on the network boots up, it retrieves the patches from the first computer and makes the network aware that it also has the patches. Subsequent computers connect to their nearest peer that has the information and also alert the network that they have it. Consequently, the information cascades through the system. Many computers on a network can process an update rapidly with little effect on the resources of any one machine.

CareScience

CareScience's mission is to use peer-to-peer technology to manage and distribute clinical information immediately and securely at the point of care.

With their Care Data Exchange, CareScience provides secure, real-time Internet access to clinical results, patient demographics, medical records, and other critical data from the owner of the original data.

The Care Data Exchange lets individual healthcare organizations continue to store and manage their own data, yet be able make it accessible to authorized users within a designated network.

Using peer-to-peer technology for this solution reduces the cost of data sharing and minimizes concern about data ownership and access privileges.

Napster

Napster caused a huge stir when it became available in late 1999. Napster provides a way to access the millions of .MP3 files music fans have stored on their computers. Napster maintains a database that includes the name, file size, and type of Internet connection of the file's owner. The program then establishes a peer-to-peer connection between your computer and the owner's. When you have finished downloading the file, you are entered into the database as a source for the file.

Other distributed network services companies include Ejacent, 3Path, and ExactOne.

Decentralized Collaboration

Engenia develops an enterprise collaboration tool called Unity. It is a virtual distributed file system that lets users share information in local or remote locations. Users can communicate and interact with customers and suppliers via a Web browser interface. It is also possible to integrate B2B solutions and back-end data services with Unity.

Information in Unity is stored in objects with sets of properties and methods. These objects interact with each other without the need of a centralized administrator.

Other players in this space are Consilient, Ikimbo, NextPage, and, of course, Groove.

The previous cases represent only a sampling of the peer-to-peer activity and applications that are emerging today.

Summary

In this chapter, you have seen how distributed processing, distributed storage, distributed network services, and decentralized collaboration are all coming together to move computing, storage, and collaboration out where it belongs—next to the user.

And we have hardly talked about Groove! In the next chapter, we'll see how Groove fits into the peer-to-peer landscape and take a look at some of the Groove tools.

What Is Groove?

CHAPTER

2

IN THIS CHAPTER

In this chapter, we will look at the history of Groove—why and how it was developed. We will describe the product and present a case study of its ability to solve an actual business problem. The chapter concludes by showing why Groove is particularly useful to intermediate programmers or advanced beginners wanting to program in the peer-to-peer space.

In the Beginning. . .

It is nearly impossible to talk about Groove without talking about Ray Ozzie. His vision, experience, personality, and technical wizardry define not only Groove as a product, but also Groove as a company.

Unlike many of today's high-visibility innovators, Ray Ozzie is a veteran. He worked with Dan Bricklin at VisiCalc. He was intensely involved in the development of Lotus Symphony. In 1984, he convinced CEO Mitch Kapor to fund Iris Associates. Iris Associates developed Lotus Notes. After IBM bought Lotus, Ray stayed long enough at Iris to bring out another version of Notes, but he was already thinking about his lifelong passion.

Ray earned a bachelor's degree in computer science at the University of Illinois Urbana-Champaign in 1979 (the same place Marc Andreesen was when he and others developed the Mosaic browser in 1993). While there, Ray had the opportunity to work on the newly formed education-based network PLATO (Programmed Logic for Automated Teaching Operations) . PLATO let researchers post messages to bulletin boards and type messages to each other on computer screens well before the advent of email and instant messaging.

The significance of what he was watching was not lost on him, and he soon began to speculate how businesses could communicate and collaborate with each other as seamlessly and naturally as possible. The facilitating of small group collaboration has been a significant theme throughout his entire career.

After he left Iris, he wondered what to do next to advance his dream. In the meantime, he wired his house with a computer network connected to a T-1 line. He then watched to see what his children would do with it.

His daughter used instant messaging to keep in constant communication with her friends. His son played Quake. And played Quake. And played Quake.

About the time his son's near obsession with Quake (a multiplayer game networked over the Internet) was threatening family tranquility, Ray noted, "These kids ran their own servers, and self-organized into teams. They talked to each other in real time over speakers. It was so much more effective than the way people in business used PCs."

In October 1997, Ray started Groove Networks to address the needs of business to collaborate in an easy, meaningful, and effective way.

Stealth Mode

For the next three years, Groove operated in "stealth mode." There was no public information on the goal the company was pursuing. Prospective employees were interviewed, screened, and hired without any idea of the nature of the project they would be developing. The majority of the new hires came as a result of employee referrals, and most had worked with Ray in the past.

Ray felt that stealth mode allowed the technical wizards at Groove to solve the formidable technological barriers of his vision without having to account to the public, or even, for the first year, outside investors. And those barriers were formidable. Groove relies heavily on cutting-edge technologies like eXtensible Markup Language (XML), whose working group was established in 1996; Microsoft's Component Object Model (COM), released in 1995; Active Template Library (ATL), released in 1995; and Open Software Description (OSD), whose specification was written three months before Groove was formed. In 1997, these were cutting-edge technologies indeed.

Ease of Use

It is one thing to employ cutting-edge technologies and quite another to make the product so easy to use that the advanced technology is hidden from the user. In this, Groove succeeds admirably. The program is designed from the ground up to be easy to set up, nearly automatic to maintain, and intuitive to use. That's what users found out in October 2000 when Groove finally went public. In April 2001, Groove released version 1.0.

What It Is

On its most basic level, Groove is an application to facilitate collaboration and communication among small groups. Most users will see Groove as an application, but to developers, it is a rich and robust peer-to-peer platform.

A key concept in the Groove paradigm is the *shared space*. A Groove user creates a shared space and then invites other people into it. Each person who responds to an invitation becomes a member of that shared space and is sent a copy that is installed on his or her hard drive. From that moment on, Groove keeps all the copies synchronized via the Internet or network. When any one member makes a change to the space, that change is sent to all copies for update.

The Groove application consists of a top-level controller called a transceiver. The transceiver, through its connections to Groove's underlying services, provides communications, security, and account maintenance, as well as a container for running tools. Groove's transceiver is shown in Figure 2.1.

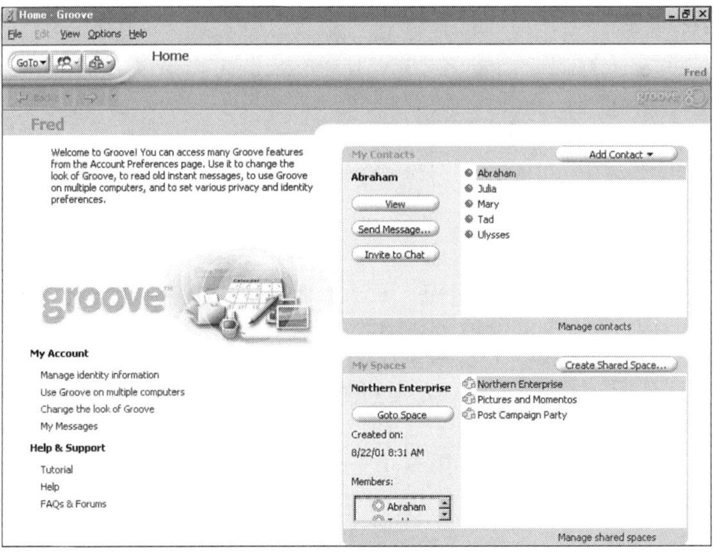

FIGURE 2.1

The Groove transceiver.

You use the transceiver to create and manage your Groove account, maintain a list of contacts, send instant messages or chat with your contacts, and add or access shared spaces. Figure 2.2 shows a typical shared space you might access or create.

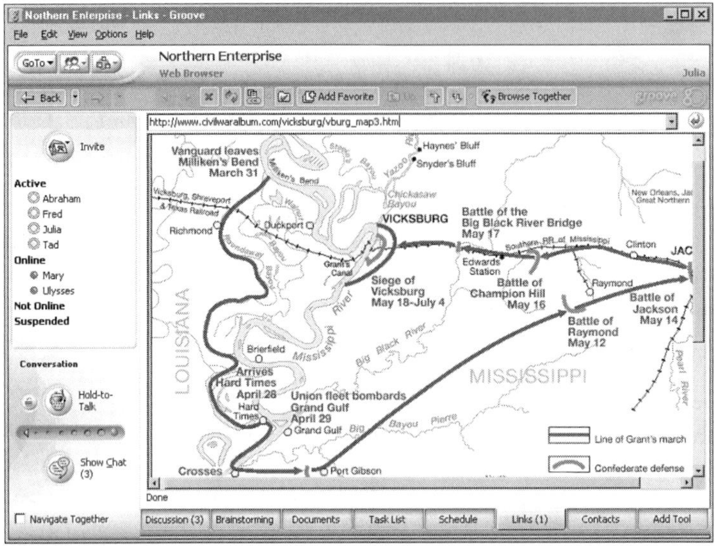

FIGURE 2.2

A strategy space.

Tools

The tabs along the bottom of the screen represent tools. Tools are mini-applications that rely on Groove's underlying functionality to disseminate and synchronize their content with other members' copies of the shared space.

Groove provides many tools that can be used in the shared spaces you create in order to customize the functionality of each space. The current list of provided tools includes the following:

- Groove Calendar Tool
- Groove Discussion Tool
- Groove Files Tool
- Groove Chess Game Tool
- Groove Tic-Tac-Toe Game Tool
- Groove Outliner Tool
- Groove Pictures Tool
- Groove Notepad Tool
- Groove Sketchpad Tool
- Groove Web Browser Tool

The Groove Calendar Tool

You can use the Groove Calendar Tool to remember important dates and to create collaborative schedules. You can assign individual dates and times, or you can select ranges. You can view your calendar in any of five views: day, week, month, business week, and business month. The calendar supports unread marks so that you can quickly scan for events that have been scheduled in your space by others. The Groove Calendar Tool is shown in Figure 2.3.

The regular release of Groove has a feature called roles and permissions that allows the creator of a shared space to assign roles to the people he invites. Invitees can be designated as managers, participants, or guests. Different permissions can be assigned to different roles. In the Preview Edition, the one that comes with this book, roles and permissions are not fully implemented. Basically, everyone is a manager with all manager permissions. Because this feature is significant to the operation of the regular release, roles and permissions will be covered whenever appropriate.

The Groove Development Kit, which you will download later in the book, contains a trial license you can use to temporarily upgrade the Preview Edition.

The Calendar Tool supports roles and permissions, so managers, participants, and guests can have varying degrees of control over the information. The Calendar Tool has permissions for adding, editing, or deleting entries.

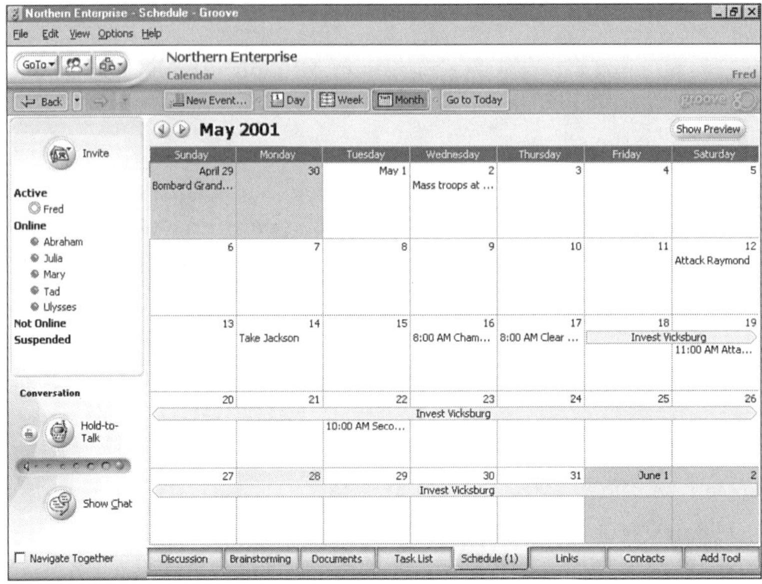

FIGURE 2.3

The Groove Calendar Tool.

The Groove Discussion Tool

The Groove Discussion Tool allows you to maintain a discussion within your space among the members, similar to using a newsgroup over the Internet. You can create and respond to topics to create threads. One of the advantages of using the Discussion Tool is that you can maintain a permanent history of the conversations and discussions. You can also attach files to a discussion topic or response entry, or create links to any of the Groove Tools that support rich text, such as Notepad, Discussion, Outliner, or Chat.

This tool also supports roles and permissions, so managers, participants, and guests may have different capabilities. The Groove Discussion Tool is shown in Figure 2.4.

The Groove Files Tool

You can use the Groove Files Tool to share and store any type of computer file. For some file types, you do not even need the appropriate application program to view them. Groove currently allows you to view Microsoft Word, Excel, and Outlook files. Additional viewers may become available at `www.groove.net/downloads`. Figure 2.5 shows the Groove Files Tool.

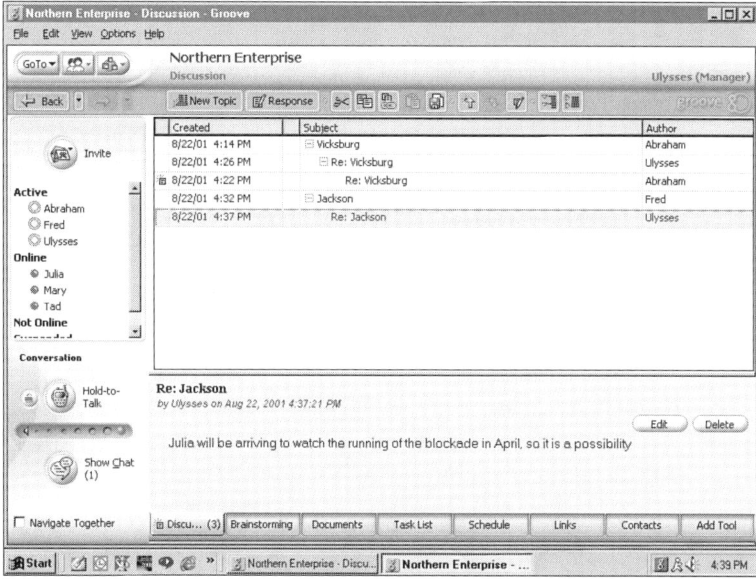

FIGURE 2.4

The Groove Discussion Tool.

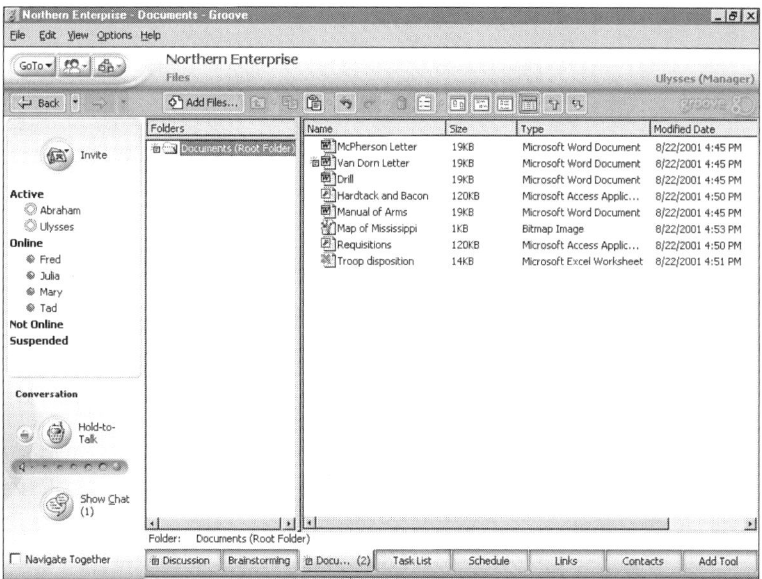

FIGURE 2.5

The Groove Files Tool.

You add files to the tool by using the Add Files button, which opens a file browser, or you can copy-and-paste or drag-and-drop from Windows Explorer.

One of the advantages of having a file-sharing tool is that two or more members can have the file open at the same time and be editing it. When that happens, the member who saves the file first has his or her changes added to the shared file. Subsequent savers get an alert that a file conflict exists and their files are added to the space under a different name, for example, `Current Needs.doc` (Maureen's copy). This should alert participants to use one of Groove's communication tools to resolve the conflict. Again, roles and permissions apply, so some members might not be able to do any editing at all.

The Groove Outliner Tool

The Groove Outliner Tool is a brainstorming tool that lets you and other members of your space quickly add topics to the tool and then organize those topics into coherent hierarchies by promoting or demoting them. Figure 2.6 shows the Groove Outliner Tool.

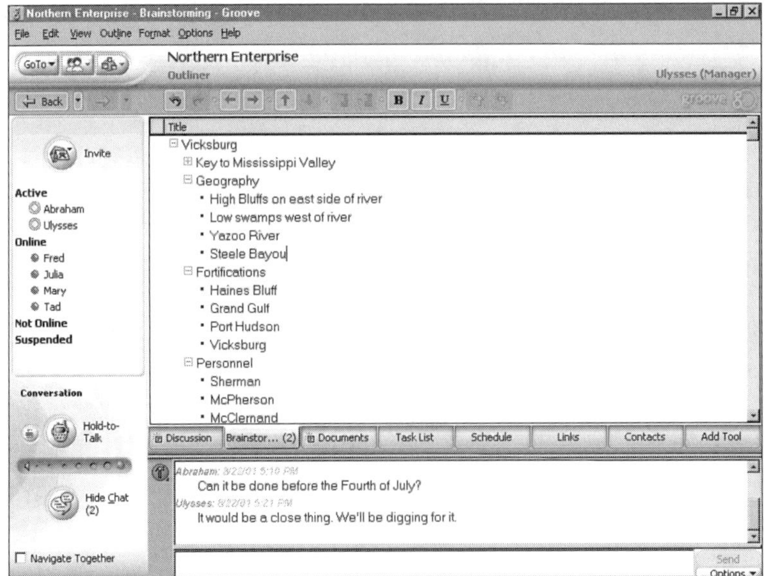

FIGURE 2.6
The Groove Outliner Tool.

You can move entries up or down the list, as well as expand and contract parts of the hierarchy. You can establish links from Outline Tool elements to other outlines, Notepad entries, Discussion Tool topics, or Chat records. Roles and permissions are supported.

The Groove Pictures Tool

The Groove Pictures Tool lets you display pictures and share the picture files in `.BMP` or `.JPG` format. The tool automatically scales all the pictures you add to fit within the current picture viewer window. Figure 2.7 shows the Groove Pictures Tool.

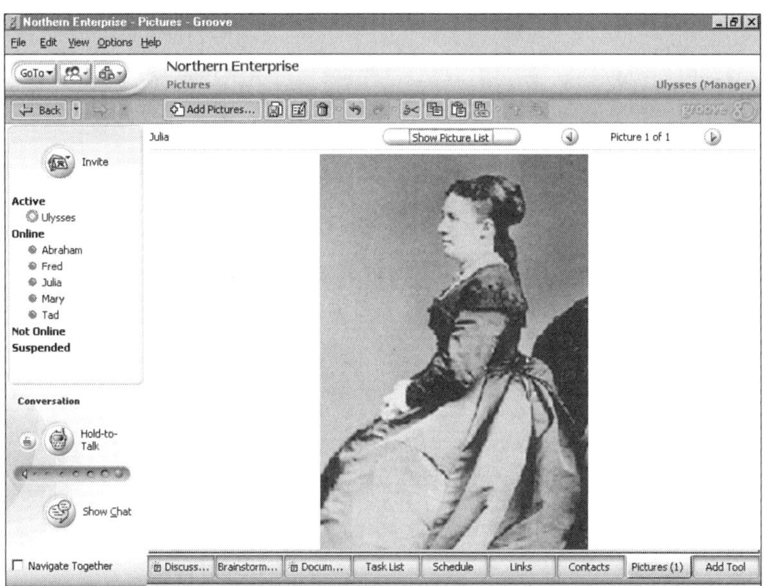

FIGURE 2.7
The Groove Pictures Tool.

The Pictures Tool has a button named Show Picture List. Clicking this button brings up a list of all the picture files you or other members have added to the space.

You can add pictures by opening a file browser from the Add Pictures button, or by copying and pasting into the picture list. You can also drag-and-drop files into the viewing area from Windows Explorer. The picture viewer automatically adds the pictures to the end of the list and updates the picture count on the viewer.

If you have an application that supports editing of `.JPG` or `.BMP` files, you can right-click on one of the pictures and select Open to launch your image editor. After you have edited the picture, you can see the results of your edit by reselecting it in the picture list. Like the other tools, the Groove Pictures Tool supports roles and permissions, and links to other rich-text tools.

The Groove Notepad Tool

The Groove Notepad Tool is a collaborative text editor. With this tool, you and other members of your space can enter, format, and edit text. The Groove Notepad Tool is shown in Figure 2.8.

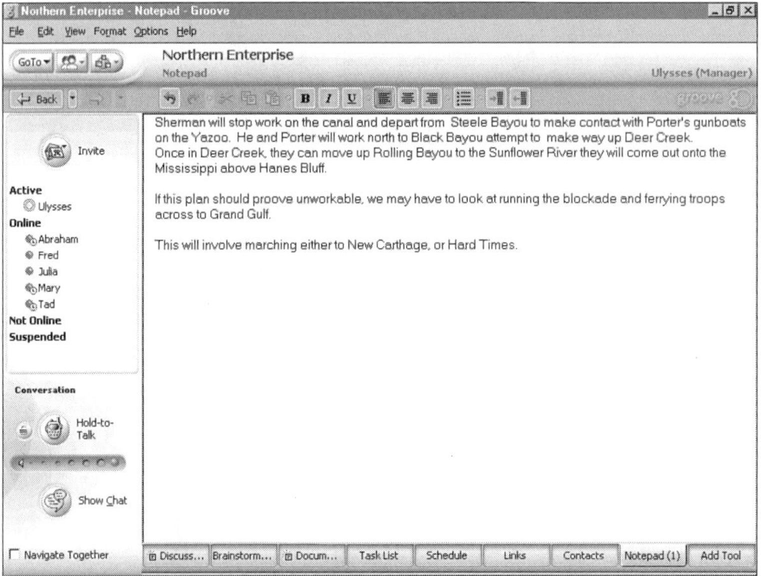

Figure 2.8

The Groove Notepad Tool.

Because this is a collaborative tool, it is possible for two or more members in a shared space to be working on the same document at the same time while connected to the Internet. If the members are offline, the moment they reconnect the document gets updated with their edits. Notepad merges the edits whenever possible. If there are conflicts, Notepad attempts to resolve them. If two members insert a word into the document, both words will be inserted. If both members edit the same word, the most recent edit is retained.

Although it is possible to construct a document with all members at the same time, performance suffers substantially, because every change is being immediately promulgated. Used judiciously, however, the Groove Notepad Tool can be invaluable in producing collaborative documents.

The Notepad Tool recognizes Uniform Resource Locators (URLs) and automatically formats them to links that members can click to open a Web browser to that address.

When you have a good start on the document, you can copy-and-paste it into a word processing program and save it in the Files Tool for future editing.

The Groove Sketchpad Tool

Whoever said “a picture is worth a thousand words” was probably talking about a collaborative environment. The Groove Sketchpad Tool allows you to create those essential “cocktail napkin” drawings.

You can bring a `.jpg` or `.bmp` image into the tool and then draw over it. You can draw freehand, or make drawings from polygons, ovals, circles, straight lines, and regular and rounded-corner rectangles. You can set line color and fill color for your shapes. You can also add text to your drawing.

The best part is that Sketchpad is a collaborative tool. You can say to another member of your space, “Oh yeah, but how about this?” and then circle “this.” Another member can say, “Well, it’s not as good as that!” and draw an arrow to “that.” If you can’t agree, maybe you can find what you both like on the Web.

The Groove Web Browser Tool

The Groove Web Browser Tool lets any of the members of a shared space browse the Web together. It is shown in Figure 2.9.

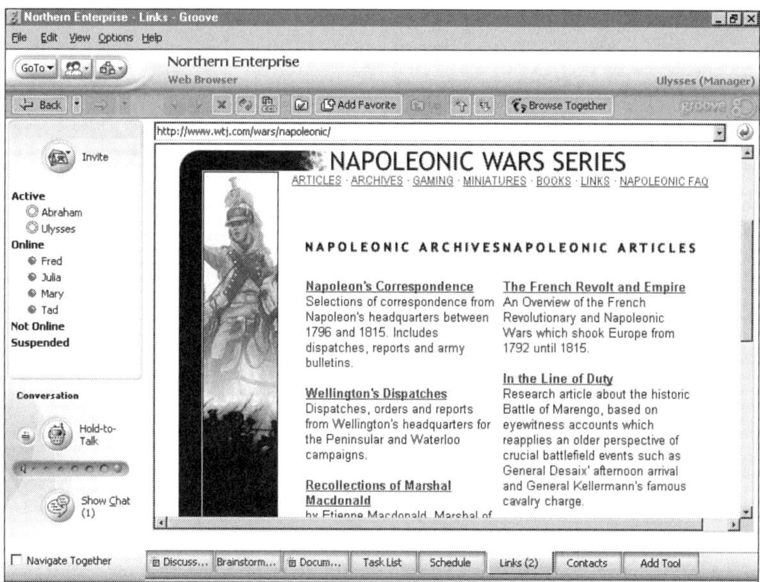

FIGURE 2.9
The Groove Web Browser Tool.

The Groove Web Browser acts just like your default Web browser, except that it can be in a shared space. Because it is in a shared space, you and other members can navigate the Web together by clicking the Browse Together button. If you navigate to `www.groove.net`, every other member's browser will point to Groove's Web site.

There are a few limitations in the Web Browser Tool that recognize its collaborative role:

- If you fill out Web forms in a shared space, the values you enter into the fields will not be shown to other members. You can be assured that when you buy that new Mercedes over the Net, not only will the others not see your debit card number, but they won't be surprised by duplicate deliveries of the car you ordered.
- If you subscribe to a password-protected site, your password will not allow the rest of the members to follow.
- You cannot lead your members to a secure (`hpps:\\`) site.

Instant Messaging, Text Chat, and Audio Chat

In addition to the tools described so far, three other services are always available throughout Groove: Instant Messaging, Text Chat, and Audio Chat.

Instant Messaging

Figure 2.10 shows Groove's Instant Messenger.

FIGURE 2.10
The Groove Instant Messenger.

You can send an instant message to any of your Groove contacts and can attach files, including a voice message or annotation, and URL links.

When you send an instant message, all you have to do is pull down the Select a Contact menu to fill in the To: line. If you haven't established your contact list yet, or the person you want to send the message to does not appear in the pull-down menu, you can click the Recipients button to bring up the Select Recipients dialog box. Select your contact in the dialog to fill in the To: line.

The From: line is filled in for you automatically. Type your message, attach a file, record a message, or include a URL link, and then click Send Message.

You will then receive a series of notifications, depending on the circumstances of the sender and recipient:

- If the sender is offline, the first message will be `Message for (whoever is in the To: line): Waiting to send.`
- If Groove is online, the first notification will be `Message for (whoever is in the To: line): Sending....`
- The next notification will be `Message for (whoever is in the To: line): Sent, waiting for delivery`. This means the message has left your computer and will be delivered immediately if the recipient is online. If a message cannot be delivered, it is forwarded to Groove's relay server, a store-and-forward message queue. The message will be delivered when the recipient next comes online.
- The notification that confirms that the message has reached the recipient's computer is `Message for (whoever is in the To: line): Delivered.`
- And finally, you will be notified when the recipient has opened the message, with `Message for (whoever is in the To: line): Opened.`

Text Chat

There are three ways to use Text Chat in Groove. You can open a chat window in a shared space that is open in the Groove transceiver. Figure 2.11 shows a chat window open in a shared space.

Using chat in this way makes sense if the chat is about tools currently open in the shared space. But sometimes your chat might have nothing to do with what is open in the transceiver. In this case, you can display chat in its own window. The advantage is that you can close or minimize the transceiver window and continue to chat.

A third option is to create a chat space. A chat space is similar to a shared space except that it is dedicated to chat and talk. Sometimes performance is better in a chat space because it avoids the overhead of supporting transceiver tools.

Audio Chat

Audio chat is voice over IP. It is available in all chat modes and is useful if some or all of your members have microphones and speakers attached to their PCs.

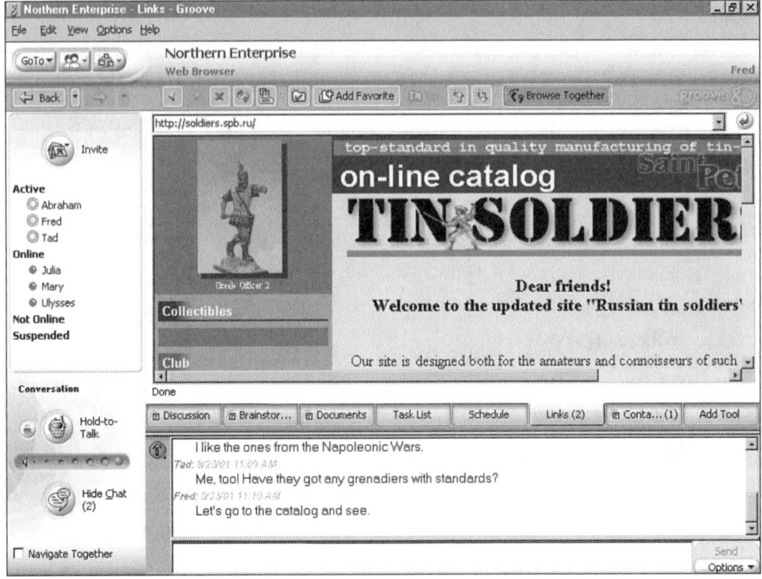

FIGURE 2.11

A chat window open in a shared space.

To talk, you press the Hold-To-Talk button. You will hear a short tone and see the button label turn to Talk. You can then talk until you release the button. When you press the Hold-To-Talk button, a status window appears to all the members in your space that tells who is speaking.

The default mode of talk is one-to-all, but you can conference on talk. Select Conference from the Audio Options menu, and all members who have this option selected can talk simultaneously.

Mix, Match, and Customize

With these tools, messaging, and chat, you can create shared spaces that address many collaborative needs and situations. One situation might need one set of tools; another might need something entirely different. Let's look at a couple of examples.

Example: Great Schools Now, Inc.

The fictitious Great Schools Now, Inc., is an educational consultancy that specializes in turning around public schools that are failing by introducing new curricula, providing teacher training, and improving their technological resources. Servicing the entire United States, they contract with specialists in these three areas to form project teams, and often have as many as 10 members to a team.

The project is sold to the schools, managed and financed by Great Schools Now. Some of the specialists on the team are local to the failing school and visit it frequently, whereas others are geographically remote from both the school and company headquarters. Typically, the project is divided into three phases: the assessment phase, the implementation phase, and the follow-up phase, in which progress is assessed.

Tom Rees is responsible for the company's contract with Brian Bell Elementary School in Frick, Illinois, and he decides to manage the highly collaborative project with an out-of-the-box Groove solution. He first creates a Bell School space and invites all the team members into it. Because several of the team members have never met, he asks them for photographs and places those into the Pictures Tool with their names as captions.

In the Files Tool, he places a Microsoft Word document that provides background on the Bell School, and then a Calendar Tool to schedule the assessment. He meets with each team member in the space, using audio or text chat, and each member enters his or her available dates. Offline, Tom resolves the conflicts in the assessment visit schedule. The next time he goes back online, the new schedule appears in the shared space of all team members.

When one of the team members asks Tom a question, he realizes that other team members might also need his answer, so he adds a Discussion Tool to act as a permanent FAQ database of the project. All the members of the assessment team visit the school and write memoranda of their visits, and those are placed in the Files Tool. Using the Brainstorming Outline Tool, all members cooperatively organize their evaluations into a meaningful hierarchy that can be easily converted into an assessment report for the school.

Some of the problems of the school can be addressed with Web-based learning programs, so Tom adds a Web browser and schedules a group meeting in Groove. Using the Browse Together button, Tom demos these programs to the team members.

The assessment report outline also forms the basis for Tom's Master Calendar, on which he schedules the project's milestones. When the Bell School accepts the assessment and is ready to move forward, Tom follows through on the Master Calendar and manages the entire project through Groove.

As nice as this solution is, it can be improved on through adding custom tools to the space. For instance, most of Great Schools Now's costs come from the hourly rates of its team members. Thus a Groove tool developer could create for Tom a timesheet application that would provide a permanent record of labor costs, and an expense report that would quantify expenses of the team members. Tom could add these tools to his existing space, greatly enhancing the power of his project management suite. After the tools are added, Tom could establish labor and expense targets in the Master Calendar and track the targets against the actual data in his two custom tools.

Because Groove is a platform for peer-to-peer applications, the developer does not have to be concerned about many of the underlying services Groove provides, but can instead concentrate on addressing Tom's needs.

Let's look at another example.

Example: American Wooden Widgets

American Wooden Widgets (AWW) has been making great widgets for 150 years. Its supplier, Continental Widget Materials (CWM), has been in business nearly as long and has established an excellent relationship with AWW.

American Wooden Widgets prides itself on its just-in-time inventory of widget-making materials, just as Continental Widget Materials prides itself on its intensive quality-control system. CWM has been written up in various magazines and is often featured as the company that provides the best quality widget materials in the industry.

Because of its outstanding quality, Continental Widget Materials maintains an extremely low inventory level. But mistakes happen. . ..

Betsy Dowd, quality assurance manager for CWM, gets a call from Jerry Remy, chief widget materials inspector for American Wooden Widget. Jerry explains that about 3% of this morning's shipment have a one-eighth-inch groove around the circumference and are unusable by AWW. He has relayed this information to his boss, Jeff Soames, the VP of operations, who told him that the rejected shipment was needed on the assembly line by 10 a.m. the next day.

Betsy calls her boss, CWM's plant manager, Terry Bunson, and tells him the situation. She also tells him that she has created an out-of-the-box Groove shared space for exactly this kind of emergency.

Into this space Betsy invites CWM's plant manager and Gerry Fritz, the production manager. She also invites American Widget's VP of operations; Brad Shears, AWW's production manager; and Jerry, AWW's chief inspector. They all meet online at 1:30 p.m.

Using the conference mode of audio chat, Terry apologizes to AWW for the problems his company has caused. Materials designed for another widget maker were inadvertently mixed in the shipment. He explains that the purpose of this meeting is to determine the best way to ensure that AWW experiences no downtime on its assembly lines. He asks AWW what time tomorrow they would have to have the replacement widget materials to keep the line from shutting down.

Brad looks at his production control database, looks at the current schedule, and tells everyone that AWW could take a shipment as late as 9:30 a.m. Gerry, Continental Widget Materials' production manager, also pulls up her schedule and confirms what she already knows: The line is producing the widget materials with the one-eighth-inch groove. The machines cannot be reset until the night shift arrives at 4:00 p.m. That will not leave enough production time to meet a full shipment by 9:30 a.m. the next day.

Betsy asks Jerry if he could put a copy of the inspection report in the Files Tool. He does, and she looks at his test results. She can see from the report the rate of defectives, and she suggests to Terry, the plant manager, that between the partial shipment that Gerry can make and the number of good widgets in the current shipment, the deadline could be met.

Terry asks AWW's VP of operations if AWW would allow a team of two packers and a QC inspector to come to AWW's plant and cull the defectives. The results of that operation, plus an emergency shipment of tonight's production, will ensure that AWW's line does not go down. AWW's VP agrees and thanks CWM for their response, and the crisis is averted.

The out-of-the-box solution worked well here, but it too can be improved with custom tools. In Chapter 13, "Data Integration and Groove Bots," you will learn about Groove *bots*. Groove bots are agents that can join shared spaces just like any other participants. One of the jobs they can perform is to access information from enterprise databases and make information available in shared spaces. Brad and Gerry could have used a Groove bot to connect the information they wanted to share to a shared space. All members would then have had access to the two companies' critical production schedules.

The function of Groove is to put the right people together at the right time with the right tools. You will be developing those right tools.

How to Think

When you think about creating your own Groove tools, think about the dynamics of small group interaction—what works and what doesn't.

For example, 10 people can effectively brainstorm about how to make a new kind of cake. They can come up with different ingredients to try, different combinations of ingredients, and novel techniques for baking. Imagine, however, 10 people in the same kitchen baking the same cake.

Writing a novel with 10 authors all working on Chapter 1 at the same time would be a nightmare, but 10 proofreaders each proofing a chapter might not be a bad idea.

Also think about whether the function of your tool is to publish information to a large group of people or to provide information a group needs in order to accomplish a goal. For example, Steven King should publish his latest e-novel on the Web. However, if one chapter were included in a book-study shared space and each of the members was asked to comment on it, the publication of that chapter in the shared space would be meaningful and appropriate.

When you create tools, think about the nature of small-group collaboration. Think about tools that enhance the group members' ability to interact with each other.

Let's install Groove and get started!

Exploring the Groove Application

CHAPTER

3

IN THIS CHAPTER

In this chapter, you will install Groove, establish identities and accounts, and experience peer-to-peer interaction. You will see and use Groove tools similar to the ones you will be building. If you are already a Groove user, you may already know the material in this chapter. Be sure to read the "Grooviness" sections of the tool descriptions, however, before moving on.

Installing Groove

To install and use Groove, your system must meet the following minimum requirements:

- Operating system:
  - Microsoft Windows Millennium Edition, 2000, 98, or NT 4.0 (with Service Pack 3 or later)
- Hardware requirements:
  - Pentium (233MHz or higher) processor
  - 64MB system RAM, with 40MB of available hard disk storage
  - Display resolution 800×600, 15-bit (32,768) color minimum
  - Sound card, speakers, and microphone required to use voice features
- Software requirements:
  - Microsoft Internet Explorer 4.0 or greater (IE 5.0 or greater recommended)
- Internet connection:
  - 56Kbps modem (LAN with Internet access, DSL, or cable modem preferred)

These requirements are subject to change. For the latest, go to `http://www.groove.net`.

If your system meets these minimum requirements, installing Groove could not be easier. Simply insert the CD included with this book into your CD-ROM drive and watch as the Groove installer launches. Respond to the prompts and you're done!

Creating an Account

After the installer launches Groove, you are presented with the Create Account dialog box (see Figure 3.1).

Enter your name and a passphrase. A passphrase can consist of letters and numbers, and for maximum security should consist of 8 to 10 random words. The passphrase is used to keep your account and any shared spaced you create secure. Note that passphrases are not recoverable, so if you were to forget your passphrase, your only option would be to delete your old account and the identities in it and create a new one, losing all your tools and spaces in the old account. You could recover these spaces, however, by asking another member of the space to re-invite you.

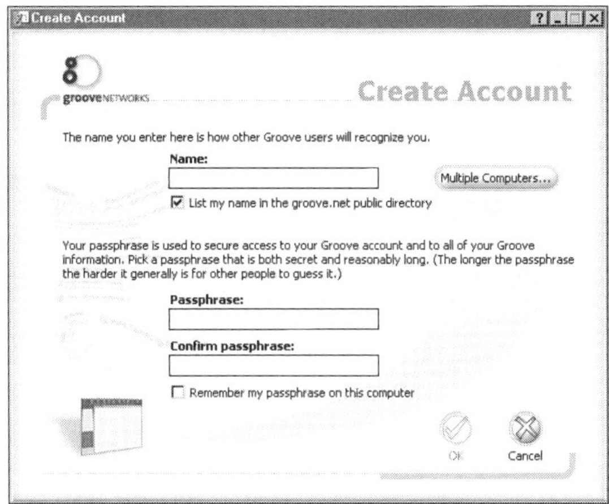

FIGURE 3.1
The Create Account dialog.

A passphrase serves the same purpose as a password except that it is generally much longer and can include punctuation, including spaces. The words in the passphrase should be random, and the longer you make your passphrase (up to 10 random words), the more secure it will be.

Passphrases are local to each device, so if you move your account to another computer, you will have to enter a new passphrase on the new system. If you want, you can check Remember My Passphrase on This Computer, but be aware that anyone with physical access to your computer can also access any of the shared spaces of which you are a member if you have enabled this option.

Accept the option List My Name in the Groove.net Public Directory. Others can then find you and start Groove activities with you.

Your Groove account is a file stored on your computer that holds your Groove identity, the private keys that Groove uses to protect your account, and a master key that is used to protect your shared spaces. It identifies the computer systems on which you run other copies of Groove, and it contains information about the people with whom you communicate.

About Identities

The name you entered in the Create Account dialog box is now your identity, or Groove screen name. A Groove identity uses a pair of cryptographic keys, a private key and a public key, to uniquely identify you, and to make sure that communications between you and other Groove identities are secure. You can also think of it as the name that appears in the shared spaces of which you are a member, and the name under which you are listed on the groove.net directory.

You might have several different identities, and you may use any one of them in shared space. In other words, someone might want to appear as Fred Williams to his professional contacts, as Fred to the members of his golf space, and as Dad in the space he shares with his children. Each of these names corresponds to an identity.

When you have finished creating your account, you can click Manage Identity Information or choose View, Go To, My Account, and then click the Identities tab to see your vCard. If you click the vCard button, you will be able to edit the information that appears on it. You can include as little information as you'd like, but keep in mind that this information will let others know whether they have the right person. For example, if your account identity is Donna M, information in your vCard will separate you from other Donna M's in the directory.

Your identity also includes a digital fingerprint. Groove automatically generates a long random number and character string, and associates it with each of your identities. Others can use this information to authenticate your identity. Let's say that Marjorie calls you on the telephone and tells you that her digital fingerprint is 1bg5-3184:2g3-8081:30b-5166:6g8-3184:4r6. You ask her a question that only she would know, or otherwise confirm her identity. You can click on the digital fingerprint line on her vCard in My Contacts and compare that number against the one she gave you on the telephone. You can then be assured that she is not an imposter. This assurance may be important if the space is used to discuss highly confidential material.

Multiple Devices

If you have more than one computer and want to use Groove on each, you can install the software, then use the same account you previously created on each of the other devices. Your Groove account includes your contact and identity information, and references to any shared spaces of which you are a member. It does not include, however, the shared space itself.

You can copy (or move if you wish) your account information to another computer in one of two ways. The first way is to create a file on a local drive of your computer and copy it to the second computer. Second, you can upload your account information to Groove.net and download it from the second computer.

To save your account to a file, open My Account and then click the Computers tab. Click on the Multiple Computers button, which launches the Multiple Computers Wizard. Figure 3.2 shows the wizard.

Click the Manually, Through a File radio button, and then Next, and you are presented with a standard Save dialog. Save the file to a floppy, or a folder you share with the system on which you want to install your account.

If you follow the Via the Internet branch, you are prompted for your passphrase to secure your account information on `Groove.net` and an email address. Click Next, and Groove uploads your account to `Groove.net` in an encrypted form accessible only by you.

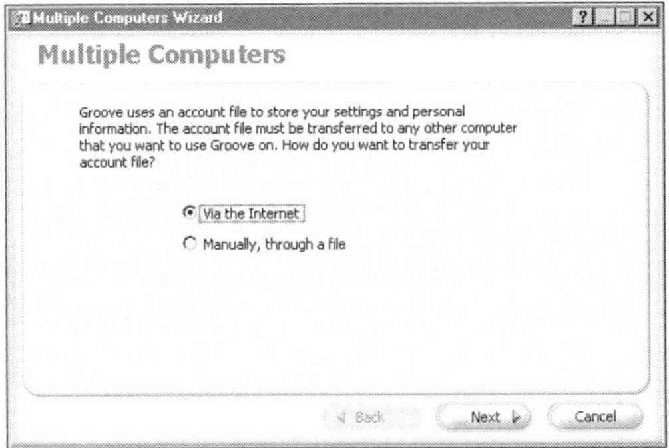

FIGURE 3.2
The Multiple Computers Wizard, launched from the computer without an account established.

To use the account on a second computer, install the Groove software on the new device, and then click the Multiple Computers button of the Create Account dialog, which launches another version of the Multiple Computers Wizard. Figure 3.3 shows the wizard.

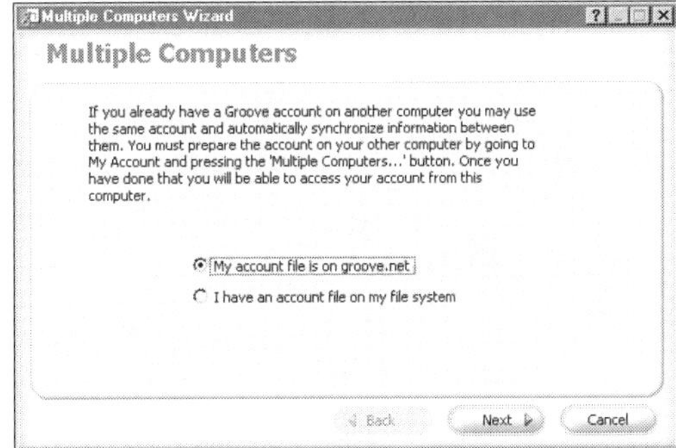

FIGURE 3.3
The Multiple Computers Wizard, launched from the computer with an account established.

If you saved your account information to a file, select I Have an Account File on My File System. You then are prompted to locate the file. Make sure that the floppy or network drive is accessible. When you click Open, your account is loaded into the second computer and you receive notification that it was successful.

If you uploaded your account to `Groove.net`, click the My Account Is on Groove.net option. Enter the account name, passphrase, and email address that you supplied when you uploaded your account, and click OK. When your account has been downloaded, the wizard presents you with instructions on how to fetch any shared spaces to which you belong.

To fetch a space, open your transceiver and select View, Go To, My Spaces in your Groove home page. When the My Spaces window opens, you will see that although your spaces are listed, the status is shown as Not on This Computer. Select a shared space from the list and click Fetch Space.

If you and the computer from which you requested the space are both online and running Groove, Groove fetches the space from the other computer, and the status indicates Fetching. When the download is complete, the status indicates Ready and the shared space is accessible from the second device.

If either of you is not online, or if the remote computer is not running Groove, the status line changes to Fetching, but the download won't begin until the remote user signs on and opens Groove. When that happens, the space downloads and the status changes to Ready.

Those multiple computers will remain synchronized by Groove as long as the two are online in Groove together with reasonable frequency, approximately once every few weeks. If you go beyond that time, Groove will stop updating the dormant machine and will post a synchronization alert.

If you see the alert, you need to delete your account from the unsynchronized computer and re-install the account from the computer with current information following the earlier steps for using the Multiple Computers Wizard.

As you can see, creating an account in Groove has consequences beyond the obvious.

Creating a Shared Space

As you saw in Chapter 2, "What Is Groove?" shared spaces are the essence of the Groove platform. They are the private playgrounds on which you and your peers will meet to use tools and share information. You can text and audio chat, and send instant messages from the base Groove application, but you can't really "groove" without a shared space.

To create a shared space, you can do any of the following:

- From the File menu, select Create Shared Space.
- Open My Spaces, and click the Create Shared Space button.
- Click the Create Shared Space button on the Home page, and select Create Shared Space from the drop-down menu.
- Pick a contact from your contact list that you would like to invite, click Invite to Space, and then click Create Shared Space from the drop-down menu.

For now, let's just go to the File menu and select Create Shared Space to bring up the Create Space Wizard. Figure 3.4 shows this wizard.

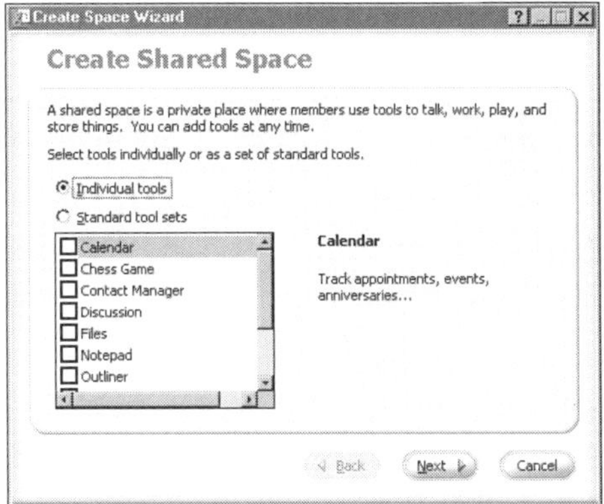

FIGURE 3.4
The Create Space Wizard.

The Create Space Wizard walks you through the steps needed to create a space. The radio button defaults to Individual Tools.

You will see that the Individual Tools radio button is highlighted, but no tools are selected in the check boxes. Checking the boxes will populate your space with each of the tools checked.

If you click the Standard Tool Sets radio button, you will notice that the dialog now lists toolsets. Click on each of the toolsets in the scrolling window to see a synopsis of their use and the individual shared tools they contain.

When you have finished looking, click the No Tools selection, and click Next. Name your space My First Space.

If you have several identities, you can choose the identity you want associated with this space by clicking on the Options button and selecting your identity from the drop-down list. For now, click the Invite No One at This Time radio button and click Next, then Finish.

Groove then creates the space and navigates you to it. In spite of the No Tools option you chose, your new space does have one tool as indicated by the tab—the Add Tool tool. All spaces always have this tool. The "(1)" on the tab shows you that one person in this space is using the Add Tool tool. The panel on the left indicates only one person listed as Active in the space, so the person using the Add Tool tool must be you.

The hammer-and-pencil icons representing the individual tools that can be added are at the top of the list; the toolset icons are at the bottom and are accessible by scrolling down the list.

Adding Tools

Let's add an individual tool to your space, the Sketchpad Tool. Highlight Sketchpad and click Add Selected Tool. The tool is added to the space to the left of the Add Tool tab, and you are navigated to it.

Go ahead and play with the tool for a second, and then add the Notepad Tool, the Discussion Tool, and the Outliner, in that order. You should now have a shared space with five tabs.

Perhaps you don't like that order. Don't worry. You can rearrange the tab order by simply dragging the tabs. Rearrange the tools now to Outliner, Notepad, Discussion, Sketchpad, and Add Tool. Notice that you cannot change the order of the Add Tool tool.

Maybe you think the Sketchpad Tool should be named Whiteboard. It's easy enough to change. Just select the Sketchpad tab, and then pull down the File menu. Find and click Rename Sketchpad Tool. Enter **Whiteboard** and you no longer have to deal with Sketchpad in this space. Notice that the change refers only to this space. Now add a new Sketchpad Tool. The name applies only to the renamed instance of Sketchpad in the space.

You certainly don't need both a Whiteboard Tool and a Sketchpad Tool, so let's delete the sketchpad you just added. Select it, pull down the File menu, and choose Delete Sketchpad Tool. Confirm the operation, and your Sketchpad is gone.

Deleting and renaming options are also available when you right-click the tool tab.

In Groove, as in other rich and complex programs, screen real estate is sometimes at a premium. Groove helps mitigate that problem by allowing you to open a tool in its own window. If you right-click on the Whiteboard Tool and select Open Tool in New Window, you can maximize the Whiteboard Tool. Make a few changes to your drawing and then close the window. You'll see that your changes update in the original window.

Deleting a Shared Space

Now that you're through playing, let's delete this space. Choose File, Delete Shared Space, From This Computer. Confirm the dialog, and you'll see that the space is gone. Or is it?

In this case, it is gone, but only because you did not invite anybody to it. If you had, the space would have been deleted only from your computer, not from those of the people you invited. The other invitees can continue to use the space even without your participation.

Inviting Others

Thanks to the Internet, you can invite anyone in the world to Groove with you, provided that they have an Internet connection and a computer that meets Groove's system requirements.

To create a new space and invite others, choose a toolset from the Add Tool menu and name your space Invitation Space. Check the Invite No One at This Time option.

You can invite others to your new shared space in one of three ways:

- Send an instant invitation on Groove's Instant Messenger, AOL Instant Messenger, ICQ, Yahoo! Messenger, or MSN Messenger Service
- Send an email invitation
- Save a message as a file and make it available to your invitees

Issuing an Invitation

In your new Invitation Space, click the Invite button. Doing so brings up the Groove Send Invitation dialog. The name of the space is already filled in, and the To: line holds a pull-down menu of your current Groove contacts. If your invitee is on the list, you can simply select that person, include a message, and click Invite.

In this case, you have no contacts in your contacts list, so you need to click the Recipients button. The Select Recipients dialog lets you address Groove identities from several different sources: My Contacts, Known Groove Contacts, your Local Network Directory, and the Groove.net Directory. There is also an option for entering an email address. You do not have any Known Groove Contacts. (Known Groove Contacts include people in your Contacts list plus people who are members in your shared spaces.) You'll be looking for invitees in the remaining three categories.

The Local Network Directory lists all Groove users on your local area network (if you belong to one).

The `Groove.net` directory lists all Groove users who have opted to list one or more of their identities in the Groove public Web directory. The `Groove.net` directory is quite large, and some LAN directories can be as well; so Groove provides a capacity for searching for specific names. Type the name you are searching for, click the Search button, and you will get a listing of identities that meet your search criteria. You may be able to find out more information on users if they have filled out their vCards. Even if they haven't, you can click on their vCard and be able to tell whether they are online.

Unless you have a lot of Groove users on your LAN, you will probably opt to invite people by email until you develop a lot of contacts. Select the Enter Email Address option and enter the email address of someone you'd like to invite to your space; then click OK.

You are returned to the Send Invitation dialog and the recipient's email address appears in the To: field. Click the Invite button, and you're prompted to enter your email address. Enter it and click OK.

If you use a mail program that has its own client, such as Outlook Express, Netscape Messenger, or Eudora, and have that client listed as the default mail program for your browser, you can invite people by instant mail as easily as you used Groove Instant Messenger. Simply click the Invite button again, and this time select Invite by Email. Groove fills in the subject line, writes a message stating the reason for the email, and provides a link to a Groove Web page that tells the recipient how to accept the invitation in Groove, as well as how to get Groove if the invitee doesn't have it. It automatically attaches the shared space `.grv` file to the email.

One last feature requires an explanation. Groove has a tremendous focus on security and is expected to be used by businesses, medical personnel, and government agencies that must operate in an absolutely secure environment. For that reason, Groove has a Require Acceptance Confirmation check box on the Enterprise version of the email invitation dialog. If Require Acceptance Confirmation is checked, a different notification and delivery procedure occurs.

When the invitation is accepted, you get a notification that says *(whoever is in the To: line)*: `is accepting an invitation - please confirm`. When you click this notification, a confirmation dialog appears that gives you several options. If you click the From: button, you can see the recipient's vCard. Clicking the digital fingerprint line brings up the digital fingerprint, which you can use to compare with the recipient's digital fingerprint that you received from a different channel. If the fingerprints match and you click Confirm, the shared space is delivered, and you can be absolutely sure that it is being delivered to the right person.

When you click OK, you then receive a series of notifications designed to keep you informed of the progress and outcome of your invitation:

- The first message you see is `Inviting` *(whoever is in the To: line)*: `Waiting to send`. Usually you get this message if the invitee is offline.
- The next message, `Inviting` *(whoever is in the To: line)*: `Sending...`, appears when the invitation is going either to the invitee's computer or to the relay server if the invitee is offline.
- The message `Inviting` *(whoever is in the To: line)*: `Sent` tells you that the invitation is off of your computer.
- When the invitation gets to the other person's computer, you see the message `Inviting` *(whoever is in the To: line)*: `Delivered, waiting for invitee to open.`
- When the invitee opens the invitation and is deciding whether to accept or decline it, you see `Inviting` *(whoever is in the To: line)*: `Opened, waiting for reply...`
- If the invitee accepts the invitation, your notification reads `Inviting` *(whoever is in the To: line)*: `Accepted, waiting to send space.`

- When the shared space is being sent to the invitee's computer, the notification is `Inviting` *`(whoever is in the To: line)`*`: Accepted: Sending shared space, x% complete.`
- `Inviting` *`(whoever is in the To: line)`*`: Waiting for delivery` means that the shared space has been uploaded from the inviter's computer.
- The last message is `Inviting` *`(whoever is in the To: line)`*`: Shared space delivered!`
- Of course, if the invitee declines the invitation, you are notified of that, too, with *`(Whoever is in the To: line)`*`: Declined (no message)`. If there is a message, it explains the decline.

This may seem like a lot of feedback, but waiting for shared spaces to be disseminated is one of the most frustrating parts of the Groove experience. You have created this beautiful shared space and want to use it now! But networks being what they are, and with no guarantee that the invitee is even online, the results are seldom instant, and the notifications certainly keep you informed.

Receiving Invitations

When you receive an invitation, your experience and your notifications are much different.

If you have Groove installed, the first thing you see is a notification in the form `Invitation for` *`(invitee)`* `from` *`(inviter)`* *`(date and time)`*—for example, `Invitation for The Fly from Ima Spider (02/02/02 3:27 p.m.)`. Clicking on this notification brings up the Groove-Respond to Invitation dialog box, giving you the choice to accept or decline. In addition, there is an Info button that, when clicked, displays the inviter's vCard. In addition, there is a space to include a message to the inviter. If you click the Accept button, you receive some or all of the following notifications:

- `Waiting for` *`(shared space)`*`: Waiting to send acceptance`
- `Waiting for` *`(shared space)`*`: Sending acceptance`
- `Waiting for` *`(shared space)`*`: Acceptance set`
- `Downloading` *`(shared space)`*`: x% complete`
- `Installing` *`(shared space)`*
- *`(shared space)`* `ready  (click to open)!`

Receiving an email invitation is similar. You simply double-click the attachment and the same notification sequence begins. After the space has downloaded, you will see the *`(shared space)`* `ready (click to open)!` message. Clicking it launches Groove into the shared space.

If you have been unable to locate someone to send the Invitation Space to, create a new identity in the My Account section and send the space to yourself. It certainly is not as good as grooving with others, but it will give you some of the experience of grooving.

Shared Space Members

The member panel on the left in the Groove window shows a list of the members in your space and provides status information on all of them. Figure 3.5 shows a sample member panel from another space.

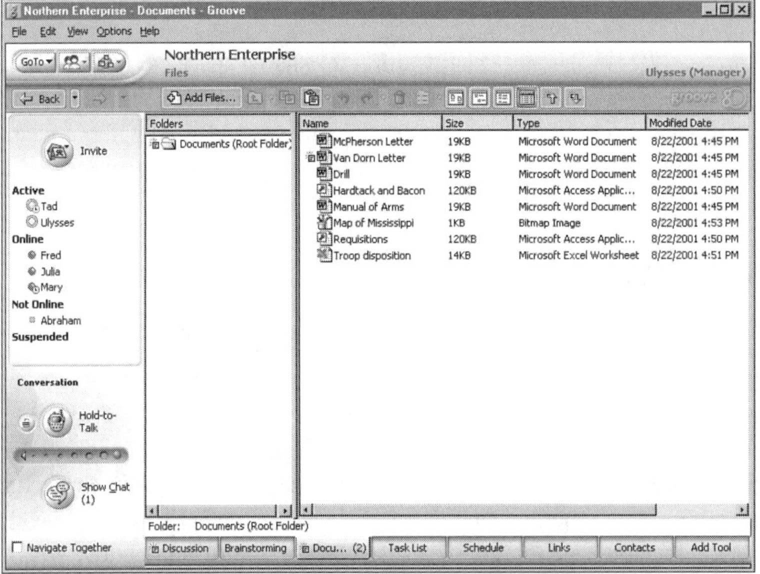

FIGURE 3.5
The member panel.

The larger double circle (yellow and green on your screen) indicates that a member is online and running Groove, and is currently active in Invitation Space. If you hover your mouse over this icon, you see a message that reads `Active in this shared space`. If you hover your mouse over the invitee's name, you see a message similar to this:

```
(Invitee) Role: Manager is viewing the following tool(s): Discussion

Chat.
```

The same icon with an offset clock face indicates a member who is online and running Groove, is in Invitation Space, but has been idle for more than 15 minutes. Hovering over this icon, you see the message similar to `Idle for 1 hour and 22 minutes`.

The smaller icon (solid green on your screen) indicates a member who is online and running Groove but does not currently have this shared space open. Over the icon, the hover message reads `Online, but not in this shared space`. Hovering over the name shows the member's name and role.

The square (gray) box icon indicates a member who is offline. The member may actually be disconnected from the Internet, may have chosen the Work Offline menu selection from the Groove icon in the system tray, or may have unchecked Show Your Online Presence to All Groove Users in Your Shared Spaces in My Account. The member also may not be running Groove.

A suspended member is one whose computer is no longer synchronized to the shared space data due to several weeks of inactivity in the space. The member needs to be re-invited if he or she is to participate in this space again.

You can also see the presence of members in the shared space tool tabs, and from the vCard. If you put your mouse over any tool tab that indicates it has members present, you get a status message that looks like this:

```
Discussion members:
(invitee 1)
(invitee 2)
```


Finally, as you may remember seeing when we were discussing the `Groove.net` directory, a member's vCard (which can be accessed by double-clicking the member's name in the member panel) has a status line that tells whether a member is online. If the member is online, the status line tells the space in which he or she is active.

As with notifications, you will come to appreciate the wealth of information on member presence. When you enter a meeting in a face-to-face collaborative situation, you can easily tell who is there and who isn't. You can tell who is on the same page and who is distracted. Presence information is Groove's way of trying to give you the same feedback.

Groove Tools

In this section we'll take a more in-depth look at the standard Groove tools. As a developer, you will be creating tools and toolsets of your own to solve specific problems. A careful study of these tools will help you develop the peer-to-peer mindset, keep you from reinventing the wheel, and give you an appreciation of what constitutes a "groovy" tool. The first tool you'll look at is the Calendar Tool.

Calendar Tool

Let's go to the Schedule tab of your Invitation space and schedule an event. You may want to hide the overview and hide chat to give yourself more room. Make sure you're in the Month view.

You'll notice that today's date is already highlighted. Now, follow these steps:

1. Click the New Event button at the top of the screen to bring up the New Calendar Event dialog. Notice that you can enter an event by manually editing the date and time entries. You can also add the date by clicking on the calendar icons, and can edit the time with the pull-down menus.
2. Create an event by typing **My First Event** in the Description field and editing the start time to be 8:26 a.m.
3. Go to the Day view. You can see that the Day view is marked off into half-hour blocks, yet the appointment start time clearly shows that the event starts before 8:30, alerting you to the unusual start time.
4. Go back to the Month view and highlight a range of days, right-click, and then select New Event. This brings up the New Calendar Event dialog with the range filled in. Give it a really creative name such as Test Event, leave the All Day Event check box checked, and click OK.
5. Select one of the days in the range, and go to the Day view. The first line below that date alerts you to your all-day event. Use the buttons in the upper-left area to scroll to a day outside the range, and you see the All Day line go away.
6. Edit the details of your event by double-clicking on the event to bring up the Edit Calendar Event dialog. You can also change the date by dragging the event to another day in the Month or Week views. In the Day view, you can drag the event to change the hour.
7. Drag the top margin of the event to change the start time. Drag the bottom margin to change the stop time. Both actions change the duration of the event accordingly. You can also cut and paste events.
8. Highlight the event and press the Delete key. The Delete Calendar Entry dialog comes up for you to confirm the deletion. Right-clicking the event and choosing Delete has the same effect. You can also cut, copy, and paste events.

Both the Month view and the Week view may not provide you with as much information as you would like about a particular event, so the Calendar Tool accommodates you in various ways.

If you hover your mouse over an event in any view, the details of that event appear in a yellow-shaded box. If you are in the Month view and want more information on a particular day's events, you can highlight the day of interest, then either pull down the View menu and choose

Show Preview, or click the Show Preview button. This splits the Month view in the current window and opens a Day pane on the right. You can then interact with the Day view.

In addition to the Day, Week, and Month views, there are two others. Business Week is the same as the weekly view, but allows more space for the business weekdays. Likewise, Business Month provides more space for Monday through Friday events.

Unread Marks

Because the Calendar Tool was designed to be used in a collaborative environment, it supports Unread Marks. An Unread Marker indicates that a calendar entry is either new or changed since you were last in the Calendar Tool. This symbol makes it easy to keep up with changes when many people are using the tool. You can change this status from Unread to Read by reading the entry or by right-clicking the event and choosing Mark Read, or, to change all calendar markers at once, by choosing Mark All Unread from the Edit menu. You can also mark all read in a space from the Home page.

Creating Links

While using some of the other tools in Groove, you might want to refer other members to a particular event in the Calendar Tool. Highlight the event, and then, from the Edit menu, choose Copy Event as Link. Your link can then be pasted into any of the rich-text tools, such as Notebook, Discussion, Outliner, or Chat.

Exporting and Importing

An entire calendar or a single calendar event can be exported as an `.XML` file. Highlight an event to be exported, and choose Export and Selected Event from the File menu. A file browser appears that lets you specify the location of the event's `.XML` file. Choose All Events to export the entire calendar contents.

Importing is equally simple. Choosing Import from the File menu brings up a file browser. Locate the `.XML` file for the calendar or calendar entry and click Open.

The Calendar Tool is rich, robust, and redundant. There are many ways to accomplish every action, and the tool is wonderfully intuitive.

Calendar Tool Grooviness

The Calendar Tool is a good peer-to-peer application because it is an entity that is jointly constructed by the shared space members. It allows all participants in the shared space to see the constraints on each member's time. It defines the timing for any activity that takes place among the participants. The tool supplants the countless emails and telephone calls that would be necessary to accomplish the same objective without the tool. Unlike a server-based scheduler, you can make changes offline and they will be incorporated in all connected members' calendars when you connect.

Each Groove tool has a view, which is a visual representation of the data that the tool contains. That information is arranged within the view through the use of layouts. The Calendar Tool is a great example of the use of multiple layouts to present the same information.

Contact Manager

Groove's Contact Manager manages contacts inside a shared space. It is different from My Contacts, the Contact Manager for the Groove Application. If you have established a shared space named Troubled Teen-aged Boys, you might not want to share your personal contact information for your teen-aged niece.

Although it is both possible and easy to move contact information between My Contacts and a shared space's Contact Manager, My Contacts are never shared with others, whereas the Contact Manager shares contact information with members of a particular shared space. Your Troubled Teen-aged Boys shared space might display a contact for Dr. Brendan Leeds, noted psychologist specializing in adolescence, but Dr. Leeds might not be in your My Contacts at all.

One of the first things you and members of your shared space will want to do is add contacts to your Contact Manager. You can add contacts in one of three ways: by adding a Groove contact, copying and pasting a vCard, or importing a vCard.

Adding a Groove Contact

The first and easiest way to add a contact is to add one of your Groove contacts. If you click the Add Contact button, the Select Contacts dialog box appears.

You have seen this dialog before when you were adding contacts to My Contacts. Select a directory from the Look In: pull-down menu, and then add search text, if necessary. Highlight the contact information you want to add to the shared space, click the Add button, and then click OK. The contact now appears in the contacts pane of the Contact Manager and is shared with all members of your space. Selecting your new contact from the contacts pane displays that contact's vCard.

If you choose the Add Email Contact line from the File menu, you open the New Contact dialog. Enter all the information you want or have into this form, and a display card is created for the new contact.

Copying and Pasting a vCard

The second method involves adding contacts by copying and pasting a vCard. Open the shared space you want to add the contact from, and right-click on the name. Select the Copy option to copy the vCard. Next, open the space you want to add the contact to, and paste.

Importing a vCard

The third way to add a contact is to import a vCard. You might have an email from a contact that includes a `.VCF` vCard file from Microsoft Outlook in the person's mail, or includes it as an attachment. Go to the File menu and select Import to bring up a file browser, select the `.VCF` file, and click Open. The contact appears in your Contact Tool.

Keeping Track of Changing Information

Remember that you or any member of the shared space can add contacts, so, again, Groove provides a way to alert you of changing contact information in the space with Unread Markers. The Edit menu provides the tools you need in order to manage Unread Markers, and the last three icons on the right are tools to scroll the contact list to find Unread Markers. The far-right icon toggles all selected contacts as read or unread.

Managing Contacts

After you have Groove contacts entered into your shared space Contact Tool, you can use the tool to manage many aspects of communication in the shared space.

If you highlight a Groove contact and click the Send Message button, the Groove-Send Message dialog is launched. You can send your contact a Groove Instant Message with either a text message or an audio message and can attach URLs and/or file attachments. If your contact is an email contact, you can right-click on the selected contact to launch the message window of your default mail program. The Invite to Chat button lets you choose one of your identities to initiate a chat with a contact. Invite to Chat is, of course, available only to Groove contacts.

The Invite to Space button brings down a list of the spaces of which you are a member and automatically issues an invitation to that space.

The Add to My Contacts button lets you include in your My Contact database contacts that others add to the space. It's an easy way for you to leverage the useful contacts of the members of your shared spaces.

The More button contains various utilities, some of which we have already covered:

- Send vCard lets you email a vCard to someone not in your space. It brings up the message window of your default mail application and attaches the selected vCard.
- Alias is an interesting feature that allows you to rename one of your contacts for display to distinguish between two people with the same name, or to jog your memory about who they are. You could cause someone to appear in your contact list as Numbskull {Johnny}, or as The Fly Fisherman {Tom Hodges}.

If you are using the regular version of Groove and you were the one who created the space, you will be able to assign permissions to members and uninvited members. If you uninvite a member, Groove revokes the membership and removes the member's name from the Member panel.

Finally, if you are using the regular edition of Groove, you can start a Microsoft NetMeeting conference by selecting the members you want in the conference, going to the Contact menu, choosing the Launch menu item, and selecting Microsoft NetMeeting. Microsoft NetMeeting launches and calls your selected members.

Contact Manager Grooviness

The Contact Manager is a good peer-to-peer tool because it creates a shared resource. All participants now have the information that was previously known to perhaps only one of the members. Because each contact is important to the subject matter of the shared space, the shared space becomes more powerful.

The Contact Manager uses an IGrooveVCardViewer that is constructed in the controlling code of the tool. When you click on the arrow keys, the scripted IGrooveVCardViewer clears all the information in a card layout and replaces it with new information. This approach is different from using multiple layouts, and demonstrates some of the power of the code.

Discussion Tool

The Groove Discussion Tool looks like an Internet message board. Like a message board, the Discussion Tool lets you create a main topic with responses to that topic, and responses to the responses. Because of its hierarchical nature, the Discussion Tool maintains a thread of conversation. Unlike chat, whose conversations tend to be less structured, the Discussion Tool lets you keep a permanent history of the conversations among shared space members.

Using the Discussion Tool

To try this tool, follow these steps:

1. To create a topic in the Discussion Tool, click the New Topic button. In the Subject: line put in some neat text like **Test Subject;** then move your cursor down to the message area and type some supporting text. At the end of the text, type **`www.groove.net`**.

   Notice that the `www.groove.net` is now a live link to the Groove Web site. Clicking the link launches your default Web browser to the linked page.
2. Select one of the words from the supporting text you just entered, and right-click on it. Under the menu items Font and Paragraph, you see enough formatting tools to keep your entries quite beautiful.
3. Save your topic. After your topic has been saved, you can still edit it. Click the Edit button, delete the link to `Groove.net`, and click Save again. This method works for simple word edits, but for more complex tasks you can double-click the topic to open it in a maximized edit window. Here, you can use the Attachment button to bring up a file browser and attach a file to your topic. Save your topic.

4. You use a similar procedure to respond to a topic. Click the Respond button, and you see the maximized edit window with the subject line already filled in. Respond to the topic with some text and click Save.
5. Notice that the response is indented from the topic, clearly showing the hierarchy. Create another response to the topic by highlighting the topic and then clicking the Response button.
6. When you save your second response, you see that it is at the same level as the first. Create a third response, but this time highlight the last response you saved. Save this one, and you find that you have responded to a response, not to the main topic.
7. It is quite easy to create links to this discussion response that can be followed from other Groove tools. Double-click your last response and then click the Copy as Link button. As you do, a link to this response is placed on the Clipboard. This link can be pasted into any of the Groove tools that support rich text: Chat, Discussion, Notepad, and Outliner.
8. Edit the main topic, paste the link (Ctrl+V), and save. Now clicking the link in the main topic brings you directly to the response.

Unlike the Outline Tool we'll cover later, the Discussion Tool does not allow you to move or promote responses. If you respond to the wrong topic, all you can do is copy the body text of the response, create a new response to the right topic, paste the body text, and then delete the incorrectly placed response.

The Topics List and the Body Window

The Discussion Tool has two main windows: the Topics List window and the Body window. Between the two is a splitter. Moving the splitter bar changes the relative sizes of the Topics List and Body windows. Enlarging the Body window makes it easier to read long responses without scrolling.

The Topics List can be sorted on each of the three columns. Click the column to switch the sort order between descending, chronological, and by order of creation (that is, the order in which topics were added to the discussion).

You can expand and collapse the Topics List to show only the topics or to show the topics with their responses, with the two buttons on the far right. You can also hide or show responses for each topic by clicking on the plus or minus signs to the left of the subject.

Unread Markers

The Discussion Tool supports Unread Markers. Of all the Groove tools, Unread Markers are the most valuable here. A discussion can grow quite large in a space with many members, and it can rapidly become difficult to keep up. Unread Markers let you scan only the changes rather than rereading entire discussions.

Exporting and Importing

You can export discussion topics to a file into three different formats: Structured Text, Tabular Text, and XML. Structured Text is a format that includes all the information in the file, even information useful only to Groove. Tabular Text exports a tab-delimited ASCII file that contains only the information contained in the Topics List. Binary XML exports an XML file that Groove can use to re-create a discussion topic in another shared space.

The Binary XML file can be imported into other shared spaces. To import, select the topic under which you want the new topic to appear, and choose Import from the File menu. This opens the Import File dialog box. You can browse to the appropriate .XML file and click Open to place the topic in the current discussion.

Deleting Topics

You can delete a discussion topic by selecting it and clicking Delete. Deleting a topic also deletes all of its associated responses.

In the regular version, in which Roles and Permissions are enforced, your ability to accomplish some of the preceding tasks may be limited or non-existent, depending on your role.

Discussion Tool Grooviness

The Discussion Tool is included in Groove's core tools because it enhances the group's ability to interact. By providing a persistent record of a discussion, and the capability to refer to a specific part of it through links, this tool allows participants in the shared space to remain focused on the shared space's objective. Unlike an Internet Message board, this discussion takes place in a secure environment among invited members.

Groove tools use engines to save the tool's data model and to reflect the changes in remote instances of the shared space. The Discussion Tool is one of the best examples of the use of Groove's Record Set Engine, a Groove-supplied database component widely used throughout Groove to persist and disseminate data.

Files Tool

The Groove Files Tool lets you manage, store, and share any type of computer file with members of a shared space. Of course, the members' ability to open and use the file depends on whether they have an application appropriate to the file type. You will find that the Files Tool is one of the most frequently included tools in your own shared spaces.

In the regular version of Groove, a few file viewers are included so that people without Microsoft Word, for example, can read the file even though they do not have the application.

The regular version also supports Roles and Permissions so that permissions can be applied to different actions in the Files Tool. You might not want everyone in the space to be able to edit or delete the mission statement your members labored over for three weeks.

In the Files Tool, permissions can be set on a per–file-folder basis. In the regular version, you can right-click on a folder and select Permissions to see the actions your role allows you to take within the selected folder.

File Organization

Files in the Files Tool are organized into folders. The default folder for the tool takes its name from the tool tab. For example, if the tool tab is labeled Documents, the default folder is called `Documents (Root Folder)`. You can place files directly into this folder, or you can create a new folder by right-clicking on the files pane and selecting New, then Folder. A new folder will be created that you will be prompted to name. This Windows Explorer–like functionality makes it easy to keep your shared files in each space organized.

You can add files in the Files Tool by selecting the folder in the Folder List and clicking the Add Files button. A file browser opens and you can select the files you want to add. Clicking Open puts the selected files into the selected folder.

You can also add files by copying them in Windows Explorer and pasting them into the appropriate folder of the Files Tool. You can also drag-and-drop from Windows Explorer.

Opening a single file is simple—just double-click it. If you have the required application, it launches. If you don't, the Windows Open With dialog box is shown. If you want to open several files simultaneously, you can select the files, right-click, and select Open. You can also right-click and select Quick View if you have the regular version of Groove.

Working with Files

A right-click and a Print choice cause the application that created the file to launch and print the file. Selecting the files with Shift-click or Ctrl-click prints multiple files.

As with Windows Explorer, you can copy, paste, or delete selected files, either from the icon buttons on the toolbar or from the File menu. You can also change the display of files to the common choices in the View menu of Windows Explorer: Large Icons, Small Icons, List, or Details.

You can also right-click on a folder or file and select Copy as Link to designate the link target. That link can then be pasted into any of the rich-text tools of Groove.

Conflicts

One intriguing problem that comes up as a result of using the Files Tool in a shared space is conflicts. There is nothing to keep you and other members with proper permissions from editing the same file at the same time. When the first person finished saves the file, the file is simply saved. But how about when the second person or subsequent authors save?

Groove deals effectively with this potential conflict. The second or subsequent author sees a Conflict Resolution notification, shown in Figure 3.6.

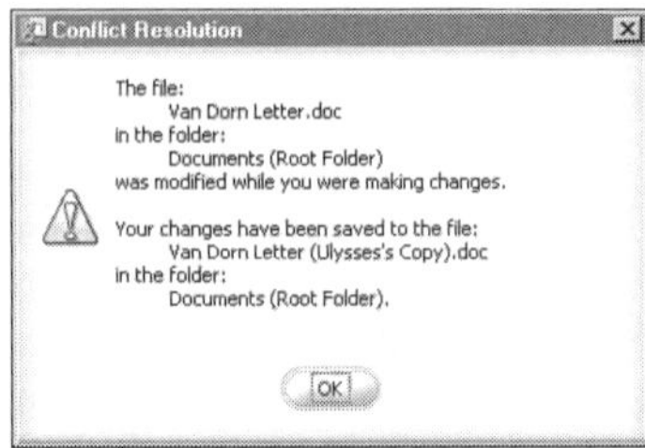

FIGURE 3.6
The Conflict Resolution notification.

The Conflict Resolution notification tells you who changed the document last, and tells you that your changes are being saved in another file with your name appended to it. When conflicts occur, it is essential that the authors meet and discuss how the changes will be merged. This is much easier to do at the beginning of the conflict than it is when many authors have made many changes to many copies.

When changes have been made to documents that do not result in conflicts, an Unread Marker appears. You can then open the document and find the changes. Managing of Unread Markers is the same here as it is in other Groove tools.

Files Tool Grooviness

The Files Tool is probably the tool that is the most visible expression of the peer-to-peer movement. Napster's sharing of music files put peer-to-peer on the public's radar. Although the purpose of Groove is not to serve as a vehicle for the evasion of copyright, its use of file sharing is no less significant. Shared files, especially those that can be jointly created and edited, are core to the whole concept of online collaboration.

The Files Tool uses a special-purpose engine called the GrooveDocumentShareEngine. The controlling code, or glue code, for this tool is substantial and relies on several Groove Script Library (`.GSL`) files and TYPELIBS. `.GSL` files allow developers to move script out of the templates and into separate files containing only glue code.

Outline Tool

The Groove Outline Tool is a very robust outlining tool that has been designed to work in a collaborative environment. It makes a great brainstorming tool. All members of the space can generate ideas and include links to resources by entering new records. Then, those records can be manipulated to force the unstructured ideas into a formal, hierarchical outline.

Ideas are entered into records. The first record is ready to have data entered into it when the tool appears, but subsequent records must be inserted. To insert any record after the first, press either the Enter key or the Insert key, and then type the idea and press Enter again to complete the record and begin a new one. You can continue to do this until all your ideas have been entered, or you can select a record and press the Enter key to begin a record below the selected record. After all records have been entered, you can very easily manipulate the hierarchical structure.

Working with Records

You can select individual records by clicking anywhere in the record and pressing the F2 key. You can then select records contiguous to the first either by pressing the Shift+up-arrow/down-arrow keys, or by Shift-clicking. Noncontiguous records can be selected with a Ctrl-click.

To promote (move to the left) a selected record, you can either press the Shift+Tab keys or click the left-arrow button located on the tools panel. To demote records (move to the right), either click the Right Arrow button on the tool panel or press the Tab key.

You can also move selected records up or down the list with the Up or Down buttons. Moving an entry up or down the list maintains that record's hierarchy. A record can be moved up or down only if it can do so without violating its hierarchical level. As with the Discussion Tool, an outline can be collapsed or expanded by clicking on the +/- buttons of parent records, or by clicking the Expand or Collapse icon buttons on the toolbar.

In some situations, it might be necessary to know which of the space's members added the record and when. If so, this information is available from the View menu. Choose Show/Hide Details to see this information.

Records can be deleted by highlighting the record and pressing the Delete key, or by selecting Delete from the Edit menu.

You can make any record the target of a link by using the Copy Row as Link selection from the Edit menu. This command places the link on the Clipboard to be pasted later into any rich-text Groove tool.

Importing and Exporting

You can also import or export records. You can export selected records as an XML file (File, then Export Rows as XML) if you want to use these outline entries in the Outline Tool of another shared space, or as a text file (File, then Export Rows as Text) if you want to move the outline to a text editor. Each record in the text file is separated by a carriage return, and hierarchy is preserved with tabs. Author and creation time and date also are exported.

If you choose Export Rows as XML, a binary XML file is created that can be imported through the File menu. Text files can also be imported. Each carriage return becomes a new record and each tab is translated to hierarchy, or indentation. The author of each record is whoever imported it, and the creation date and time are the date and time of the import.

Unread Markers

When changes have been made to the outline by other authors, an Unread Marker appears beside the changed record. Management of Unread Markers is the same here as it is in other Groove tools.

Outline Tool Grooviness

One of the primary reasons for collaboration is to bring the thoughts of people to bear on a problem or an opportunity. A synergy develops in which the collective thinking of the group is often far more creative than the thinking of individuals. The Outline Tool facilitates and formalizes group thinking.

The GrooveDataViewerTool controls the visual structure of the outline data. The GrooveDataViewerTool provides a collection of interfaces for accessing, modifying, and displaying Groove record-based data, and it is made up of a DataViewer and ModelGlue. The DataViewer provides for display and editing of hierarchical record data, whereas the ModelGlue provides interfaces for modification of the underlying data set.

In the case of the Outline Tool, the underlying data is persisted and disseminated by a `RecordSetEngine`.

Pictures Tool

The Groove Pictures Tool lets you share and manage pictures with the other members of your shared space in either `.JPG` or `.BMP` format. You can use the Pictures Tool as a slideshow in your shared space, or you can link pictures to other Groove rich-text tools such as Chat, Discussion, Notepad, and Outline Tools. You can use these links to illuminate difficult-to-describe portions of your written documents.

Using the Pictures Tool

When you first bring up the Pictures Tool, you are presented with a blank picture viewing area. Click the Show Picture List button and the window is split into two areas: the Picture List and the Viewing Area. Pictures that are moved into the Viewing Area are automatically scaled to fit.

Click the Add Pictures button. You are presented with a Windows Explorer–style file browser where you can designate a file or files to be added.

You can drag-and-drop pictures from Windows Explorer into either the Picture List or the Viewing area. You can also copy and paste files into either area.

When you drag-and-drop or paste files from the Clipboard into the viewing area, the image presented does not change. The pasted image is inserted at the end of the current file list, so you can see the image only if you either scroll to the last picture or select the file from the Picture List.

Although it is possible to paste an actual image into the Picture List, this is not a good idea because the image is always pasted in `.BMP` format and is uncompressed. Your Picture Tool can be quickly swamped by multimegabyte files that are inconvenient on your own computer but a huge mistake in a shared space that depends on bandwidth for performance. Anyone who downloads your shared space will appreciate well-compressed `.JPG`s.

You can view the pictures by selecting one from the Picture List or by scrolling through the pictures with the arrow keys in the Viewing Area. If you change the names, either by clicking in the title box or by choosing Rename Picture from the Edit menu, you can convert the filenames to captions and create an effective slideshow.

Editing Pictures

If you have a picture-editing program that has Windows file associations with `.BMP` or `.JPG` files, you can edit the pictures in the Pictures Tool by right-clicking the picture, then choosing Open. Your image-editing program then launches with the picture open. After editing, save the file.

Inside the Pictures Tool, the image will not have reflected your edits. You need to manually refresh the image by selecting another image, then reselecting the first. Your changes are then reflected in the image.

You can save individual pictures to their own files by using the Save Picture As dialog box, which can be accessed from an icon on the toolbar or through the Export choice from the File menu.

Copying and Deleting Pictures

You can copy pictures by placing the picture on the Clipboard. To do so, click the Copy icon button on the toolbar or select the Copy choice from the Edit menu. These can then be pasted into an external image-editing program.

You can also copy pictures by file. Right-click one or more pictures in the Picture List and select Copy from the Edit menu. Navigate to the desired location for the file in Windows Explorer, and paste.

If you want a copy to remain in the Pictures Tool, click Paste from the Edit menu. The file, prefaced by Copy Of, is added to the end of the file list.

You can delete files from the Pictures Tool by selecting the picture or pictures from the Picture List and clicking the Delete icon button. You can also cut the files.

Creating Links to Pictures

Creating links to pictures is very similar to the way it is done in the other Groove Tools. Select the picture and right-click it. Choose the Copy as Link option. Then navigate to the rich-text location of your choice. Insert the cursor and right-click again. Choose the Paste option. Pictures as links in rich-text documents can be extremely powerful tools.

Unread Markers

When other authors make changes to a picture or to the Pictures Tool, an Unread Marker appears beside the changed picture. You can use the Next Unread and Previous Unread choices in the View menu and their associated keyboard shortcuts to quickly scan your spaces for changed or new pictures.

Pictures Tool Grooviness

The Pictures Tool creates a shared visual repository to which every member can contribute. Images can frequently mean the difference between understanding and confusion. Providing pictures within a shared space is another example of facilitating collaboration through shared resources.

The Pictures Tool uses the Groove Image Control to display the pictures. The layout that displays both the pictures and the Picture List contains a splitter. A splitter divides a window horizontally or vertically and can be adjusted to resize the windows.

Notepad Tool

The Groove Notepad Tool is a text editor that was designed for collaboration over the Net. If you are in the Notepad Tool in a shared space with another member, you see the letters appear in your instance of Notepad when the other person types.

There is nothing to stop you from typing, formatting, or making edits to the shared document at the same time other members are also using the tool. Because every change to the document is immediately promulgated to all the other members, both the performance of the system and the efficiency of communication can suffer. Most often, it makes sense to use this tool either one at a time or offline.

If you click the Groove button in the system tray and select Work Offline, you can write, format, or edit your document. When you have finished, toggle the Work Offline choice back on. At that moment, your edits are relayed and synchronized in the shared space, and other members can see your work.

The Groove Notepad Tool synchronizes the shared space by merging your changes to the document. Because it is possible for two members to edit the same word at nearly the same time, Groove uses the most recent edit.

The behavior of the Notepad Tool differs from Chat: Notepad is simultaneous communication whereas Chat is sequential.

If you are working in the regular edition of Groove, you can use Roles and Permissions to manage the number of people who can edit a Notepad document.

Using the Notepad Tool

Enter text into the Notepad Tool by typing or copying and pasting text from another program. After the text is entered, you can format the font or the paragraph style of your selected text. The Format menu contains choices for Typeface, Size, and Color. The More Colors choice from the Color entry in the Format menu launches a Windows Color dialog box that allows you to choose from an unlimited number of colors.

The Format menu also contains bold, italic, underline, and strikeout styles. The More Fonts choice from the Format menu launches a standard Windows font dialog box. Paragraph formatting can also be done from the Format menu. Choices include left, center, and right alignments; indent controls; and bullets.

You can also use the bold, italic, or underline icons from the toolbar for font formatting, and the left, center, and right alignment icons for quick paragraph formatting. Bullet and indenting icons are also on the toolbar.

The Notebook Tool makes it easy to include links to URLs in Notepad documents. The Detect URLs choice in the View menu causes URLs like `www.groove.net` to appear as live links.

You cannot print from the Notepad Tool. Instead, select all text in the document and then cut-and-paste into another program.

Notepad Tool Grooviness

If you have a Microsoft Word document in your Files Tool, you might want to create/edit a paragraph for it in real-time with other members of the shared space. You can jointly compose the text and then paste it into the shared document. That is a Groovy use for the Notepad Tool.

The Notepad Tool uses the GrooveTextTools component, which contains interfaces and classes for manipulating and rendering rich text. The formatting of the text is controlled through the Groove toolbar at the top of the window. The glue code for the Notepad Tool is controlling the images that appear in the toolbar and the functions of the buttons.

Sketchpad Tool

The Groove Sketchpad Tool is used to create and share sketches in a shared space. Like a whiteboard at an in-person meeting, the Sketchpad can be extremely valuable to an across-the-Web meeting. It is a full-featured tool with enough options to support your artistic talents.

Using the Sketchpad Tool

To try using the Sketchpad Tool, follow these steps:

1. You can begin your drawing by setting a background image. When you click on the background image icon, a file browser launches. Locate the `.BMP` or `.JPG` you want to use as a background image and click Open. The image is automatically scaled to fit in the current drawing. You can use the image as part of your drawing, or trace it with the drawing tools, and then remove it later. Use the Remove Background Image option in the File menu, or click the Remove Background Image icon button.
2. You'll want to set your line color and your fill color for the shapes you'll draw. Click on the Line Color or Fill Color icon buttons or choose those options from the Draw menu. In addition to the 16 standard colors, the More Colors entries launches a standard Windows Color dialog, allowing you to set unlimited colors if the standard colors are too restrictive.
3. Choose a shape from the menu of shapes: rectangle, rounded rectangle, circle or ellipse, or polygon. Click and drag on the drawing surface to draw all the shapes except the polygon. Use the polygon tool by clicking and dragging to form line segments. Click at the end of a line segment to continue the shape; when you have connected the end of a line segment to the beginning of the first segment, the shape is completed and filled with the selected fill color.
4. Use the text tool to add text to your sketches.

Working with Lines and Shapes

The Sketchpad Tool gives you two options for lines. Use the straight-line tool for straight lines, and use the freehand tool as you would use a pencil.

You can select shapes using the selection tool either by clicking on a shape or by dragging a rectangular marquee around one or more shapes. Deselect shapes by Shift-clicking with the selection tool. A selected shape displays eight resize points around it. Click and drag on these points to resize the shape vertically, horizontally, or diagonally.

Click in the center of the shape and drag to move a shape. You can move multiple shapes if they have all been selected. You can delete any shape by selecting it and either selecting the Delete option from the Edit menu or pressing the Delete key.

Naming and Deleting a Drawing

When you are finished, you may want to name your drawing. Double-click in the title box in the upper-left part of the drawing area, or select the Rename Sketch option from the Edit menu.

When you click the New Sketch button, a new drawing area appears and the scroll status text changes to `2 of 2`. You can click the left scroll arrow to redisplay your sketch.

You may want to erase your drawing and start over. Use the Delete Sketch choice from the Edit menu to delete the current sketch.

Unread Marks

The Sketchpad Tool supports Unread Marks, so you can use the icons on the toolbar or the Next Unread and Previous Unread choices from the View menu to step through the changed sketches.

Sketchpad Tool Grooviness

The Sketchpad Tool is an extremely Groovy tool. Nothing assists collaboration more than a tool that lets people interact with each other in a graphic way. This electronic shared whiteboard allows people to communicate with each other in a manner nearly impossible, except face to face.

The Sketchpad Tool uses multiple engines. It uses its own custom engine to disseminate and persist sketches. The Background Image importer uses the Document Share engine, and the Navigation Bar uses an Artifact Engine.

Web Browser

The Groove Web Browser Tool lets you browse the Web alone or with other members of your shared space. If you choose to Browse Together, all members of the shared space have their browsers synchronized with each other, and all see the same pages. Use this option for shared Web tours.

Most of the features that display in your Web browser are derived from your default Web browser. For example, if your default browser is Internet Explorer 4 or higher, you can avoid typing the `www.` part of a Web address in the address box. If your default browser is Netscape, you can't.

Saving Favorites

In the Groove Web Browser you can save the current page as an Internet shortcut or favorite. To do so, follow these steps:

1. Click the Favorites icon button to open the Favorites pane, and then click the Add Favorite button. The Add Favorite dialog box is launched.
2. Click the New Folder button to keep your favorites organized. Select the folder you created in the folders pane and click Add. Your new shortcut now resides in your newly created folder.

3. You can put a link to this favorite on the Clipboard by clicking the Copy as Link icon button on the toolbar. The link can then be pasted into any Groove rich-text tool.
4. Close the Favorites pane by clicking the Favorites icon again.

Navigating

As with other browsers, you can use the arrows on the toolbar to navigate through your Web page history. The back arrow is available only if you have opened at least two Web pages. The forward arrow is available only if you have clicked the back arrow at least once.

As with other browsers, you can also pull down a list of the pages you have visited by clicking the arrow icon at the end of the address box.

The Stop Transmission icon button lets you stop the retrieval of a Web page if it is taking a very long time and you suspect problems.

The Refresh icon button lets you refresh the current Web page.

Browsing Together

The whole reason for having a Web browser in a collaborative environment is to be able to browse together. There are two ways to do this:

- If you click the Browse Together button on the toolbar, the browser synchronizes for all members in the shared space, and a member can lead others on a Web tour. Members can then discuss the contents of the Web pages without worrying whether all members are on the same page.
- If you click the Navigate Together check box under the leftmost panel, the shared spaces of members whose check box is checked are synchronized, and all tools for those members are in identical states. When one person moves to another tool, all move.

Unread Marks

The Web Browser Tool supports Unread Marks for favorites. You can scroll through new or changed favorites from the icons on the toolbar, or from the last two entries on the View menu.

Security Issues

Because it was designed to be a collaborative tool, the Web Browser has a few limitations due to security. If you fill out forms in the Web Browser Tool, other members will not be able to see your entered information.

Also, you cannot access password-protected sites that are open only by subscription, nor can you browse to any secure site.

Web Browser Grooviness

The Web Browser Tool is at its grooviest in the Browse Together mode. Operated in this mode, the tool becomes a joint resource for the membership of the shared space to surf the Web together in real-time. Used in normal mode, the Web Browser Tool allows you to put links on the Clipboard that can be pasted into rich-text tools so that exterior Web sites can become internal resources for the shared space.

The Web Browser Tool is a good example of the capability to extend Groove with custom engines. This tool uses its own custom Web engine to display the HTML pages. The tool's glue code is mostly concerned with the toolbar choices, and most of that is necessary to support the DocumentShareEngine that is used in the Add Favorite button.

Summary

Now that we have examined the tools that are standard in Groove, we can begin to study how they work. To understand them, you first need a thorough understanding of the revolutionary Groove architecture. We'll examine this architecture in the next chapter.

Understanding Groove Architecture

CHAPTER

4

IN THIS CHAPTER

In this chapter, we will look under the hood of Groove. You will learn the concept of a shared space and explore the underlying services of the Groove application. You will study the services that take care of the security, persistence, and dissemination of data. You will find out how automatic dissemination of Groove tools and components takes place.

This chapter will help you gain a fundamental understanding of how Groove works and will expose you to Groove as a platform, rather than as an application. Finally, this chapter will give you an appreciation for all the things that need to be done in a peer-to-peer application—things you don't have to do. Groove allows you to concentrate on your tool rather than on the plumbing necessary to make it function in a peer-to-peer space.

The Model-View-Controller Structure

The early computers we talked about in the Internet history section of Chapter 1, "Why Peer-to-Peer?" had a very simple structure for their operation. This structure is shown in Figure 4.1.

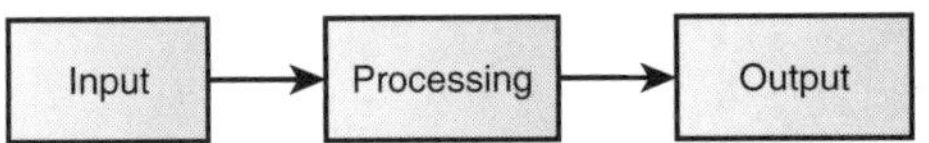

FIGURE 4.1
The Input-Processing-Output structure.

Data was input through magnetic tape or punched cards. It was then processed, and the output was printed or displayed on a CRT monitor. The processing was sequential and linear.

The advent of the graphical user interface (GUI) changed that model. The computer was no longer a machine that began, operated, and quit. Now, it spent most of its time in an idle loop, waiting for the user to respond to the computer through input devices. As a result, a new structure evolved that has been the mainstay of many applications developed since, called the Model-View-Controller (MVC) structure. Figure 4.2 illustrates this system, in which the three parts interact with each other continuously.

The Model represents all the routines that store, retrieve, or manipulate data. It corresponds to the Processing term in the Input-Processing-Output structure.

The View constantly monitors the Model and makes changes to itself to alert the user. The View corresponds to the Output function of the Input-Processing-Output structure.

The Controller monitors input devices on the computer and translates the user's gestures into commands that create changes in the Model, the View, or both. When the user types a *T*, for example, both the data in the Model and the presentation of that data on the screen update. The Controller is analogous to Input in the Input-Processing-Output structure.

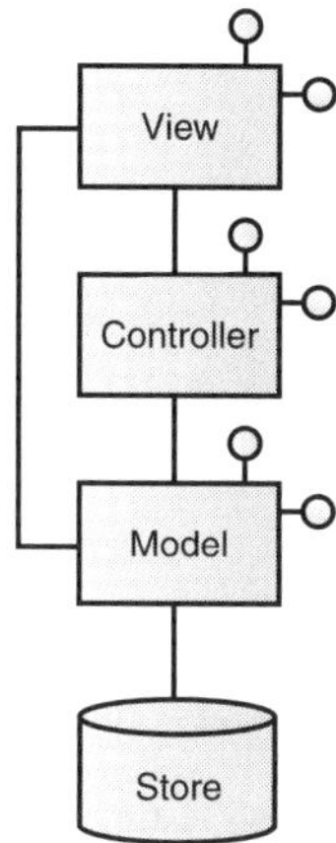

FIGURE 4.2
The Model-View-Controller structure.

The Store in the diagram is simply storage media that the Model can use as a repository for persistent data.

The Groove Structure

Because Groove was designed to let multiple users interact with the same tool and data simultaneously, the Groove platform uses an augmented version of the traditional Model-View-Controller.

First, a Command Processor is utilized to moderate between the Controller and the Model. The Command Processor intercepts the commands, which in Groove are XML objects, and processes the recording, sequencing, and playback of those commands. That processing is necessary because the application not only must respond to the commands of its own Controller, but also must respond to the commands that arrive from the Controllers of its remote peers.

Next, a Virtual Message Queue is needed to store and forward command messages from and to other computers. The Virtual Message Queue is designed to be asynchronous because commands may be sent or received simultaneously; and because members might not always be connected, Groove uses a store-and-forward design.

The XML objects that Groove uses need to travel between peers as optimally as possible over different protocols, through firewalls and proxies, and over varying bandwidths. In addition, these XML object routing mechanisms must operate without any user or administrator participation. Consequently, Groove developed a new set of methods for moving the commands around the network.

Finally, intense 192-bit encryption ensures the confidentiality and integrity of data, both on the user's hard disk and over the network.

Figure 4.3 shows the resulting structure.

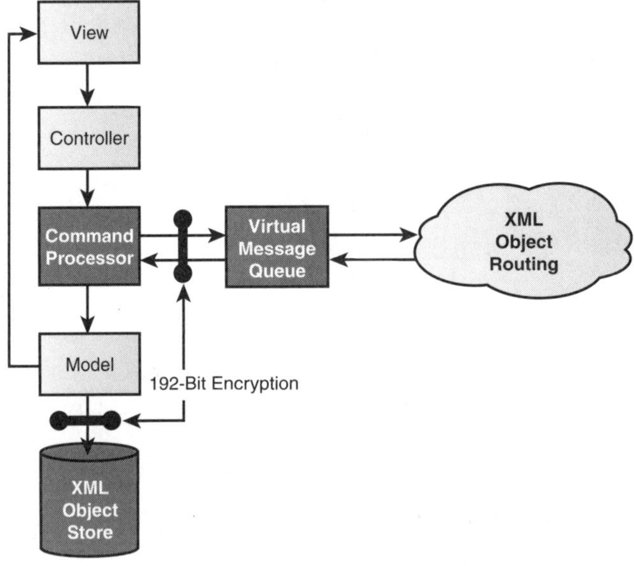

FIGURE 4.3
The Groove structure.

In Groove, the Model consists of components that store and manipulate data. These components also expose interfaces to data manipulation methods that other objects can use. The collection of components that accomplishes this task is called an *engine*.

The Controller forms the connection between the Model, or engine, and the View. In Groove, it is referred to as *glue*. Glue code can be written in either a scripting language (such as JavaScript) or any COM-compliant language. You, as a Groove developer, will soon be writing a lot of glue code in JavaScript.

A View in Groove is the collection of a tool's user interface design elements. The View operates on a UI thread.

The Shared Space

Understanding the concept of a shared space is critical to appreciating the design of Groove. A shared space contains a hierarchical database that is a collection of eXtensible Markup Language (XML) documents that contain XML objects. If a shared space member is online, the shared space document collection describes the state of all online members' interactions with each tool.

A shared space contains one or more tools, composed of tool components: views, engines, and controlling code, or glue. Each tool maintains an XML document in the shared space that holds the tool's persistent data.

The database of XML documents in a shared space has a dynamic part, which contains the data for the tool, and a static part, which maintains a list of components required by the tool, as well as the data that is specific to the tool's engine.

The dynamic part of the tool's XML database contains changes to the tool state. When any member of a shared space takes an action that results in a change to the shared space, a delta is created. A *delta* is Groove terminology for a unit of change to the model.

The commands that correspond to the delta are executed and stored in the user's shared space document. Then they are sent to all the other members of the shared space. After the deltas have been disseminated, the dynamic part of the database is updated for all remote members, and all members see the change.

Deltas are created in tools through the capture of a user's gestures. The tool itself determines the granularity of the delta, and different tools can create different-sized deltas. For the Notepad Tool, for example, the delta size might be a letter, whereas for the Outline Tool it might be a record.

Shared space services work with the engine to asynchronously coordinate local and remote changes to the data model and maintain shared space consistency.

There are two top-level parts to the Groove application: Instant Groove and the transceiver.

Instant Groove

Instant Groove is a system tray application that includes the components TaskbarIcon, Messager, Hot Key, and Notifier. These components can be used to launch and shut down the Groove application, and to provide chat, voice chat, and instant messaging. Instant Groove also supports distribution of invitations to shared spaces.

The Transceiver

The transceiver is a collection of dedicated tools and components running in a container application. The transceiver uses underlying services to provide system-level functionality, such as communications, security, and account maintenance. Its UI enables the user to create and maintain shared spaces, change skins, or make changes to his or her account. It houses tools that manage the presence status of members; provides communication services such as voice-over-IP, instant messaging, and chat; and manages changes in security levels. The transceiver also has a window that hosts the Groove tools, so those tools can leverage the transceiver's functionality.

As a Groove developer, you will be developing the tools that the transceiver houses.

Tools

Tools are special-purpose applications that leverage the underlying services of the Groove platform to accomplish specific useful activities. Tools can be aggregated into toolsets to create complex applications dedicated to a specific purpose. For example, Groove's Project toolset includes a calendar, contact list, documents, and so on.

Groove Platform Services

Instant Groove, the Groove transceiver, and Groove tools rely on underlying services supplied by the Groove platform. These services are used to manage accounts and identities, the user interface, components, shared spaces, communications, storage and XML, security, and Web integration.

Account and Identity Services

Each instance of Groove has a local Account Subsystem that maintains each user's account. It is responsible for listing the device on the network, publishing the presence information of local users, and sensing the presence of remote users. It is responsible for the creation, change, deletion, and maintenance of identities, and for publishing the identity, along with its state information. It maintains a database of accounts and account information on every device. There can be as many accounts on a device as memory allows, and an account can be used on many individual devices. These services interact with the security, communications, and storage services.

Account Services can also provide other services such as licenses, security policy, and/or security key management. It provides support for both the device and user vCards.

Account Services also provide account information to other tools and subsystems. It maintains this information in an account database that lists account information for each identity in an account, and for each account on the device. It also keeps track of the online status of each identity.

The Account Database

The Account Database is actually a special-purpose shared space that contains tools for managing personal contacts, managing the templates of any tools you have installed, managing skins, and managing identities. An account holder's database contains the following information:

- Groove identity or identities (in particular, their public/private identity keypairs) and preferences for each identity
- Awareness information based on identity preferences

- Identifiers for all the devices on which the account is used
- A vCard for each identity
- A directory of references to the user's shared spaces
- A shared space identifier (a GUID), a filename, a storage service, and a security bulk storage master key for protecting the user's shared spaces on disk
- The user's personal contacts
- Any sent and/or received instant messages

Because the Account Database is a special-purpose shared space, any changes in an account or identity are distributed to all the user's other devices through Groove's shared space synchronization, so an individual user's account file contains the same data on all his devices.

Any invitations or other messages received by the account in one device are automatically relayed to the user's other devices.

UI Services

Groove tools are developed by writing templates in XML. Templates define all the components of the tool and describe how the components interact. The tool contains logic in the form of *glue code* that defines the tool's function and how the tool manipulates its data.

The tool presents a user interface through the use of a view. The view uses a layout that describes the location of the components the view contains.

UI Services provide a rich set of UI components, including buttons, text input, combo boxes, image and text containers, menus, and toolbars. UI Services also support common layout styles such as HTML Table, multi-cell, and X/Y positioning. The Groove Component Catalog provides a detailed description of these components and layouts, and includes XML fragments that can be used by developers in the construction of templates.

UI Services also support skins. Skins provide a way for the user to change the basic look of Groove. Skins can include different layouts, button styles and backgrounds, sounds, and even behaviors.

Individual tools may or may not be "skin aware," depending on the needs of the developer. Skins are described in XML and are implemented in templates. Tools can call the Skin Manager to get the properties that describe the current skin setting.

The Windows Manager is called to open or close windows. This allows the underlying Groove application to keep track of all open windows so that they can be managed and disposed of properly when the user quits Groove. Window Services can be called from tools to open a tool's own windows and dialogs.

An Idle Manager allows tools to subscribe to it to receive notification of available idle time. The Idle Manager then allows the tool to use idle time for that tool's processing needs.

When you properly describe a component in a tool template, Component Services will ensure that the component is available for use.

Component Services

As a tool developer, you will become extremely familiar with Groove Component Services. The Component Services Subsystem manages the download of all software components needed to run Groove. Every Groove process has a dedicated Component Services Subsystem.

OSD

A *component* is any file that Groove may need to retrieve, install, or update for which an Open Software Description (OSD) file can be written. OSD is a W3C standard that provides a vocabulary in XML for describing software packages and their dependencies. It was originally developed in 1997 by Microsoft and Marimba to install components over the Internet.

Software installation packages that use OSD have some real advantages over earlier installation systems:

- They are easy to use and can be made transparent to the user.
- They do not require the reinstallation of previously installed base software.
- Components required for update can be distributed over the Internet.
- Standard instruction file formats can be used cross-platform to locate components, to tell where to install those components, and to describe how those components relate to others.

Groove uses OSD to tell the Component Manager where to get software components, what other components they depend on, and where and how to install them. We will devote more time to OSD in Chapter 6, "Essential OSD."

Downloading, Installing, and Activating Components

The Component Manager can get components from the Web, or from Groove shared spaces. It can retrieve components automatically, in the case of updates, or it can retrieve them in response to user action, such as the installation of a new tool into a shared space.

When the Component Subsystem for a Groove process loads, it checks the version of its components against the version contained in a descriptor file. If it finds a match, the process continues. It then checks the Groove Manifest to see whether the component has ever been installed in any local user's account before. If it has, Component Manager installs the component from its local source.

If it does not find the component listed in the Manifest, and its version of the component does not match the descriptor file, the Component Manager checks the OSD and asks the Download Manager to retrieve the component. In addition to providing components in response to versioning, the Component Manager can identify a missing component in response to finding a new data type in the shared space.

The Download Manager then retrieves files from the Internet. There is only one Download Manager per device. The Download Manager goes to the location specified in the OSD and downloads the required components.

After the needed components are downloaded, the Install Manager installs them. If the component is required by the system, a separate process called the System Install Manager handles installation. The SIM is capable of upgrading system components even if Groove is not running.

Even after the component is downloaded and installed, it is not yet ready to be used. A separate step, activation, is needed. *Activation* is the instantiation of an installed component by a factory. To activate a component, the Component Manager calls the appropriate factory to produce an instance of the installed component in the tool.

The Component Manager also implements security for components and may also control a component's use. It may restrict the component to a single shared space or enforce some arbitrary time limit for use.

Groove peer-to-peer tools need shared spaces in which to function.

Shared Space Services

The Shared Space Services manage the interaction of tools with the Dynamics Manager. Remember that a tool is composed of a view; controlling code, or glue; and an engine. The user initiates a *gesture*, or action, that results in a change to the data model in the engine. The change occurs as a result of the execution of commands. The change needs to be acted on both locally and remotely to affect the change in the data model of every member in the shared space. Groove's mechanism for formalizing the remote and local handling of those commands is the Dynamics Manager.

When the tool calls the Dynamics Manager, it requests a container called a *delta*. The delta is a container into which the commands that need to be processed in order to affect the data model can be placed. The tool puts the commands into the supplied delta and then submits the delta to the Dynamics Manager for execution and eventual dissemination.

The creation of the delta, the placing of the commands into the delta, and the execution of the delta on the local system are synchronous. The application does not wait for delta dissemination and delta execution on remote computers.

Dynamics Services

Every shared space on a device has a dedicated Dynamics Manager, which is responsible for executing the changes to the shared space data in response to requests by the tool. Along with the Communications Manager, it disseminates the local deltas to remote computers for their processing. The Dynamics Manager maintains a model of the changes in the shared space and makes sure that those changes result in identical versions of the data in all shared spaces. It resolves any conflicts in a deterministic, rather than semantically correct, way. It also provides automatic recovery of deltas in case of communications failure.

The Dynamics Manager controls the execution of commands contained in both local and inbound deltas. It processes a delta by interpreting each command in it, instantiates engines if needed, and then delivers the command to the appropriate engine. Shared spaces can be updated even when the user is not active in the application because engines do not have UIs.

When the engine receives the commands from the Dynamics Manager, it makes the consequent changes to the data model of the engine in the shared space. Then it notifies any views that have asked to be notified when the engine's data model changes. The view can then update and reflect the changes that resulted from the execution of the delta. When all shared space members are online and active in their spaces, these changes occur nearly simultaneously.

Coordinating Execution of Deltas

It is not unusual for two or more members to be working in the same space at the same time, and even on the same data at the same time. One of the responsibilities of the Dynamics Manager is to coordinate and sequence the execution of deltas in the shared space. Those deltas may be inbound from remote computers, or they may be local.

Every local Dynamics Manager makes the changes to the shared space in exactly the same way. Groove makes these changes deterministically, which means that there are established rules for processing and sequencing deltas, and for resolving conflicts.

Let's say, for example, that two of us are working on a document in the Notepad Tool. I type the word *Hello* and you type the word *world*. The result might be *Hello world* or *world Hello*, depending on who made the first change. Whichever sequence occurs, it will be identical in all shared spaces after all deltas have been processed.

When we say that it will be identical in all spaces, we are speaking of the data in the store. Tools can present data in several ways or not present it at all, so we cannot say that every instance of the shared space is identical in view. We can, however, say that the data of every shared space is identical.

What about this case? I decide to delete the word *world* and you decide to apply a bold style to it. Most likely, the word *world* would be deleted because there is no way to bold a deleted word, but whatever happened, it would be the same in the shared spaces of all members.

Groove resolves conflicts to consistency, but not to correctness or accuracy. It is up to individual tool developers, like you, to provide the tool or engine the logic it needs in order to provide correct, as well as consistent, solutions.

Data Recovery and Cleanup

The Dynamics Manager is also responsible for data recovery and delta cleanup. If one member gets out of synch with other members' data, Dynamics Manager can resynchronize the spaces.

Groove constantly checks the shared spaces to ensure consistency. If it finds an inconsistency, it can request that the Dynamics Manager of the original sender of the information resend the appropriate deltas. If that sender is offline, it can ask another member of the shared space to provide the necessary information.

Authenticators

To ensure that the information sent from the requested member is authentic, Groove sends each delta with an *authenticator*, that is, integrity-protected with the sender's digital signature. Thus, when Groove checks to see whether the delta was sent from the requested member's space, it can also check to see whether the data is unmodified (that is, the same as was sent by the originator of the data). All deltas are protected in this way.

In the event of a communications failure of a remote device, Groove can resynchronize the shared space data. Dynamics Manager also purges data from the system on a regular basis to conserve memory.

Dynamics Manager interacts with the Communications Subsystem.

Communications Subsystem

The Communications Subsystem manages all communications among devices running Groove, including deltas. It routes information to the proper resources, whether those resources are local or remote. It must specify how a particular instance of Groove sends and receives messages, and must manage the asynchronous receipt and delivery of data between instances. It manages both outbound and inbound deltas.

The Communications Manager chooses communication protocols, usually Groove protocols, to arrange the most direct communications possible. It can, however, convert Groove protocols to HTTP to provide firewall transparency. It can peacefully coexist with other protocols on the network so as not to interfere with other network traffic, and it can also manage indirect, or relay communications, when Groove users of a shared space are offline or are available only through a firewall or when fanout is utilized.

The Communications Manager can sense bandwidth availability and can tailor communications to optimize the available bandwidth. For example, if a user disseminates a large delta over a 9600-baud dial-up connection to five other members, the Communications Manager can decide to send one copy of the delta to Groove's relay server, which then duplicates the delta and *fans out* the deltas to other members over faster transmission lines, instead of sending five separate deltas directly to each of the members.

The Communications Manager is responsible for determining the method of routing communications with other members of a shared space. Groove currently supports *unicasting* (point-to-point communications to a single device of a member), *multicasting* (point-to-point communications to a several devices), and *omnicasting* (transmission to all listening devices).

A *presence server* on each device running Groove announces its availability online. *Presence* can refer to either a user or a device. User presence is announced with a Groove protocol based on Rendez-Vous (RDV) protocol. Groove uses Device Presence Protocol (DPP) for devices. Groove tools use user presence protocols, whereas the Groove applications use device presence protocols.

Based on the availability of the devices with which it needs to communicate, and the bandwidth available to each device, the Communications Manager can determine the most efficient communication method.

Available and Unavailable Devices

Devices can be online and connected, or they can be unavailable or unreachable. Unavailable devices are ones that are not currently connected to the Internet, whereas unreachable devices are available but are behind a firewall, or are otherwise incommunicado due to transmission protocols.

Groove's Communications Manager deals with unavailable devices by forwarding communications to the relay server, which then forwards the data the next time the target device reconnects. If, for some reason, a relay is unavailable, the Communications Manager can store the data for a period, and then send the data when the device becomes available again. In the case of unreachable devices, the Communications Manager again utilizes a relay, but this time uses a different protocol.

Let's look at how the Communications Manager actually communicates deltas.

Communicating Deltas

When the Communications Manager receives a local delta from the Dynamics Manager, it searches the delta for all the target endpoint IDs and determines the exact device and address of each. After the target devices have been identified, the Communications Manager tries to send the delta directly to each device. Let's assume that all devices are available, so it sends copies of the delta to every identified device.

Now, what does the receiving device do with it? On the target device, the responsibility of the Communications Manager is to receive those deltas and route them to the proper resource. Typical Groove tools would not use these services directly.

After the delta is disseminated, it needs to be stored.

Storage and XML Services

Groove uses XML as its primary storage format. XML was chosen because the language allows format extensibility, supports device independence, and provides interoperability with other systems.

Every active instance of Groove has a Storage Manager. The Storage Manager's job is to maintain all the XML documents for all services and shared spaces on one instance of Groove. It is constantly receiving data from other members of each shared space, and it makes sure that all the stored data is continually updated, current, and consistent. The Storage Security Manager makes sure that all shared space and account data is encrypted before it is written to disk.

The Storage and XML Services provide access to methods for manipulating XML, and provide Groove schemas, which are XML documents that describe other XML documents. Groove schemas can define attributes and describe indexing. We will study schemas in Chapter 5, "Essential XML."

The Storage and XML Services expose interfaces for indexing strings, dates, and integers; provide support for different document types, such as collections; and provide mechanisms for linking data both within a single database and between databases. The Storage and XML Services also provide support for collections. Collections can provide tools with abstractions of records. A collection is efficiently indexed so that designated portions of the data can be manipulated effectively.

A good example of the use of collections is the Outline Tool. When outline topics are collapsed or expanded, the tool is using a different view from the collection without affecting the underlying XML document database. Collection services can also sort, move, or group data.

Handling Transactions

Groove also supports transactions. A good example of a transaction is banking, a transfer from your savings account to your checking account.

Let's say we handle your transfer like this: First we'll remove the money from your savings account balance. Then we'll add that amount to your checking account balance. If the computer crashes between the two operations, you will lose the amount of money you transferred, because the money was debited but never credited.

Transactions prevent that from happening by ensuring that all operations are atomic. That means that the database is adjusted only after all the operations of a transaction have been completed. In our example, both the debit and the credit operations would have to complete before the results of the operation could be written to disk. The transfer would either happen correctly or, in the event of a crash, not happen at all.

Groove transactions are atomic, consistent (meaning that operations must occur in the proper order), and independent (meaning that operations do not interfere with each other).

Traditional requirements of transactions include a requirement for durability. A *durable* transaction means that after the transaction occurs, it must be committed, or locked in the database. Because Groove transactions always stay in process to allow asynchronous updates, they are not, in the classic sense, durable, but a tool developer could ensure durability.

Now that we have created data, transported it, and stored it, let's talk about how Groove keeps it secure.

Security Manager

Security was one of the most important design goals of Groove. In any distributed application or platform running in an untrusted communications environment (such as the Internet), security is essential and must be implemented by the application itself. Data not only must be secure in transmission, but also has to be secure on the user's local storage and be accessible to the shared space member alone. The application must authenticate each user's identity to other users, verify the source of components, and ensure confidentiality and integrity of messages and data. To be as secure as possible, security must be always on, and require no administration. And it has to do all this while operating in a multitude of network configurations, on- and offline and behind firewalls.

To accomplish this kind of security, Groove relies on cryptographic technology. There are two services to Groove security: encryption/integrity and authenticity/confidentiality. Encryption/integrity determines who can read data in a shared space, whereas authenticity/integrity assures users that the data came from the purported sender and has not been tampered with.

Two types of cryptographic technologies and keys are used: *secret-key technology* (using symmetric keys) and *public-key technology* (using asymmetric keypairs). Symmetric keys are single keys that must be shared between the communicating parties, whereas asymmetric keypairs consist of a private key and a public key. The private key (which must be known only to one party) is for decrypting data and signing messages; the public key (which can be known by any number of parties) is for encrypting data and verifying signatures.

Groove operates in a mutually suspicious security environment. In a mutually suspicious environment, members know the originator of all data and all communications. Groove uses keys that not only guarantee that the data came from a member of a shared space, but also guarantee that it came from a particular member.

Lifetime of a Shared Space

Security begins when a user of Groove establishes his or her account. When a user establishes an account, the person is prompted for a passphrase. That passphrase produces a passphrase-derived symmetric key that is used to protect the storage key for the account file. The passphrase is used for nothing else in Groove; in particular, the passphrase is not stored on disk (unless the user explicitly requests Groove to memorize the passphrase, which is convenient but discouraged, for security reasons).

Each shared space and the account file have their own storage key, which is used to encrypt/decrypt data stored on disk. When a new user establishes a passphrase, the user is protecting his or her own account.

We know that accounts are not the same as identities. An identity is a collection of data that defines one persona for a user. The name for the default identity is the account name. The collection includes a Groove identity Uniform Resources Identifier (URI), a vCard, and two more keys: an asymmetric key pair for signature generation and verification, and an asymmetric key pair to encrypt/decrypt symmetric keys.

The signature key pair is used to authenticate invitations, instant messages, and some special-purpose public keys we'll discuss later. The encryption keypair is used to decrypt invitations and instant messages. The public halves of the key pairs are stored in the identity's contact and are shared when the contact is shared. If you want, you can actually see your own public keys by exporting your vCard and then opening it with a text editor. Your digital fingerprint is created from the public halves of your identity's signature key pair and encryption keypair.

Creating the Shared Space

Now that you have established your account and have at least your default identity, you can create a shared space. Creating a shared space triggers the creation of a special type of key pair called an ESIGN key pair. The public half of this shared-space–specific ESIGN key will be exchanged in the shared-space invitation protocol as described in the following text.

Inviting and Authenticating

After you have the shared space, you can invite someone. Let's say that the first person you invite does not currently use Groove. You will need to send the person an email invitation.

If you use the Invite By Email option from the Invite button in the shared space, you'll generate an email that contains a `.GRV` file as an attachment. The body of the message will be populated with a link to the download area of the `groove.net` Web site, in case your invitee does not have the Groove software. The recipient downloads and installs the Groove software, if necessary.

When the recipient double-clicks the `.GRV` file, that invitee sends you a message with a one-time key encrypted with your public key, and the invitee's ESIGN public key for the shared space. The ESIGN public key is digitally signed with the invitee's identity signature private key. The shared space is then transferred to the invitee.

For the users to authenticate one another, they must display one another's digital fingerprints and validate them to one another out-of-band (for example, by personal presence or a telephone call). This is called *end-entity authentication* (as opposed to the *data-origin authentication* involved in message-integrity). For example, when Abraham invites Mary for the first time, Mary needs to be able to authenticate him. If she doesn't know Abraham from Adam, she can ask for his telephone number. She can then talk to him on the telephone and assure herself that she is really communicating with Abraham. If she is so convinced, she can ask him for his digital fingerprint information. Then, when she receives the invitation, she can check the digital fingerprint to validate that the communicating entity really is Abraham.

The shared space includes a symmetric group key that is to be used for encrypting subsequent messages in the space. It also includes the ESIGN public keys for all members in the shared space.

Disseminating and Writing Data

You now have exchanged keys (per member ESIGN key and the group encryption key) between the members of the space. It's time to open the Notepad Tool and type a word.

As you type, deltas are being created that need to be disseminated to the other members' copies of the shared space and written to your own hard drive. Let's consider the dissemination first.

The encrypt/decrypt group key stored in the shared space encrypts the data, and the signer's ESIGN private key provides integrity for the delta message. Figure 4.4 shows a typical delta message from a shared space. It is then sent over the network to the invitee's copy of the shared space, where the ESIGN signature is verified with the sender's public key to ensure the delta's integrity. Finally, it is decrypted with the group cipher key and displayed in the invitee's Notepad Tool view.

As the delta is being disseminated, it is being written to the encrypted object store on disk. Encryption on disk is handled on a per-member, per–shared-space symmetric storage key, which is protected by the symmetric storage master key you established when you created your account.

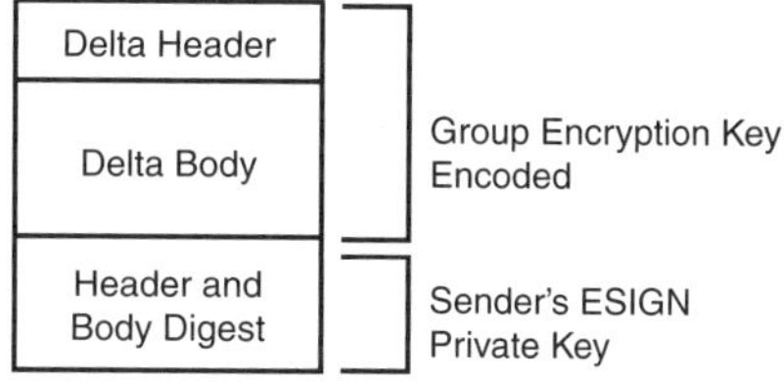

FIGURE 4.4
A typical delta sent to a shared space.

Each Groove instance constantly monitors communications. Because Groove messages are sequenced, Groove knows when it has not received a message. The software can assume that a message is lost and can recover the message from other members of the shared space. Groove will try to recover the message from the original sender, or from any of the other members. However, to provide data-origin authenticity, the fetcher of the message must be able to authenticate the author of the message even though it may be forwarded by another member of the space. (This prevents message forwarders from modifying the original message before forwarding it.) To accomplish this job, the message author's original authenticator (the author's ESIGN signature) is preserved in all copies of the message, so even when a copy is received from any other member, it contains information that authenticates the originator.

You now have a working, shared space with security in place for all data, both on the disk and on the wire.

Uninviting

Just as members can be invited into a shared space, they can also be uninvited out of it. Without getting into the social or political aspects of uninviting, you can see that the security needs of the space will change. You don't want an uninvited person to have access to the shared space, so keys will need to change. Actually, the solution is pretty simple—send out a new group key to each of the remaining members' shared spaces encrypted with the public keys of each member.

Of course, networks are not always as linear as we would like, and it is possible to receive a delta encrypted with a key before receiving the key itself. Groove gets around this problem by versioning keys. Messages announce their dependency on particular versions of keys. If a message arrives that is encrypted with a version of a key that a copy of Groove doesn't have, it waits for the delivery of the proper key before it processes the new version encrypted delta.

With Groove's strong security support, you can feel comfortable operating on the insecure Web.

Web Services

Groove is a hybrid peer-to-peer application, so the use of the Web is integral to its design. Communications are normally peer-to-peer, but Groove may use specialized server services, especially when one or more members of a shared space are offline.

As you have seen, Web Services also provide component farms that allow you to download, install, and instantiate components. Your contact information is stored in a special directory on `groove.net` that lets you contact other Groove members.

These obvious uses of the Web are part of a whole package that tightly integrates the Web with Groove.

Relay

As you have seen, Groove uses the Relay Server three ways:

- To store and forward messages to Groove devices that are offline
- To fan-out messages to conserve bandwidth on slow connections
- To facilitate Groove communication through firewalls

Groove's Communications Manager deals with offline devices by sending any messages destined for the offline device to the relay server. When the device reconnects, those stored messages are forwarded to the device and all shared spaces are updated.

The Communications Manager can also sense bandwidth and make allowances for slow throughput. Rather than communicating directly with peers, the Communications Manager can choose to send the message to the relay server, and then fan-out the messages to the other members of the shared space.

The Communications Manager can forward messages to the relay server when it detects that other instances of Groove are unreachable due to firewalls. The relay server can act as a proxy server. If the firewall blocks Groove's Simple Symmetrical Transport Protocol (SSTP), the relay server can deliver the messages using HTTP.

Presence

One of the mission-critical tasks performed by Web Services is device presence. Peer-to-peer systems have significant autonomy from servers, and they operate in an environment characterized by intermittent connection and unpredictable IP addresses. Consequently, the Internet's DNS system is not reliable for identifying peers. Presence, or the address and available status of a peer, becomes essential to peer-to-peer computing.

Groove divides presence into two areas: presence of the user and presence of the device. For the user, Groove uses a proprietary peer-to-peer protocol called the Rendez-Vous Protocol (RVP). Groove's RVP Protocol is serverless, so it exists outside Web services.

Groove uses two different protocols for device presence: LAN Device Presence Protocol (DPP), which uses the User Datagram Protocol (UDP), and WAN DPP, which uses SSTP to communicate with relay servers.

Tools work with user presence; the Groove application uses device availability.

Component Services Subsystem

As you saw in the section "Downloading, Installing, and Activating Components," the Component Services Subsystem manages the download of all software components needed to run Groove. In addition to updates and new tool installations, the Web site contains some additional skins that can be downloaded and installed.

My Groove Services

Last, the Web site contains a searchable database of Groove users, and utilities to make moving of account information between devices across the Internet easier.

Customer Services Subsystem

The Customer Services Subsystem is a set of components that gather data, diagnose, and handle errors in the Groove application. Some of these components reside in the application and some on a Web site. The Web site, depending on the error, can be either Groove's Web site or a third party's.

Running in the background, these services can provide error resolution and remote diagnostics, and can even recover crashes automatically. You will use a Groove tool, `GrooveCSMViewer.exe`, to access some of this information to troubleshoot the injection of tools.

Summary

Do not feel that you have to memorize this chapter. Reading this chapter should have given you an intuitive feel for the environment in which your tools will function. Most of these services take place in the background, and, in general, you won't have to deal with them directly. If for some reason you do have to interact with them, Groove provides API access through various type libraries. Don't feel that you have to thoroughly understand these systems, but you should be aware of how your tools interact with them.

In this chapter you will certainly have noticed the emphasis that Groove architecture places on XML. It is a thread that runs throughout Groove development, from the underlying services of the application to the individual tools like those you will be creating. Consequently, a short review of XML programming won't hurt any potential Groove Tool developer. You'll get that review in the next chapter.

Essential XML

CHAPTER

5

IN THIS CHAPTER

In this chapter, we will study one of Groove's most pervasive technologies. We will take a short history break to examine XML's roots, and we will discuss how XML solves some of the difficulties inherent in HTML. We will walk through the construction of a typical XML document, and build and display a sample XML catalog. We'll see how we can validate the data in our catalog, using both Document Type Definitions (DTDs) and XML Schema.

If you are already comfortable using XML you can browse this information and skip ahead to "Groove's Use of XML" near the end of the chapter.

XML History

Back before the days of computers, publishers would mark up manuscripts describing how type was to be set for the resulting book. A chapter head, for example, might be set in 24-point Goudy Old Style Black with 30 points of leading. A section heading might be set in 16-point Helvetica Bold, with 19 points of leading. Margins and indents would also be indicated in the *markup*.

Of course, you could just mark up the document with markup like `Chapter Head` and `Section Heading`, and have a separate document for each book that specified exactly what those terms meant. That idea occurred to Charles Goldfarb.

Standard Generalized Markup Language (SGML)

In 1969, Charles Goldfarb was working for IBM on a project to develop an integrated system for a law office. He needed a means of allowing the text editing, formatting, and information retrieval subsystems to share documents. The result was Generalized Markup Language (GML), a language IBM used for many years to publish its documents.

Nine years later, when the American National Standards Institute (ANSI) committee on Information Processing established the Computer Languages for the Processing of Text committee, they asked Goldfarb to join the committee and lead a project for a text description language standard based on GML. Goldfarb's basic language design for SGML was developed into a standard.

The first working draft of the SGML standard was published in 1980. By 1983, the sixth draft was recommended. Another year of review and comment went by before the final text was published in record time after approval. The record time was due to using an SGML system developed by Anders Berglund, then of the European Particle Physics Laboratory (CERN). One of the early major adopters was the United States Department of Defense (DOD).

In those days, electronic documents were a hodge-podge of incompatible file formats structured and formatted by a great number of incompatible, proprietary computer systems and applications. Nowhere was this more of a problem than at the DOD.

The DOD had hundreds of major weapons programs that were designed and supported by thousands of vendors. Simple tasks such as producing operating manuals for a system that was co-designed by six different vendors operating six different computer systems were nightmares for DOD personnel. As a result, the Computer-aided Acquisition and Logistic Support (CALS) program was born. The military standard (MIL-M-28001) that resulted in February 1988 assured the DOD that all defense contractors' documentation would adhere to SGML.

HTML

Two years after the publication of the SGML standard, Tim Berners-Lee built his Web browser and server. He needed small, simple language to format documents for display. Berners-Lee envisioned thousands of researchers publishing works on the Web, so the markup language had to be much simpler than the complex and arcane vocabulary of SGML. He just happened to have an expert in SGML at CERN, Anders Berglund, whom you read about earlier.

Between them, they developed HTML.

HTML focused on marking up presentation and left the users of the system, not the author, to determine how they wanted the document to be displayed. Users could determine what point size, color, and font a "heading 1" would be displayed in. Content was king.

With the explosion of the Web, however, many authors felt too constrained. They wanted control not only of content, but of presentation as well. That factor, and the competing browser technologies that emerged, resulted in incremental and chaotic changes to the HTML language. In addition, HTML had some serious drawbacks when it came to describing content.

XML

The first people to recognize the seriousness of these drawbacks were the developers who had been laboring in SGML. SGML experts realized that HTML was going to be neither powerful enough nor flexible enough to easily manage large, industrial, database-driven applications on the Web, and they were petitioning W3C to develop a way to use SGML on the Web. One of those experts was Jon Bosak, of Novell, who is now with Sun Microsystems.

Bosak had successfully used SGML to put 150,000 pages of Novell technical manuals on the Web, and knew firsthand how difficult it was. He petitioned W3C to investigate how the process could be made easier. W3C's Dan Connelly was especially interested, but W3C did not have the resources necessary to develop the language. Connelly asked Bosak whether Sun Microsystems would be interested in underwriting the effort. Sun was, and did, and Bosak went on to head the Web SGML Activity.

From the end of August 1996 through November of that year, Bosak and his team of international experts pared and simplified SGML into XML. It took another year to fill out the details and bring it to the point of a W3C specification. How successful the team was in simplifying SGML is best demonstrated by the page counts of the specifications: 26 pages for XML, 500-plus for SGML.

What XML Is

On one level, eXtensible Markup Language (XML) can be thought of as a meta-language, or a system of rules that describe how a language is to be constructed. The language is extensible, which means that, as long as you remain compliant with XML's rules, you can invent different vocabularies to describe all kinds of systems and information. You can write an XML document to describe aircraft systems, and another to describe butcher-shop inventories.

On another level, an XML document is a storage medium. A document contains data and a description of that data. XML uses tags like HTML does, but unlike in HTML, those tags describe the data that is enclosed in them, and the XML document as a whole describes the relationship of that data to other data in the document.

In XML, the basic building block is an *entity*. An entity is a unit of storage that consists of parsed or unparsed data. Parsed data is either markup or parsed character data (PCDATA). Unparsed character data (CDATA) is ignored by the parser. Here is an example of an XML entity:

```
<street_address>171 South Hart Street</street_address>
```

`<street_address>` and `</street_address>` are markup, and `171 South Hart Street` is character data.

By itself, XML really doesn't do much. It needs an application to use the data it contains in some way. Just as a browser uses HTML to display a page, an application uses XML for whatever the application is designed to do. Because applications, not humans, deal with XML, XML's structure and syntax are very precise.

The application relies on an XML Processor to provide access to XML data and its syntax. You'll be using the XML Processor in Microsoft Internet Explorer.

Using Microsoft Internet Explorer 5.0 or higher, you can parse XML and verify that it is well formed. *Well formed* means that the document conforms to the correct XML structure. You will be using Microsoft Internet Explorer to check the well formedness of the documents we write.

An XML Document

XML documents are generally written top-down, making it easier to define the hierarchical structure of the document. You'll design a sample document the same way, and examine what you're doing at each stage. Your finished document will be a small catalog of books.

At the simplest level, an XML document can consist of a prolog, an optional DTD, and a root element.

Prolog

A prolog can consist of comments and processing instructions. Comments begin with `<!--` and end with `-->`, and processing instructions start with `<?` and end with `?>`.

The simplest and most often-used processing instruction simply tells the XML Processor what type of document this is and what version of XML you are using. The sample catalog begins with a processing instruction and a comment:

```
<?xml version="1.0"?>
<!-- An XML Book Catalog -->
```

Save these lines into a Notepad document and call it `catalog.xml`.

If you try to look at `catalog.xml` in Microsoft Internet Explorer, you'll find that it isn't a well-formed XML file and that the XML Processor will throw an error: `XML document must have a top level element`. That's because your document contains only a prolog.

DTD

The next part of an XML document is the DTD. Most often a DTD element calls an external file, a Document Type Definition, written with a `.dtd` extension.

DTDs are the rules of grammar for a particular XML document. They can contain element declarations, attribute declarations, notations declarations, and entity declarations. We'll cover these later when you fill in your DTD. A DTD can be external, as with the example's `.dtd` file, or it can be internal to the XML document.

There are two classifications of grammar conformity in XML: well formed and valid. As we have seen, *well formed* means that the syntax is consistent with the XML specification. Valid means that it is well formed and consistent with the DTD.

Let's add a DTD to your XML file. The code inside the square brackets is the internal DTD:

```
<?xml version="1.0"?>
<!-- An XML Book Catalog -->
<!DOCTYPE catalog SYSTEM "catalog.dtd">
```

You know that this isn't going to run in Internet Explorer after you save it to `catalog.xml` because you still don't have a root element, but if you did try the code in Internet Explorer, you would get the error `The system cannot locate the resource specified. Error processing resource 'catalog.dtd'. Line 5, Position 3.`

This is, of course, because you haven't actually written a `.dtd` file. Do that now. Using Notepad, create a file at the same location as your `catalog.xml` file. At this point, the DTD doesn't need to have any content; just save an empty file with the filename `catalog.dtd`. Open `catalog.xml` in Internet Explorer and you'll see our old favorite, `XML document must have a top level element.`

Well, maybe you'd better add that top-level element. Your root element will start out empty, but it can contain comments, processing instructions, other elements, entity references, and CDATA sections.

Believe it or not, you have already committed to the name for the element. DTDs define the structure and grammar of the element they are named after, so `catalog.dtd` defines the element `catalog`. Here's the code with the root element added:

```
<?xml version="1.0"?>
<!-- An XML Book Catalog -->
<!DOCTYPE catalog SYSTEM "catalog.dtd">

<catalog></catalog>
```

Open the document in Internet Explorer, and you'll find that this is a well-formed XML document.

It may be well formed, but it is really pretty useless. Let's try to make it more useful by adding some information.

Adding Elements

You do this by adding elements to hold that information. Elements can contain parsed character data, attributes, and entity references.

Let's start by modeling the information you would like to have included in the catalog and deciding how to structure it. Your catalog will represent a collection of books, so you'll need a `book` element. Some of the information you'll want in the `book` element are the author, title, description, publisher, ISBN number, and price. Figure 5.1 shows a preliminary structure.

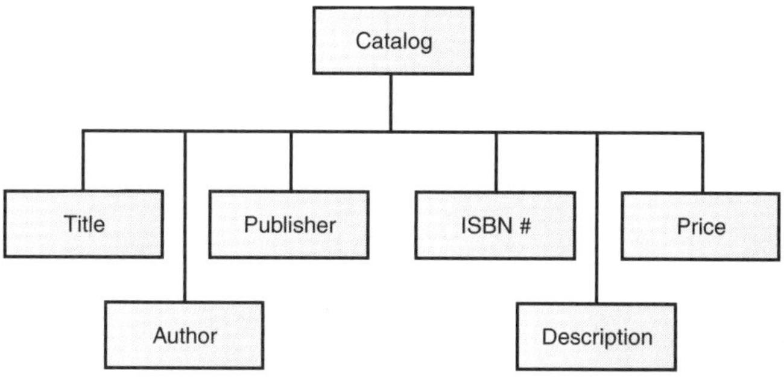

FIGURE 5.1
A possible catalog structure.

Inside your catalog tags, you can add elements to describe data in your XML document. Entities are added in angle brackets, just as with the root element. Here's the code with the added elements:

```
<?xml version="1.0"?>
<!-- An XML Book Catalog -->
<!DOCTYPE catalog SYSTEM "catalog.dtd">
<catalog>
     <book>
          <title></title>
          <author></author>
          <publisher></publisher>
          <ISBN_Num></ISBN_Num>
          <description></description>
          <price></price>
     </book>
</catalog>
```

Check your typing by opening the document in Internet Explorer. You should be able to open the file without error.

This is a good start, but it looks as though we need a little more detail in two of the elements: `author` and `description`. You'll want to break down the `author` element into first name and last name so that the application that uses this data can search on first name, last name, or both. Also, the `description` element is really too broad. You need to add categories for a synopsis, a picture of the cover, and the number of pages. Figure 5.2 shows the new structure. The changes are shown in the following code:

```
<?xml version="1.0"?>
<!-- An XML Book Catalog -->
```

```
<!DOCTYPE catalog SYSTEM "catalog.dtd"><catalog>
     <book>
          <title></title>
          <author>
               <first_name></first_name>
               <last_name></last_name>
              </author>
          <publisher></publisher>
          <ISBN_Num></ISBN_Num>
          <description>
               <synopsis></synopsis>
               <picture></picture>
               <page_count></page_count>
              </description>
          <price></price>
     </book>
</catalog>
```

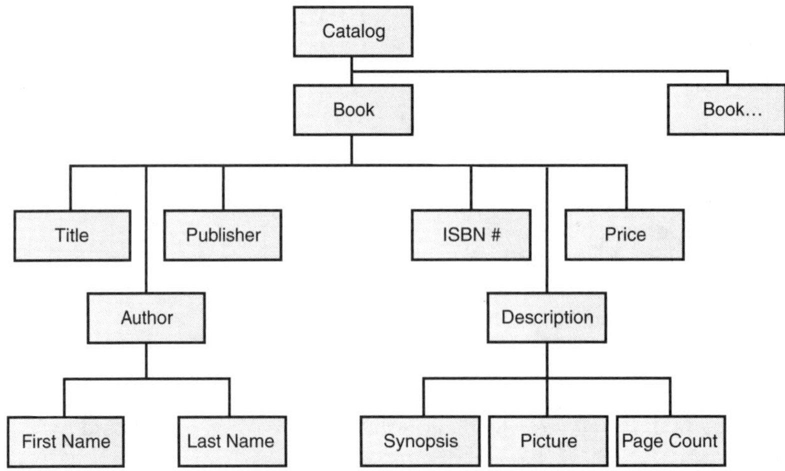

FIGURE 5.2
A refined catalog structure.

If you are satisfied with the structure, you can duplicate it for a three-book catalog and begin to load your data. Listing 5.1 shows the result.

LISTING 5.1 Loading the Data

```
<?xml version="1.0"?>
<!-- An XML Book Catalog -->
<!DOCTYPE catalog SYSTEM "catalog.dtd">
```

LISTING 5.1 Continued

```
<catalog>
       <book>
          <title>Sams Teach Yourself ASP.NET in 21 Days </title>
              <author>
               <first_name>Chris</first_name>
               <last_name>Payne</last_name>
              </author>
              <author>
                <first_name>Scott</first_name>
               <last_name>Mitchell</last_name>
              </author>
          <publisher>Sams</publisher>
          <ISBN_Num>0672321688</ISBN_Num>
          <description>
               <synopsis>The book introduces the ASP.NET Framework,
➥Visual Basic .NET, and C#, the new COM framework. </synopsis>
               <picture>21asp-net.jpg</picture>
               <page_count>1024</page_count>
              </description>
          <price>39.99</price>
     </book>
       <book>
          <title>Flash for the Real World: E-Commerce Case Studies</title>
          <author>
               <first_name>Steve</first_name>
               <last_name>Street</last_name>
              </author>
          <publisher>Sams</publisher>
          <ISBN_Num>0672320797</ISBN_Num>
          <description>
               <synopsis>e-commerce case studies directed to intermediate,
➥ advanced and professional Flash developers.</synopsis>
               <picture>flashRW.jpg</picture>
               <page_count>304</page_count>
              </description>
          <price>49.99</price>
     </book>
       <book>
          <title>Perl Developer's Dictionary</title>
          <author>
               <first_name>Clinton</first_name>
               <last_name>Pierce</last_name>
              </author>
```

LISTING 5.1 Continued

```
        <publisher>Sams</publisher>
        <ISBN_Num>0672320673</ISBN_Num>
        <description>
            <synopsis>Perl Developer's Dictionary is a complete,
➥ well-organized reference to the Perl language and environment</synopsis>
            <picture>pdd.jpg</picture>
            <page_count>640</page_count>
           </description>
        <price>39.99</price>
    </book>
</catalog>
```

Notice that the first book has two authors.

You now have a well-formed XML document that describes the data structure. It can be made considerably more concise, however, through the use of attributes.

Using Attributes

Elements are logical units of information, whereas attributes are characteristics of the information. If you think of elements as information objects, attributes are properties of the information object.

A decision about whether to model a unit of information as an element or an attribute depends on many factors. The primary consideration is context. Elements should be independent information units, whereas attributes should clarify the information of an element.

Another consideration is how the information will be used. Attributes can be more tightly constrained than elements. For example, if you have a piece of information that can take one of three possible values, an attribute is the logical choice because attributes can be constrained against a predefined list.

Attributes have other advantages as well. They can have default values, they can be constrained to limited data types, they are very concise, and they are easier to parse than elements. Because of these advantages, attributes should be used as much as possible.

Attributes have some disadvantages, though, that modify our data model thinking. Because of the way attributes are entered in elements, they are very inconvenient for long strings of text. Also, they cannot contain nested information.

If you take a look at your XML document, you can see several places where it makes sense to use attributes. Within the `book` element, `publisher`, `ISBN_Num`, and `price` are candidates, and within the `description` element, `picture` and `page count` are possible choices. Let's replace these elements with attributes. Listing 5.2 shows the replacements.

LISTING 5.2 Using Attributes

```
<?xml version="1.0"?>
<!-- An XML Book Catalog -->
<!DOCTYPE catalog SYSTEM "catalog.dtd">
<catalog>
     <book publisher="Sams" ISBN_Num ="ISBN0672321688" price="39.99" >
          <title>Sams Teach Yourself ASP.NET in 21 Days </title>
          <author>
               <first_name>Chris</first_name>
               <last_name>Payne</last_name>
          </author>
          <author>
               <first_name>Scott</first_name>
               <last_name>Mitchell</last_name>
          </author>
          <description picture="21asp-net.jpg" page_count="1024">
               <synopsis>The book introduces the ASP.NET Framework,
➥ Visual Basic .NET, and C#, the new COM framework. </synopsis>
          </description>
     </book>
     <book publisher="Sams" ISBN_Num ="ISBN0672320797" price="49.99">
          <title>Flash for the Real World: E-Commerce Case Studies</title>
          <author>
               <first_name>Steve</first_name>
               <last_name>Street</last_name>
          </author>
          <description picture="flashRW.jpg" page_count="304">
               <synopsis>E-commerce case studies directed to intermediate,
➥ advanced and professional Flash developers.</synopsis>
          </description>
     </book>
     <book publisher="Sams" ISBN_Num ="ISBN0672320673" price="39.99">
          <title>Perl Developer's Dictionary</title>
          <author>
               <first_name>Clinton</first_name>
               <last_name>Pierce</last_name>
          </author>
          <description picture="pdd.jpg" page_count="640">
               <synopsis>Perl Developer's Dictionary is a complete,
➥ well-organized reference to the Perl language and environment</synopsis>
          </description>
     </book>
</catalog>
```

Again, notice that your document parses in Internet Explorer. This means you have well-formed XML and valid XML. The document is valid because you check the validity against your DTD, and your DTD is empty.

Writing the DTD

But you now have enough background to be able to proceed to write the DTD. Remember that DTDs are the rules of grammar for a particular XML document. One of the things a validating parser checks against the DTD is that no elements are used in the XML document that haven't been declared in the DTD.

To declare an element in a DTD, you have to know what the element contains.

Empty Elements

First, elements can be empty. If an empty element contains any information, it must be contained in attributes. Here is an example of an empty element containing data:

```
<contact telephone="1-800-555-1212"></contact>
```

This can also be written in XML this way:

```
<contact telephone="1-800-555-1212"/>
```

Empty elements in the DTD are declared using the following syntax:

```
<!ELEMENT contact EMPTY>
```

In this case, you don't have any empty elements.

Elements-Only Elements

Second, elements can contain nothing but other child elements. Elements-only elements are declared using a format like this:

```
<!ELEMENT ElementName (ContentModel)> .
```

Your element `catalog` is an example of an elements-only element. The document model for `catalog` is `(book)`. Note the parentheses. They define the group of elements that the declared element contains. The enclosed elements are separated with commas. You can declare the `catalog` element like this:

```
<!ELEMENT catalog (book)>
```

Various characters can be used to further constrain the content model enclosed in the parentheses:

- If there is no symbol, it means that a particular enclosed element can occur only once.
- A question mark (`?`) says that a particular enclosed element can occur exactly once, or not at all.

- An asterisk (`*`) indicates that the child element can occur any number of times.
- A plus sign (`+`) indicates that a particular child element must occur once.
- A pipe (`|`) says that one element must occur from a choice of elements.

In this case, you want the catalog to contain at least one book, so your declaration becomes this:

```
<!ELEMENT catalog (book+)>
```

Go ahead and paste that line into your empty `catalog.dtd` file.

Next, you'll do the `book` element. The `book` element contains the `title`, `author`, and `description` elements. Because you must have one title and one description per book but you may have multiple authors, you'll declare the `book` element like so:

```
<!ELEMENT book (title, author+, description)>
```

The `book` element contains `title`, `author`, and `description` elements that need to be declared. `Title` contains nothing but `PCDATA`, so we can declare it with the following code:

```
<!ELEMENT title (#PCDATA)>
```

The `author` element contains `first_name` and `last_name` elements:

```
<!ELEMENT author (first_name, last_name)>
```

The `description` element holds the `synopsis` element:

```
<!ELEMENT description (synopsis)>
<!ELEMENT synopsis (#PCDATA)>
```

You can also declare the `author` element's `first_name` and `last_name` child elements now:

```
<!ELEMENT first_name (#PCDATA)>
<!ELEMENT last_name (#PCDATA)>
```

Declaring Attributes

Your `book` element has attributes, so you need to declare them in DTD as well. Attributes are declared differently from elements. Attributes follow the form

```
<!ATTLIST ElementName AttributeName AttributeType Default>
```

Instead of symbols, attributes have more defined attribute types. Attribute types can be any of the following:

- `CDATA`—Unparsed character data.
- `Enumerated`—A series of string values.
- `ID`—A unique identifier.

- `IDREF`—A reference to an ID that appears somewhere else in the DTD.
- `IDREFS`—Several references to IDs that appear elsewhere in the DTD.
- `NMTOKEN`—A name consisting of letters, numbers, periods, colons, dashes, and underscores.
- `NMTOKENS`—Multiple `NMTOKEN`s.
- `ENTITY`—An external binary entity.
- `ENTITIES`—Multiple occurrences of `ENTITY` separated by whitespace.

For now, you'll only worry about `CDATA` and `Enumerated`.

Attributes also have four default types:

- `#REQUIRED` means that the attribute must be included.
- `#IMPLIED` means that the attribute is optional.
- `#FIXED` means that the attribute's value is a fixed value.
- `default` is the default value of the attribute.

The `book` element has three attributes: `publisher`, `ISBN_Num`, and `price`. You need to declare all three. First, you'll declare `ISBN_Num`. ISBNs are unique to each book, so your catalog shouldn't have two books with the same ISBN. To ensure that it doesn't, you'll assign your `ISBN_Num` attribute an ID type. ID types must begin with a letter (A–Z), an underscore, or a colon. Begin your ID with the letters *ISBN*.

For pricing, let's say that the standard prices are $49.99, $39.99, or $29.99. You can use an enumerated data type for the price attribute to ensure that your XML file does not accept a nonstandard price.

Fortunately, you can declare multiple attributes within a single attribute list. You do that like this:

```
<!ATTLIST book
     publisher CDATA "Sams"
     ISBN_Num ID #REQUIRED
     price (29.99|39.99|49.99) #REQUIRED>
```

Paste this text into `catalog.dtd`.

The `description` element holds the `picture` and `page_count` attributes:

```
<!ELEMENT description (synopsis)>
<!ATTLIST description
     picture CDATA #REQUIRED
     page_count CDATA #REQUIRED>
<!ELEMENT synopsis (#PCDATA)>
```

Add this last code to `catalog.dtd`, and you should have a well-formed, valid XML document. Listing 5.3 shows all the code.

LISTING 5.3 Catalog.dtd

```
<!ELEMENT catalog (book+)>
<!ELEMENT book (title, author*, description)>
<!ATTLIST book
     publisher CDATA "Sams"
     ISBN_Num ID #REQUIRED
     price (29.99|39.99|49.99) #REQUIRED>
<!ELEMENT title (#PCDATA)>
<!ELEMENT author (first_name, last_name)>
<!ELEMENT description (synopsis)>
<!ATTLIST description
     picture CDATA #REQUIRED
     page_count CDATA #REQUIRED>
<!ELEMENT synopsis (#PCDATA)>
<!ELEMENT first_name (#PCDATA)>
<!ELEMENT last_name  (#PCDATA)>
```

Testing the XML

To check the validity of your XML, you need a validating parser. Point your browser to `http://msdn.microsoft.com/library/default.asp?url=/library/en-us/dnxml/html/xmlpaddownload.asp` and download the Microsoft XML Notepad.

After you have installed the utility, open your `catalog.xml` in it. If you have typed correctly, the document will open without error and give you a nice picture of your document structure along with all the values of your elements and attributes.

Let's try to break the document in a couple of places and see what happens:

1. When you declared your `title` element, you said that one title was required. Open `catalog.xml`, cut the title and its enclosing tags out of the third book element, and save. Open the document with XML Notepad. What happens?

   XML Notepad will complain and refuse to process the file because book three doesn't have a title, and you told XML Notepad, through `catalog.dtd`, that it would.

   Paste the `title` element back into `catalog.xml` and save.

2. Open `catalog.XML` again. Let's try to get a good deal on Clinton Pierce's book, *Perl Developer's Dictionary*. Go into book three of `catalog.xml` and change `39.99` to `17.50`. Save the file, and then open it with XML Notepad.

XML Notepad won't allow your purchase! You told the XML Processor that the price could only be $29.99, $39.99, or $49.99—$17.50 doesn't check out. Be sure to change the price in `catalog.xml` back to its original, nonbargain state, and resave.

3. Cut the ISBN number on book two, type book one's number into it, and save. Open the file in XML Notepad and note the error; then paste the correct ISBN back into `catalog.xml`.

Namespaces

Because XML is an extensible language, there are no restrictions on the names you can choose for your element tags. A tag derives its meaning from its context. For example, in `catalog.xml`, you used the tag `Title` to describe the name of a book in your document. Let's say that your catalog contained law books instead of computer books and you wanted to flag those that related to the legal principle of "title." Especially if two different organizations were working on this document (one of the advantages of XML), you could very well end up with two `title` tags that meant two entirely different things. How would the XML Processor or your application know which was which?

The answer is namespaces. When W3C made the namespace recommendation in January 1999, they wrote:

> We envision applications of Extensible Markup Language (XML) where a single XML document may contain elements and attributes (here referred to as a "markup vocabulary") that are defined for and used by multiple software modules. One motivation for this is modularity; if such a markup vocabulary exists which is well-understood and for which there is useful software available, it is better to re-use this markup rather than re-invent it.

Reusability of DTDs and schema, which we'll take a look at next, was the principle motivation for the development of namespaces. But there are other benefits, too.

Declaring that a particular tag belongs to a given namespace makes it possible to write DTDs that refer to specific parts of a complex XML document. If your `catalog.xml` were a part of an e-commerce application, you might have an entirely different namespace for the currency exchange sections, and yet another one for shipping, where `Title` might mean Mr., Mrs., or Ms. Namespaces allow you to modularize XML code.

Namespaces are consistent with the vision of XML's extensibility. Different DTDs and schemas can be designed for unforeseen applications yet incorporated easily into documents through namespaces.

Namespaces are simple to declare. The namespace declaration takes the following form:

```
xmlns: Prefix = Namespace
```

The keyword xmlns alerts the XML Processor that a namespace exists and is used in the document. The prefix part is a short name for a placeholder to indicate where in the document the namespace is being used. An element or attribute name that includes the prefix is said to be *qualified*, that is, it explicitly uses the namespace. Unqualified names are assumed to be in the namespace if a namespace is declared.

For example, xmlns:b="http://books-unlimited.com" could define all element names that begin with b: as belonging to the namespace uniquely derived from http://books-unlimited.com. The names of those elements might be defined in an external DTD that could be located at http://books-unlimited.com/catalog.dtd, but it is not necessary to point to a DTD or schema in order to declare a namespace. In the following example, author is a qualified name, and first_name and last_name are unqualified. The fact that the child element, first_name, is unqualified means that the namespace that applies to first_name is the namespace applicable to its parent, author:

```
<author xmlns:b="http://books-unlimited.com">
     <first_name>Scott</first_name>
     <last_name>Mitchell</last_name>
</author>
```

If your code declared a separate namespace for first_name like

```
<author xmlns:b="http://books-unlimited.com">
     <xmlns:l=http://lawbooks.com first_name>Scott</first_name>
     <last_name>Mitchell</last_name>
</author>
```

first_name would now be qualified and would be in the l namespace.

Namespaces can map to URIs, URLs, or URNs. Each of these establishes a unique mapping of a prefix to a namespace declaration.

Usually, namespace declarations point to DTDs or schemas that provide the rules for the namespaces. For example, all Microsoft XML Schemas must include the namespace dt for datatypes. Here is a sample declaration:

```
<Schema name="MySchema" xmlns="urn:schemas-microsoft-com:xml-data"
xmlns:dt="urn:schemas-microsoft-com:datatypes">
<!--Schema content-->
</Schema>
```

You'll find that nearly any XML document that is designed to be used by more than one organization, department, or even individual will use namespace declarations.

XML Schema

DTDs have a long and rich history with roots that extend to SGML. Despite their longevity, however, DTDs have their limitations. First, the language is not very intuitive, and at times it's downright cryptic. Second, DTDs do not address data typing, so we can't constrain price in our catalog to a decimal value, for example. Third, you cannot really constrain how many times an element occurs. You can specify that it occurs at least once, or that it doesn't occur at all, or that it can occur any number of times, but you can't set the element to occur three times and three times only.

XML Schema addresses all these points and more.

Like DTDs, XML schemas are used to describe elements and their contents so that XML documents can be validated. XML schemas, though, use XML as their language. Everything you have learned about XML is applicable to XML schemas.

XML Schema supports a large number of data types, including not only most number types, but calendar, time, and Boolean values as well. Because XML schemas are written in XML, those data types can be extended by the XML schema author to produce extremely rich, custom data types.

XML schemas can describe elements with `minOccurs` and `maxOccurs` keywords that let you tightly constrain the range of element occurrences. If you want three occurrences, you can have three occurrences.

Unfortunately, it's not all good news when it comes to XML schemas.

Background

XML Schema had its origins in a W3C note on XML-Data in January 1998. The note proposed an XML vocabulary for describing XML documents. Another note in July proposed an idea known as Document Content Description (DCD) for the same purpose.

It's important to know that W3C notes are really just ideas that announce some of the things W3C is thinking about. Microsoft thought both those ideas were good and began development of their own system while W3C created a committee to write a working draft of the specification.

Microsoft finished development of XML Schema early enough to put it into Internet Explorer 5.0 when it was released in March 1999. W3C released its Working Draft, the second-highest stage for a W3C specification, on September 24, 1999. The W3C working Draft became a recommendation on May 2, 2001.

What does all that mean? It means we currently have more than one XML Schema de facto specification. More important, any applications that support XML Schema which were created before May 2, 2001, probably do not adhere to the W3C recommendation. Because XML Schema support is built into Internet Explorer 5.0, we'll discuss that implementation.

Building a Schema

We will discuss XML Schema in the context of catalog.dtd. You'll use your DTD to develop the XML Schema for catalog.xml.

Because it is an XML document, your schema needs to start the file with the same processing instruction you used in catalog.xml:

```
<?xml version="1.0"?>
```

Then you need to use the Schema element to indicate to the XML Processor that this document is to be used to validate other XML documents. The Schema element contains the name of the schema and its namespace:

```
<Schema name="catalogSchema"
     xmlns:"urn=schemas-microsoft-com:xml-data"
     xmlns:dt="urn:schemas-microsoft-com:datatypes">
     <!--Schema content-->
</Schema>
```

The schema declares two namespaces: one for xml-data and one for datatypes. The default namespace is urn:schemas-microsoft-com:xml-data, so everything in the document, except what's prefixed with dt:, belongs to this namespace. Elements using the datatypes namespace will need to be qualified. In addition to the types specified in DTDs, XML Schema currently supports the following types: string, bin.base64, bin.hex, boolean, char, date, dateTime, dateTime.tz, fixed.14.4, float, int, number, time, time.tz, i1, i2, i4, r4, r8, ui1, ui2, ui4, uri, and uuid.

Elements and Attributes

The ElementType element and the AttributeType elements form the basic structure of XML schemas. It may be helpful to think in object-oriented terms when approaching ElementTypes and AttributeTypes, elements and attributes. You can think of ElementTypes and AttributeTypes as abstract classes, and elements and attributes as concrete classes derived from the Types. The ElementType can contain attribute, AttributeType, datatype, description, element, and group child elements.

If you look at catalog.xml, you'll see that the first element you need to describe is the catalog element. Before you can do that, though, you need to describe the catalog ElementType:

```
<ElementType name="catalog" content="eltOnly" order="seq">
     <element type="book" minOccurs="1" maxOccurs="*"/>
</ElementType>
```

The content attribute of the ElementType is set to eltOnly, so catalog can contain only elements; and the order attribute states that catalog orders its enclosed elements sequentially. The minOccurs and maxOccurs attributes say that you must have at least one book, but you can have as many as you want. Now, you need to declare an ElementType for your book element, but first you need to describe the types of the attributes that your book element will hold. Your book has three attributes—publisher, ISBN_Num, and price—but those attributes have not been described. You need to describe them with an AttributeType:

```
<AttributeType name="title" dt:type="string" required="yes"/>
<AttributeType name="ISBN_Num" dt:type="id" required="yes"/>
<AttributeType name="price" dt:type="enumeration"
➥ dt:values="29.99 39.99 49.99" required="yes"/>
```

Your title attributeType is declared to be of type string; ISBN_Num is an ID type and the type of your price attribute is enumeration, with the allowable values of 29.99, 39.99, and 49.99. You also specify that values for all three attributes must be supplied.

With the AttributeTypes described, you can now write your ElementType:

```
<ElementType name="book" content="eltOnly" order="seq">
     <element type="title" minOccurs="1" maxOccurs="1"/>
       <element type="author" minOccurs="1" maxOccurs="*"/>
       <element type="first_name" mimOccurs="1" maxOccurs="1"/>
       <element type="last_name" mimOccurs="1" maxOccurs="1"/>
       <element type="description" minOccurs="1" maxOccurs="*"/>
       <attribute type="publisher"/>
       <attribute type="ISBN_Num"/>
       <attribute type="price"/>
</ElementType>
```

The content tag says that your book element contains elements only, and the order tag tells the XML Processor that the XML document lists those elements sequentially. The elements are Title, which must occur once; author, which must occur at least once but can occur as many times as necessary; first_name and last_name which must occur once and only once, and description, which must occur once. The book will contain three attributes: publisher, ISBN_Num, and price.

Now, you need to create ElementTypes for the child elements Title, Author, first_name, and last_name:

```
<ElementType name="title" content="textOnly"/>

<ElementType name="author" content="textOnly"/>

<ElementType name="first_name" content="textOnly"/>

<ElementType name="last_name" content="textOnly"/>
```

Here, you declare element `title`, `author`, `first_name`, and `last_name` to be text-only attributes. Before you can write your `ElementType` for `description`, though, you have to write your `AttributeTypes` for `picture` and `page_count`.

You'll use the filename of the picture, so give it a string type. `PageCount` type will be an integer. A `picture` may be optional, but a `pageCount` will always be `required`; so add the two attributes like this:

```
<AttributeType name="picture" dt:type="string" required="no"/>
<AttributeType name="pageCount" dt:type="int" required="yes"/>
```

Next, you need to declare an `ElementType` for your synopsis element. You do that like this:

```
<ElementType name="synopsis" content="textOnly"/>.
```

Now, the components for your `description ElementType` are complete, so you can describe it:

```
<ElementType name="description" content="textOnly">
     <element name="synopsis" content="textOnly"/>
     <attribute type="picture"/>
     <attribute type="page_count"/>
</ElementType>
```

You now have a validating XML Schema document for `catalog.xml`. Listing 5.4 shows all the code for `catalogSchema.xml`.

LISTING 5.4 `CatalogSchema.xml`

```
<?xml version="1.0"?>

<Schema name="catalogSchema"
     xmlns="urn:schemas-microsoft-com:xml-data"
     xmlns:dt="urn:schemas-microsoft-com:datatypes">

     <ElementType name="catalog" content="eltOnly" order="seq">
          <element type="book" minOccurs="1" maxOccurs="*"/>
     </ElementType>

     <AttributeType name="publisher" dt:type="string" required="yes"/>
     <AttributeType name="ISBN_Num" dt:type="id" required="yes"/>
     <AttributeType name="price" dt:type="enumeration"
          dt:values="29.99 39.99 49.99" required="yes"/>

     <ElementType name="book" content="eltOnly" order="seq">
          <element type="title" minOccurs="1" maxOccurs="1"/>
          <element type="author" minOccurs="1" maxOccurs="*"/>
          <element type="description" minOccurs="1" maxOccurs="*"/>
```

LISTING 5.4 Continued

```
        <attribute type="publisher"/>
        <attribute type="ISBN_Num"/>
        <attribute type="price"/>
    </ElementType>
    <ElementType name="title" content="textOnly"/>

    <ElementType name="author" content="textOnly"/>
    <ElementType name="first_name" content="textOnly"/>
    <ElementType name="last_name" content="textOnly"/>

    <AttributeType name="picture" dt:type="string" required="no"/>
    <AttributeType name="page_count" dt:type="int" required="yes"/>

    <ElementType name="description" content="eltOnly">
        <element type ="synopsis" minOccurs="1" maxOccurs="1"/>
        <attribute type="picture"/>
        <attribute type="page_count"/>
    </ElementType>

    <ElementType name="synopsis" content="textOnly"></ElementType>

</Schema>
```

In your XML file, you'll remove the `!DOCTYPE` declaration, and add an `xmlns` attribute to the catalog tag. Listing 5.5 shows the changes to the `catalog.xml` file.

LISTING 5.5 Final `catalog.xml`

```
<?xml version="1.0"?>
<!-- An XML Book Catalog -->
<catalog xmlns="x-schema:catalogSchema.xml">
    <book publisher="SAMS" ISBN_Num ="ISBN0672321688" price="39.99">
        <title>Sams Teach Yourself ASP.NET in 21 Days </title>
        <author>
            <first_name>Chris</first_name>
            <last_name>Payne</last_name>
        </author>
        <author>
            <first_name>Scott</first_name>
            <last_name>Mitchell</last_name>
        </author>
        <description picture="21asp-net.jpg " page_count="1024">
            <synopsis>The book introduces the ASP.NET Framework,
➥ Visual Basic .NET, and C#, the new COM framework. </synopsis>
        </description>
```

LISTING 5.5 Continued

```
    </book>
    <book publisher="SAMS" ISBN_Num ="ISBN0672320797" price="49.99">
        <title>Flash for the Real World: E-Commerce Case Studies</title>
        <author>
            <first_name>Steve</first_name>
            <last_name>Street</last_name>
        </author>
        <description picture="flashRW.jpg " page_count="304">
            <synopsis>E-commerce case studies directed to intermediate,
➥ advanced and professional Flash developers.</synopsis>
        </description>
    </book>
    <book publisher="&SP;" ISBN_Num ="ISBN0672320673" price="39.99">
        <title>Perl Developer's Dictionary</title>
        <author>
            <first_name>Clinton</first_name>
            <last_name>Pierce</last_name>
        </author>
        <description picture="pdd.jpg" page_count="640">
            <synopsis>Perl Developer's Dictionary is a complete,
➥ well-organized reference to the Perl language and environment</synopsis>
        </description>
    </book>
</catalog>
```

As you can see, `catalogSchema.xml` is much more verbose than `catalog.dtd`, but its structure is considerably more well-defined.

It is important to understand that we developed both the schema and the DTD backward for teaching purposes. Normally, because they describe and constrain documents, DTDs and schema are written before the XML document and serve as a blueprint for it.

Keep in mind that XML Schema specifications vary and represent a moving target. You will certainly see schema that do not conform to this specification, but the principle of defining structure, logic, and content will be the same.

Groove's Use of XML

Groove uses XML to define a class of data objects and the behavior of the applications that process them. It also uses XML as its storage medium. Groove specifically chose XML for several reasons, including the capability to interoperate with other systems and storage models, and the fact that XML is an open and well-understood language.

Groove uses the namespace `xmlns:g="urn.groove.net"` and precedes all Groove-specific uses of XML with the opening tag `<g:`.

Virtually everything about Groove is stored in an XML database. If you are in a shared space with members you have invited and are using a suite of tools, all of that data is persisted in a Groove XML file. If you are in the Calendar Tool and you enter an appointment, that data is stored in an XML document unique to that tool. When you write a tool template, you write it in XML. You describe the components you will use, how those components are arranged on the screen, how those components behave and interact, and where and how any user input is stored.

Here is some XML you might use in constructing a tool. It defines a button that will be used in the tool's UI:

```
            <g:Component Name="NextButton">
                <g:ComponentResource FingerprintID="Groove"
➥URL="http://components.groove.net/Groove/Components/Root.osd?
➥Package=net.groove.Groove.ToolComponents.GrooveCommonComponents_DLL&amp;
➥Version=0&amp;Factory=Button"/>
                <g:PropertyList Version="1">
                    <g:Property Name="Label" Value="Next"/>
                    <g:Property Name="Style" Value="StandardIconButton"/>
                    <g:Property Name="Enabled" Value="true"/>
                    <g:Property Name="OverrideLabelPosition"
➥ Value="InsideLeft"/>
                    <g:Property Name="ImageURL"
➥ Value="grooveFile:///ToolBMPs\Arrows16x16Images.jpg"/>
                    <g:Property Name="ImageMaskURL"
➥ Value="grooveFile:///ToolBMPs\Arrows16x16ImagesMask.bmp"/>
                    <g:Property Name="ImageOffset" Value="16"/>
                    <g:Property Name="ImageHeight" Value="16"/>
                    <g:Property Name="ImageWidth" Value="16"/>
                </g:PropertyList>
            </g:Component>
```

This piece of XML code is named `nextButton`. It provides the location and the method of instantiation for a button COM object.

The property list describes the properties of the button, the button's style and its image resources, and its label. It is typical of the XML you will be writing as a Groove developer.

Groove Schemas

Groove does not support DTDs or Microsoft's XML Schema, but instead, it has its own version of schemas. Groove schemas are stored in an XML database called `schemas.xss`.

All Groove schemas can define attributes, provide indexing, and specify bindings. Groove schemas support a wide variety of datatypes. Even though data in XML is text, storage services filter the data through schema when writing to disk in order to store the data using the appropriate data type.

Here is a sample schema that serves as a default schema, the `groovestandardrecordschema2.xml`:

```
<g:Schema Version="1,0,0,0" URL="GrooveStandardRecordsSchema2.xml"
➥ xmlns:g="urn:groove.net">
    <g:ElementDecl ElementTemplate="true" Name="urn:groove.net:Record">
        <g:AttrGroup>
            <g:AttrDef Type="Double" Name="_RecordID"/>
            <g:AttrDef Type="Date" Name="_Created"/>
            <g:AttrDef Type="String" Name="_CreatedBy"/>
            <g:AttrDef Type="String" Name="_CreatedByURL"/>
            <g:AttrDef Type="Date" Name="_Modified"/>
            <g:AttrDef Type="String" Name="_ModifiedBy"/>
        </g:AttrGroup>
    </g:ElementDecl>
    <g:ElementDecl ElementTemplate="true"
➥ Name="urn:groove.net:HierarchicalRecord">
        <g:ElementRef IsChildElement="0" Element="urn:groove.net:Record"/>
        <g:AttrGroup>
            <g:AttrDef Type="Double" Name="_ParentID"/>
            <g:AttrDef Type="Double" Name="_NewParentID"/>
            <g:AttrDef Type="Double" Name="_PreviousSiblingID"/>
        </g:AttrGroup>
    </g:ElementDecl>
    <g:ElementDecl Name="urn:groove.net:RecordWrapper">
        <g:AttrGroup>
            <g:AttrDef Index="True" Type="Double" Name="_RecordID"/>
        </g:AttrGroup>
    </g:ElementDecl>
</g:Schema>
```

This schema provides definitions for system-generated fields, like `_recordID`, as well as hierarchical records.

Summary

As you can see, Groove's use of XML is pervasive. You need to thoroughly understand XML or you won't grasp Groove.

Let's put XML aside for a moment and move on to another technology you will need to know in order to develop Groove tools: OSD.

Essential OSD

CHAPTER

6

IN THIS CHAPTER

In this chapter, we will study the technology that lets Groove install the tools you will develop from the Web. You will learn the history of Open Software Description (OSD) and look at Microsoft's implementation. We will walk through the structure and elements of a typical OSD file and present an example. We'll then see how Groove uses OSD and see how and why Groove has extended the OSD specification. We'll view a sample Groove OSD file and talk about object structure and file hierarchy.

The History of OSD

Software was installed on the first personal computers through magnetic "floppy" disks. First 5 1/4-inch, then 3 1/2-inch drives were used to load installation programs which made sure that the right resources went to the right places. As software packages became larger and larger, though, and CD-ROM drives became more ubiquitous, CDs became the standard medium for software distribution and installation.

With the explosion of the Internet, Microsoft and others began to think about distribution of software over networks. The concept made sense especially for upgrades to programs that already assumed an Internet connection—browsers, for example.

Marimba Incorporated had been experimenting with "push" technology, or automatic distribution of content from servers to clients over the Net. In August 1997, Microsoft and Marimba submitted a note to W3C describing "The Open Software Description (OSD) Format."

Looking at the conditions as they were in 1997, Arthur van Hoff of Marimba and Hadi Partovi and Tom Thai of Microsoft saw some serious problems with how software was then being installed from the Web. The problems boiled down to three: Users had to find the correct software for their system, they had to determine whether the upgrade pertained to their particular configuration, and they had to make sure that they had downloaded all the dependent software. The authors saw an opportunity to take the user totally out of the equation and automate download and installation of software packages. What was needed was a language for describing the composition of software packages in a standard, platform-independent way.

XML was an obvious choice, but the XML would need a very specialized vocabulary to accommodate software package descriptions—descriptions that could include applications, COM components, Web applets, or JavaBeans.

OSD needed to convey information about the machine and about the platform on which the software was designed to run, on which packages the installation depended, which languages the package supported, and how much memory and disk space were required to install it. Intentionally left out was any mention of how the software was going to be distributed. OSD simply described what the required software packages were and where they were located.

One huge advantage of using XML for OSD was extensibility. The OSD specification could evolve easily as conditions changed.

Microsoft first supported OSD in Internet Explorer 4.01 in December 1997.

Microsoft's OSD Specification

The best way to understand OSD is to look at Microsoft's OSD specifications. Microsoft's current specifications have been extended from the August 1997 note, and they include some alternative XML constructs. Microsoft OSD served as a starting point for Groove and is not a very active specification for Microsoft today, so only the elements that Groove uses are discussed in detail here.

After the XML version processing instruction, Microsoft OSD contains some lines that establish a Microsoft namespace, a DTD, and a special processing instruction. These elements are not used by Groove.

```
<?XML version="1.0"?>
<!DOCTYPE SOFTPKG SYSTEM http://msdn.microsoft.com/standards/osd/osd.dtd>

<?XML::namespace href=
➥http://msdn.microsoft.com/standards/osd/msicd.dtd as "msicd"?>
```

An OSD file is made up of major and minor elements. The minor elements are children of the major elements, and we will cover them later. The major elements are `SOFTPKG`, `IMPLEMENTATION`, and `DEPENDENCY`:

- A `SOFTPKG` element describes a general software package. It is always the root element of an OSD document.
- An `IMPLEMENTATION` further describes `SOFTPKG` in terms of the hardware, operating system, processor, language, and location of components the code requires. There can be several different `IMPLEMENTATION` elements within a `SOFTPKG` element, depending on the platforms supported.
- `DEPENDENCY` specifies a piece of code that must be present for the `SOFTPKG` to function correctly—code on which the `IMPLEMENTATION` or the `SOFTPKG` depends.

Within a `SOFTPKG` element, a Microsoft OSD file can be organized into three sections using two elements from the `msidc` namespace (`JAVA` and `NATIVECODE`) and a `DEPENDENCY` section. The `JAVA` and `NATIVECODE` elements are not used by Groove.

In addition to `DEPENDENCY`, `IMPLEMENTATION` elements can contain `ABSTRACT`, `TITLE`, `IMPLEMENTATION`, and `LANGUAGE` elements, as well as the attributes `href`, `name`, `version`, and three Microsoft-specific attributes (`ABSTRACT` is not used by Groove):

- The TITLE element designates the text that will appear in the title bar of the downloaded Web page.
- LANGUAGE elements specify language codes used for international distribution.

As noted previously, IMPLEMENTATION specifies the configuration required by the current software distribution. The IMPLEMENTATION element includes LANGUAGE, OS, PROCESSOR, and CODEBASE elements:

- The OS element specifies the operating system for which the implementation is designed. The attributes carry the values for various OS's. OS version holds the exact version of the operating system described in the OS element.
- Like the OS element, the PROCESSOR element describes the processor that the code requires. It is also an empty element with attributes describing the values.
- The CODEBASE element specifies the location of the file to be used in the installation. An empty element, it has the attributes filename, href, size, and style. Size and style refer to Channel Definition Format (CDF) files. Filename is a string value name that identifies the code to be downloaded. If filename is used, the file is expected to exist in the same archive as the Open Software Description file. If href is used, the file is expected to be available on the network.

The DEPENDENCY element contains another SOFTPKG element.

Here is an example of a Microsoft Open Software Description file:

```
<?XML version="1.0"?>
<!DOCTYPE SOFTPKG SYSTEM http://msdn.microsoft.com/standards/osd/osd.dtd>

<?XML::namespace href=
➥http://msdn.microsoft.com/standards/osd/msicd.dtd as "msicd"?>
<SOFTPKG NAME="com.allgames.www.chess" VERSION="1,0,0,0">
     <TITLE>Chess</TITLE>
     <ABSTRACT>Chess by Allgames</ABSTRACT>
     <MSICD::NATIVECODE>
          <CODE> NAME="Allgames Chess"
➥ CLASSID="84D8E454-0001-0001-0001-45EA43332000" VERSION="1,1,0,0">
               <IMPLEMENTATION>
                    <!--This implementation is for Windows NT-->
                    <OS VALUE="WINNT"/>
                    <OSVERSION VALUE="4,0,0,0"/>
                    <PROCESSOR VALUE="x86"/>
                    <LANGUAGE VALUE="en"/>
                    <CODEBASE HREF=http://www.allgames.com/chess.cab/>
```

```
                </IMPLEMENTATION>
            </CODE>
        <MSICD::NATIVECODE>
        <DEPENDENCY>
            <!-- Needs chess pieces-->
            <SOFTPKG NAME="com.allgames.www.chessPieces" VERSION="1,0,0,0">
                <TITLE>Chess Pieces</TITLE>
                <ABSTRACT>Chess Pieces by Allgames</ABSTRACT>
                <MSICD::NATIVECODE>
                    <CODE> NAME="Allgames Chess"
➥ CLASSID="84D8E454-0001-0001-0001-45EA43332000" VERSION="1,1,0,0">
                        <IMPLEMENTATION>
                        <!-- This implementation is for Windows NT-->
                            <OS VALUE="WINNT"/>
                            <OSVERSION VALUE="4,0,0,0"/>
                            <PROCESSOR VALUE="x86"/>
                            <LANGUAGE VALUE="en"/>
                            <CODEBASE HREF=
➥http://www.allgames.com/chesspieces.cab/>
                        </IMPLEMENTATION>
                    </CODE>
                <MSICD::NATIVECODE>
        </DEPENDENCY>
</SOFTPKG>
```

An `OBJECT` tag like the one that follows, embedded in an HTML page, would allow Internet Explorer to find and download all the code necessary to install our fictitious chess game onto an x86 processor machine, running Windows NT 4.0 as its operating system:

```
<OBJECT ID="AllGames Chess"
➥ CLASSID="CLSID: 84D8E454-0001-0001-0001-45EA43332000"
   CODEBASE=" http://www.allgames.com/chess.cab #Version=1,0,0,0">
</OBJECT>
```

Groove's Use of OSD

Groove uses OSD to specify the location of components to be downloaded and how they are to be installed. Groove extends OSD to identify components, not just packages, to provide a finer granularity. You can specify how to install the component, identify a specific factory for instantiating it, and use Groove's `ComponentURLProvider` to define dependencies.

Unlike Microsoft's `OBJECT` tag solution, all Groove component downloads begin with a `.GRV` file. GRV is a file type associated with Groove in the Windows Registry. It is written in XML and can be attached to email, embedded in a Web page, and even run from Windows File Explorer. When the `.GRV` is run, it *injects* a tool or a component into Groove.

There are several types of .GRV files, depending on their use. There are .GRV files for User Account transfers, Tool and Toolset .GRVs that are created by tool developers, shared space invitations, .GRVs for injecting skins, .GRVs that add or update the Groove help files, .GRVs to create a new shared space from a template, and a .GRV that injects components.

Here, the discussion is limited to the XML files that pertain to tools. As Groove tool developers, we will be writing tool templates and tool descriptors.

A boilerplate tool descriptor .GRV file is listed here:

```
<?xml version='1.0'?><?groove.net version='1.0'?>
<g:fragment xmlns:g="urn:groove.net">
<g:InjectorWrapper AccountGUID="grooveIdentity:///DefaultIdentity"
➥MessageID="d7g4v4pbmpqdu2wk6bs3hsvqsx4meamiwtk6s7c"
➥ResourceURL="grooveIdentityMessage:///ToolMessage;Version=3,0,0,0"
➥ LocalDeviceURLs="Injector">
    <g:IdentityMessageHeader>
        <g:MessageHeader MessageType="ToolMessage"
➥ MessageID="d7g4v4pbmpqdu2wk6bs3hsvqsx4meamiwtk6s7c"
➥ Version="1,0,0,0" CreateTime="9/24/00 7:41 PM"
➥ CreatorDeviceURL="dpp://friends.groove.net/0sGnePZSnu-AY-fePpNqEqzwSOPo9910">
            <g:SenderContact/>
            <g:RecipientContact/>
        </g:MessageHeader>
        <g:MessageBody BodyName="MessageBody">
            <g:ToolMessage>
                <g:ToolMessageHeader ToolURL=
➥"grooveAccountTool:;CategoryName=grooveToolCategory:
➥//Account/ToolTemplateList,ComponentName=ToolTemplateList"/>
                <g:ToolMessageBody>
                    <g:TemplateDescriptorList>
                        <g:TemplateDescriptorURL URL="YourURLGoesHere"/>
                    </g:TemplateDescriptorList>
                </g:ToolMessageBody>
            </g:ToolMessage>
        </g:MessageBody>
    </g:IdentityMessageHeader>
</g:InjectorWrapper>

</g:fragment>
```

You will remember that the leading g: identifies the element names as belonging to the Groove namespace. All Groove namespace elements are qualified with the g:.

It is interesting that almost all Groove XML files are XML documents. This one, however, is not. It is a fragment. W3C defines a fragment as "a general term to refer to part of an XML document, plus possibly some extra information, that may be useful to use and interchange in the absence of the rest of the XML document."

The significant item in this XML fragment for the tool developer is the line

```
<g:TemplateDescriptorURL URL="YourURLGoesHere"/>
```

URL is the path to your .OSD file and, usually, the package name of the tool descriptor file.

When a user clicks on the .GRV file, Groove's Component Manager downloads the tool descriptor file to the account database and to the /Data/XML files directory. The tool descriptor file contains a TemplateDescriptor. The TemplateDescriptor has several attributes, including Name, Description, Type, and Resource URL. The Name and Description attributes are displayed in the lists that are displayed in the Add Tool and Create Shared Space dialogs. The Type determines which icon appears on the list, tool, or toolset. The URL points to the tool's package and .OSD file. Here is a sample:

```
<g:Document xmlns:g="urn:groove.net">
     <g:TemplateDescriptorList>
          <g:TemplateDescriptor
               Name="My New Tool"
               Category="AllMyTools"
               Description="My New Tool"
               Author="Me"
               HelpAbout=
➥"http://MyHost.MyDomain.com/AllMyTools/MyNewTool/About.html"
               ReleaseDate="0/00/00"
               Version="0,0,0,0"
               Filename="MyNewTool.tpl"
               Type="Tool"

ResourceURL="http://MyHost.MyDomain.com/AllMyTools/MyNewTool.osd?
➥Package=com.MyDomain.AllMyTools/MyNewTool/MyNewTool_TPL&amp;
➥Version=0&amp;Factory=Open"/>
     </g:TemplateDescriptorList>
</g:Document>
```

After the tool descriptor has been copied into the account database and the /Data/XML files directory, the tool can be added to the shared space.

Often the tool template is listed as a dependency of the tool descriptor. If it is, the tool components are downloaded and installed during this step.

The Groove Manifest

The Groove application keeps track of all its installed components in a *manifest*. The manifest is a running "registry" of every component, dependency, and descriptor that has ever been installed by any user on the device. It is an XML document stored in the `components.xss` file. An `.xss` file is a collection of XML files.

Components are represented in the manifest by `SOFTPKG`. Each `SOFTPKG` listed represents a component. `SOFTPKG`s list the name and version of the component; an `IMPLEMENTATION`, which includes the `CODEBASE HREF`; and a Groove OSD extension called `g:Install` that tells where and how the component was installed. The `SOFTPKG` also has a `g:DependentsList` section that gives the name and location of every component dependency.

When the tool is selected for use, Groove inspects the local manifest to see whether the proper versions of the tool's component are installed. If the tool is installed, it is instantiated.

If not all the required components are installed, Component Services uses the `ComponentResourceURL` to find the OSD file and the tool template `SOFTPKG`. The OSD gets the location of the tool template file, and any dependent components, as well as any resources that might be necessary to run the tool, such as graphics or sound files. As we have seen, the OSD file might even include references to other OSDs.

Again, after Component Services is satisfied that all components needed by the tool are present, the tool is added to the user's account and becomes available in the Add Tool and Create Shared Space dialogs.

At this point, the user can add the tool to the shared space. As the tool is being added, Component Services scans the tool's template file and re-inspects the manifest for nondependent components.

Groove tools are most often made up of Groove components. For example, if your tool uses a button, you do not have to create one from scratch. You can use an instance of the Groove button component. You reference these components in your tool template file.

When you reference one of these components, you will include a `ComponentResourceURL` that points to that component's OSD. These components are called nondependent components or implicit dependencies.

Inside the tool template file that is being loaded is a `ComponentURLProvider`. The `ComponentURLProvider` identifies a `TemplateParser`.

The `TemplateParser` is a preprocessor that scans the tool template before the tool loads and makes sure that it has all the components referenced in the tool template. If it finds any that are not installed, it uses the `ComponentResourceURL` in the template to locate the `SOFTPKG` in the

OSD. Any components referenced in the tool template are automatically installed, if necessary. If your tool uses only the components that Groove premanifests, or custom tools you have already installed, no components are installed.

Here are a few of the premanifested components that Groove includes: `EditControl`, `ComboBox`, `ListBox`, `StaticText`, `Button`, `ImageControl`, `RichTextEngine`, `RichTextDisplay`, `CalendarEngine`, `WebBrowser`, `IconListView`, `Header`, `NavigationBar`, `Menu`, and `RTFHelpProvider`.

If you did not use the `ComponentResourceURL` and corresponding `TemplateParser`, you would have to list all component dependencies in your OSD, including every standard Groove component. Trust me, you don't want to do that.

After the `TemplateParser` completes its work, the tool is instantiated.

Figure 6.1 shows a flowchart.

Notice how important OSD is to this installation process. OSD is called from the `.GRV` file to begin the process. It is called again from the tool descriptor file to locate the tool template file, related components, other resource files, and/or additional OSD; and, finally, it is called from the tool template file to allow Component Services to locate components and make sure that they are installed.

Writing an OSD File

Let's write a simple Groove OSD file.

Like most Groove XML files, a Groove OSD file is a document. Because there is only one version of XML, Groove does not include the processing instruction

```
<?XML version="1.0"?>
```

with which you have started all your previous XML files. Groove files begin with a Groove-qualified document tag, a `Name` attribute, and a namespace declaration:

```
<g:Document Name="MyNewToolsOSD" xmlns:"urn:groove.net">
</g:Document>
```

You will have to include a component fingerprint. The component fingerprint is required by Groove's component security system for all component files:

```
    <g:ComponentSecurity>
       <g:FingerprintTable>
         <g:Entry FingerprintID="Groove"
➥ Fingerprint="4262-dcb1:4552-d303:123d-36a6:0a96-62e5:24a7-d7db"/>
       </g:FingerprintTable>
    </g:ComponentSecurity>
```

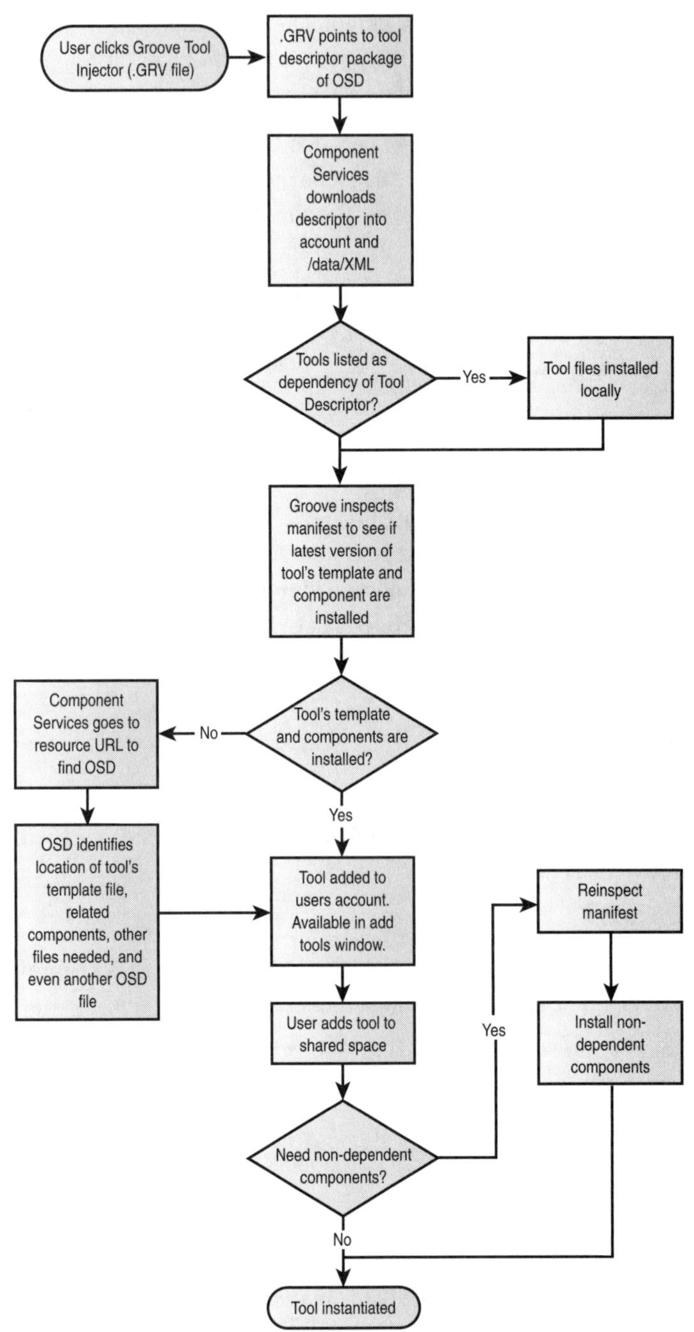

FIGURE 6.1

The Add Tool flowchart.

Your OSD must contain a SOFTPKG, so let's give it one:

```
<g:Document Name=" MyNewToolsOSD " xmlns:g="urn:groove.net">
     <g:ComponentSecurity>
        <g:FingerprintTable>
          <g:Entry FingerprintID="Groove"
➥ Fingerprint="4262-dcb1:4552-d303:123d-36a6:0a96-62e5:24a7-d7db"/>
        </g:FingerprintTable>
     </g:ComponentSecurity>
     <SOFTPKG Name="com.MyCompany.AllMyTools.MyNewTool.MyNewToolDescriptor_XML"
➥ VERSION="0,0,0,0">
               <TITLE>My New Tool Descriptor</TITLE>
     </SOFTPKG>
</g:Document>
```

SOFTPKG names are arbitrary, but to ensure that the names are as individual as possible, it is a convention to mirror the network location of the file with the reverse domain name and the file. This convention was first used to uniquely identify Java packages. SOFTPKG takes a VERSION attribute that is a string value corresponding to the major, minor, custom, and build version numbers.

What you have just written qualifies as a valid OSD file, and if you give it an .xml extension, it will parse successfully in Internet Explorer. It might be well formed and valid, but it's also useless. You want to use the OSD to tell Groove what the tool descriptor is, where to find the components to be downloaded, and what to do with them after they are downloaded. You need an IMPLEMENTATION section:

```
<g:Document Name=" MyNewToolsOSD " xmlns:g="urn:groove.net">
     <SOFTPKG Name="com.MyCompany.AllMyTools.MyNewTool.MyNewToolDescriptor_XML"
➥ VERSION="0,0,0,0">
          <TITLE>My New Tool Descriptor</TITLE>
          <IMPLEMENTATION>
          </IMPLEMENTATION>
     </SOFTPKG>
</g:Document>
```

Next, you'll tell Groove where to find your descriptor. You'll do that with an HREF attribute to a CODEBASE element, like this:

```
<g:Document Name=" MyNewToolsOSD" xmlns:g="urn:groove.net">
     <g:ComponentSecurity>
        <g:FingerprintTable>
          <g:Entry FingerprintID="Groove"
➥ Fingerprint="4262-dcb1:4552-d303:123d-36a6:0a96-62e5:24a7-d7db"/>
        </g:FingerprintTable>
     </g:ComponentSecurity>
```

```
    <SOFTPKG Name="com.MyCompany.AllMyTools.MyNewTool.MyNewToolDescriptor_XML"
➥ VERSION="0,0,0,0">
        <TITLE>My New Tool Descriptor</TITLE>
        <IMPLEMENTATION>
            <CODEBASE HREF=
➥"components.MyCompany.com/AllMyTools/MyNewTool/MyNewToolDescriptor.xml"/>
        </IMPLEMENTATION>
    </SOFTPKG>
</g:Document>
```

Now you can use some Groove extensions to OSD. One of these extensions tells Groove how and where to install your template. This is done with a `g:Install` element:

```
<g:Document Name=" MyNewToolsOSD " xmlns:g="urn:groove.net">
    <g:ComponentSecurity>
       <g:FingerprintTable>
         <g:Entry FingerprintID="Groove"
➥ Fingerprint="4262-dcb1:4552-d303:123d-36a6:0a96-62e5:24a7-d7db"/>
       </g:FingerprintTable>
    </g:ComponentSecurity>
    <SOFTPKG Name="com.MyCompany.AllMyTools.MyNewTool.MyNewToolDescriptor_XML"
➥ VERSION="0,0,0,0">
        <TITLE>My New Tool Descriptor</TITLE>
        <IMPLEMENTATION>
            <CODEBASE HREF=
➥"components.MyCompany.com/AllMyTools/MyNewTool/MyNewToolDescriptor.xml"/>
            <g:Install Type="Copy"
                      TargetDir="$GROOVEDATA$\XML Files"/>
        </IMPLEMENTATION>
    </SOFTPKG>
</g:Document>
```

The `Type` attribute tells Groove how to install the component. In this case, Groove will copy the template to the XML folder in the `Data` directory. The `$GROOVEDATA$` specifies the URI of the `Groove Data` folder.

There are seven OSD install types: Copy, Import to XSS, Unpack CAB (Win32), Install CAB (Win32), InProcServer (Win32), LocalServer, and External.

You'll also need a `factory` element that specifies a mode of instantiation for the component. In the case of a descriptor file, the mode is Open. The Component Manager uses factories (objects that know how to instantiate certain other kinds of objects) to activate components. In our file, the type of document is set to Temporary XML Document.

Here is the OSD with a `factory` element included:

```
<g:Document Name=" MyNewToolsOSD " xmlns:g="urn:groove.net">
    <g:ComponentSecurity>
       <g:FingerprintTable>
         <g:Entry FingerprintID="Groove"
➥ Fingerprint="4262-dcb1:4552-d303:123d-36a6:0a96-62e5:24a7-d7db"/>
       </g:FingerprintTable>
    </g:ComponentSecurity>
    <SOFTPKG Name="com.MyCompany.AllMyTools.MyNewTool.MyNewToolDescriptor_XML"
➥ VERSION="0,0,0,0">
         <TITLE>My New Tool Descriptor</TITLE>
         <IMPLEMENTATION>
              <CODEBASE HREF=
➥"components.MyCompany.com/AllMyTools/MyNewTool/MyNewToolDescriptor.xml"/>
              <g:Install Type="Copy"
                         TargetDir="$GROOVEDATA$\XML Files"/>
              <g:Factory
                         Name="Open"
                         Type="Temporary XML Document"
                         Filename=
➥"$GROOVEDATA$\XML Files\ MyNewToolDescriptor.xml"/>
         </IMPLEMENTATION>
    </SOFTPKG>
</g:Document>
```

An OSD file might include component dependencies. A DEPENDENCY element is used to specify one or more SOFTPKGs that are needed for the enclosing SOFTPKG to run. The enclosing SOFTPKG component depends on the enclosed SOFTPKG elements.

Dependencies can be written both inside and outside of an IMPLEMENTATION block. You can have an IMPLEMENTATION for one operating system that requires a .DLL that is not required by all. The dependency for that .DLL would go inside the IMPLEMENTATION block.

You saw before that if you write the OSD file so that the tool template is a dependency of the tool descriptor, Component Services will install the tool's components at the time of injection. Let's do that here.

First, you'll put in some DEPENDENCY tags and the tool template's SOFTPKG tags:

```
<g:Document Name=" MyNewToolsOSD " xmlns:g="urn:groove.net">
    <g:ComponentSecurity>
       <g:FingerprintTable>
         <g:Entry FingerprintID="Groove"
➥ Fingerprint="4262-dcb1:4552-d303:123d-36a6:0a96-62e5:24a7-d7db"/>
       </g:FingerprintTable>
    </g:ComponentSecurity>
```

```
    <SOFTPKG Name="com.MyCompany.AllMyTools.MyNewTool.MyNewToolDescriptor_XML"
➥ VERSION="0,0,0,0">
         <TITLE>My New Tool Descriptor</TITLE>
         <IMPLEMENTATION>
              <CODEBASE HREF=
➥"components.MyCompany.com/AllMyTools/MyNewTool/MyNewToolDescriptor.xml"/>
              <g:Install Type="Copy"
                         TargetDir="$GROOVEDATA$\XML Files"/>
              <g:Factory
                         Name="Open"
                         Type="Temporary XML Document"
                         Filename=
➥"$GROOVEDATA$\XML Files\MyNewToolDescriptor.xml"/>
         </IMPLEMENTATION>
         <DEPENDENCY>
              <SOFTPKG Name="com.MyCompany.MyNewTool.AllMyTools.MyNewTool_TPL"
➥VERSION="0,0,0,0>
              </SOFTPKG>
         </DEPENDENCY>
    </SOFTPKG>
</g:Document>
```

Let's include an `IMPLEMENTATION` and specify the language your tool supports:

```
<g:Document Name=" MyNewToolsOSD " xmlns:g="urn:groove.net">
    <g:ComponentSecurity>
       <g:FingerprintTable>
         <g:Entry FingerprintID="Groove"
➥ Fingerprint="4262-dcb1:4552-d303:123d-36a6:0a96-62e5:24a7-d7db"/>
       </g:FingerprintTable>
    </g:ComponentSecurity>

    <SOFTPKG Name="com.MyCompany.AllMyTools.MyNewTool.MyNewToolDescriptor_XML"
➥ VERSION="0,0,0,0">
         <TITLE>My New Tool Descriptor</TITLE>
         <IMPLEMENTATION>
              <CODEBASE HREF=
➥"components.MyCompany.com/MyNewTool/MyNewToolDescriptor.xml"/>
              <g:Install Type="Copy"
                         TargetDir="$GROOVEDATA$\XML Files"/>
              <g:Factory
                         Name="Open"
                         Type="Temporary XML Document"
                         Filename=
➥"$GROOVEDATA$\XML Files\ MyNewToolDescriptor.xml"/>
         </IMPLEMENTATION>
         <DEPENDENCY>
```

```
                <SOFTPKG Name="com.MyCompany.AllMyTools.MyNewTool.MyNewTool_TPL"
➥ VERSION="0,0,0,0">
                     <IMPLEMENTATION>
                          <LANGUAGE VALUE="en"/>
                     </IMPLEMENTATION>
                </SOFTPKG>
           </DEPENDENCY>
      </SOFTPKG>
</g:Document>
```

Next you'll need a `CODEBASE` element to tell Groove how to find your tool on your component farm, and another `g:Install` to cover your tool:

```
<g:Document Name=" MyNewToolsOSD " xmlns:g="urn:groove.net">
     <g:ComponentSecurity>
        <g:FingerprintTable>
          <g:Entry FingerprintID="Groove"
➥ Fingerprint="4262-dcb1:4552-d303:123d-36a6:0a96-62e5:24a7-d7db"/>
        </g:FingerprintTable>
     </g:ComponentSecurity>

     <SOFTPKG Name="com.MyCompany.AllMyTools.MyNewTool.MyNewToolDescriptor_XML"
➥ VERSION="0,0,0,0">
          <TITLE>My New Tool Descriptor</TITLE>
          <IMPLEMENTATION>
               <CODEBASE HREF=
➥"components.MyCompany.com/AllMyTools/MyNewTool/MyNewToolDescriptor.xml"/>
               <g:Install Type="Copy"
                          TargetDir="$GROOVEDATA$\XML Files"/>
               <g:Factory
                          Name="Open"
                          Type="Temporary XML Document"
                          Filename=
➥"$GROOVEDATA$\XML Files\MyNewToolDescriptor.xml"/>
          </IMPLEMENTATION>
          <DEPENDENCY>
               <SOFTPKG Name="com.MyCompany.AllMyTools.MyNewTool.MyNewTool_TPL"
➥ VERSION="0,0,0,0">
                    <IMPLEMENTATION>
                         <LANGUAGE VALUE="en"/>
                         <CODEBASE HREF=
➥"components.MyCompany.com/AllMyTools/MyNewTool/MyNewTool.tpl"/>
                         <g:Install Type="Import to XSS"
                              DatabaseURI="$TEMPLATESURI$"
                              DocumentName="MyNewTool.tpl"
                              SchemaURI="$DEFAULTSCHEMA$"/>
```

```
                    </CODEBASE>
                </IMPLEMENTATION>
            </SOFTPKG>
        </DEPENDENCY>
    </SOFTPKG>
</g:Document>
```

Notice that this `Type` attribute is different from the one you used for the descriptor file. This `Type` attribute is `Import to XSS`. In this case, Groove will copy the template to an `.xss` database file, with the URI specified in the `$TEMPLATESURI$` variable. If the engine of your tool used a custom schema, you would specify the location in the `SchemaURI` attribute. If you use the default, or no schema at all, you can use the `$DEFAULTSCHEMA$` variable.

You'll also want to specify a `ComponentURIProvider` for the use of your `TemplateParser` to scan your template for Groove components and resolve OSD to Groove standard components. Inside the tag, you specify the database to which your template has been copied (`DatabaseURI`), as well as the document name (`DocumentName`) and the type of document (`DocumentType`):

```
<g:Document Name=" MyNewToolsOSD " xmlns:g="urn:groove.net">
    <g:ComponentSecurity>
       <g:FingerprintTable>
         <g:Entry FingerprintID="Groove"
➥ Fingerprint="4262-dcb1:4552-d303:123d-36a6:0a96-62e5:24a7-d7db"/>
       </g:FingerprintTable>
    </g:ComponentSecurity>

    <SOFTPKG Name="com.MyCompany.AllMyTools.
MyNewTool.MyNewToolDescriptor_XML"
➥ VERSION="0,0,0,0">
         <TITLE>My New Tool Descriptor</TITLE>
         <IMPLEMENTATION>
              <CODEBASE HREF=
➥"components.MyCompany.com/AllMyTools/MyNewTool/MyNewToolDescriptor.xml"/>
              <g:Install Type="Copy"
                         TargetDir="$GROOVEDATA$\XML Files"/>
              <g:Factory
                         Name="Open"
                         Type="Temporary XML Document"
                         Filename=
➥"$GROOVEDATA$\XML Files/MyNewToolDescriptor.xml"/>
         </IMPLEMENTATION>
         <DEPENDENCY>
              <SOFTPKG Name="com.MyCompany.AllMyTools.MyNewTool.MyNewTool_TPL"
➥ VERSION="0,0,0,0">
```

```
                    <IMPLEMENTATION>
                         <LANGUAGE VALUE="en"/>
                         <CODEBASE HREF=
➥"components.MyCompany.com/AllMyTools/MyNewTool/MyNewTool.tpl"/>
                         <g:Install Type="Import to XSS"
                               DatabaseURI="$TEMPLATESURI$"
                               DocumentName="MyNewTool.tpl"
                               SchemaURI="$DEFAULTSCHEMA$"/>
                               <g:ComponentURLProvider
                               ProgID="Groove.TemplateParser"
                               DatabaseURI="$TEMPLATESURI$"
                               DocumentName="MyNewTool.tpl"
                               DocumentType="Template"/>
                         </CODEBASE>
                    </IMPLEMENTATION>
               </SOFTPKG>
          </DEPENDENCY>
     </SOFTPKG>
</g:Document>
```

Finally, you'll need another factory for Groove to use to instantiate the tool. The format is slightly different for the tool. Instead of a filename, it has a document name, and it has the additional `DatabaseURI` element to specify where to find the tool template.

The finished OSD file is shown here:

```
<g:Document Name=" MyNewToolsOSD " xmlns:g="urn:groove.net">
     <g:ComponentSecurity>
        <g:FingerprintTable>
          <g:Entry FingerprintID="Groove"
➥ Fingerprint="4262-dcb1:4552-d303:123d-36a6:0a96-62e5:24a7-d7db"/>
        </g:FingerprintTable>
     </g:ComponentSecurity>

     <SOFTPKG Name="com.MyCompany.AllMyTools.MyNewTool.MyNewToolDescriptor_XML"
➥ VERSION="0,0,0,0">
          <TITLE>My New Tool Descriptor</TITLE>
          <IMPLEMENTATION>
               <CODEBASE HREF=
➥"components.MyCompany.com/AllMyTools/MyNewTool/MyNewToolDescriptor.xml"/>
               <g:Install Type="Copy"
                          TargetDir="$GROOVEDATA$\XML Files"/>
               <g:Factory
                          Name="Open"
                          Type="Temporary XML Document"
                          Filename=
➥"$GROOVEDATA$\XML Files\MyNewToolDescriptor.xml"/>
```

```
            </IMPLEMENTATION>
            <DEPENDENCY>
                <SOFTPKG Name="com.MyCompany.AllMyTools.MyNewTool.MyNewTool_TPL"
➥ VERSION="0,0,0,0">
                    <IMPLEMENTATION>
                        <LANGUAGE VALUE="en"/>
                        <CODEBASE HREF="
➥components.MyCompany.com/AllMyTools/MyNewTool/MyNewTool.tpl"/>
                            <g:Install Type="Import to XSS"
                                DatabaseURI="$TEMPLATESURI$"
                                DocumentName="MyNewTool.tpl"
                                SchemaURI="$DEFAULTSCHEMA$"/>
                            <g:ComponentURLProvider
                                ProgID="Groove.TemplateParser"
                                DatabaseURI="$TEMPLATESURI$"
                                DocumentName="MyNewTool.tpl"
                                Argument="MyNewTool.tpl"
                                DocumentType="Template"/>
                            <g:Factory
                                Name="Open"
                                Type="XML Document"
                                DatabaseURI="$TEMPLATESURI"
                                DocumentName="MyNewTool.tpl"/>
                        </CODEBASE>
                    </IMPLEMENTATION>
                </SOFTPKG>
            </DEPENDENCY>
        </SOFTPKG>
</g:Document>
```

It is important to note that if the component listed in the dependency section does not load, neither does the parent SOFTPKG. It is an all-or-nothing system.

The Groove Manifest

There are two ways to describe a component dependency: by value and by reference. By value refers to the dependent SOFTPKG name, and by reference refers to the CODEBASE HREF.

The first time a component is installed, it must be installed as a dependency by reference. That's because Component Services has to physically find the SOFTPKG. After download and installation, however, a component can be specified by value. This allows you to reuse a component without having to download it again.

In a by value dependency, the dependent component uses the same SOFTPKG name as it had when it was previously downloaded. As a result, Component Services searches the Manifest for the component's SOFTPKG name and can refer to the CODEBASE HREF of the component described in the previous OSD. The component might previously have been installed from its own OSD, or it could be described as a dependency in another OSD entirely.

The Model Changes

Groove is a rapidly evolving platform. As this book is being written, major changes in the Groove OSD model are under development. Major performance efficiencies will result from these changes.

ComponentURLProviders

The first change is in the use of ComponentURLProviders. As you may remember, the ComponentURLProvider identifies a TemplateParser.

The TemplateParser is a preprocessor that scans the tool template before the tool loads and makes sure that it has all the components referenced in the tool template. If it finds any that are not installed, it uses the ComponentResourceURL in the template to locate the SOFTPKG in the OSD.

This allows Groove to download as little as possible to install a tool and lets the template developer avoid establishing dependencies to all his Groove components. Unfortunately, there are some serious side effects to this process.

When you download a tool using OSD, you frequently have dependencies to other OSD files. These can in turn point to still others. Component A begins downloading, and then finds that it need to download component B. The component B OSD file begins downloading and then runs into a dependency to component C.

This situation is a nightmare for progress reporting. When Groove starts to download component A, it initially has no idea it also needs B and C.

A progress bar would show the percent download of component A, and then stop while component B was downloaded. It could continue the start-and-stop routine several times, depending on how many dependencies there were and how they were structured.

Next, the download completes and the TemplateParser does its work. It finds that one or several of the components that were not included as dependencies in the OSD are missing. It downloads these, possibly running through more OSD dependency trees. Some of these components might also include ComponentURLProviders.

Groove has already made some headway with the progress issue. Now, when you sign your OSD (you'll be signing OSDs in Chapter 10, "Publishing a Basic Groove Tool," and Chapter 12, "Easier Groove: Modifying the Basic Groove Tool with Tool Creator and Tool Publisher"),

Groove looks through the OSD tree, collects the file sizes, and knows the size of the download. The installation process now consists of four steps: finding components, downloading any components you don't have, installing, and publishing.

But there still has to be a better way.

Groove developers reasoned that if you had core Groove installed, you must have all the components. You shouldn't have to check to see whether you have a button component if you already have Groove installed, for example. Consequently, you can expect to see tool template OSD written with a dependency to the proper version of Groove core. The use of OSD dependencies to a core component solves the problem of loopback at the very end of the download, but it doesn't help with the dependency tree difficulty.

Groove Assembly Files

The dependency to a core component eliminated the need for the developer to write OSD dependencies to Groove components, but it did nothing to eliminate the need to write OSD dependencies to non-Groove components. That's where Groove Assembly Files come in.

Groove Assembly Files are similar to `.CAB` files with some special-purpose Groove files included. They package the components together and imply dependency. You can write a dependency on a Groove Assembly File and eliminate the need to write dependencies to each of the included components separately.

A second use for Groove Assembly Files is as deployment vehicles. Instead of putting 10 files up on your Web site, you might need only one.

At some point, you might be able to write a `.GRV` to a Groove Assembly File and send non–Web hosted tools to others.

You'll still find references to `ComponentURLProviders` throughout this book, and they continue to be supported. But keep in mind that OSD references to a core component and Groove Assembly Files will be making your life easier soon.

Thinking in OSD

In a way, writing the OSD is the simplest part of the job. The more difficult part is designing the OSD.

There are various considerations. You need to name your packages, structure your file layout, and devise a reusable component strategy.

As we mentioned before, Groove uses a reverse domain notation. In the earlier examples, we used `components.MyCompany.com/AllMyTools/MyNewTool/MyNewTool.tpl` to uniquely identify the tool template. This particular notation implies that we have other tools beyond `MyNewTool` and that `MyNewTool` is in the category of `AllMyTools`, and there might be tools other than `MyNewTool` in that category.

Often, your file layout will mirror your name structure. The problems arise when your structure begins to mature into complex chains of OSD files referencing other OSD files that might reference others yet.

Let's look at an example. After developing `MyNewTool`, suppose you receive an urgent request from Paris for a French version. Your `MyNewTool.OSD` lists `MyNewTool.TPL` as a dependency of `MyToolDescriptor.XML`. The `SOFTPKG` for `MyNewTool.tpl` specifies English in the `LANGUAGE` element of the `IMPLEMENTATION` tag. You need another OSD.

The Paris version is so successful that they want a Linux version. Guess what? Your OSD does not include an `OS` element for the `IMPLEMENTATION` tag. You need another OSD.

Let's say that your `MyNewTool.osd` contains another dependency for your company logo that will be copied into `/Groove/Data/ToolData`. When you wrote your OSD for the French version, you copied the OSD into a new file, changed the `LANGUAGE` element, renamed the file `MyNewTool(French).osd`, and saved. When you wrote your OSD for the French language Linux version, you copied the OSD into a new file, changed the `OS` element, renamed the file `MyNewTool(French(Linux)).osd`, and saved. You were so successful that you were able to pay an advertising company to redesign your old, tired company logo. Guess what? Your old logo resides in the `/Groove/Data/ToolData/` directory at least once, and as many as three times, if you didn't reference the logo dependency by value in the previous two OSDs, and they are all the old logo. Yet more OSDs.

A lot of thinking early in the game can keep you out of this kind of trouble.

An obvious solution to this logo problem would be to keep the logo at the `AllMyTools` level. Each OSD could point to the logo by reference. If the logo ever changed, it could be changed just once. It would help the other problems if you had designed your hierarchy along the lines of `com.MyCompany.AllMyTools.Win32Tools.EnglishTools.MyNewTool`.

Two additional factors provide a bit of relief for OSD designers. First, OSD files can list other OSD files as dependencies. Although this kind of chaining makes OSD webs extremely complex, it can provide very flexible solutions to the problem of multiple versions. Second, Groove's Component Manager provides for OSD redirection. With properly written OSD files, the Component Manager can traverse OSD trees in search of the proper component. This is a complex topic that is treated in greater detail in Chapter 14, "Advanced Topics."

Keep in mind, too, that after you have put these components onto your Web site, you can never move them. If you do, all your `CODEBASE` elements will be wrong.

Summary

It pays great dividends to put a lot of thought into the structure of both your physical files and your component hierarchy. But enough theory. Let's go get our hands dirty. In the next chapter we'll see what resources we have at `devzone.Groove.net`, download and explore the Groove Development Kit (GDK), and set up our computers to develop tools.

Creating a Groove Development Environment

CHAPTER

7

IN THIS CHAPTER

In this chapter, we will investigate Groove's DevZone Web site to learn about the resources available to you as a developer. You will download, install, and explore the Groove Development Kit (GDK). You will then create an environment that will allow you to safely and effectively create Groove tools. Finally, we'll take a closer look at the development process.

The DevZone

Besides being the location that hosts the GDK, `http://DevZone.groove.net` contains a lot of other developer support information. Before you download and install the GDK, you should look at the site because you will certainly use its resources later.

If you point your browser at the site, you will see that it contains a lot of valuable information, including news and events, forums, a library, tech notes, FAQs, developer support, and the location of the Groove Development Kit (GDK).

The home page provides an overview of the site. It also offers late-breaking news and events such as GDK upgrades, developer training classes, technical articles from third-party sources, and general news of interest to developers.

Forums allow developers to ask questions of each other. If you cannot find some information after searching the libraries, tech notes, and tutorials, the forums can provide answers and recommendations from the Groove development community. To join the forums, you must register.

The library contains reference information on the Groove platform. The tech notes contain notes divided into several sections. These tend to vary greatly in the degree of depth in which subjects are covered, but they can be very helpful. FAQs tend to cover less weighty subjects than the tech notes. Developer support is available on the site to Groove Partners with support agreements.

The Groove Development Kit link takes you to a page that contains a download link for the GDK. You will need to fill out a license form and then download the kit. We will return to this page later to get the API Reference Guide (JavaScript) to ensure that we have the latest. Download the GDK now.

The GDK

The download gives you a `GrooveGDK.exe` file. Running that file puts a `localhost` directory in your Groove Data folder. Open the `localhost` folder when the installer is finished. In the `localhost` folder you will find enclosed folders containing resources such as documentation, licenses, registry files, samples, typelibs, and utilities.

Locate the documentation, and you'll find an `APIReference` folder. It will initially have only one file—a `readMe` file—directing you back to `http://DevZone.groove.net/GDK` to download

API reference files. The API reference files are not downloaded with the GDK because they are quite large, about 7MB each—so take only the version you need. For purposes of this book, you need the `GrooveJSAPIReference.chm` file to cover JavaScript code use. Download it now and put it into your `APIReference` folder.

The documentation consists of several other resources. Much of this information has been, or will be, covered in this book, but it is valuable material to use as additional information or as a different perspective on the material presented here.

Locate the information on licenses and you'll find a `.GRV` file that will upgrade your Preview Edition to a regular Groove version for a 90-day evaluation period. You will need this license in your developer account to test Roles and Permissions in your tools. You will be establishing a developer account a little later in the chapter.

The registry files change your registry settings to enable and disable development features in Groove. You will activate three of these a little later.

There are sample Groove tools in the GDK that contain large amounts of sample code, from simple tutorial files to code for database integration. The GDK also contains Groove typelibs that are required for C++ and Visual Basic programming.

The utilities in the GDK include the Tool Creator and the Tool Publisher Tools you will be using later in the book. Also included is the Groove Database Navigator Tool, which you will be installing shortly. A `makeGRV` ZIP file contains all the tools necessary to create the `.GRV` files that inject tools into your shared spaces. You'll also find some information on the Groove Object Model (GOM), including some HTML and XML files that describe it.

To develop Groove tools you need a development environment. Not only do you need to have Groove installed, but you need other supplemental applications, some specialized Groove tools, a few special registry settings, some strategically placed folders, and a plan to develop in such a way that, if things go wrong, you can recover as quickly and as completely as possible.

Development Account

One of the first things you will want to do is back up your `Data` folder. Many of the tools you will use in development are potentially destructive to your Groove data. To ensure that you can always recover a working version of Groove that includes your personal and business shared spaces, you need to copy your `Data` folder to another part of your hard drive or to another drive altogether.

To accomplish that task, you need to shut down Groove from the system tray application and then do the backup. Do that now. When you have finished, restart Groove.

After your Data directory is backed up, you need to establish a development account. Right-click the system tray application and choose New Account. You will follow the same procedures you did when you established your personal accounts in Chapter 3, "Exploring the Groove Application," except that you will not list your account in the Groove directory. You will use this account for all Groove tool development.

Create a shared space in this account called Development Space. At this time, you don't need to add any tools or toolsets, and you don't need to invite anyone. You also created shared spaces in Chapter 3.

Supplemental Applications

In addition to an account, you need some supplemental applications to develop Groove tools. You might want to shut down any running applications to install these tools.

First, you need a text editor that supports tabs for writing your JavaScript. WordPad, the text editor found in the Start menu, under Accessories, is sufficient. You will need to save your files in text-only format and be careful to preserve Groove extensions, but WordPad will work quite well for Groove Tool Development. If you already have a preferred IDE such as Microsoft Developer Studio, you can certainly use it.

In addition, if you didn't already download and install Microsoft XML Notepad back in Chapter 5, "Essential XML," you can point your browser to http://msdn.microsoft.com/library/default.asp?url=/library/en-us/dnxml/html/xmlpaddownload.asp. Microsoft XML Notepad is very good for helping you visualize the structure of the Groove XML files, and for verifying that your XML is well formed. You should check for well-formed XML every time you have problems in Groove tool development.

GRV files inject tools into shared spaces and are essential to the tool publication process. There are several ways to produce them. One of these ways requires Perl. If you do not already have it installed, you can download and install Perl from http://aspn.activestate.com/ASPN/Downloads/ActivePerl/index/.

Finally, if you have Microsoft Visual Interdev, you will find it very useful for debugging.

Specialized Groove Tools

There are a few specialized Groove tools you will use extensively. The first of these is the Groove Database Navigator Tool. The others, discussed a bit later, are the Tool Creator and Groove Tool Publisher Tools.

The Groove Database Navigator Tool

Groove instantiates a tool using tool template files written in XML. Those files have a .TPL extension. Collections of these files are stored in XML databases. The XML database files have an .XSS extension. XSS files are binary and are not accessible by text editors.

Consequently, Groove provides the Groove Database Navigator Tool. You can use this tool to inspect the contents of .XSS databases, and to view the code of the enclosed XML documents.

The primary purpose of the Groove Database Navigator is to "overlay" tool template files so that you can test revisions to an installed tool. We will cover this use in greater detail later.

Another use for this tool is to locate, inspect, and copy code from other templates for reuse in tools you might develop. Careful study of the code Groove engineers used to develop the core tools is one of the best ways to learn Groove programming.

Because the Groove Database Navigator Tool makes changing and deleting Groove code so easy, it is dangerous. Use it carefully.

Generally, it is not a good idea to delete anything from this tool. Deleting an essential file, or a database, will make Groove unusable. To recover, you'll need to restore your backed-up `Data` folder.

Disabling Component Authentication

The utilities and sample tools in the GDK are *unsigned*, meaning that they do not adhere to Groove's security model for secure components. Component authentication is designed to keep your Groove applications from accepting unsigned, and possibly malicious, components either from .GRV files or from other shared spaces of which you are a member.

As a result, before you install the Groove Database Navigator Tool, you will have to disable component authentication. You can use the `DisableComponentAuthentication.reg` file, located in the GDK, to do that. Locate this file and run it now. You will receive notification that the file has successfully changed your registry settings. Groove must be shut down and restarted for the registry changes to take effect.

When you are developing your tools and before they have been deployed to a server, you should keep component authentication disabled, but when you have finished your development and publishing, or whenever you receive tools from an external source, you should re-enable component authentication using the `EnableComponentAuthentication.reg` file in the same directory.

When component authentication is enabled, you'll get a dialog box warning that component authentication is disabled when you install anything (signed or unsigned). You will also see the warning when Groove starts up.

After you have disabled component authentication, you can continue with the Groove Database Navigator Tool installation.

Installing the Tool

Find the utilities in the GDK directory and locate the `GrooveDBNav` folder. Open it and launch the `GrooveDBNav.grv` file. This injects the Groove Database Navigator Tool. Choose your development account as the target account. Next, open the Development Space shared space you created previously, and add the Groove Database Navigator Tool.

After you have installed the tool, open it. You should see something similar to what's shown in Figure 7.1.

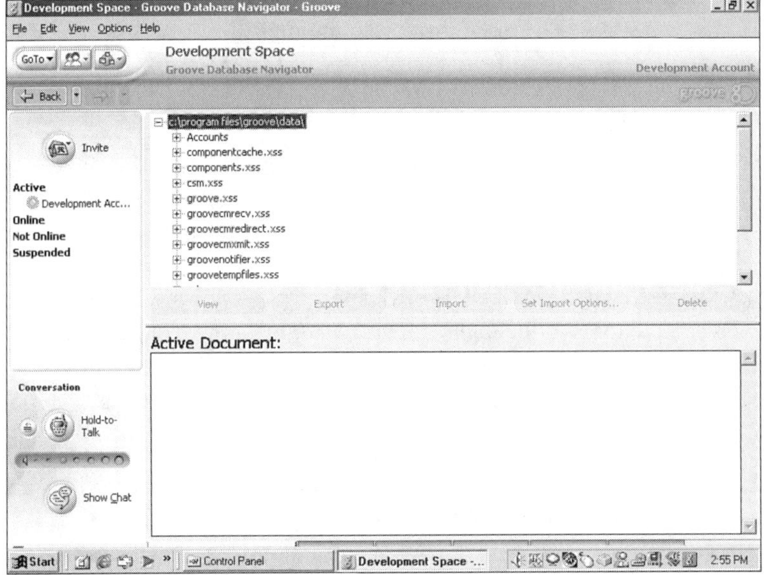

FIGURE 7.1
The Groove Database Navigator Tool.

Using the Tool

The Groove Database Navigator Tool consists of a two-pane window. Use the top pane to navigate to the `templates.xss` database. Expand the entry by clicking on the plus sign and locate `AudioTuner.tpl`. Click View Document, and you will see the XML for Groove's Audio Tuning Wizard. After you have explored the code, click the Export Document to File button and put a copy of the template on your desktop.

Open this file in Microsoft XML Notepad, and you will be able to easily view the structure of this `.TPL` file.

The Tool Creator and Groove Tool Publisher Tools

In addition to installing the Groove Database Navigator, you will install the Tool Creator Tool and the Groove Tool Publisher Tool. You will need these later in the book, but while you are installing, let's install these now. Use the same procedures you used to install the Database Navigator Tool—inject with the appropriate `.GRV` file, and then add the tools to your Development Space.

You will later use the Groove Tool Creator Tool to create and modify `.TPL` files similar to the one you explored previously. The Tool Creator builds an in-memory XML document representing a Groove tool template that contains the Groove components you add to it. When you are happy with the tool, you can save it as a `.TPL` file.

You can also use the Tool Creator Tool to modify an existing tool. You can bring in an existing template and add, delete, or modify its components. And you can use the tool to overlay existing files in your `templates.xss` file as you could with the Database Navigator Tool discussed earlier.

You will use the Groove Tool Publisher Tool to create the files necessary to stage and publish your tool templates. The Tool Publisher creates OSD files, XML tool descriptor files, and `.GRV` tool injector files. You can also use the Groove Tool Publisher to generate a unique certificate that you can use to sign your Groove tools.

You will use both of these tools extensively later in the book.

Registry Files

You already installed one of the registry files when you disabled component authentication to install the Groove Database Navigator. Let's look at some of the others.

`EnableScriptDebugging.reg`

The `RegistryFiles` folder also contains an `EnableScriptDebugging.reg` file. Because Groove uses Microsoft Windows Script Components (ActiveScripting) as the scripting engine for tools, you can use Microsoft's Visual Interdev as a script debugger. (If you do not have Visual Interdev, you can download the Microsoft Script Debugger 1.0 from `http://msdn.microsoft.com/scripting/default.htm?/scripting/debugger/default.htm`.)

To connect these debuggers with Groove, you must run the `EnableScriptDebugging.reg` file.

With debugging enabled, you can use the debugger to see which tool templates and/or script libraries Groove has open in memory, find the specific line of code that is causing problems for the Groove ScriptHost, get error messages, and set break points. You can also trace code execution. Unfortunately, you cannot edit script in the debugger and save the modified code back into a `.tpl` file.

`EnableCellBorders.reg`

The `EnableCellBorders.reg` can be used during layout development to see table borders. This is equivalent to temporarily setting cell borders in the HTML, except that you do not have to worry about removing the code when you deploy the tool. Borders are shown as red lines. The `DisableCellBorders.reg` can be used to disable the feature.

`EnableMyTemplates.reg`

In the course of Groove development, tool templates commonly are changed and modified frequently. Consequently, Groove includes a rapid prototyping facility that allows you to run Groove tool templates from a `My Templates` folder in the Groove `Data` folder without having to overlay the files into `templates.xss`. The Groove Tool Creator Tool also uses this folder. You enable rapid prototyping in Groove by running the `EnableMyTemplates.reg` file.

Rapid prototyping makes it easy to see incremental changes in your tool as you make them. It also cleanly separates tool development and publishing, which is extremely valuable in troubleshooting.

Go ahead and launch the `.reg` file now, because you will be using this facility frequently. Remember that Groove must be shut down and restarted for the registry changes to take effect.

You must manually create the `My Templates` folder before you use it, so do that now. It goes in `\Program Files\Groove\Data` and the name must include the space between `My` and `Templates`.

While you're at it, you'll need one more folder. Somewhere outside of the `Program Files` folder, create a `Groove Development` folder.

The Plan

Developing Groove tools, like any other development, requires a plan. As you have noted before, many of the tools and procedures you use can adversely affect Groove performance. It might be necessary to destroy the active Groove `Data` directory and restore your backup to get Groove working again. You develop tools by creating template files in the `My Templates` folder or by injecting the tool into the `templates.xss` file, and by writing OSD, XML tool descriptor files, and `.GRV` tool injector files. Publishing is often tested with the template, OSD, tool descriptor, and `.GRV` files staged in the `localhost` directory. Both of these folders are found inside the `\Groove\Data` folder. If you have not saved your work anywhere else, destroying the current `Groove\Data` folder will also erase all your working files.

A highly recommended development plan is to write all source files in a folder you've created elsewhere, such as the `Groove Development` folder you created previously, and then copy them to the `My Templates` folder. If you overlay tools into the `templates.xss` folder, overlay them from the `Groove Development` folder. That way, you will always have safe source files.

You also might want to back up your `\Groove\Data` directory frequently so that you don't lose nondevelopment assets, such as changes to accounts, tools, and content in shared spaces.

You should be sure that your Groove application is stable before overwriting.

Groove Tool Development

When you develop a tool, you need to write four files:

- The XML tool descriptor file points to the OSD for the tool.
- The OSD file provides the location of all the tool's resources and dependencies.
- The tool template file describes the tool's components and behavior.
- The Groove Injector file (`.GRV`) makes the tool available in Groove.

The tool descriptor, the OSD, and the injector files are used to publish the tool. The tool template is the file that Groove uses to instantiate the tool.

Thanks to Groove's rapid prototyping facility, you can begin with the development of the tool template, without having to first write a tool descriptor and your OSD.

Tool Template Development

As you know, a tool template is an XML file. Because of the rigidly hierarchical nature of XML files, you develop tools using a top-down approach.

The tool template file typically has a structure similar to that shown in Figure 7.2.

The tool begins with a document element. Inside the tool template document, you include a `ComponentSecurity` element and a `ToolTemplate` element. Groove component security makes sure that all components are authenticated as to origin. The `ComponentSecurity` element is a security section that holds the fingerprint table.

The `ToolTemplate` element contains a `ViewInfo` section and a `ComponentGroup` section. The `ViewInfo` element contains one attribute: `Lifetime`. The `ComponentGroup` is where all the heavy lifting takes place.

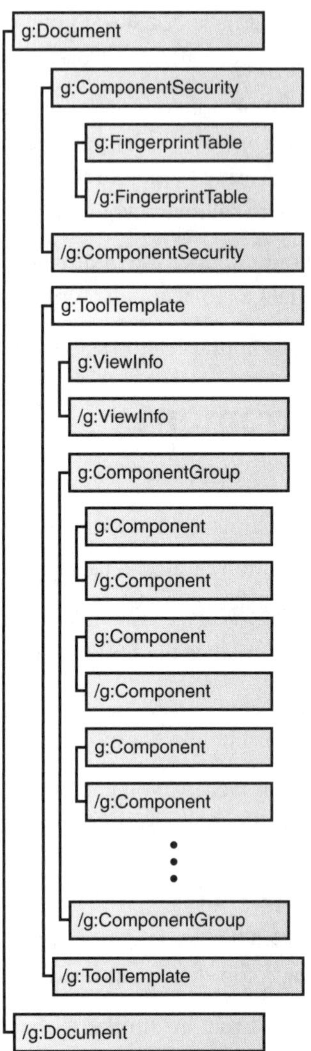

FIGURE 7.2
The typical tool template structure.

You begin writing the `ComponentGroup` element to enclose component elements, which can contain user interface components, view containers, engines, delegates, and Groove script libraries. A typical `ComponentGroup` has a structure similar to what's shown in Figure 7.3.

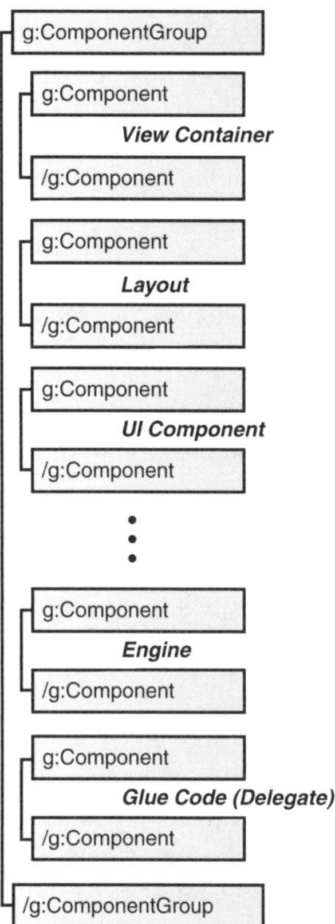

FIGURE 7.3
The typical component group structure.

The Form

Every Groove tool must contain a form, which can be defined as the visual representation of the tool, or an encapsulation of the tool's look and behavior. A form specifies at least one *view container* as the default view, and a *delegate* that defines a tool's behavior.

A view container consists of a default view and a layout. A delegate is a glue code component that determines the tool's behavior and how the components in the view interact with each other.

The View

The `ViewContainer` holds the user interface components for the tool, and arranges these components according to a layout. Groove provides various UI components, such as buttons, static text, and list boxes.

In addition, Groove provides some special components such as the `RichTextDisplay` and `RichTextEngine`, the `CalendarEngine`, the `WebBrowser`, and `IconListView`.

The Layout

You next arrange the visual components in the view container through the use of layouts. Although a view container can use only one layout at a time, the same view can use multiple layouts.

Groove provides three basic types of layouts, HTML Table, MultiCell, and XY, as well as two special-purpose layouts, SingleCell and Splitter:

- HTML Table layout provides a fast way to lay out simple tables. Written in XML, rather than HTML, HTML Table uses most of the HTML table commands, including row and column spanning, but exhibits some differences. All tags must be uppercased and XML empty tag notation can be used. Table attributes are restricted to `HSPACE`, `VSPACE`, and `CELLPADDING`, and table item attributes are restricted to `LeftPad`, `TopPad`, `BottomPad`, `HEIGHT`, and `WIDTH`. Note also that only component variable names can be placed in the cells. Cells can have `HEIGHT`, `WIDTH`, `LEFTPAD`, `RIGHTPAD`, `TOPPAD`, and `BOTTOMPAD`, as well as `COLSPAN` and `ROWSPAN`. Many of Groove's templates, including the transceiver, are in HTML Table layout.
- MultiCell layout is made up of a series of `ROW`s or `COLUMN`s, with varying numbers of `CELL`s in each. The advantage of MultiCell layout is the capability to render very complex tables. Row or column spanning is not supported, and the component variable names go into the `CELL` tags. The Calendar Tool is an example of the use of MultiCell layout.
- XY layout is used for layouts that do not fit comfortably into tables. Components are sited on the basis of x and y coordinates. X coordinates can be measured from the left or right edges of the layout, whereas y coordinates are referenced from either the top or the bottom. Percentage values can be used to allow resizing. A good example of the use of XY layout is the conversation section of the transceiver.
- SingleCell provides a view container and a layout in one component. As the name implies, it consists of one cell. It is used to enclose a component that already provides for its visual representation, such as the Chess Tool.
- The Splitter is used to divide a window into horizontal or vertical panes. Because layouts can be nested, complex structures can be built within the panes. The Groove Database Navigator Tool uses the splitter layout to separate the navigation and viewer panes of the tool.

After each UI component is included in the component group and placed according to the layout, you can add an engine.

The Engine

Engines maintain and change the tool's data model. That functionality allows for the creation and execution of the deltas that flow to and from remote instances of the tool's shared space, and provides a means to save the tool's data.

Tool developers commonly use one of the three Groove-supplied engines: Artifact, PropertyList, and Record Set.

The Artifact Engine

The Artifact engine is the simplest and least granular of the Groove engines. It simply deltas the entire data model. Each change rewrites the data model into a single element for persistence and dissemination, so you send the whole document instead of just the changes. Used improperly, the Artifact engine can cause large amounts of data to be disseminated among shared space members over the Net. The Artifact engine is used in many of the navigation bars in the Groove core tools.

The PropertyList Engine

One step up the complexity/granularity ladder is the PropertyList engine.

Every component has a property list. The list consists of name/value pairs, and can contain any number of properties. The height and width of buttons are controlled by properties, for example. The `StaticText` component has a property named `label`, and the value of the `label` property determines the text that is displayed by the component in the tool. If you created a button that changed the `StaticText`'s `label` property value, pressing the button would immediately change the displayed text in your tool. The text of your tool's `StaticText` component in a remote shared space, however, would not change.

If you want the remote values to change, you need to include a PropertyList engine to manage changes to the property lists of remote instances of your tool. You also need a PropertyList engine to persist property values, even in your local tool, and to disseminate the changes to remote instances.

When the button is pushed in your example, your glue code changes the `Label` property of the static text. The `PropertyList` engine notices the change in the `PropertyList` and fires off an `OnPropertyChanged` event containing the name of the changed property, the new value, and whether the change was generated locally. The `OnPropertyChanged` event causes the change to be disseminated to the remote instance, changing the remote property list and updating the view.

Because the PropertyList engine responds to property value changes, only the most recent value of the property is persisted. If you are persisting and/or disseminating configuration information, use of the PropertyList engine is sufficient. But if you need to keep a running record of events or store a list of database entries, you will still need more complexity and granularity. You'll need the `RecordSetEngine`.

The `RecordSetEngine`

The `RecordSetEngine` not only updates the properties of UI Components each time the tool's data model is updated, but also disseminates and persists data records, so you can build a database into your tool. The `RecordSetEngine` is the primary interface for managing persistent field-oriented data in Groove.

The `RecordSetEngine` stores a flat list of records, each identified by a unique ID number in the tool's XML database. Just as the `PropertyList` engine maintained a name/value pair for properties, the `RecordSetEngine` maintains pairs of field names and values.

The `groovestandardrecordschema.xml` acts as the default schema for the tool's records in the XML database, and supports the datatypes strings, long and double datatypes, and even elements. If you need more or different datatypes, you'll need to write a custom schema. You can see the standard fields the schema provides by reading Listing 7.1, but in addition to these, you can add string fields through your glue code.

LISTING 7.1 The Groove `groovestandardrecordschema.xml` Schema

```
<g:Schema Version="1,0,0,0" URL="GrooveStandardRecordsSchema.xml"
➥ xmlns:g="urn:groove.net">
    <g:ElementDecl ElementTemplate="true" Name="urn:groove.net:Record">
        <g:AttrGroup>
            <g:AttrDef Type="Double" Name="_RecordID"/>
            <g:AttrDef Type="Date" Name="_Created"/>
            <g:AttrDef Type="String" Name="_CreatedBy"/>
            <g:AttrDef Type="Date" Name="_Modified"/>
            <g:AttrDef Type="String" Name="_ModifiedBy"/>
        </g:AttrGroup>
    </g:ElementDecl>
    <g:ElementDecl ElementTemplate="true"
➥ Name="urn:groove.net:HierarchicalRecord">
        <g:ElementRef IsChildElement="0" Element="urn:groove.net:Record"/>
        <g:AttrGroup>
            <g:AttrDef Type="Double" Name="_ParentID"/>
            <g:AttrDef Type="Double" Name="_NewParentID"/>
            <g:AttrDef Type="Double" Name="_PreviousSiblingID"/>
        </g:AttrGroup>
    </g:ElementDecl>
</g:Schema>
```

The Discussion Tool uses a `RecordSetEngine` to maintain hierarchical records.

Next, you need to write your tool's delegate, or glue code.

The Glue Code

The *glue code* is the code you write to provide the functionality of the tool. Groove provides the following definition of glue code:

> Tool code components are the controlling code ("glue") that make the engine, view, and rest of the tool fit together as a template and function as a tool, thus giving the tool its personality, behaviors, and functionality.

Glue can be written in any COM-compliant language, such as JavaScript, VDScript, C++, or Visual Basic. Most of your effort as a tool developer will go into writing glue.

NOTE

The tool creation process is not linear as we have presented it, even for the best of Groove developers. Many iterations are usually necessary. Changes in any one area often require changes in others. Although much of the process can be streamlined with a lot of up-front thinking, revisions and revisions to revisions are inevitable.

After a tool is created and successfully tested, you are ready to move on to the publishing aspect of Groove tool development.

Publishing Your Tool

In Chapter 6, "Essential OSD," we covered in detail the steps needed to publish a Groove tool. We'll review a little here in the context of the tool publishing process.

Remember that you need to write three files, the tool descriptor file, the tool's OSD, and a `.GRV` file (needed to actually complete the installation).

The Tool Descriptor

The tool descriptor is the first file added to your account when you inject a tool. It lets you select the tool from the Add Tool/Create Shared Space tool lists. It contains parameters that help describe the tool, such as `Name`, `Description`, `Type`, and `ResourceURL`. The `Name`, `Description`, and `Type` attributes are displayed in the Add Tool/Create Shared Space tool lists, whereas the `ResourceURL` points to the tool's OSD file.

The OSD File

The tool's OSD file contains at least one `SOFTPKG` that specifies the component name, version, location, and other information for a tool. It usually has an `IMPLEMENTATION` section that specifies where your template is located, how it is to be installed, and perhaps the language and/or processor for which the tool was designed. The OSD file also points to a template parser, using the `ComponentURLProvider`, so that each of the Groove components you used in your template can also be found.

Because your tools may be hosted on servers that are case sensitive, it is important to maintain case awareness when writing OSD.

The .GRV File

As you will remember from Chapter 6, a .GRV file is associated with Groove through the Windows Registry. When your .GRV file is launched, it injects your tool, toolset, or skin into Groove. The .GRV can appear as an attachment to an email, or as link from a Web site. It can even be launched from Windows Explorer.

There are several types of .GRV files. The files you will be writing will be for tools, toolsets, and skins, but Groove also uses .GRV files for accounts, shared space invitations, additions and updates to Groove help files, and upgrades to Groove components. One type can create a new shared space from a template.

.GRV files are written in XML, and Groove provides various methods for writing them:

- The most basic way is to copy and modify an existing .GRV file. Groove provides one in the makeGroove.zip file in the GDK. You modify the TemplateDescriptorURL element. Here is a sample:

  ```
  <g:TemplateDescriptorURL
  URL="http://components.yourcompany.com/YourTools/YourNewTool/YourNewTool.osd?
  ➥Package=com.yourcompany.YourTools.YourNewTool.YourNewToolDescriptor_XML&amp;
  ➥Version=0&amp;Factory=Open"/>
  ```

- Use a Perl script provided in the makeGroove.zip file in your GDK.
- Use the Groove Tool Publisher.

We will cover the last two methods in detail in later chapters.

Summary

Now that you have established a Groove tool development environment and have developed a plan to create tools, you are nearly ready to create a tool of your own. But first, let's take a short detour.

In the next chapter, you'll take a look at skins, and how Groove uses them. You'll see how resources are managed in Groove, and you will get an opportunity to study some Groove glue code. Hopefully, you will become more familiar with Groove programming while learning how to do something really useful—modify the look of Groove.

Customizing Groove

CHAPTER

8

IN THIS CHAPTER

In this chapter, you will change the look of the Groove transceiver and will learn how skins are applied to Groove tools. In the process, you'll see how to use properties in Groove programming and become more familiar with Groove XML code. You will learn the names of many Groove components and how they are instantiated and used. You will also become familiar with the use of the Groove Database Navigator Tool.

Groove Skins

Users have the ability to change the look of the Groove transceiver through the use of skins. Launch Groove now and click on the Change the Look of Groove link button on the Home page.

Select the Redmond Gray skin, click Apply, and then go to the Home page. The transceiver will look very different from the Groove Default skin, but the layout of the transceiver will be only slightly different.

If you go back and select the Cellular skin, you'll see that the colors, graphic shapes, and layout of the transceiver have all changed dramatically.

Two XML files and a folder of image and sound resources control the look and sounds for each skin. One of the files, the `groovedefaultskinresources.xml` file, identifies the resources that the Default skin uses as properties for various components of the transceiver. In the case of graphic or sound resources, the file points to the graphic or sound. Changes to layout and functionality are defined in the second file, `standardtransceiver.tpl`. You're going to change some of those image resources and watch the effects of those changes on the look of Groove.

The layout and functionality of each transceiver is specified in the template file. The Groove Default skin uses the `standardtransceiver.tpl` template, Redmond Gray uses `redmondgrayskintransceiver.tpl`, and Cellular uses the `cellularskintransceiver.tpl`. We will look at the `standardtransceiver.tpl` file to see how it uses the resources you will be changing.

Getting Ready

Before you begin changing code for the Groove transceiver, you had better take the safe course and back up the files you will use. You also may want to restore the originals after you are finished with this exercise.

Shut down Groove from the icon in the system tray, and then open the `\Groove\Data` folder. Locate a folder called `Skins`. Open it, and then the `groove.net` folder, and you'll see three enclosed folders. Create a copy of the `GrooveDefault` folder and call it `OriginalGrooveDefault`.

Now you can safely change the files in the `Images` folder of the Groove Default skin because you have backups of the files you will be modifying. You can restore these when you are finished with this exercise, or if you get in trouble.

Next, launch Groove with your Development account, go to your Development Space, and open the Groove Database Navigator Tool. Find the `themes.xss` database and open it. Select the `groovedefaultskinresources.xml` file, and then click the Export Document to File button. You are presented with a file browser. Locate the `Groove Development` folder you created in the preceding chapter and save the file to it. You will be studying and modifying this file soon.

A little later you're going to publish your new skin so that others can use it. To make it easier for others to download the resource files, you'll put them into a cabinet (CAB) file. You'll need a utility to create CAB files, so point your browser to `http://msdn.microsoft.com/workshop/management/cab/cabdl.asp`.

Finally, you'll need a new folder in your `localhost` directory. In this case, call it `mySkin`, the name of the skin you will be creating. You will use this folder to stage the files you want to publish.

Modifying the Images

You can now start modifying the images that define the Groove Default skin. If you look at the images in the `Images` folder, you'll see that they are either `.jpg` or `.bmp` files. Because of the long filenames, it is easiest to view the image files in a list view in Windows Explorer. The JPGs are the actual images, whereas the BMPs are masks. Most images and masks are 72 dpi images. The masks are 1-bit monochrome images, whereas the image files are 24-bit RGB files.

In this exercise you will not be modifying the sizes of the individual images, so you will not need to change the masks at all. If you later decide to modify the sizes of the images in your skin, you'll need to change the mask to change the size or shape. You will also need to create a custom transceiver and a skin resources file, and make changes to the layouts of the templates that use your skin. You will be taking the easy way out. You will simply alter the images and change the properties of the Default skin files.

If you want, you can create new images, respecting the current sizes. Because the aim of this exercise is to explore skins, you will change the colors of the existing images and see the effects of your changes in the Groove transceiver as you make them.

To do this, you'll need an image editor like Adobe Photoshop. If you don't have access to an editor that will let you globally change the colors of the images, you will have to invert the images in Microsoft Paint.

Image Editing

If you have an image editor with a Hue/Saturation control, let's go ahead and change just one of the files in the `Images` folder and see what happens. The `MemberPaneBackground.jpg` is the left vertical pane of the transceiver shown when users are in a shared space. It is the background you see below the Invite button, the members list, and the conversation subform. Its dimensions are 150 pixels high by 115 wide, in case you're creating your own.

Open `MemberPaneBackground.jpg` in your image editor, and change the Hue to a value of `-180`. Save this file.

Now, let's look and see what you've done. Go to your Groove application icon in the system tray and shut down Groove. Relaunching the application to your Development account will refresh all the images.

You should now see that the Member pane background has changed to an off-white, or light tan background, and that the graphic behind the Conversation subform has changed from shades of green and blue to a graphic with shades of orange and purple.

Open the Development space you created in the preceding chapter, and use the Groove Database Navigator Tool to open the `themes.xss` database. Find the `groovedefaultskinresources.xml` file and export it to your `Groove Development` folder. Next, find the `standardtransceiver.tpl` file in the `templates.xss` database and export it too.

Understanding the Changes

As part of this exercise, you should not only see the changes your editing makes, but understand how Groove is using these resources. To do that, you need to do some searching and examination of Groove code. Let's trace the file we just changed, `MemberPaneBackground`, through the code.

With Wordpad, open the `groovedefaultskinresources.xml` file you put into your `Groove Development` folder, and then search for *MemberPaneBackground*. `MemberPaneBackground` is the name of a Background Renderer component that is instanced from the `GrooveTechnoVogueTheme.dll` located in the root directory of Groove. The `MemberPaneBackground` component has several properties, including a `BackgroundImageURL` whose value points to the file you have just edited. Notice that it also has properties for `ImageHeight`, `ImageWidth`, `MaxWidth`, `StretchMarginTop`, and `StretchMarginBottom`. The stretch margins identify the areas of the image protected from tiling. In the case of the `MemberPaneBackground`, all the tiling takes place between 67 pixels from the top and 235 pixels from the bottom. The border does not tile while the rest of the image does. Setting the `maxWidth` property to the value of the `ImageWidth` ensures that the image won't stretch in the horizontal direction.

Now open the `standardtransceiver.tpl` file in your WordPad application and do a search for *MemberPaneBackground*. You'll find that it is the value of the `Style` property of the `BackgroundStyle` element of the `Background` element of the `TitleBarFormView1` component.

If you check the Layout of this `TitleBarSubform1`, you'll see that the section for which `MemberPaneBackground` is the background contains the `InviteButton`, the `MemberAwarenessSubForm`, the `ConversationPaneTitle`, the `TalkWithPeopleSubForm`, the `ChatButton`, and the `FollowModeButton`. See whether you can identify these components in the Development Space.

Working between the files in the `Images` folder and the `standardtransceiver.tpl`, you can make changes and make sure that the changes occur correctly. You can see also how the images' filenames relate to the values of various properties. You will repeat this method several times as you complete the transformation of the Groove Default skin.

Let's make another change and trace it through the code.

Changing `TransceiverWindowBackground.jpg`

The `TransceiverWindowBackground.jpg` forms the background for the entire transceiver. It is 500 pixels high by 230 wide. The `DefaultToolBarBackground.jpg` is a 27×27 pixel tile that serves as the background for the toolbar buttons that appear in many of the Groove tools. Follow these steps to change `TransceiverWindowBackground.jpg` and trace its use:

1. Open `TransceiverWindowBackground.jpg` and `DefaultToolBarBackground.jpg` in your image editor. Change the hue to –180 in each file and save. Use the refresh procedure previously described, and the toolbar now appears brown with blue buttons.
2. Search for *TransceiverWindowBackground* in `groovedefaultskinresources.xml` and you'll see that it is the `BackgroundStyle` for the transceiver window opened by the Groove application.
3. If you search for *DefaultToolBarBackground*, you'll find that it is the `BackgroundStyle` for the `ToolCommandsToolBar` component.
4. Find `ToolCommandsToolBar` in `standardtransceiver.tpl`, and you'll see that it is the style for a `ToolCommandContainer` component that is part of `TitleBarSubForm2`. Looking at the standard transceiver, you can see that `TitleBarSubForm2` is located to the right of the `NavigationSubForm` that includes the forward and back arrows.
5. Change the hue of `NoviceModeBackground.jpg`. Novice Mode was the original name for Overview. The image is an 80×80-pixel tile.

As you might suspect by now, `NoviceModeBackground.jpg` is the `BackgroundImageURL` for the `NoviceModeBackground` component in `groovedefaultskinresources.xml`.

NoviceModeBackground is the BackgroundStyle for the HelpModeViewContainer in standardtransceiver.tpl.

Change the hue of HeaderBackground.jpg, a 45×45-pixel 96 dpi tile. You won't see the change reflected in the transceiver, nor will you find it in the standardtransceiver.tpl. This file is used as the background for list headers in many Groove tools, such as discussion or outliner. This is an example of a component that is defined in groovedefaultskinresources.xml but is used in Groove tools.

Notice that, so far, you have changed only backgrounds. Looking at your skin, it becomes pretty obvious what you have changed and what you haven't. Especially glaring are your buttons.

Before getting into the buttons, though, let's change the look of your tabs. Edit the hue of the StandardTabs.jpg file and save. The StandardTabs.jpg file contains two sets of four images. In the groovedefaultskinresources.tpl file, the URL to StandardTabs.jpg is used by the StandardTabControlSelectedTab as the value of a StateImagesURL property. The four images of the first set (in this case, identical) represent the various states of the Tab button.

There is also a StandardTabControlUnselectedTab. It also uses StandardTabs.jpg as the value of a StateImagesURL property. The only difference in code between the two controls is the value of the ImageIndex property. The value for the selected tab is 0 and the value for the unselected tab is 1. The index tells the selected tab control to use the first set of images, and the unselected tab control to use the second.

As with the HeaderBackground, tabs aren't used in the standardtransceiver.tpl. The images you just edited are used by the SelectToolTabControl and are implemented in groovetoolwindow.tpl to manage the tool tabs in shared spaces.

Let's move on to buttons.

Changing the Look of Buttons

Buttons come in the following Groove-standard styles: StandardButton, StandardIconButton, LargeButton, SmallTextButton, SmallIconButton, SmallIconTextButton, Checkbox, Radiobutton, and LinkButton. Many custom buttons are displayed throughout Groove using these standard buttons as starting points. Refer to the Groove Component Catalog at http://docs.groove.net/gdk/client/currentbuild/.

The groovedefaultskinresources.xml file defines these styles for the transceiver when it is using the Groove Default skin. In addition, the groovedefaultskinresources.xml file defines several special-purpose buttons for the Groove transceiver. The graphics for all of these buttons are stored in the TransceiverButtonImages.jpg file.

Open that file now, and you see a series of button shapes arranged horizontally across the page. The images are also arranged in rows, with each row representing a button state, corresponding to button down, button up, hover, and disabled.

The first set of images represents the button states of a `GoToButton` component defined in the `groovedefaultskinresources.tpl` This button is in turn used as the `Style` property of the `GlobalGoToButton` in the `QuickAccessSubForm` of the standard transceiver, defined in the `standardtransceiver.tpl` file. The GoTo label of this button is set using the `Label` property of the `GlobalGoToButton`.

The second set of images consists of the graphics for the button states of a `MyContactsButton` that is used as the `Style` property of the `PersonalContactsButton` in the standard transceiver.

The third set is for the `MySpacesButton`, which is used for the `TelespaceListButton`.

Here is the code that defines these buttons in the `groovedefaultskinresources.tpl`:

```
<g:Component Name="GotoButton">
   <g:ComponentResource FingerprintID="Groove"
➥URL="http://components.groove.net/Groove/Components/Root.osd?
➥Package=net.groove.Groove.ToolComponents.GrooveTechnoVogueTheme_DLL&amp;
➥Version=0&amp;Factory=ButtonUI"/>
   <g:PropertyList Version="1">
       <g:Property Name="DisplayLabel" Value="true"/>
       <g:Property Name="LabelAlignment" Value="Center"/>
       <g:Property Name="LabelOutside" Value="false"/>
       <g:Property Name="LabelFont">
           <g:FontDesc Color="#000000" Typeface="Tahoma" Height="11"/>
       </g:Property>
       <g:Property Name="MaxHeight" Value="27"/>
       <g:Property Name="MaxWidth" Value="52"/>
       <g:Property Name="StateImagesURL"
➥ Value="grooveFile:///Skins\groove.net\GrooveDefault\Images\
➥TransceiverButtonImages.jpg"/>
       <g:Property Name="ImageOffset" Value="0"/>
       <g:Property Name="ImageHeight" Value="27"/>
       <g:Property Name="ImageWidth" Value="52"/>
       <g:Property Name="PushSoundURL"
➥ Value="Skins\groove.net\GrooveDefault\Sounds\Action.wav"/>
   </g:PropertyList>
           </g:Component>

           <g:Component Name="MyContactsButton">
   <g:ComponentResource FingerprintID="Groove"
➥ URL="http://components.groove.net/Groove/Components/Root.osd?
➥Package=net.groove.Groove.ToolComponents.GrooveTechnoVogueTheme_DLL&amp;
➥Version=0&amp;Factory=ButtonUI"/>
```

```
   <g:PropertyList Version="1">
       <g:Property Name="MaxHeight" Value="27"/>
       <g:Property Name="MaxWidth" Value="37"/>
       <g:Property Name="StateImagesURL"
➥ Value="grooveFile:///Skins\groove.net\GrooveDefault\Images\
➥TransceiverButtonImages.jpg"/>
       <g:Property Name="ImageOffset" Value="52"/>
       <g:Property Name="ImageHeight" Value="27"/>
       <g:Property Name="ImageWidth" Value="37"/>
       <g:Property Name="PushSoundURL" Value="Skins\groove.net\GrooveDefault\
➥Sounds\Action.wav"/>
   </g:PropertyList>
            </g:Component>

            <g:Component Name="MySpacesButton">
   <g:ComponentResource FingerprintID="Groove"
➥ URL="http://components.groove.net/Groove/Components/Root.osd?
➥Package=net.groove.Groove.ToolComponents.GrooveTechnoVogueTheme_DLL&amp;
➥Version=0&amp;Factory=ButtonUI"/>
   <g:PropertyList Version="1">
       <g:Property Name="MaxHeight" Value="27"/>
       <g:Property Name="MaxWidth" Value="39"/>
       <g:Property Name="StateImagesURL"
➥ Value="grooveFile:///Skins\groove.net\GrooveDefault\Images\
➥TransceiverButtonImages.jpg"/>
       <g:Property Name="ImageOffset" Value="89"/>
       <g:Property Name="ImageHeight" Value="27"/>
       <g:Property Name="ImageWidth" Value="39"/>
       <g:Property Name="PushSoundURL" Value="Skins\groove.net\GrooveDefault\
➥Sounds\Action.wav"/>
   </g:PropertyList>
            </g:Component>
```

If you take a look at the properties of these buttons, you'll find that each contains an `ImageOffset` property. The offset for `GoToButton` is `0`; for `MyContactsButton`, `52`. For the `MySpacesButton`, the value of the `ImageOffset` property is `89`. These values represent the number of pixels from the left edge of the image file to the start of each image. Using this number and the `ImageHeight` and `ImageWidth` properties, an image area in the `TransceiverButtonImages.jpg` is defined. Groove can use this image area to set the graphics for each button and state.

The GoTo button properties contain label information. The value `true` for the `DisplayLabel` property ensures that the label can be seen. The `LabelAlignment` property for this button is `Center`, and the `LabelOutside` is set to `false` so that the label will appear inside the button. Notice that the actual label contents are not set here. The GoTo label that you see is set with the `Label` property in the `GlobalGoTo` button component in the `standardtransceiver.tpl`.

Select the first three sets of images in your image editor and set the hue to -180; then check out the results by refreshing the Groove Default skin. Try the buttons to see the changes in the other states.

The next image in the tranceiverButtonImages.jpg file is for a button called TransceiverPushToTalkButton. If you search Groove DefaultSkinResources for TransceiverPushToTalkButton, you'll find the following component:

```
<g:Component Name="TransceiverPushToTalkButton">
   <g:ComponentResource FingerprintID="Groove"
➥ URL="http://components.groove.net/Groove/Components/Root.osd?
➥Package=net.groove.Groove.ToolComponents.GrooveTechnoVogueTheme_DLL&amp;
➥Version=0&amp;Factory=ButtonUI"/>
   <g:PropertyList Version="1">
       <g:Property Name="DisplayLabel" Value="true"/>
       <g:Property Name="LabelAlignment" Value="right"/>
       <g:Property Name="LabelOutside" Value="true"/>
       <g:Property Name="LabelFont">
           <g:FontDesc Color="#000000" Typeface="Tahoma" Height="11"/>
       </g:Property>
       <g:Property Name="MaxHeight" Value="40"/>
       <g:Property Name="MaxWidth" Value="40"/>
       <g:Property Name="StateImagesURL"
➥Value="grooveFile:///Skins\groove.net\GrooveDefault\Images\
➥TransceiverButtonImages.jpg"/>
       <g:Property Name="StateImagesMaskURL"
➥ Value="grooveFile:///Skins\groove.net\GrooveDefault\Images\
➥TransceiverButtonImagesMask.bmp"/>
       <g:Property Name="ImageOffset" Value="201"/>
       <g:Property Name="ImageHeight" Value="40"/>
       <g:Property Name="ImageWidth" Value="40"/>
   </g:PropertyList>
          </g:Component>
```

Like the other buttons, the StateImagesURL points to the tranceiverButtonImages.jpg file. The button image size is indicated through the ImageHeight and ImageWidth properties, 40 pixels by 40 pixels. The ImageOffset property locates the LargeButton image 201 pixels from the left edge of the JPG file. If you go to your image editor and measure, you'll find that these properties properly identify the TransceiverPushToTalkButton images.

Select this set of images in your image editor and change the hue setting to -180. Refresh the Groove Default skin and look for the changes in your Development Space. You'll see changes in the Invite button and the ShowChat button in addition to the Hold to Talk button. You'll find a GroovieTalkie button, and a Chat button defined in the standardtransceiver.tpl file. The Invite button is defined in the groovedefaultskinresources.tpl file, and all three have TransceiverPushToTalkButton as the Style property.

The next set of images is referenced in the `LockButton` component of the `groovedefault skinresources.tpl`. The `LockButton` is used as the `Style` property of the `GroovieTalkieLockButton`.

Select this set of images in your image editor and change the hue setting to `-180`. Refresh the Groove Default skin again and then find the Lock button near the Push to Talk button. Notice that the button's outline hue has changed and that there is a lock icon on the button.

Now take a look at the `GroovieTalkieLockButton` component:

```
<g:Component Name="GroovieTalkieLockButton">
    <g:ComponentResource FingerprintID="Groove"
➥ URL="http://components.groove.net/Groove/Components/Root.osd?
➥Package=net.groove.Groove.ToolComponents.GrooveCommonComponents_DLL&amp;
➥Version=0&amp;Factory=Button"/>
    <g:PropertyList Version="1">
        <g:Property Value="grooveFile:///ToolBMPs\QuickAccessIconImages.jpg"
➥ Name="ImageURL"/>
        <g:Property Value="grooveFile:///ToolBMPs\
➥QuickAccessIconImagesMask.bmp" Name="ImageMaskURL"/>
        <g:Property Value="389" Name="ImageOffset"/>
        <g:Property Value="11" Name="ImageHeight"/>
        <g:Property Value="11" Name="ImageWidth"/>
        <g:Property Value="Click to talk live to other members of this shared
➥space; click again to stop broadcasting (Alt+F12)" Name="Tooltip"/>
        <g:Property Value="LockButton" Name="Style"/>
        <g:Property Value="ALT+0x7B" Name="Mnemonic"/>
    </g:PropertyList>
</g:Component>
```

The Lock button picks up its button graphic from the `tranceiverButtonImages.jpg` file, and then the `GroovieTalkieLockButton` gets its icon image from the `QuickAccessIconImages.jpg` file, resulting in a button with layered images.

The `Style` of this button is `LockButton`. If you click a lock button, it maintains its down state until it is clicked again.

The next image series contains the images for the Groove-standard `SmallIconButton`. The `SmallIconButton` is defined in `groovedefaultskinresources.tpl`. Change its hue and use the refresh procedure previously described.

In Groove, go to the Options menu and choose Send Message. The Record Voice Memo button has a `SmallIconButton` style. This button can be found in the `messagerTool.tpl` file. Like the Lock button, it picks up its icon from a different file. In this case, it takes the icon from the `Shared16x16Images.jpg` file in the `ToolBMPs` folder.

The next image series is the StandardButton, the most ubiquitous button in Groove. If you change its hue and refresh Groove, you'll also see changes in the StandardIconButton. That's because both buttons reference the same graphic. You can see a StandardIconButton when you look at the navigation arrows at the bottom of the Audio Tuning Wizard. Launch the wizard from the Options menu.

The next series is the LargeButton. Change the hue on this graphic set, restart Groove, and you will see the change on the Groove Login dialog.

You'll get two changes for the price of one when you change the ninth series. These graphics are for the SmallTextButton and the SmallIconTextButton. As you might expect, the SmallIconTextButton also contains an icon. An example of the SmallTextButton is on the Home view of Groove. If you have at least one contact, you will see that all the buttons in the My Contacts section are SmallTextButtons. You might think that the Add Contact button is a SmallIconTextButton, but it isn't. It is a SmallTextButton with a Menu property. The code looks like this:

```
<g:Property Name="Menu" Value="PersonalContactMenu"/>
```

The down triangle icon is automatically added if the button has a Menu property. You can look at the direction arrows on the Audio Tuner Wizard to see some real SmallIconTextButtons. Change those graphics now and take a look.

The last images in the file are the graphics for the TranceiverBackButton, the TransceiverForthButton, the TranscieverBackHistoryButton, and the TransceiverForthHistoryButton. These are all defined in groovedefaultskinresources.tpl. They are used in the standardtransceiver.tpl file as Style properties for BackButton, ForwardButton, BackHistoryButton, and ForthHistoryButton, respectively.

When you have changed those graphics and refreshed Groove, you will have changed all of Groove's graphic buttons.

While we're on the subject of buttons, you should talk about the other three standard Groove buttons: the Checkbox, the RadioButton, and the link button, or LaunchURL button. They are defined in groovedefaultskinresources.tpl. The text entries under My Account and Help & Support on the Home view are link buttons. A check box is in your Development Space for Navigate Together, and the volume buttons for Hold-to-Talk are radio buttons.

Those are all the buttons in the transceiver, but you still have more to do. If you add the Calendar Tool to your Development Space, you'll see that the toolbar buttons don't match your skin. They are located in the DefaultToolBarButtonImages.jpg file. They are called by the individual tools. Change those images now.

You have now changed all the backgrounds and buttons on your skin, so while you have your image editor out, let's change one other file. It's called `Preview.jpg`. This graphic is shown in the Skins Tool of the Account Tool. Change it now, and you'll give fair warning to whoever might want to try your skin.

Sounds

Sounds in the Groove Default skin are pretty subtle. The `TransceiverGoToButton` has a sound called `Action.wav`, played when you press the GlobalGoTo button. Let's change it in your skin:

1. Go to your `\WINDOWS\media\` folder and copy the file `CHIMES.WAV`; then shut down Groove.
2. Go to the `Data\Skins\groove.net\groovedefault\Sounds\` folder and rename `Action.wav` to `OldAction.wav`.
3. Paste your copy of `CHIMES.WAV` into the `Sounds` folder and rename it `Action.wav`.
4. Relaunch Groove and try the GoTo button. You should hear chimes.

So far, you have changed only the resources that the `groovedefaultskinresources.tpl` identifies. Next, you'll change the template itself.

When you make changes to the template, you won't be able to see them until you publish the skin, so before you do anything else, do some preliminary housekeeping:

1. Shut down Groove.
2. Copy the `GrooveDefault` folder from the `Skins` folder into your `Groove Development` folder, and then rename your `Original Groove Default` folder in your `Skins` folder `GrooveDefault`.
3. Go to your `localhost` folder and create a new folder named `MySkin`, and copy the `groovedefaultskinresources.xml` file from your `Groove Development` folder into your new `mySkin` folder.
4. Start Groove again, and you'll find that the `GrooveDefault` skin is back to normal.

Now you can edit the `groovedefaultskinresources.xml` file.

Because you are modifying an existing skin rather than developing one, you are going to be very careful not to change anything that could affect the layouts of `standardtransceiver.tpl`.

First, you will edit the `FontStyles` section. You have seen a `FontStyle` property defined in the `TransceiverPushToTalkButton` code previously. The `FontStyles` section defines variables for type styles used throughout the skin.

For example, the space name that appears to the right of the `QuickAccessSubForm` has the `FontStyle TelespaceHeader`. Let's change the color of that space name:

1. Find the `TelespaceHeader` property in the `FontStyles` section of the `groovedefaultskinresources.tpl`. Change its color from hexadecimal #193A62 to hexadecimal #624119. Hexadecimal #624119 is a dark brown that goes with your overall tan look.
2. Change the ToolHeader font style that is used by the `CurrentToolName` and `MemberName`. `CurrentToolName` appears under the space name when you are in a tool. `MemberName` is shown to the right of the `QuickAccessSubForm`. The `groovedefaultskinresources.tpl` file defines the color of `ToolHeader` as hexadecimal #436C99. Change that to hexadecimal #997043, a slightly lighter color than the `TelespaceHeader` change you made previously.
3. You could change the `TelespaceHeader` and `Tool Header TypeFace` attributes to `TimesNewRoman` if you were daring. You're not. Changing typefaces could affect one of the layouts of `standardtranceiver.tpl`. You really don't want any ugly wraps in your skin, so play it safe and stop here. Save `groovedefaultskinresources.xml`.

For others to be able to use your skin, you have to publish it.

Publishing a Skin

To make it as easy as possible for others to download your skin, you need to create a `.CAB` file to hold your skin's changed resources. Use the CAB utility you downloaded previously to create a `.CAB` file named `mySkin` that contains the graphic and sound resources you edited earlier and placed in your development directory. As you create your `.CAB`, be sure to preserve the folder names `Images` and `Sounds`.

Use the command

```
cabarc -p -r n mySkin.cab Images\*.* Sounds\*.*
```

from an MS-DOS prompt.

You might want to extract the `.CAB` to a test folder to make sure that it creates your two folders. That way you can be sure that any problems you may have in injecting the skin do not involve your `.CAB`.

Now, follow these steps:

1. Name the CAB `mySkin.cab` and place it into the `\localhost\mySkin\` folder you created in the "Getting Ready" section.

2. Change the document URL on the first line of the `groovedefaultskinresources.xml` file you just edited from `groovedefaultskinresources.xml` to `myskinresources.xml`; then change every reference of `Skins\groove.net\GrooveDefault` to `Skins\myCompany.com\mySkin`.
3. Rename the `groovedefaultskinresources.xml` file to `myskinresources.xml` and copy it to the `mySkin` folder.

You won't be putting this skin on your Web site, so don't worry if you do not have one. You will still be able to test injection of your skin. In Chapter 12, "Easier Groove: Modifying the Basic Groove Tool with Tool Creator and Tool Publisher," you'll learn how to stage your files and make your injectables available to others.

When Groove sets out to find the OSD and descriptor files, it checks the `localhost` directory first. If it doesn't find the files there, it tries to obtain the files from the designated Web site.

When you do move your files onto your Web site, you will have to do some additional housekeeping. As long as you have the OSD and descriptor files in your `localhost` directory, your tools and skins will install from there. After you have tested installation from the `localhost` file and have moved all files to your Web site, erase the files from `localhost`. If this step is neglected, you will not be able to test your ability to install from the Web.

You should now have your resources and your edited resource file inside the `myTool` folder.

Creating the Descriptor File

Next, you have to create a descriptor file for your skin. The skin descriptor serves the same function for the skin that the tool descriptor serves for the tool.

Create a new file named `mySkinDescriptor.xml` and put it into the `\localhost\mySkin` folder. Enter the following code into it. If you type this code from the book, be aware that all quoted strings need to be on a single line without hard or soft returns. For example, the `Value` for `ResourceURL` is a quoted string that needs to be on a single line. The critical line is the `resourceURL` element, which points to the `mySkin.OSD` file:

```
<g:Document xmlns:g="urn:groove.net">
   <g:ThemeDescriptionList>
      <g:ThemeDescriptionRecord>
         <g:ThemeDescription Name="Name" Value="urn:groove.net:Core.mySkin"/>
         <g:ThemeDescription Name="DisplayName" Value="My Skin"/>
         <g:ThemeDescription Name="Category" Value="\groove\starter"/>
         <g:ThemeDescription Name="Description" Value="My First Skin."/>
         <g:ThemeDescription Name="Author" Value="My Company"/>
         <g:ThemeDescription Name="HelpAbout" Value="Created by My Company"/>
         <g:ThemeDescription Name="ReleaseDate" Value="January 01, 2002"/>
```

```
         <g:ThemeDescription Name="Version" Value="0,0,0,0"/>
         <g:ThemeDescription Name="ContentTemplateURL"
➥ Value="http://components.groove.net/Groove/Components/Root.osd?
➥Package=net.groove.Groove.Skins.GrooveDefaultSkinTools_XML&amp;
➥Version=0&amp;Factory=Open"/>
         <g:ThemeDescription Name="ResourceTemplateURL"
➥ Value="GrooveDocument:///GrooveXSS/$PersistRoot/Themes.xss/
➥myskinresources.xml"/>
         <g:ThemeDescription Name="ResourceURL"
➥ Value="http://components.mycompany.com/mySkin/mySkin.osd?
➥Package=com.mycompany.mySkin&amp;
➥Version=0&amp;Factory=Skin"/>
         <g:ThemeDescription Name="PreviewImage"
Value="grooveFile:///Skins\mycompany.com\mySkin\Images\Preview.jpg"/>
      </g:ThemeDescriptionRecord>
   </g:ThemeDescriptionList>
</g:Document>
```

The ContentTemplateURL points to the GrooveDefaultsSkinsTools.XML file. This file identifies the location of the standard transceiver file and the proper shared space display tool. If you were to develop a skin that was specific to your own custom transceiver, you would have to write a custom version of GrooveDefaultsSkinsTools.XML.

Next, you'll need to write the following .OSD file:

```
<g:Document Name="mySkin.osd" xmlns:g="urn:groove.net">
   <SOFTPKG NAME="com.mycompany.mySkin.mySkinDescriptor_XML" VERSION="0,0,0,0">
      <TITLE>My Skin Descriptor</TITLE>
      <ABSTRACT>My Skin Descriptor</ABSTRACT>

      <IMPLEMENTATION>
         <CODEBASE HREF="http://components.mycompany.com/mySkin/
➥mySkinDescriptor.xml"/>
         <g:Install Type="Copy" TargetDir="$GROOVEDATA$\Skins\
➥mycompany.com"/>
         <g:Factory Name="Open" Type="Temporary XML Document"
➥ Filename="$GROOVEDATA$\Skins\mycompany.com\MySkinDescriptor.xml"/>
      </IMPLEMENTATION>

      <DEPENDENCY>
         <CODEBASE HREF="http://components.mycompany.com/mySkin/mySkin.osd?
➥Package=com.mycompany.mySkin&amp;Version=0"/>
      </DEPENDENCY>

   </SOFTPKG>
```

```
   <SOFTPKG NAME="com.mycompany.mySkin" VERSION="0,0,0,0">
      <IMPLEMENTATION>
         <CODEBASE HREF="http://components.mycompany.com/mySkin/mySkin.cab"/>
         <g:Install Type="Unpack CAB" TargetDir="$GROOVEDATA$\
➥Skins\mycompany.com\mySkin"/>
         <g:Factory Name="Skin" Type="ProgID" ProgID="Groove.DefaultSkin"/>
      </IMPLEMENTATION>
      <DEPENDENCY>
         <SOFTPKG NAME="com.mycompany.mySkin.mySkinResources_XML"
➥ VERSION="0,0,0,0">
            <IMPLEMENTATION>
               <CODEBASE HREF="http://components.mycompany.com/mySkin/
➥mySkinResources.xml"/>
               <g:Install Type="Import To XSS" DatabaseURI="$THEMESURI$"
➥ DocumentName="mySkinResources.xml" SchemaURI="$DEFAULTSCHEMA$"/>
               <g:ComponentURLProvider ProgID="Groove.TemplateParser"
➥ DatabaseURI="$THEMESURI$" DocumentName="mySkinResources.xml"
Argument="mySkinResources.xml"
➥ DocumentType="Template"/>
               <g:Factory Name="Open" Type="XML Document"
DatabaseURI="$THEMESURI$"
➥ DocumentName="mySkinResources.xml"/>
            </IMPLEMENTATION>
         </SOFTPKG>
      </DEPENDENCY>
   </SOFTPKG>
</g:Document>
```

Again, be aware that all quoted strings need to be on a single line without hard or soft returns. For example, the `Value` for the `CODEBASE HREF` attribute is a quoted string that needs to be on a single line.

This OSD file contains three `SOFTPKG`s. The first tells Groove to copy the skin descriptor file to a `\Skins\mycompany.com` folder that Groove will create. The `SOFTPKG` lists the OSD file as a dependency.

This dependency means that the OSD file is required by the tool descriptor for the tool descriptor to function properly. The tool descriptor will not be copied if the OSD file is not present.

The second `SOFTPKG` tells Groove to unpack the `.CAB` you created and install the `Images` and `Sounds` folders into a `\Skins\mycompany.com\mySkin` folder.

The third `SOFTPKG` is listed as a dependency of the second. It tells the application to import `mySkinResources.xml` into Groove's `themes.xss` XML database.

As a result of the dependency, the .CAB will not be unpacked, and the Sounds and Images folders will not be installed if the mySkinResources.xml is not successfully imported into the themes.xss database.

When we do inject the skin later, you can expect to see a folder in your Skins folder named mycompany.com. Within that folder you should see a mySkinDescriptor.xml file and a mySkin folder. Within the mySkin folder should be folders named Images and Sounds. If you open themes.xss in Database Navigator after the installation, you should see a mySkinResources.xml file.

Creating the Injector File

Now you need to write a .GRV file to start all of this installation rolling. For this exercise, you are going to create the .GRV by modifying the line that reads Your URL goes here in the ThemeBoilerplate file. Your finished MySkin.GRV file should look like this:

```
<?xml version='1.0'?><?groove.net version='1.0'?>
<g:fragment xmlns:g="urn:groove.net">
<g:InjectorWrapper AccountGUID="grooveIdentity:///DefaultIdentity"
➥ MessageID="qk992d4bwqywywgunpwm7ri9bijg7chkewrw7e6"
➥ ResourceURL="grooveIdentityMessage:///ToolMessage;Version=3,0,0,0"
➥ LocalDeviceURLs="Injector">
   <g:IdentityMessageHeader>
       <g:MessageHeader MessageType="ToolMessage"
➥ MessageID="qk992d4bwqywywgunpwm7ri9bijg7chkewrw7e6"
➥ Version="1,0,0,0" CreateTime="9/24/00 7:44 PM"
➥ CreatorDeviceURL="dpp://friends.groove.net/0sGnePZSnu-AY
➥fePpNqEqzwSOPo9910">
           <g:SenderContact/>
           <g:RecipientContact/>
       </g:MessageHeader>
       <g:MessageBody BodyName="MessageBody">
           <g:ToolMessage>
               <g:ToolMessageHeader ToolURL="grooveAccountTool:;
➥ CategoryName=grooveToolCategory://Account/
➥ThemeList,ComponentName=SkinManager"/>
               <g:ToolMessageBody>
                   <g:ThemeDescriptorList>
                       <g:ThemeDescriptorURL
➥ URL="http://components.mycompany.com/mySkin/mySkin.osd?
➥Package=com.mycompany.mySkin.mySkinDescriptor_XML&amp;
➥Version=0&amp;Factory=Open"/>
                   </g:ThemeDescriptorList>
               </g:ToolMessageBody>
           </g:ToolMessage>
```

```
        </g:MessageBody>
    </g:IdentityMessageHeader>
</g:InjectorWrapper>

</g:fragment>
```

Again, be aware that all quoted strings need to be on a single line without hard or soft returns. The URL Values are quoted strings that need to be on a single line.

Save the file as mySkin.GRV.

Your mySkin folder in your localhost directory should now hold five files: mySkin.cab, myskinresources.xml, mySkinDescriptor.xml, mySkin.osd, and mySkin.GRV.

Testing Injection

You are almost ready for the big moment, but first, shut down Groove and make a backup of your Data folder. If you run into problems during injection, or have difficulty with your new skin, you can simply shut down Groove, delete the current Data folder, copy in the backup, and relax. When you restart Groove, the application will be the same as it is now.

To inject your skin, you will have to run the registry file DisableComponentAuthentication.reg in the RegistryFiles folder of the GDK. Because component authentication protects you from installing unsigned tools, you should generally work with component authentication on, unless you are testing injection with one of your own unsigned tools.

Okay, take a deep breath, restart Groove, open your Development Account, navigate to your .GRV file, and launch it.

Next, you will see a progress bar as the skin injects.

Click on the Change the Look of Groove link to go to the Skins tab of the Account Tool. The skin listing should include mySkin, and you should be able to see a preview in the preview pane.

Hover your mouse over mySkin, and you should see My First Skin in the Tooltip. This message came from the Description element of the skin descriptor. Click the Apply button to change Groove to your skin.

Hopefully, everything worked. If it didn't, open each of the files you changed in XMLNotepad to make sure that they are all valid XML. If they are, reread every file, looking for misspellings, extra whitespace, and misplaced returns. Correct the errors and try it again.

If you are still having problems, keep in mind that injection problems usually come from two sources: either Groove cannot download the file, or your OSD is faulty. Groove won't be able to download the file if you are not connected to the Internet, or if the file is not in the location you specified. OSD errors are usually due to incorrect component URLs. Check your URLs for case and spelling, and make sure that the URLs match the directory structure.

Groove provides a debugging utility called Groove CSM Viewer that can help determine the component having difficulty with the OSD. A technote at `http://devzone.groove.net` explains its use.

You have now looked at and manipulated two of the three elements that describe a skin—the images and the skin resources descriptor. Before you leave this discussion of Groove skin development, you should explore the third element.

The Transceiver Template

The transceiver template defines the layout and functionality of the transceiver. In the Groove-supplied transceivers, the things they do remain pretty consistent across all skins, but the appearance can vary greatly. Check out the differences between the cellular skin and the Groove Default skin.

Let's first take a look at the layout component of the `standardtransceiver.tpl` file. The top-level layout component is a MultiCell layout. MultiCell is a series of either columns or rows of cells. It is like an HTML table, but each row or column could have a different number of cells. Unlike with an HTML table, however, there is no spanning. Components are placed into `CELL` elements.

Here is the layout component of the `standardtransceiver.tpl` file:

```
<g:Component Name="Layout">
                <g:ComponentResource FingerprintID="Groove"
➥ URL="http://components.groove.net/Groove/Components/Root.osd?
➥Package=net.groove.Groove.ToolComponents.GrooveCommonComponents_DLL&amp;
➥Version=0&amp;Factory=MultiCellLayout"/>
   <g:PropertyList Version="1">
       <g:Property Name="Layout">
           <g:PropertyValue>
               <MULTIROW>
      <ROW>
          <CELL HEIGHT="23">
              StdMenuBarForm
          </CELL>
      </ROW>
      <ROW>
          <CELL HEIGHT="44">
              QuickAccessSubForm
          </CELL>
      </ROW>
```

```
        <ROW>
            <CELL HEIGHT="29" WIDTH="165">
                NavigationSubForm
            </CELL>
            <CELL>
                TitleBarSubForm2
            </CELL>
            <CELL WIDTH="88"/>
        </ROW>
        <ROW>
            <CELL WIDTH="1" NAME="TELESPACE_PANE_TOOLS"/>
            <CELL TabOrder="1">
                ContentViewContainer
            </CELL>
        </ROW>
                </MULTIROW>
            </g:PropertyValue>
        </g:Property>
    </g:PropertyList>
</g: Component>
```

This layout contains five components:

- The `StdMenuBarForm` component holds the File, View, Options, and Help menus across the top of the transceiver.
- Just below it is the `QuickAccessSubForm`, which contains the `GlobalGoToButton`, the `PersonalContactsButton`, and the `TelespaceListButton`. To the right of those components are the `SpaceName`, the `CurrentToolName`, and the `MemberName`.
- Below that is the `NavigationSubForm` that consists of the `BackButton`, `BackHistoryButton`, `ForwardButton`, and `ForwardHistoryButton`.
- To the right of the `NavigationSubForm` is the `TitleBarSubForm2`. `TitleBarSubForm2` is a subform component used by the tools in the shared space. That is where the Calendar Tool buttons reside, for example.
- Below these two components are a cell named `TELESPACE_PANE_TOOLS` and the `ContentViewContainer` component. `TELESPACE_PANE_TOOLS` is a placeholder for `TitleBarSubForm1`, and you saw earlier that the subform contains the `InviteButton`, the `MemberAwarenessSubForm`, the `ConversationPaneTitle`, the `TalkWithPeopleSubForm`, the `ChatButton`, and the `FollowModeButton`. The `ContentViewContainer` holds the `Content` component and the `HelpModeViewContainer`. `Content` is a cell that houses individual tools, and `HelpModeViewContainer` holds the help information that is shown in the Overview for a tool, either when the tool is first shown or when it is opened from the View menu.

If you launch Groove and change to the Groove Default skin, you should be able to identify all these components.

Except for some slight changes in cell sizes, the top-level layout for the Redmond Gray skin is identical to Groove Default. Most of the skin's changes in appearance are the result of changes in graphics.

The Cellular skin makes much greater changes in the layout. Here is the layout for the `cellularskintransceiver.tpl` file:

```
<g:Component Name="Layout">
   <g:ComponentResource FingerprintID="Groove"
➥ URL="http://components.groove.net/Groove/Components/Root.osd?
➥Package=net.groove.Groove.ToolComponents.GrooveCommonComponents_DLL&amp;
➥Version=0&amp;Factory=MultiCellLayout"/>
   <g:PropertyList Version="1">
       <g:Property Name="Layout">
           <g:PropertyValue>
               <MULTICOL>
      <COL>
          <CELL HEIGHT="16" WIDTH="140"/>
          <CELL HEIGHT="89" WIDTH="140" TabOrder="0">
              NavigationSubForm
          </CELL>
          <CELL WIDTH="140">
              BlankTitleBar
          </CELL>
          <CELL HEIGHT="64" WIDTH="140" TabOrder="0"/>
          <CELL HEIGHT="18" WIDTH="140"/>
      </COL>
      <COL>
          <CELL HEIGHT="3"/>
          <CELL HEIGHT="16">
              StdMenuBarForm
          </CELL>
          <CELL HEIGHT="6"/>
          <CELL HEIGHT="26">
              TitleBarSubForm2
          </CELL>
          <CELL TabOrder="1">
              ContentViewContainer
          </CELL>
          <CELL HEIGHT="3"/>
      </COL>
      <COL>
          <CELL WIDTH="25" TabOrder="0">
              WindowFrameControlsSubForm
```

```
            </CELL>
            <CELL HEIGHT="272" WIDTH="25" TabOrder="0">
                GripSubForm
            </CELL>
            <CELL WIDTH="25"/>
        </COL>
                </MULTICOL>
            </g:PropertyValue>
        </g:Property>
    </g:PropertyList>
            </g:Component>
```

Groove Cellular uses a MultiCell layout that is a series of three columns. The column layout is not as intuitive as the row layout, so you might want to use the registry file `EnableCellBorders.reg` from the `Registry Files` folder of the GDK to help you follow along. You have to shut down and restart Groove for the registry changes to take effect. The purple borders correspond with MultiCell layout.

The second cell of the first column contains the `NavigationSubForm` component, like you had in the `standardtransceiver.tpl` file, but that's where the similarity ends. Groove Cellular incorporates the functionality of both the `NavigationSubForm` and the `QuickAccessSubForm` components described in `standardtransceiver.tpl`. The menu on the cellular GoTo button is programmatically initialized in a way that is quite different from the one in `standardtransceiver.tpl`.

Notice in the following code that the position of the `ForwardButton`, `ForwardHistoryButton`, `BackButton`, `BackHistoryButton`, and `GoToButton` is in XY layout:

```
<g:Component Name="Layout">
        <g:ComponentResource FingerprintID="Groove"
➥ URL="http://components.groove.net/Groove/Components/Root.osd?
➥Package=net.groove.Groove.ToolComponents.GrooveCommonComponents_DLL&amp;
➥Version=0&amp;Factory=XYLayout"/>
    <g:PropertyList Version="1">
            <g:Property Name="Layout">
        <g:PropertyValue>
            <g:Control Left="20" Height="40" Top="13"
➥ Name="BackButton" Width="23"/>
            <g:Control Left="18" Height="13" Top="54"
➥ Name="BackHistoryButton" Width="16"/>
            <g:Control Left="86" Height="40" Top="13"
➥ Name="ForwardButton" Width="23"/>
            <g:Control Left="94" Height="13" Top="54"
➥ Name="ForwardHistoryButton" Width="16"/>
            <g:Control Left="35" Height="21" Top="64"
➥ Name="GoToButton" Width="59"/>
```

```
        </g:PropertyValue>
           </g:Property>
           </g:PropertyList>
</g:Component>
```

XY layout is used for the precise positioning of elements, usually in spaces that do not scale. If you enabled cell borders, you can tell XY layout by the red borders.

The third cell contains a `BlankTitleBar` component. It is a static component with a blank label. It serves as a placeholder for `TitlebarSubform1`. `TitlebarSubform1` holds all the components from the Invite button to the Navigate Together check box.

The first cell in the second column holds the `StandardMenubarForm` and `TitlebarSubform2`. The `StandardMenubarForm` functions exactly as it did in the `standardtransceiver.tpl` file. The cellular `TitlebarSubform2` is similar but does not hold the space name. The `ContentViewContainer` is identical to its counterpart in the `standardtransceiver.tpl` file.

The transceiver window for Cellular is defined in `cellularskinresources.xml` and has its `CaptionVisible` and `BorderVisible` properties set to `false`. That means Groove, rather than Windows, has to handle the minimize, restore, and close functions. The cellular skin needs room to site these controls, so it includes the third column and integrates the controls with a Grip graphic.

As you can see, modifying the transceiver template file can result in dramatic changes in the look and feel of a Groove application. Eventually, your ability to transform the look and functionality of Groove will be limited only by your imagination.

In the meantime, you don't have to start with the Groove Default skin. You can use the same procedures you used earlier with Cellular, or any new skins that appear on `groove.net`. Even with what you already know, you can create lively and interesting Groove skins.

Summary

Now that you have seen someone else's Groove programming, you should do some of your own. In the next chapter we will begin to develop tools.

Building a Basic Groove Tool

CHAPTER

9

IN THIS CHAPTER

In this chapter, you'll begin to program Groove tools. We will first review what a tool template is and how it is constructed. You will then begin creating your own. You will start with an XML skeleton and then add components and code until you have a very basic Groove tool. You will use this tool as the foundation for a group trivia-game application you'll work on over the next few chapters.

Tool Templates

A Groove tool is an instantiation of a tool template. Groove uses the template to instantiate the components, arrange them in space, and connect them with the tool's controlling code. The tool template represents the tool.

As you learned in the discussion of Groove tool development in Chapter 7, "Creating a Groove Development Environment," a tool template is an XML file that has the structure shown in Figure 9.1.

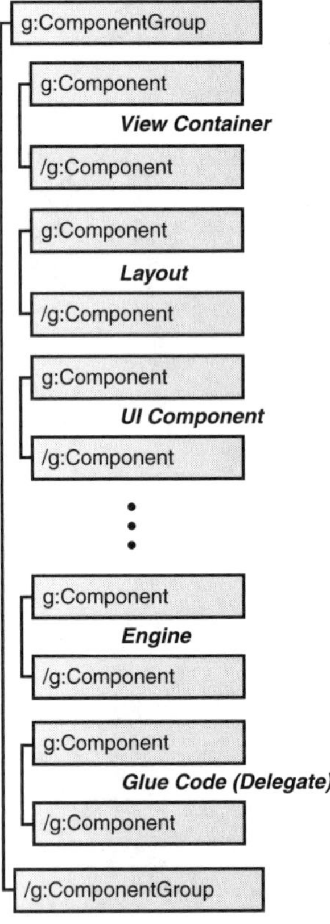

FIGURE 9.1
The typical tool template structure.

The outer brackets represent an XML document element. This element is the container for your tool. Inside the document are a ComponentSecurity element and a ToolTemplate element. You will remember that the ComponentSecurity element holds the fingerprint table with which components are signed. For now, you will use Groove's ComponentSecurity element contents because you will be using Groove components.

The ToolTemplate element contains a view info element that is used to tell Groove how to hold the template in memory. In the case of your tools, the Lifetime attribute will always be Limited.

The ComponentGroup element contains a series of Groove components. Components are referenced by a ComponentResource URL element. You start construction of a resource URL element with the <g:ComponentResource /> tag. You then add the Fingerprint ID="Groove" attribute/value pair to describe these components as having originated with Groove. You then add the URL attribute:

```
<g:ComponentResource Fingerprint ID="Groove" URL= />
```

The URL itself begins with the location of the Root.osd file, which is http://components.groove.net/Groove/Components/Root.osd:

```
<g:ComponentResource Fingerprint ID="Groove" URL=
"http://components.groove.net/Groove/Components/Root.osd"/>
```

This is followed by a query to find the correct package:

```
<g:ComponentResource Fingerprint ID="Groove" URL= "http://components.groove.net
➥/Groove/Components/Root.osd?Package=net.groove.Groove.ToolComponents"/>
```

Finally, add the DLL, the factory name, and the name of the factory to be used to instantiate the component:

```
<g:ComponentResource Fingerprint ID="Groove"
➥ URL= "http://components.groove.net/Groove/Components/Root.osd?
➥Package=net.groove.Groove.ToolComponents.GrooveCommonComponents_DLL&amp;
➥Version=0&amp;Factory=Button"/>
```

This ComponentResource URL identifies a button component and will allow Groove to instantiate it when Groove accesses the tool template.

The components include the view container, UI, engine, and glue code.

View Container Components

A template has a ViewContainer as one of its components in the ComponentGroup and one or more layouts in the component group. At design time you define a connection in your ViewContainer to a single layout component. It is the Layout component that describes the arrangement of the visual components of a Groove tool.

So far, we have seen and studied the MultiCell and XY layouts. We have also mentioned the HTMLTable layout that we will be using shortly. Other layouts include SingleCell and Splitter.

UI Components

The Groove UI components are `Static`, `Image`, `Button`, `Menu`, `ToolBar`, `ListBox`, `ComboBox`, `Edit`, `Tab Control`, `Header`, `ListView`, `TreeView`, `IconListView`, and `DataViewer`:

- A `Static` component is used to display simple text that is referenced from its `Label` property.
- An `Image` component, as you might expect, displays an image that it references either by URL or by element. Some of the properties of this component can allow the image to scale, accept only certain image types, or launch a URL by clicking the image.
- `Buttons` in Groove usually trigger tool code. They have numerous properties to change both their appearance and their functionality.
- `Menu` components display a list of choices. They have a `UICommands` property that allows you to set an initial set of commands that the component will display.
- The `ToolBar` can take images and associate UI commands with them to create toolbars. The `style` property determines the look of the toolbar by using a skin-defined style. We saw this in Chapter 8, "Customizing Groove," with the `NavigationSubForm` of the standard transceiver.
- A `ListBox` displays a list of items. It has a very simple interface that does not allow for much complexity.
- The `ComboBox` component provides a drop-down selection list. The Select Account section of the Groove Logon dialog is a good example of the use of a combo box.
- An `Edit` component provides a way to contain text user input. The Discussion Tool uses an Edit component in the New Topic dialog to accept a subject.
- `Tab` controls have properties to hold images as well as text, and can be set to allow rearranging via drag and drop.
- A `Header` component displays one or more columns and is normally used with other components.
- `ListView` components have the capability to display text and images in multiple columns, so they are much more powerful than `ListBox` components. The many properties for this component determine both the look and functionality of the container and the presentation of its contained media.
- The `TreeView` component is used to display a hierarchical list. An example of a `TreeView` component is the Subject area of the Discussion Tool.

- The `IconListView` is similar to ListView but can also display icons. An example of a `IconListView` component is the Member Awareness panel Groove Home page.
- The `DataViewer` provides a grid control for Groove Record-based data and is used with the RecordSetEngine described in the next paragraph.

Engine Component

As we discussed earlier, engines maintain and change the tool's data model, which allows for persistence and the dissemination of deltas to synchronize the data models of all participants in a shared space.

You have already had experience with one of these engines: the property list. All the components we examined in the `groovedefaultskinresources.xml` file had property lists. In fact, every component has a property list. If a component description in XML does not include a property list, Groove gives it an empty one. Your first efforts at persisting data in the tutorial application will use property lists. Later, you will migrate to a `RecordSetEngine`.

The `RecordSetEngine` is the primary component for managing persistent field-oriented data in Groove. It not only maintains user data, but also updates and disseminates tool state data. The `RecordSetEngine` stores a flat list of records, each identified by a unique ID number in the tool's XML database. A schema is used to describe the recordset's data.

The Discussion Tool is an obvious example of the use of this engine. The Discussion Tool also uses the `DataViewer` and `ModelGlue Components`. `DataViewer` provides a grid control for Groove Record-based data. It must be used with `ModelGlue`, because the `ModelGlue` component provides the application logic for record access. `ModelGlue`, in turn, connects to a `Tool CollectionsComponent` that manages the lifetime of the data collections that `DataViewer` and `ModelGlue` create.

Glue Code Components

The glue code is code that connects the view, UI components, engines, and engine helpers and transforms the collection of components into a working tool. To add glue code to the template, you need to add the Groove `ScriptHost` component. The `ScriptHost` component allows your script to call and interact with Groove interfaces. This component also defines the component connections, and can include TypeLIBs or Groove Script Library (GSL) files.

You will be writing your glue code in JavaScript, but glue can also be written in any COM-compliant language such as VBScript, C++, VisualBasic, and Python.

Creating a Tool Template Skeleton

Using what you have just learned, you can create a basic tool template skeleton. The tool skeleton will serve as a template you can use to rapidly develop tools later. Open your text editor and create a file named ToolSkeleton.tpl. Then you can create a `document` element:

```
<g:Document Name="ToolName.tpl" xmlns:g="urn:groove.net">
</g:Document>
```

Again, if you are typing this code from the book, be aware that all quoted strings need to be on a single line without a hard or soft return. For example the Value for Name is a quoted string that needs to be on a single line.

Next, you add a `ComponentSecurity` element. Remember that the `ComponentSecurity` element provides the fingerprint of the signer of the Groove components. You also need to add a comment to make it easier to navigate the template later:

```
<g:Document Name="ToolName.tpl" xmlns:g="urn:groove.net">
<!--Component Signing -->
<g:ComponentSecurity>
        <g:FingerprintTable>
            <g:Entry Fingerprint=
➥ "4262-dcb1:4552-d303:123d-36a6:0a96-62e5:24a7-d7db" FingerprintID="Groove"/>
        </g:FingerprintTable>
    </g:ComponentSecurity>
</g:Document>
```

Below the `ComponentSecurity` element, you will add a `ToolTemplate` element.

The `ToolTemplate` Element

The `ToolTemplate` element takes three attributes: the name of the `ToolTemplate` component, the `DefaultToolDisplayName` that will provide the tool's label in the transceiver, and the `TemplateDisplayName`. The name that appears in the Add Tool tool comes from the XML Descriptor file:

```
<g:Document Name="ToolName.tpl" xmlns:g="urn:groove.net">
<!--Component Signing -->
<g:ComponentSecurity>
        <g:FingerprintTable>
            <g:Entry Fingerprint=
➥"4262-dcb1:4552-d303:123d-36a6:0a96-62e5:24a7-d7db" FingerprintID="Groove"/>
        </g:FingerprintTable>
    </g:ComponentSecurity>
    <!-- Start Tool Template -->
    <g:ToolTemplate Name=" ToolName.Tool" DefaultToolDisplayName="ToolName"
➥ TemplateDisplayName="ToolName"
```

```
    </g:ToolTemplate>
</g:Document>
```

Inside the ToolTemplate element, you will place a pair of ViewInfo tags, followed by the tags for the ComponentGroup:

```
<g:Document Name="ToolName.tpl" xmlns:g="urn:groove.net">
<!--Component Signing -->
<g:ComponentSecurity>
        <g:FingerprintTable>
            <g:Entry Fingerprint=
➥"4262-dcb1:4552-d303:123d-36a6:0a96-62e5:24a7-d7db" FingerprintID="Groove"/>
        </g:FingerprintTable>
    </g:ComponentSecurity>
    <!-- Start Tool Template -->
    <g:ToolTemplate Name=" ToolName.Tool" DefaultToolDisplayName="ToolName"
➥ TemplateDisplayName=" ToolName ">
    <g:ViewInfo Lifetime="Limited"/>
        <!-- Start Component Group -->
        <g:ComponentGroup DefaultView="ToolViewContainer">
        </g:ComponentGroup>
    </g:ToolTemplate>
</g:Document>
```

The ViewInfo component takes a lifetime attribute that tells Groove how to manage memory for the tool. Your tools will always have a value of Limited.

ComponentGroup Elements

You can specify four ComponentGroup elements:

- The DefaultView indicates the UI of the group.
- The Delegate is the glue code component that the group uses.
- The HelpInfoProvider lists the component that provides help information to the user.
- The DataModelDelegate indicates the component that exposes interfaces to the engine that maintains the data model for the group.

Each tool must have a default view, so you will include a DefaultView attribute in your skeleton code. The value for the DefaultView attribute will be the name of your ViewContainer component, the first of five components we are using that you will need to place in your ComponentGroup. Those five are a view container, a layout, a UI component, an engine, and glue code:

```
<g:Document Name="ToolName.tpl" xmlns:g="urn:groove.net">
<!--Component Signing -->
```

```
<g:ComponentSecurity>
        <g:FingerprintTable>
            <g:Entry Fingerprint=
➥"4262-dcb1:4552-d303:123d-36a6:0a96-62e5:24a7-d7db" FingerprintID="Groove"/>
        </g:FingerprintTable>
    </g:ComponentSecurity>
    <!-- Start Tool Template -->
    <g:ToolTemplate Name=" ToolName.Tool" DefaultToolDisplayName="ToolName"
➥ TemplateDisplayName=" ToolName ">
    <g:ViewInfo Lifetime="Limited"/>
        <!-- Start Component Group -->
        <g:ComponentGroup DefaultView="ToolViewContainer">
           <!-- The View Container -->
           <!-- The Layout -->
           <!-- A UI Component -->
          <!-- The Engine -->
          <!-- The Glue Code -->
        </g:ComponentGroup>
    </g:ToolTemplate>
</g:Document>
```

ViewContainer

A `ViewContainer` is a component that works in conjunction with the layout to define the look of a Groove tool. Within the `Component` element, a resource URL references the `ViewContainer` component and is constructed by combining the path to the `root.osd` file and a query to find the correct package. A `ViewContainer` component has three properties you can set, so you will need a `PropertyList` component.

Within the `PropertyList` component, you'll add a property to describe the background of the view container, and you will give it a `BackgroundStyle` element with a `Style` attribute of `SectionBackground`. In the skin resource file, font styles, colors, buttons, and backgrounds are defined and given names. Those names can be used as the style attributes for components.

You can specify the height and width of the window as `PreferredHeight` and `PreferredWidth` properties. For the skeleton, you'll include only the `SectionBackground` property.

The view container will also hold component connections. The ViewContainer's connection to the Layout component must use the value 0 (zero) as its ID, and the connection to the form delegate component must use the value 1 (one) as its ID.

Your completed `ViewContainer` component looks like this:

```
<g:Component Name="YourViewContainer">
   <g:ComponentResource FingerprintID="Groove"
➥ URL="http://components.groove.net/Groove/Components/Root.osd?
```

```
➥Package=net.groove.Groove.ToolComponents.GrooveCommonComponents_DLL&amp;
➥Version=0&amp;Factory=ViewContainer"/>

   <!-- View Property List -->
   <g:PropertyList Version="1">

      <g:Property Name="Background">
         <g:BackgroundStyle Style="SectionBackground"/>
      </g:Property>

   </g:PropertyList>

   <!-- Connections -->
   <g:ComponentConnections>
      <g:Connection ConnectionID="0" Name="YourLayout"/>
      <g:Connection ConnectionID="1" Name="ToolGlue"/>
   </g:ComponentConnections>

</g:Component>
```

The Layout

The view container works with a layout to size and place components in the view. You will use the `HTMLTableLayout` in your skeleton.

After including the resource URL, you will add a property to the component's property list. The property will be named `Layout`. The property's value will be the series of tags that make up the HTML table. Those tags appear to be HTML and are identical in most respects, but because the code is XML, there are a few differences.

One difference is that all tags in XML must be uppercase. Another is that XML conventions, rather than HTML, apply, so single-element XML tags are allowed if they are empty—for example, `<TD/>` rather than `<TD></TD>`. Also, only variable names can appear in table cells—you cannot display raw text. When you use this skeleton, you will place the names of your UI component in these tags.

The `<TABLE>` tag can take only `HSPACE`, `VSPACE`, `COLSPAN`, `ROWSPAN`, `NAME`, and `CELLPADDING` attributes, and you can put only `LeftPad`, `TopPad`, `RightPad`, `BottomPad`, `HEIGHT`, and `WIDTH` attributes in the `<TD>` tags. <TR> tags do not have attributes.

You'll put enough tags into your shell code to start an HTML table and to facilitate modification with cut and paste. The resulting `Layout` component in XML looks like this:

```
<!-- Layout -->
   <g:Component Name="YourLayout">
```

```
    <g:ComponentResource FingerprintID="Groove"
➥ URL="http://components.groove.net/Groove/Components/Root.osd?
➥Package=net.groove.Groove.ToolComponents.GrooveCommonComponents_DLL&amp;
➥Version=0&amp;Factory=HTMLTableLayout"/>
    <!-- Layout Property List -->
    <g:PropertyList Version="1">
        <g:Property Name="Layout">
            <g:PropertyValue>
                <TABLE>

                    <TR>
                        <TD/>
                        <TD/>
                    </TR>

                    <TR>
                        <TD/>
                        <TD/>
                    </TR>

                    <TR>
                        <TD/>
                        <TD/>
                    </TR>

                </TABLE>
            </g:PropertyValue>
        </g:Property>
    </g:PropertyList>
</g:Component>
```

The Button

Next, you will want some shell code to use with a typical UI component: a button. Each UI component has its own set of properties. You will give yours a name, a component resource URL, and a property list. Inside the property list, you'll specify `Style`, `Label`, `Tooltip`, and `Mnemonic` properties:

- The `Style` property is just like the `style` element you saw earlier with backgrounds. You'll use the `StandardButton` style defined in the skin resources file.
- Then you will use a value of `Press to &Initiate Action` for the `Label` property. The `&` tells Groove to underline the following letter to indicate the button's mnemonic, or keyboard shortcut.

- The `Tooltip` property determines the message displayed if the user hovers the mouse over the button. You'll put in a value of `The tool's tooltip`, just to see it work when you display your skeleton code later.
- The `Mnemonic` property sets the Alt key combination that simulates a button click. In your case, the value is `Alt+I`.

Here is the button code:

```
<g:Component Name="ToolButton">
   <g:ComponentResource FingerprintID="Groove"
➥ URL=http://components.groove.net/Groove/Root.osd?
➥Package=net.groove.Groove.ToolComponents.GrooveCommonComponents_DLL&amp;
➥Version=0&amp;Factory=Button/>

   <g:PropertyList Version="1">
      <g:Property Name="Style" Value="StandardButton"/>
      <g:Property Name="Label" Value="Press to &amp;Initiate Action"/>
      <g:Property Name="Tooltip" Value="The tool's tooltip"/>
      <g:Property Name="Mnemonic" Value="ALT+I"/>
   </g:PropertyList>
</g:Component>
```

We will discuss both the button properties and the properties of all the other UI components in much greater detail as you use them in upcoming code.

The Engine Component

Next, you will put an engine component into your skeleton code. You'll use a `RecordSetEngine` because that is the most commonly used engine in Groove. A `RecordSetEngine` stores a set of records, each of which is identified by a unique record ID. A record is a comprised of one or more fields, each of which holds a value. The field values can be strings, longs, or doubles or a Groove element.

In addition to the `name` attribute, the `RecordSetEngine` component takes a `SingleInstance` attribute that is set to `true` and a `Category` attribute of `Engine`.

The `SingleInstance ="True"` attribute signifies that there should only be a single instance of this component created for each process running Groove. This allows multiple instances of the tool's view to render the same data model.

Categories are used by the `IGrooveToolContainer` interface for finding a particular tool.

A `RecordSetEngine` has an `EnginDesc` element with a `Tag` attribute set to `urn:groove.net:RecordSetEngine`. A `RecordSetEngine` also has a `ClassInfoList` element. The `ClassInfo List` property takes a `Name` attribute and a `URL` attribute. The value for `Name` is the class of record that will be stored in the engine, and the value for the URL to the factory that implements the record.

You will be using urn:groove.net:Record as the Name value, and

```
http://components.groove.net/Groove/Components/Root.osd?
➥Package=net.groove.Groove.ToolComponents.
➥GrooveListComponents_DLL&amp;Version=0&amp;Factory=Record
```

as the URL value.

As you use the RecordSetEngine later, you will see more properties, and we'll go into more detail about how to use the ClassInfoList.

Here is what your finished engine component looks like:

```
<!--Engine Component -->
<g:Component SingleInstance="True" Category="Engine" Name="RecordSetEngine">
   <g:ComponentResource FingerprintID="Groove"
➥ URL="http://components.groove.net/Groove/Components/Root.osd?
➥Package=net.groove.Groove.ToolComponents.GrooveListComponents_DLL&amp;
➥Version=0,4&amp;
Factory=RecordSetEngine3"/>
   <g:EngineDesc Tag="urn:groove.net:RecordSetEngine"/>
   <g:PropertyList Version="1">
     <g:Property Name="ClassInfoList">
        <g:PropertyValue>
           <g:ClassInfo Name="urn:groove.net:Record"
➥ URL="http://components.groove.net/Groove/Components/Root.osd?
➥Package=net.groove.Groove.ToolComponents.GrooveListComponents_DLL&amp;
➥Version=0&amp;Factory=RecordSetEngine3"/>
Factory=Record"/>
        </g:PropertyValue>
     </g:Property>
  </g:PropertyList>
</g:Component>
```

The Glue Code

The last component of your shell is for your glue code. For the component's Name attribute, you'll use ToolGlueCode. Your resource URL will be similar to those of the previous components, except you'll use a ScriptHost3 factory, the current script host component at the time of this writing.

After your component URL, add your component connections. A component connection is the mechanism through which glue code is made aware of other components it may use.

ScriptHost is the component that implements the necessary interfaces for your scripts to execute. Your glue code uses ScriptHost to listen to the outgoing interfaces of your components. For any component listed in your component connections, you can handle its callback functions by naming routines in your script in the following manner: *ComponentName_MethodName*. A typical button press, for example, can be handled by the following code:

```
function ToolButton_OnCommand(i_pIUICommand)
   {
      DoSomething();
   }
```

In this case, the method name is OnCommand. OnCommand can take an interface pointer as an input parameter, i_pIUICommand, for use inside your delegate code if you wish.

NOTE

Groove naming conventions tell us that the lowercase i indicates that it is an input parameter. i_p tells us that it is an input parameter of type pointer, in this case to UICommand.

ScriptHost lets your code know when the tool has been loaded and a valid property list has been created, and that all component connections have been processed, by calling your Initialize method. Likewise, ScriptHost calls the Terminate method to tell you that your component is being unloaded. When it is called, the property list is still valid and all components you have been connected to are still valid; so it is a good idea to use this method for any cleanup you may need to do.

The OnViewContainerShow and OnViewContainerHide methods let your code know that the view container to which you have a component connection is being shown or hidden. OnPropertyChanged lets you know that a property in your property list has been modified, whereas OnPropertyRemoved tells your code that a property in your property list has been deleted. In addition to these methods, there are others you can use to learn about different conditions in the UI components to which you are connected through component connections.

Establish component connections to the button you included in your layout, and to the RecordSetEngine component using the following code:

```
<g:ComponentConnections>
   <g:Connection ConnectionID="0" Name="ToolButton"/>
   <g:Connection ConnectionID="1" Name ="RecordSetEngine"/>
</g:ComponentConnections>
```

Note

These connections do not have to be in order, need to start with 0, or need to be a particular value for a particular component. This is unlike the earlier connections between the view container and the layout and form delegate, which must be 0 and 1, respectively.

Next, include an empty `PropertyList` for your use.

Note

At this point in the code, you could add a `TYPELIB`. For this skeleton code, you are not going to, but if you did, it would take this form:

```
<TYPELIB LIBID="{FB1EBAB1-C159-11d3-80B6-00500487887B}"
➥ NAME="GrooveCollectionComponents" MAJORVER="1"
➥ MINORVER="0"/>.
```

After the `TYPELIB`, you could add a Groove Script Library file like `GrooveGlobalHelperFunctions.gsl`. GSL files are enclosed in `<SCRIPT>` tags. The `SCRIPT` element takes an `SRC` attribute that is similar to a resource URL. You would add `GrooveGlobalHelperFunctions.gsl` to your code using the following format:

```
<SCRIPT
SRC="http://components.groove.net/Groove/Components/Root.osd?Package=
➥net.groove.Groove.ToolComponents.GrooveGlobalHelperFunctions_GSL&amp;
➥Version=0,1&amp;Factory=Open" />
```

You are finally ready to include your glue code. You will put it inside `<SCRIPT>` tags and put the actual code inside a `CDATA` element. Because you haven't written any glue code, you'll leave the `CDATA` element empty for now. The completed glue code component looks like this:

```
<!-- Glue code -->
<g:Component Name="ToolGlue">

   <g:ComponentResource FingerprintID="Groove"
➥ URL="http://components.groove.net/Groove/Components/Root.osd?
➥Package=net.groove.Groove.ToolComponents.GrooveCommonComponents_DLL&amp;
➥Version=0&amp;Factory=ScriptHost3"/>

   <g:ComponentConnections>
      <g:Connection ConnectionID="0" Name="ToolButton"/>
      <g:Connection ConnectionID="1" Name ="RecordSetEngine"/>
```

```
   </g:ComponentConnections>

   <g:PropertyList Version="1"/>

   <SCRIPT>
      <![CDATA[

      ]]>
   </SCRIPT>
</g:Component>
```

The Completed Skeleton

Putting it all together, you can look at your tool template skeleton code in Listing 9.1.

LISTING 9.1 The Tool Skeleton

```
<g:Document Name="ToolName.tpl" xmlns:g="urn:groove.net">
<!-- Component Signing -->
   <g:ComponentSecurity>
      <g:FingerprintTable>
         <g:Entry Fingerprint=
➥"4262-dcb1:4552-d303:123d-36a6:0a96-62e5:24a7-d7db" FingerprintID="Groove"/>
      </g:FingerprintTable>
   </g:ComponentSecurity>

   <!-- Start Tool Template -->
   <g:ToolTemplate Name=" ToolName.Tool" DefaultToolDisplayName="ToolName"
➥ TemplateDisplayName="ToolName">
   <g:ViewInfo Lifetime="Limited"/>
   <!-- Start Component Group -->
      <g:ComponentGroup DefaultView="ToolViewContainer">
         <!-- The View Container -->
         <g:Component Name="ToolViewContainer">
            <g:ComponentResource FingerprintID="Groove"
➥ URL="http://components.groove.net/Groove/Components/Root.osd?
➥Package=net.groove.Groove.ToolComponents.GrooveCommonComponents_DLL&amp;
➥Version=0&amp;Factory=ViewContainer"/>

            <!-- View Property List -->
            <g:PropertyList Version="1">

               <g:Property Name="Background">
                  <g:BackgroundStyle Style="SectionBackground"/>
               </g:Property>
```

Listing 9.1 Continued

```
        </g:PropertyList>

        <!-- Connections -->
        <g:ComponentConnections>
            <g:Connection ConnectionID="0" Name="ToolLayout"/>
            <g:Connection ConnectionID="1" Name="ToolGlue"/>
        </g:ComponentConnections>

    </g:Component>

    <!-- The Layout -->
    <g:Component Name="ToolLayout">

    <g:ComponentResource FingerprintID="Groove"
➥ URL="http://components.groove.net/Groove/Components/Root.osd?
➥Package=net.groove.Groove.ToolComponents.GrooveCommonComponents_DLL&amp;
➥Version=0&amp;Factory=HTMLTableLayout"/>
    <!-- Layout Property List -->
        <g:PropertyList Version="1">

            <g:Property Name="Layout">
            <g:PropertyValue>
                <TABLE>

                    <TR>
                        <TD>ToolButton</TD>
                        <TD/>
                    </TR>

                    <TR>
                        <TD/>
                        <TD/>
                    </TR>

                    <TR>
                        <TD/>
                        <TD/>
                    </TR>

                    </TABLE>
                </g:PropertyValue>
            </g:Property>
        </g:PropertyList>
    </g:Component>
```

LISTING 9.1 Continued

```
        <!-- A UI Component -->
        <g:Component Name="ToolButton">
           <g:ComponentResource FingerprintID="Groove"
➥ URL="http://components.groove.net/Groove/Root.osd?
➥Package=net.groove.Groove.ToolComponents.GrooveCommonComponents_DLL&amp;
➥Version=0&amp;Factory=Button"/>

           <g:PropertyList Version="1">
              <g:Property Name="Style" Value="StandardButton"/>
              <g:Property Name="Label" Value="Press to &amp;Initiate Action"/>
              <g:Property Name="Tooltip" Value="The tool's tooltip"/>
              <g:Property Name="Mnemonic" Value="ALT+I"/>
           </g:PropertyList>
        </g:Component>

        <!-- The Engine -->
        <g:Component SingleInstance="True" Category="Engine"
➥ Name="RecordSetEngine">
           <g:ComponentResource FingerprintID="Groove"
➥ URL="http://components.groove.net/Groove/Components/Root.osd?
➥Package=net.groove.Groove.ToolComponents.GrooveListComponents_DLL&amp;
➥Version=0,4&amp;Factory=RecordSetEngine3"/>
           <g:EngineDesc Tag="urn:groove.net:RecordSetEngine"/>
              <g:PropertyList Version="1">
                 <g:Property Name="ClassInfoList">
                    <g:PropertyValue>
                       <g:ClassInfo Name="urn:groove.net:Record"
➥ URL="http://components.groove.net/Groove/Components/Root.osd?
➥Package=net.groove.Groove.ToolComponents.GrooveListComponents_DLL&amp;
➥Version=0&amp;Factory=Record"/>
                    </g:PropertyValue>
                 </g:Property>
              </g:PropertyList>
           </g:Component>

        <!-- The Glue Code -->
        <g:Component Name="ToolGlue">

           <g:ComponentResource FingerprintID="Groove"
➥ URL="http://components.groove.net/Groove/Components/Root.osd?
➥Package=net.groove.Groove.ToolComponents.GrooveCommonComponents_DLL&amp;
➥Version=0&amp;Factory=ScriptHost3"/>

           <g:ComponentConnections>
```

LISTING 9.1 Continued

```
                <g:Connection ConnectionID="0" Name="ToolButton"/>
                <g:Connection ConnectionID="1" Name="RecordSetEngine"/>
            </g:ComponentConnections>

            <g:PropertyList Version="1"/>

            <SCRIPT>
                <![CDATA[
                  function ToolButton_OnCommand(i_pIUICommand)
        {
        }

                ]]>
            </SCRIPT>
        </g:Component>
    </g:ComponentGroup>
  </g:ToolTemplate>
</g:Document>
```

Save your `ToolSkeleton.tpl` file and place it into the `My Templates` folder inside the `Data` folder of your Groove application. Be sure that there is no whitespace in the component URLs, and that there are no hard or soft wraps in the code.

Launch `XML Notepad` and make sure that the file is valid XML. Correct any typing errors you find until it validates, after which, you can add the tool to your Groove Development Space.

When you look at the tool in Groove, it's not too exciting. If you've used the `EnableCellBorders.reg` file, you'll see six cells in the tool space, arranged into three rows of two columns each. You'll see a Press to Initiate Action button that appears to work because you have provided a component connection and a function in your glue code to handle the button event, even though your function does nothing. Because you are not yet using an engine, your tool will neither persist data nor disseminate it to remote members of your Development Space. Whether it's impressive or not, you now have a complete tool template that you can begin populating and modifying to produce a considerably more sophisticated tool.

Let's save a copy of `ToolSkeleton.tpl` in your `MyTemplates` folder as `TriviaQuiz1.tpl` and begin some serious tool development.

TriviaQuiz1

You will want to do some preplanning and pre-thinking about your Trivia Quiz. In `TriviaQuiz1`, you are going to decide on some components to use. You will place them into your view container using your Layout component, and you will write some more empty handlers to catch your `UIComponent` calls.

> **NOTE**
>
> This section walks through the process of building the trivia quiz step-by-step. The finished code for `TriviaQuiz1.tpl` appears in Listing 9.2 at the end of the section.

Let's make a tool that shows a screen with a question and four possible answers. You'll include some buttons you can use to choose your answer. If you get the correct answer, you can go on to the next question. Figure 9.2 shows a cocktail-napkin rendition of the game screen.

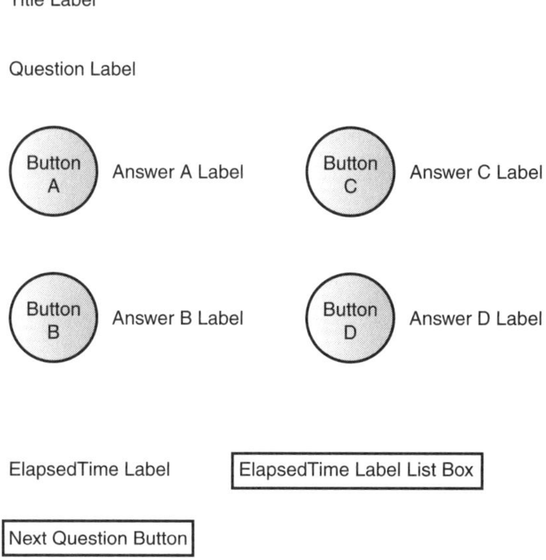

FIGURE 9.2
Our trivia game.

Looking at the illustration, you can determine what you need for a layout. You will use `HTMLTableLayout` to begin your tool, and if you leave some spacer rows and columns between the elements, it looks as though you need 11 rows and 8 columns. You need to span enough columns on the first row to keep the name of your game shown in the Title Label from wrapping when you resize the screen.

Likewise, you need to support some fairly long questions, so you'll span the last seven columns of the third row. Finally, you'll span the first through the third columns of the last row to make enough space for your Next Question Button.

Creating the Layout

While you're creating the TABLE element, you will assign names for your components—`TitleLabel`, `QuestionLabel`, `AnswerAButton`, `AnswerALabel`, `AnswerBButton`, `AnswerBLabel`, and so on. You'll call the last three components `ElapsedTimeLabel`, `ElapsedTimeListBoxControl`, and `NextQuestionButton`.

Start the `table` element of the `TriviaQuiz1` layout with the following values:

```
<TABLE CELLPADDING="2">

   <TR>
        <TD HEIGHT = "30" COLSPAN="4">TitleLabel</TD>
        <TD WIDTH="2%"></TD>
        <TD WIDTH="10%"></TD>
        <TD WIDTH="2%"></TD>
        <TD WIDTH="35%"></TD>
   </TR>
   <TR>
        <TD HEIGHT = "30" WIDTH="6%"></TD>
        <TD WIDTH="10%"></TD>
        <TD WIDTH="2%"></TD>
        <TD WIDTH="35%"></TD>
        <TD/>
        <TD/>
        <TD/>
        <TD/>
   </TR>
</TABLE>
```

The three rows with buttons will have `HEIGHT="60"` attributes. The height is set in the first cell in the row, which automatically sets the rest. Continue to make all the changes necessary to produce the 11×8 table.

Next change the document name in the document element and the `ToolTemplate` element's `DefaultToolDisplayName` to `TriviaQuiz1`. Set the component's `Name` to `TriviaQuiz1.Tool`, and its `TemplateDisplayName` to `TriviaQuiz1`. Change the default view of the component group to `TriviaQuiz1ViewContainer`, and change the name of the view component to `TriviaQuiz1ViewContainer` as well.

When you have finished, you can add the tool to your Development Space to make sure that the syntax is correct, but you won't see anything except SectionBackground, the background you specified for the Background property of your view container. Your template's layout consists only of empty cells.

The TitleLabel Component

Let's add a Groove Static component for the title label and see what happens. Start with an opening component tag and give the component the name TitleLabel. Next, add a resource URL to the Static factory, like this:

```
<g:ComponentResource FingerprintID="Groove"
➥ URL="http://components.groove.net/Groove/Components/Root.osd?
➥Package=net.groove.Groove.ToolComponents.GrooveCommonComponents_DLL&amp;
➥Version=0&amp; Factory=Static"/>
```

You can use Groove's Static component to display simple text, such as a label. This component's properties allow you to specify its appearance and behavior. In this example, you will use the Normal value for the Style property, rather than Button or Header. You will control the horizontal alignment with the HAlignment property, but you won't use the VAlignment property until later. To control how breaks occur if the label wraps, you'll use WordBreak for the BreakType, and you'll specify your LabelFont because you do not want to use the Standard Font Descriptor described in the skin resources file, which, for a Static component, is EditText font. EditText would be too light and too small for this one line of text.

The Label property is where the actual words you want to display go.

Here is the completed TitleLabel Static component. The bolded code shows the additions:

```
<g:Component Name="TitleLabel">
   <g:ComponentResource FingerprintID="Groove"
➥ URL="http://components.groove.net/Groove/Components/Root.osd?
➥Package=net.groove.Groove.ToolComponents.GrooveCommonComponents_DLL&amp;
➥Version=0&amp;Factory=Static"/>
   <g:PropertyList Version="1">
      <g:Property Name="Style" Value="Normal"/>
      <g:Property Name="HAlignment" Value="Left"/>
      <g:Property Name="BreakType" Value="WordBreak"/>
      <g:Property Name="Label" Value="Our Trivia Game"/>
      <g:Property Name="LabelFont">
         <g:FontDesc Color="#000000" Typeface="Tahoma" Height="18"/>
      </g:Property>
   </g:PropertyList>
</g:Component>
```

NOTE

In addition to the properties described earlier, a Static control has properties to use a Tooltip, accept events, or function as a link, allowing Static text to function much like a button. It has two more properties—one that affects how text is truncated, and one that displays ampersands in XML. Static components can also take skin-defined backgrounds and use RGB or skin-defined colors in their backgrounds.

Add the TitleLabel component to the end of the ComponentGroup immediately after the ToolLayout component.

The QuestionLabel Component

The QuestionLabel Static component is exactly like TitleLabel with two exceptions. The label value for it is This is the question to answer. The Height attribute of the FontDesc value for the LabelFont property is 14 rather than 18.

Create your QuestionLabel component now, and add it to the component group immediately below the TitleLabel component.

The AnswerLabel Components

The next component to add is your AnswerAButton. We discussed some of the button properties when you placed your button into the skeleton code.

You use a property in AnswerAButton that you haven't seen before: OverrideLabelPosition. The Style property for this button is LargeButton, which is defined in the skin resource file as having a label outside and to the right of the button. Because you want your labels inside the button, you have to specify an OverrideLabelPosition with a value of Center, which will override the default appearance of the LargeButton style button. The LargeButton is defined in the skin resource file as having a label outside and to the right of the button:

```
<g:Component Name="AnswerAButton">
   <g:ComponentResource FingerprintID="Groove"
➥ URL="http://components.groove.net/Groove/Root.osd?
➥Package=net.groove.Groove.ToolComponents.GrooveCommonComponents_DLL&amp;
➥Version=0&amp;Factory=Button"/>
   <g:PropertyList Version="1">
      <g:Property Name="Style" Value="LargeButton"/>
      <g:Property Name="OverrideLabelPosition" Value="Center"/>
      <g:Property Name="Label" Value="A"/>
      <g:Property Name="Tooltip" Value=""/>
```

```
        <g:Property Name="Mnemonic" Value="ALT+A"/>
    </g:PropertyList>
</g:Component>
```

AnswerALabel is similar to the QuestionLabel except that the Label text is This is Answer A. Also, you are no longer using a FontDesc property but are using the FontStyle property to utilize one of your skin-defined styles, LabelText:

```
<g:Component Name="AnswerALabel">
<g:ComponentResource FingerprintID="Groove"
➥ URL="http://components.groove.net/Groove/Components/Root.osd?
Package=net.groove.Groove.ToolComponents.GrooveCommonComponents_DLL&amp;
➥Version=0&amp;Factory=Static"/>
    <g:PropertyList Version="1">
        <g:Property Name="Style" Value="Normal"/>
        <g:Property Name="HAlignment" Value="Left"/>
        <g:Property Name="VAlignment" Value="Center"/>
        <g:Property Name="BreakType" Value="WordBreak"/>
        <g:Property Name="Label" Value="This is answer A"/>
        <g:Property Name="FontStyle" Value="LabelText"/>
    </g:PropertyList>
</g:Component>
```

Add these components to your ComponentGroup after the QuestionLabel component. Copy and paste to create the rest of the buttons. The order is not important, but to echo the layout it should go A, C, B, and D.

The Elapsed Time Components

The ElapsedTimeLabel is the same as the button label, except for the label text. Create the ElapsedTimeLabel and place it under AnswerDLabel in the component group.

The ElapsedTimeListBoxControl component is a ListBox component used to display a list of items in a simple way. You'll be using it, of course, to display the time it takes a user to answer. The ListBox has various properties to determine both its function and its appearance.

In this example, you'll use ListBox properties to set sorting and selection behavior. You can specify that the ListBox sort the items in the list by setting the Sort property value to TRUE. A user can select items in three ways, depending on the value of the SelectionMode property: Multiple, Extended, and SingleSelection.

In terms of appearance, the ListBox can use its Visible property to be initially hidden or shown. It can use skin resource styles and colors, or RGB colors to control the color of its background and font, show or hide a border, and display a Tooltip using the appropriate properties. It can also list initial values in the box.

The `ElapsedTimeListBoxControl` component looks like this:

```
<!-- ElapsedTimeListBox -->
   <g:Component Name="ElapsedTimeListBoxControl">
      <g:ComponentResource FingerprintID="Groove"
➥ URL="http://components.groove.net/Groove/Components/Root.osd?
➥Package=net.groove.Groove.ToolComponents.GrooveCommonComponents_DLL&amp;
➥Version=0&amp;Factory=ListBox"/>

      <g:PropertyList Version="1">
         <g:Property Name="Sort" Value="false"/>
         <g:Property Name="SelectionMode" Value="SingleSelection"/>
      </g:PropertyList>

</g:Component>
```

Add the `ElapsedTimeListBoxControl` component shown below to your `ComponentGroup` after the `ElapsedTimeLabel`.

The `NextQuestionButton` Component

The `NextQuestionButton` is a little different from the previous buttons because it has `StandardIconButton` as the value for its `Style` property. Consequently, you have to identify the icon image and mask by URL using `ImageURL` and `ImageMaskURL` properties. The values of these properties are URLs that point to individual files in the `ToolBMPs` folder in the `Data` folder of Groove. As with other images, you need to specify the height, width, and offset to properly identify the icon in the image file.

Set the `Enabled` property of the button to `false` because you are going to turn the button on after a guess. Here is what that component looks like:

```
<!-- Next Question Button -->
<g:Component Name="NextQuestionButton">
   <g:ComponentResource FingerprintID="Groove"
➥ URL="http://components.groove.net/Groove/Root.osd?
➥Package=net.groove.Groove.ToolComponents.GrooveCommonComponents_DLL&amp;
➥Version=0&amp;Factory=Button"/>
   <g:PropertyList Version="1">
      <g:Property Name="Style" Value="StandardIconButton"/>
      <g:Property Name="Enabled" Value="false"/>
      <g:Property Name="OverrideLabelPosition" Value="InsideLeft"/>
      <g:Property Name="ImageURL"
➥ Value="grooveFile:///ToolBMPs\Arrows16x16Images.jpg"/>
      <g:Property Name="ImageMaskURL"
➥ Value="grooveFile:///ToolBMPs\Arrows16x16ImagesMask.bmp"/>
      <g:Property Name="ImageOffset" Value="16"/>
```

```
      <g:Property Name="ImageHeight" Value="16"/>
      <g:Property Name="ImageWidth" Value="16"/>
      <g:Property Name="Label" Value="Press for &amp;next question"/>
      <g:Property Name="Tooltip" Value=""/>
      <g:Property Name="Mnemonic" Value="ALT+N"/>
   </g:PropertyList>
</g:Component>
```

Put it under the `ListBox` component you created earlier.

The Glue Code

Next, you'll modify your glue code component.

You can establish component connections to each of the components you will need to interact with in the glue code. Those connections will include connections to the `QuestionLabel`, the answer buttons, the answer labels, the elapsed time list box, and the next question button. Those connections are shown here:

```
<g:ComponentConnections>
   <g:Connection ConnectionID="0" Name="QuestionLabel"/>
   <g:Connection ConnectionID="1" Name="AnswerALabel"/>
   <g:Connection ConnectionID="2" Name="AnswerAButton"/>
   <g:Connection ConnectionID="3" Name="AnswerBLabel"/>
   <g:Connection ConnectionID="4" Name="AnswerBButton"/>
   <g:Connection ConnectionID="5" Name="AnswerCLabel"/>
   <g:Connection ConnectionID="6" Name="AnswerCButton"/>
   <g:Connection ConnectionID="7" Name="AnswerDLabel"/>
   <g:Connection ConnectionID="8" Name="AnswerDButton"/>
   <g:Connection ConnectionID="9" Name="ElapsedTimeListBoxControl"/>
   <g:Connection ConnectionID="10" Name="NextQuestionButton"/>
</g:ComponentConnections>
```


Next, you need an empty property list to hold properties you will add later in your glue code:

```
<g:PropertyList Version="1"/>
```

At this point in the code, you add your `TYPELIB`s.

You will use the `GrooveGlobalHelperFunctions.GSL`, so include it like this:

```
<SCRIPT SRC="http://components.groove.net/Groove/Components/Root.osd?
➥Package=net.groove.Groove.ToolComponents.GrooveGlobalHelperFunctions_GSL
➥&amp;Version=0,1&amp;Factory=Open"/>
```

The next element is your `script` element. This is the container for your JavaScript code, and it has a CDATA child element. Inside the `CDATA` element, you will put a series of empty functions that you will add code to later:

```
<SCRIPT>
      <![CDATA[

         function Initialize()
         {
         }

         function AnswerAButton_OnCommand(i_pIUICommand)
         {
         }

         function AnswerBButton_OnCommand(i_pIUICommand)
         {
         }

         function AnswerCButton_OnCommand(i_pIUICommand)
         {
         }

         function AnswerDButton_OnCommand(i_pIUICommand)
         {
         }

         function NextQuestionButton_OnCommand(i_pIUICommand)
         {
         }

         function OnPropertyChanged(
                                 i_Key,
                                 i_pValue,
                                 i_LocallyGenerated
                                 )
     {
         }
      ]]>
   </SCRIPT>
</g:Component>
```

This concludes your code for the time being, so be sure that there is no whitespace in the component URLs, and that there are no hard or soft wraps in the code. Listing 9.2 shows the complete `TriviaQuiz1` code.

LISTING 9.2 `TriviaQuiz1.tpl`

```
<g:Document Name="TriviaQuiz1.tpl" xmlns:g="urn:groove.net">

    <!-- Component Security -->
```

LISTING 9.2 Continued

```
    <g:ComponentSecurity>
        <g:FingerprintTable>
            <g:Entry FingerprintID="Groove"
➥ Fingerprint="4262-dcb1:4552-d303:123d-36a6:0a96-62e5:24a7-d7db"/>
        </g:FingerprintTable>
    </g:ComponentSecurity>

    <!-- Tool Template -->
    <g:ToolTemplate DefaultToolDisplayName="TriviaQuiz1"
➥ Name="TriviaQuiz1.Tool" TemplateDisplayName="TriviaQuiz1">

        <!-- Tool View -->
        <g:ViewInfo Lifetime="Limited"/>

        <!-- Component Group -->
        <g:ComponentGroup DefaultView="TriviaQuiz1ViewContainer">

            <!-- View -->
            <g:Component Name="TriviaQuiz1ViewContainer">
                <g:ComponentResource FingerprintID="Groove"
➥ URL="http://components.groove.net/Groove/Components/Root.osd?
➥Package=net.groove.Groove.ToolComponents.GrooveCommonComponents_DLL&amp;
➥Version=0&amp;Factory=ViewContainer"/>

                <!-- View Property List -->
                <g:PropertyList Version="1">

                    <g:Property Name="Background">
                        <g:BackgroundStyle Style="SectionBackground"/>
                    </g:Property>

                </g:PropertyList>

                <!-- Connections -->
                <g:ComponentConnections>
                    <g:Connection ConnectionID="0" Name="TriviaQuiz1Layout"/>
                    <g:Connection ConnectionID="1" Name="TriviaQuiz1Glue"/>
                </g:ComponentConnections>


            </g:Component>

            <!-- Layout -->
            <g:Component Name="TriviaQuiz1Layout">
```

LISTING 9.2 Continued

```
                <g:ComponentResource FingerprintID="Groove"
➥ URL="http://components.groove.net/Groove/Components/Root.osd?
➥Package=net.groove.Groove.ToolComponents.GrooveCommonComponents_DLL&amp;
➥Version=0&amp;Factory=HTMLTableLayout"/>
                <!-- Layout Property List -->
                <g:PropertyList Version="1">
                    <g:Property Name="Layout">
                        <g:PropertyValue>
                            <TABLE CELLPADDING="2">

                                <TR>
                                  <TD HEIGHT = "30" COLSPAN="4">TitleLabel</TD>
                                  <TD WIDTH="2%"></TD>
                                  <TD WIDTH="10%"></TD>
                                  <TD WIDTH="2%"></TD>
                                  <TD WIDTH="35%"></TD>
                                </TR>
                                <TR>
                                    <TD HEIGHT = "30" WIDTH="6%"></TD>
                                    <TD WIDTH="10%"></TD>
                                    <TD WIDTH="2%"></TD>
                                    <TD WIDTH="35%"></TD>
                                    <TD/>
                                    <TD/>
                                    <TD/>
                                    <TD/>
                                </TR>
                                <TR>
                                    <TD/>
                                    <TD HEIGHT = "30"
➥ COLSPAN="7">QuestionLabel</TD>
                                </TR>
                                <TR>
                                    <TD HEIGHT = "30"></TD>
                                    <TD/>
                                    <TD/>
                                    <TD/>
                                    <TD/>
                                    <TD/>
                                    <TD/>
                                    <TD/>
                                </TR>
                                <TR>
                                    <TD HEIGHT = "60"></TD>
```

LISTING 9.2 Continued

```
                <TD>AnswerAButton</TD>
                <TD/>
                <TD>AnswerALabel</TD>
                <TD/>
                <TD>AnswerCButton</TD>
                <TD/>
                <TD>AnswerCLabel</TD>
            </TR>
            <TR>
                <TD HEIGHT = "30"></TD>
                <TD/>
                <TD/>
                <TD/>
                <TD/>
                <TD/>
                <TD/>
                <TD/>
            </TR>
            <TR>
                <TD HEIGHT = "60"></TD>
                <TD>AnswerBButton</TD>
                <TD/>
                <TD>AnswerBLabel</TD>
                <TD/>
                <TD>AnswerDButton</TD>
                <TD/>
                <TD>AnswerDLabel</TD>
            </TR>
            <TR>
                <TD HEIGHT = "30"></TD>
                <TD/>
                <TD/>
                <TD/>
                <TD/>
                <TD/>
                <TD/>
                <TD/>
            </TR>
            <TR>
                <TD HEIGHT = "60"></TD>
                <TD>ElapsedTimeLabel</TD>
                <TD/>
                <TD>ElapsedTimeListBoxControl</TD>
                <TD/>
```

LISTING 9.2 Continued

```
                                <TD/>
                                <TD/>
                                <TD/>
                            </TR>
                            <TR>
                                <TD HEIGHT = "30"></TD>
                                <TD/>
                                <TD/>
                                <TD/>
                                <TD/>
                                <TD/>
                                <TD/>
                                <TD/>
                            </TR>
                            <TR>
                                <TD HEIGHT = "60"
➥ COLSPAN="3">NextQuestionButton</TD>
                                <TD/>
                                <TD/>
                                <TD/>
                                <TD/>
                                <TD/>
                            </TR>

                        </TABLE>
                    </g:PropertyValue>
                </g:Property>
            </g:PropertyList>
        </g:Component>

        <!-- TitleLabel -->
        <g:Component Name="TitleLabel">
            <g:ComponentResource FingerprintID="Groove"
➥ URL="http://components.groove.net/Groove/Components/Root.osd?
➥Package=net.groove.Groove.ToolComponents.GrooveCommonComponents_DLL&amp;
➥Version=0&amp;Factory=Static"/>
            <g:PropertyList Version="1">
                <g:Property Name="Style" Value="Normal"/>
                <g:Property Name="HAlignment" Value="Left"/>
                <g:Property Name="BreakType" Value="WordBreak"/>
                <g:Property Name="Label" Value="Our Trivia Game"/>
                <g:Property Name="LabelFont">
                            <g:FontDesc Color="#000000"
➥Typeface="Tahoma" Height="18"/>
                        </g:Property>
```

LISTING 9.2 Continued

```
            </g:PropertyList>
        </g:Component>

        <!-- QuestionLabel -->
        <g:Component Name="QuestionLabel">
            <g:ComponentResource FingerprintID="Groove"
➥ URL="http://components.groove.net/Groove/Components/Root.osd?
➥Package=net.groove.Groove.ToolComponents.GrooveCommonComponents_DLL&amp;
➥Version=0&amp;Factory=Static"/>
            <g:PropertyList Version="1">
                <g:Property Name="Style" Value="Normal"/>
                <g:Property Name="HAlignment" Value="Left"/>
                <g:Property Name="VAlignment" Value="Center"/>
                <g:Property Name="BreakType" Value="WordBreak"/>
                <g:Property Name="Label"
➥ Value="This is the question to answer"/>
                <g:Property Name="LabelFont">
                            <g:FontDesc Color="#000000"
➥ Typeface="Tahoma" Height="14"/>
                        </g:Property>
            </g:PropertyList>
        </g:Component>

        <!-- Answer A Button -->
        <g:Component Name="AnswerAButton">
            <g:ComponentResource FingerprintID="Groove"
➥ URL="http://components.groove.net/Groove/Root.osd?
➥Package=net.groove.Groove.ToolComponents.GrooveCommonComponents_DLL&amp;
➥Version=0&amp;Factory=Button"/>
            <g:PropertyList Version="1">
                <g:Property Name="Style" Value="LargeButton"/>
                        <g:Property Name="OverrideLabelPosition"
➥ Value="Center"/>
                <g:Property Name="Label" Value="A"/>
                <g:Property Name="Tooltip" Value=""/>
                <g:Property Name="Mnemonic" Value="ALT+A"/>
            </g:PropertyList>
        </g:Component>

        <!-- Answer A Label-->
        <g:Component Name="AnswerALabel">
            <g:ComponentResource FingerprintID="Groove"
➥ URL="http://components.groove.net/Groove/Components/Root.osd?
➥Package=net.groove.Groove.ToolComponents.GrooveCommonComponents_DLL&amp;
➥Version=0&amp;Factory=Static"/>
```

LISTING 9.2 Continued

```
            <g:PropertyList Version="1">
                <g:Property Name="Style" Value="Normal"/>
                <g:Property Name="HAlignment" Value="Left"/>
                        <g:Property Name="VAlignment" Value="Center"/>
                <g:Property Name="BreakType" Value="WordBreak"/>
                <g:Property Name="Label" Value="This is answer A"/>
                <g:Property Name="FontStyle" Value="LabelText"/>
            </g:PropertyList>
        </g:Component>

        <!-- Answer B Button -->
        <g:Component Name="AnswerBButton">
            <g:ComponentResource FingerprintID="Groove"
➥ URL="http://components.groove.net/Groove/Root.osd?
➥Package=net.groove.Groove.ToolComponents.GrooveCommonComponents_DLL&amp;
➥Version=0&amp;Factory=Button"/>
            <g:PropertyList Version="1">
                <g:Property Name="Style" Value="LargeButton"/>
                        <g:Property Name="OverrideLabelPosition"
➥Value="Center"/>
                <g:Property Name="Label" Value="B"/>
                <g:Property Name="Tooltip" Value=""/>
                <g:Property Name="Mnemonic" Value="ALT+A"/>
            </g:PropertyList>
        </g:Component>

        <!-- Answer B Label-->
        <g:Component Name="AnswerBLabel">
            <g:ComponentResource FingerprintID="Groove"
➥ URL="http://components.groove.net/Groove/Components/Root.osd?
➥Package=net.groove.Groove.ToolComponents.GrooveCommonComponents_DLL&amp;
➥Version=0&amp;Factory=Static"/>
            <g:PropertyList Version="1">
                <g:Property Name="Style" Value="Normal"/>
                <g:Property Name="HAlignment" Value="Left"/>
                        <g:Property Name="VAlignment" Value="Center"/>
                <g:Property Name="BreakType" Value="WordBreak"/>
                <g:Property Name="Label" Value="This is answer B"/>
                <g:Property Name="FontStyle" Value="LabelText"/>
            </g:PropertyList>
        </g:Component>

        <!-- Answer C Button -->
        <g:Component Name="AnswerCButton">
```

LISTING 9.2 Continued

```
                <g:ComponentResource FingerprintID="Groove"
➥ URL="http://components.groove.net/Groove/Root.osd?
➥Package=net.groove.Groove.ToolComponents.GrooveCommonComponents_DLL&amp;
➥Version=0&amp;Factory=Button"/>
                <g:PropertyList Version="1">
                    <g:Property Name="Style" Value="LargeButton"/>
                            <g:Property Name="OverrideLabelPosition"
➥ Value="Center"/>
                    <g:Property Name="Label" Value="C"/>
                    <g:Property Name="Tooltip" Value=""/>
                    <g:Property Name="Mnemonic" Value="ALT+A"/>
                </g:PropertyList>
            </g:Component>

            <!-- Answer C Label-->
            <g:Component Name="AnswerCLabel">
                <g:ComponentResource FingerprintID="Groove"
➥ URL="http://components.groove.net/Groove/Components/Root.osd?
➥Package=net.groove.Groove.ToolComponents.GrooveCommonComponents_DLL&amp;
➥Version=0&amp;Factory=Static"/>
                <g:PropertyList Version="1">
                    <g:Property Name="Style" Value="Normal"/>
                    <g:Property Name="HAlignment" Value="Left"/>
                            <g:Property Name="VAlignment" Value="Center"/>
                    <g:Property Name="BreakType" Value="WordBreak"/>
                    <g:Property Name="Label" Value="This is answer C"/>
                    <g:Property Name="FontStyle" Value="LabelText"/>
                </g:PropertyList>
            </g:Component>

            <!-- Answer D Button -->
            <g:Component Name="AnswerDButton">
                <g:ComponentResource FingerprintID="Groove"
➥ URL="http://components.groove.net/Groove/Root.osd?
➥Package=net.groove.Groove.ToolComponents.GrooveCommonComponents_DLL&amp;
➥Version=0&amp;Factory=Button"/>
                <g:PropertyList Version="1">
                    <g:Property Name="Style" Value="LargeButton"/>
                            <g:Property Name="OverrideLabelPosition"
➥Value="Center"/>
                    <g:Property Name="LabelFont">
                        <g:FontDesc Color="#000000" Typeface="Tahoma"
➥Height="14"/>
```

LISTING 9.2 Continued

```
                    </g:Property>
                <g:Property Name="Label" Value="D"/>
                <g:Property Name="Tooltip" Value=""/>
                <g:Property Name="Mnemonic" Value="ALT+A"/>
            </g:PropertyList>
        </g:Component>

        <!-- Answer D Label-->
        <g:Component Name="AnswerDLabel">
            <g:ComponentResource FingerprintID="Groove"
➥ URL="http://components.groove.net/Groove/Components/Root.osd?
➥Package=net.groove.Groove.ToolComponents.GrooveCommonComponents_DLL&amp;
➥Version=0&amp;Factory=Static"/>
            <g:PropertyList Version="1">
                <g:Property Name="Style" Value="Normal"/>
                <g:Property Name="HAlignment" Value="Left"/>
                        <g:Property Name="VAlignment" Value="Center"/>
                <g:Property Name="BreakType" Value="WordBreak"/>
                <g:Property Name="Label" Value="This is answer D"/>
                <g:Property Name="FontStyle" Value="LabelText"/>
            </g:PropertyList>
        </g:Component>

        <!-- Elapsed Time Label-->
        <g:Component Name="ElapsedTimeLabel">
            <g:ComponentResource FingerprintID="Groove"
➥ URL="http://components.groove.net/Groove/Components/Root.osd?
➥Package=net.groove.Groove.ToolComponents.GrooveCommonComponents_DLL&amp;
➥Version=0&amp;Factory=Static"/>
            <g:PropertyList Version="1">
                <g:Property Name="Style" Value="Normal"/>
                <g:Property Name="HAlignment" Value="Left"/>
                        <g:Property Name="VAlignment" Value="Center"/>
                <g:Property Name="BreakType" Value="WordBreak"/>
                <g:Property Name="Label" Value="Elapsed Time: "/>
                <g:Property Name="FontStyle" Value="LabelText"/>
            </g:PropertyList>
        </g:Component>

        <!-- ElapsedTimeListBox -->
        <g:Component Name="ElapsedTimeListBoxControl">
            <g:ComponentResource FingerprintID="Groove"
➥ URL="http://components.groove.net/Groove/Components/Root.osd?
➥Package=net.groove.Groove.ToolComponents.GrooveCommonComponents_DLL&amp;
➥Version=0&amp;Factory=ListBox"/>
```

LISTING 9.2 Continued

```
                <g:PropertyList Version="1">
                    <g:Property Name="Sort" Value="false"/>
                    <g:Property Name="SelectionMode" Value="SingleSelection"/>
                </g:PropertyList>

            </g:Component>

            <!-- Next Question Button -->
            <g:Component Name="NextQuestionButton">
                <g:ComponentResource FingerprintID="Groove"
➥ URL="http://components.groove.net/Groove/Root.osd?
➥Package=net.groove.Groove.ToolComponents.GrooveCommonComponents_DLL&amp;
➥Version=0&amp;Factory=Button"/>
                <g:PropertyList Version="1">
                    <g:Property Name="Style" Value="StandardIconButton"/>
                            <g:Property Name="Enabled" Value="false"/>
                            <g:Property Name="OverrideLabelPosition"
➥ Value="InsideLeft"/>
                            <g:Property Name="ImageURL"
➥ Value="grooveFile:///ToolBMPs\Arrows16x16Images.jpg"/>
                            <g:Property Name="ImageMaskURL"
➥ Value="grooveFile:///ToolBMPs\Arrows16x16ImagesMask.bmp"/>
                            <g:Property Name="ImageOffset" Value="16"/>
                            <g:Property Name="ImageHeight" Value="16"/>
                            <g:Property Name="ImageWidth" Value="16"/>
                    <g:Property Name="Label"
➥ Value="Press for &amp;next question"/>
                    <g:Property Name="Tooltip" Value=""/>
                    <g:Property Name="Mnemonic" Value="ALT+A"/>
                </g:PropertyList>
            </g:Component>


            <!-- Glue code -->
            <g:Component Name="TriviaQuiz1Glue">

                <g:ComponentResource FingerprintID="Groove"
➥ URL="http://components.groove.net/Groove/Components/Root.osd?
➥Package=net.groove.Groove.ToolComponents.GrooveCommonComponents_DLL&amp;
➥Version=0&amp;Factory=ScriptHost3"/>
                <g:ComponentConnections>
                    <g:Connection ConnectionID="0" Name="AnswerAButton"/>
                    <g:Connection ConnectionID="1" Name="AnswerAButton"/>
                    <g:Connection ConnectionID="2" Name="AnswerBButton"/>
```

LISTING 9.2 Continued

```
                    <g:Connection ConnectionID="3" Name="AnswerCButton"/>
                    <g:Connection ConnectionID="4" Name="AnswerDButton"/>
                    <g:Connection ConnectionID="5"
➥ Name="ElapsedTimeListBoxControl"/>
                    <g:Connection ConnectionID="6" Name="NextQuestionButton"/>

                </g:ComponentConnections>

                <g:PropertyList Version="1"/>

                <TYPELIB LIBID="{FB1EBAB1-C159-11d3-80B6-00500487887B}"
➥ NAME="GrooveCollectionComponents" MAJORVER="1" MINORVER="0"/>
                <SCRIPT
➥ SRC="http://components.groove.net/Groove/Components/Root.osd?
➥Package=net.groove.Groove.ToolComponents.GrooveGlobalHelperFunctions_GSL&amp;
➥Version=0,1&amp;Factory=Open"/>
                <SCRIPT>

                    <![CDATA[

                        function Initialize()
                        {
                        }

                        function AnswerAButton_OnCommand(i_pIUICommand)
                        {

                        }

                        function AnswerBButton_OnCommand(i_pIUICommand)
                        {

                        }

                        function AnswerCButton_OnCommand(i_pIUICommand)
                        {

                        }

                        function AnswerDButton_OnCommand(i_pIUICommand)
                        {

                        }
```

LISTING 9.2 Continued

```
                         function NextQuestionButton_OnCommand(i_pIUICommand)
                         {

                         }


                         function OnPropertyChanged(
                                 i_Key,
                                 i_pValue,
                                 i_LocallyGenerated
                                 )
                         {

                         }

                         function OnPropertyRemoved
                         (
                         i_Key,
                         i_LocallyGenerated
                         )
                     {

                     }
                 ]]>

             </SCRIPT>
         </g:Component>

     </g:ComponentGroup>

 </g:ToolTemplate>

</g:Document>
```

The Finished Tool

Launch XMLNotepad and make sure that the file is valid XML. Correct any invalid XML, and then add the tool to your Groove Development Space. When you open your tool, you should see something similar to what's shown in Figure 9.3.

Your buttons should react properly. Of course, they won't do anything yet. If you have the `EnableCellBorders` registry settings enabled, you will be able to clearly see the layout.

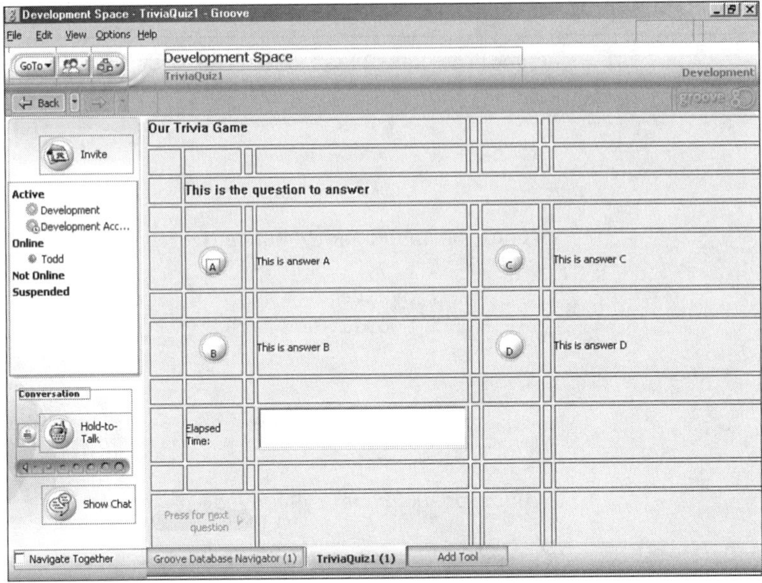

FIGURE 9.3

The `TriviaQuiz1` *screen.*

After you have this tool working properly in your Development Space, save it as `TriviaQuiz2`. Open your new `TriviaQuiz2` file and change the value of the document's `name` property, and the tool template component's `Name`, `DefaultToolDisplayName`, and `TemplateDisplayName` to reflect `TriviaQuiz2`. Also rename the tool template's component connections and the layout and glue components.

TriviaQuiz2

In the `TriviaQuiz2` tool, you will explore several ways to get your questions and answers into the template, and you'll set up a mechanism for measuring and displaying the time between the presentation of a question and the choosing of an answer.

NOTE

The finished glue code for `TriviaQuiz2.tpl` appears in Listing 9.3 at the end of this section. The code up to the glue code portion is identical to that for `TriviaQuiz1.tpl`, with the exception of the tool name. In Listing 9.3, new code appears in bold.

The simplest way to display your questions is to replace the question label's `Label` property with the question, and then put the answers into each of the `Label` properties of the answer labels.

Here is a trivia question for you to use:

What animal has the heaviest brain?

a) Man c) Elephant

b) Sperm whale d) Grizzly bear

Make the above changes and check out the results.

This method is quite simple and would be appropriate for providing help in a series of steps. Because view components can have multiple layouts, each step could be a different layout, and the Next button could set a new layout for the view. In this case, we are changing the properties of the existing labels, but we could also change to a different group of components.

The method has a couple of disadvantages, however. The first disadvantage is that, if you changed components, you would have to write as many layouts as you had questions, which would result in a very large template. The second disadvantage is that you still need to store a key somewhere that lets your glue code know the correct answer. Ideally, you would like to store your questions, answers, and correct answer code in one structure.

The `PropertyList`

Your layout remains constant throughout the entire quiz, regardless of the number of questions in the quiz, so you can repopulate your existing tool with new data. One place you could store your question and answer data is in the `PropertyList` of the glue component. Let's set up a data structure that looks like this:

```
<g:PropertyList Version="1">
   <g:Property Name="Question1" Value="What animal has the heaviest brain?"/>
   <g:Property Name="Answer1a" Value="Man"/>
   <g:Property Name="Answer1b" Value="Sperm whale"/>
   <g:Property Name="Answer1c" Value="Elephant"/>
   <g:Property Name="Answer1d" Value="Grizzly bear"/>
   <g:Property Name="CorrectAnswer" Value="b"/>
</g:PropertyList>
```

Replace the property list in the `TriviaQuiz2Glue` component with this code.

Setting the Question and Answer Labels

Next, you will write a JavaScript function to set the values of the question and answer labels to the properties in the property list. You will trigger your function in response to the `Initialize` method of the tool. Here is the new `Initialize` function:

```
function Initialize()
   {
      ChangeLabels();
   }
```

> **TIP**
>
> As you write your glue code, you're going to want to refer to the Groove JavaScript API Reference that you downloaded and put into `\Data\localhost\GDK\Documentation\API_Reference`. You should make a shortcut to this file and open it now.

The first thing you want to do is change the text of a `Static` component:

1. Go to the Index tab of the Groove JavaScript API Reference, type **GrooveCommon Components**, and click on the found line to bring up a list of components. Scroll down to GrooveStatic in the right-hand pane and click on it.
2. This brings up information on the `GrooveStatic` component, and indicates its supported interfaces. Under Supported Interfaces is a link to the `IGrooveStatic` interface. Click on that and you get a list of the methods, read-only properties, read/write properties, and write-only properties supported by the interface.
3. Click on the `SetText` method and you will see a code example and an explanation of the method's parameters. In this case, you want to implement the `QuestionLabel`'s `SetText` method. Include the text you would like the component to hold in parentheses. Your finished line might look like this:

   ```
   QuestionLabel.SetText("What animal has the heaviest brain?")
   ```

   But you can certainly do better than that, because you already have that question as a property.
4. Looking again at the Groove JavaScript API Reference, type **GroovePropertyList** into the Keyword box and click on the found item to see that `GroovePropertyList` has an `IGroovePropertyList` interface with many useful methods. One of those methods is `OpenProperty`.

5. Click on `OpenProperty` and you get a usage sample. To retrieve the value of your `Question1` property of `PropertyList`, you need this line of code:

   ```
   PropertyList.OpenProperty("Question1");
   ```

6. Combining `QuestionLabel.SetText` and `(PropertyList.OpenProperty("Question1"))` produces a sample line of code you can use to finish your `ChangeLabels` function:

   ```
   QuestionLabel.SetText(PropertyList.OpenProperty("Question1"));
   ```

   And here is the complete `ChangeLabels()` function:

   ```
   function ChangeLabels()
      {
         QuestionLabel.SetText(PropertyList.OpenProperty("Question1"));
         AnswerALabel.SetText(PropertyList.OpenProperty("Answer1a"));
         AnswerBLabel.SetText(PropertyList.OpenProperty("Answer1b"));
         AnswerCLabel.SetText(PropertyList.OpenProperty("Answer1c"));
         AnswerDLabel.SetText(PropertyList.OpenProperty("Answer1d"));
      }
   ```

7. Make the changes to the code, and then replace the value of the `Label` properties of each of the question and answer labels with an empty string (`""`).

8. Save the `TriviaQuiz2` file and open Groove. Delete the old `TriviaQuiz2` from the space and re-add it. You should see the question and answer labels properly filled in.

Changing Labels

Next, you'll develop a mechanism to change all of these labels for each question. At the top of your script code, you'll add a global variable `questionNumber`. This will let you use the variable in place of the `1` in your `ChangeLabels` function. Change the function to look like this:

```
function ChangeLabels()
   {
      QuestionLabel.SetText(PropertyList.OpenProperty
➥("Question"+questionNumber));
      AnswerALabel.SetText(PropertyList.OpenProperty
➥("Answer"+questionNumber+"a"));
      AnswerBLabel.SetText(PropertyList.OpenProperty
➥("Answer"+questionNumber+"b"));
      AnswerCLabel.SetText(PropertyList.OpenProperty
➥("Answer"+questionNumber+"c"));
      AnswerDLabel.SetText(PropertyList.OpenProperty
➥("Answer"+questionNumber+"d"));
   }
```

TIP

Groove developers use the convention `g_numQuestionNumber` to identify the variable as both a global and holding a variant of type number. Use that construct if you wish.

Now you can add more questions to the `propertyList`:

- For question 2, use "What note do most US cars beep in?" and use A, B, D, and F for the four possible answers. Question 2's correct answer is F, which is answer d.
- For question 3, use "How many men were killed in the Battle of Lexington?" as the question, and 4, 8, 16, and 32 as the possible answers. Question 3's correct answer is 4, which is answer a.

You are going to change the correct question properties to `CorrectAnswer1`, `CorrectAnswer2`, and `CorrectAnswer3`, and you'll also have to change the numbers of the other properties accordingly. Change the `questionNumber` variable to `2` and save the file. When you add the tool to Development Space, you'll see the new questions and answers.

Elapsed Time

Next, let's work on your elapsed time:

1. To do the timing, you need a start time and an end time. To get the start time, you will create a JavaScript `Date` object and then use the `GetTime()` function on it later. The end time will be set in another function, using a `startTime` and a `nowTime` variable. To be able to use `startTime` later, you must declare it as a global variable:

   ```
   var thisDate = new Date();
   var startTime;
   ```

   Put these below `questionNumber` in the `TriviaQuiz2` file.

2. Elapsed time is going to be the difference between the time the question is shown and the time the question is answered. You know that the first question will be shown when your tool is initialized, so, for the time being, you will set your start time there. Put

   ```
   startTime = thisDate.getTime();
   ```

   into your `Initialization` function to establish `startTime`.

3. You need a new function to determine and display the elapsed time. You will cleverly call it `ShowElapsedTime`. To determine the current time, you need a new `Date` object. You can get the current time from it and subtract your `startTime` variable to get the elapsed time. Start your `ShowElapsedTime()` function with these lines:

```
function ShowElapsedTime()
   nowDate = new Date();
   nowTime = nowDate.getTime();
   elapsedTime = nowTime - startTime;
```

All that remains is to put it into the `ElapsedTimeListBoxControl`.

4. If you look up the list box in Groove JavaScript API Reference (it is a `GrooveCommonComponent`), you will see that its `IGrooveListBox` interface has an `AddItem method`, which takes a string value as its input parameter. You can cast time into a string value when you programmatically add it into the `PropertyList`, because when you look up `IGroovePropertyList`, you see that it has a `SetPropertyAsString` method. Add a `Time` property to your property list like this:

   ```
   PropertyList.SetPropertyAsString("Time", nowTime);
   ```

5. With the `Time` property in your `PropertyList`, you can use the list box's `AddItem` method to display the `Time` property's value. Add this line to your function:

   ```
   ElapsedTimeListBoxControl.AddItem(PropertyList.OpenProperty("Time"));
   ```

6. Add the `ShowElapsedTime` function to your `TrivaQuiz2` code, right below the `ChangeLabels` function. It should look like this:

   ```
   function ShowElapsedTime()
      {
         nowDate = new Date();
         nowTime = nowDate.getTime();
         elapsedTime = (nowTime - startTime)/1000;
         //Convert microseconds to seconds
         PropertyList.SetPropertyAsString("Time", elapsedTime);

   ElapsedTimeListBoxControl.AddItem(PropertyList.OpenProperty("Time"));
   }
   ```

7. You would like to enable the `NextQuestionButton` when any answer button is pressed. That way the user can move on to the next question. (You'll deal with multiple guesses later.) You can cause that to happen in a `UserGuess` function. There will be other consequences for guessing, of course, but to get started, just enable the `NextQuestionButton`. The function will be called from any of the answer buttons, so you might as well add `UserGuess()` to each of the answer button functions.

8. In `UserGuess`, change the button's `enabled` property to `true`:

   ```
   NextQuestionButton.Enabled = true;
   ```

9. Also call the elapsed time function from within the `UserGuess functon`.

10. Let's give users 20 seconds to answer the question. If the guess is wrong, or if they take longer than 20 seconds, they will receive an elapsed time of 20 seconds.

11. You can check to see whether the answer is correct in the Question button code, and set a flag if it is. Set the `correctFlag` to `0` when you initialize it at the top of your glue code:

    ```
    var correctFlag = 0;
    ```

12. Add this code to the Question A button:

    ```
    if (PropertyList.OpenProperty("CorrectAnswer"+questionNumber)== "a")
    {
          correctFlag = 1;
       }
    ```

13. Add this code to the remaining buttons as well, changing the last letter.

14. Now that your flag is set, modify your `ShowElapsedTime` function like this:

    ```
    //Penalize for more than 20 seconds or incorrect answer
    if ( (elapsedTime > 20) | (correctFlag == 0))
       {
          elapsedTime = 20.0;
       }
    ```

15. Store this information in a property called `GameTime` that you can use for scoring. You will determine whether the property exists, and if it does, you'll add `elapsedTime` to it. If it doesn't, you'll initialize it to `elapsedTime`. You will have to open the `GameTime` property as a `long` in order to cast it from a string to do the math:

    ```
    if (PropertyList.PropertyExists("GameTime"))
       {
          var newTime = PropertyList.OpenPropertyAsLong("GameTime");
          var propertyValue = newTime + elapsedTime;
          PropertyList.SetProperty ("GameTime", propertyValue);
       } else {
          PropertyList.SetProperty("GameTime", propertyValue );
       }
    ```

As a result of these modifications, your `ShowElapsedTime` function looks like this:

```
function ShowElapsedTime()
   {
      nowDate = new Date();
      nowTime = nowDate.getTime();
      //Convert milliseconds to seconds
      elapsedTime = (nowTime - startTime)/1000;
      //Penalize for more than 20 seconds or incorrect answer
      if ( (elapsedTime > 20) | (correctFlag == 0))
      {
      elapsedTime = 20.0;
      }
      //set or add to "GameTime" property
      if (PropertyList.PropertyExists("GameTime"))
```

```
{
newTime = PropertyList.OpenPropertyAsLong("GameTime");
newTime = newTime + elapsedTime;
PropertyList.SetProperty ("GameTime", newTime);
} else {
PropertyList.SetProperty("GameTime", elapsedTime );
}

PropertyList.SetPropertyAsString("Time", elapsedTime);
ElapsedTimeListBoxControl.AddItem(PropertyList.OpenProperty("Time"));
}
```

Handling Multiple Guesses

Make one last change to the `UserGuess` function. After the user has made a guess, you don't want him guessing again, so disable all the answer buttons. The completed `UserGuess` function is as follows:

```
function UserGuess()
   {
      NextQuestionButton.Enabled = true;
      ShowElapsedTime();
      DisableQuestionButtons()
   }
```

`DisableQuestionButtons()` is quite straightforward:

```
function DisableQuestionButtons ()
   {
      AnswerAButton.Enabled = false;
      AnswerBButton.Enabled = false;
      AnswerCButton.Enabled = false;
      AnswerDButton.Enabled = false;
   }
```

Now, after answering the first question, your poor user can't do anything but look at the screen, so you'd better build some functionality into the `NextQuestionButton`:

1. Reset your globals. Set a new `startTime` and reset the `correctFlag` to `0`.
2. Increment the `questionNumber` global so that you can see more questions.
3. You want to know whether there are any more questions, so add another variable above `questionNumber` for `totalQuestions`. For now, initialize it with a value of `3`:

   ```
   var totalQuestions = 3;
   ```

4. In the `NextQuestionButton` code, test to see whether you are at the last question. If you are, do nothing. If you aren't, increment the `questionNumber` and change the labels.

5. You want to enable all the question buttons and disable the `NextQuestionButton`. Write an `EnableQuestionButtons` function that mirrors your `DisableQuestionButtons` routine.

The new `NextQuestionButton` code looks like this:

```
function NextQuestionButton_OnCommand(i_pIUICommand)
   {
      thisDate = new Date();
      startTime = thisDate.getTime();
      correctFlag = 0;

      if (totalQuestions > questionNumber )
      {
         questionNumber = questionNumber + 1;
         ChangeLabels();
         EnableQuestionButtons();
         NextQuestionButton.Enabled = false;
      }
   }
```

The Revised Tool

Listing 9.3 shows the glue code for `TriviaQuiz2`, with new code shown in bold. If you try this new code, you'll find that you now have a somewhat functional trivia game, but it's a long way from being groovy. Right now you have a one-person tool that can be shared in a Groove shared space, but there is no interaction among the members, and no persistence of the game state.

After you have this tool working properly in your Development Space, save it as `TriviaQuiz3`.

To disseminate the data from the game game to other users and to maintain state, you can use a `PropertyList`. In `TriviaQuiz3`, you'll modify your code to listen for changes of properties and to send those changes on to other users.

LISTING 9.3 `TriviaQuiz2.tpl` Glue Code

```
            <!-- Glue code -->
            <g:Component Name="TriviaQuiz2Glue">

                <g:ComponentResource FingerprintID="Groove"
➥ URL="http://components.groove.net/Groove/Components/Root.osd?
➥Package=net.groove.Groove.ToolComponents.GrooveCommonComponents_DLL&amp;
➥Version=0&amp;Factory=ScriptHost3"/>
                <g:ComponentConnections>
                    <g:Connection ConnectionID="0" Name="QuestionLabel"/>
```

LISTING 9.3 Continued

```
                    <g:Connection ConnectionID="1" Name="AnswerALabel"/>
                    <g:Connection ConnectionID="2" Name="AnswerAButton"/>
                    <g:Connection ConnectionID="3" Name="AnswerBLabel"/>
                    <g:Connection ConnectionID="4" Name="AnswerBButton"/>
                    <g:Connection ConnectionID="5" Name="AnswerCLabel"/>
                    <g:Connection ConnectionID="6" Name="AnswerCButton"/>
                    <g:Connection ConnectionID="7" Name="AnswerDLabel"/>
                    <g:Connection ConnectionID="8" Name="AnswerDButton"/>
                    <g:Connection ConnectionID="9"
➥Name="ElapsedTimeListBoxControl"/>
                    <g:Connection ConnectionID="10" Name="NextQuestionButton"/>
                </g:ComponentConnections>

                <g:PropertyList Version="1">
                    <g:Property Name="Question1"
➥Value="What animal has the heaviest brain?"/>
                    <g:Property Name="Answer1a" Value="Man"/>
                            <g:Property Name="Answer1b" Value="Sperm whale"/>
                    <g:Property Name="Answer1c" Value="Elephant"/>
                    <g:Property Name="Answer1d" Value="Grizzly bear"/>
                    <g:Property Name="CorrectAnswer1" Value="b"/>
                    <g:Property Name="Question2"
➥Value="What note do most US cars beep in?"/>
                    <g:Property Name="Answer2a" Value="A"/>
                            <g:Property Name="Answer2b" Value="B"/>
                    <g:Property Name="Answer2c" Value="D"/>
                    <g:Property Name="Answer2d" Value="F"/>
                    <g:Property Name="CorrectAnswer2" Value="d"/>
                    <g:Property Name="Question3"
➥Value="How many people were killed at the Battle of Lexington?"/>
                    <g:Property Name="Answer3a" Value="4"/>
                            <g:Property Name="Answer3b" Value="8"/>
                    <g:Property Name="Answer3c" Value="16"/>
                    <g:Property Name="Answer3d" Value="32"/>
                    <g:Property Name="CorrectAnswer3" Value="a"/>
                </g:PropertyList>


                <TYPELIB LIBID="{FB1EBAB1-C159-11d3-80B6-00500487887B}"
➥ NAME="GrooveCollectionComponents" MAJORVER="1" MINORVER="0"/>
                <SCRIPT
➥ SRC="http://components.groove.net/Groove/Components/Root.osd?
➥Package=net.groove.Groove.ToolComponents.GrooveGlobalHelperFunctions_GSL&amp;
➥Version=0,1&amp;Factory=Open"/>
```

LISTING 9.3 Continued

```
                    <SCRIPT>

                        <![CDATA[
                            var totalQuestions = 3;
                            var questionNumber = 1;

                            var thisDate = new Date();
                            var startTime;
                            var correctFlag = 0;

                            function Initialize()
                            {
                                startTime = thisDate.getTime();
                                ChangeLabels();
                            }

                            function ChangeLabels()
                            {
                                QuestionLabel.SetText(PropertyList.OpenProperty
➥("Question"+questionNumber));
                                AnswerALabel.SetText(PropertyList.OpenProperty
➥("Answer"+questionNumber+"a"));
                                AnswerBLabel.SetText(PropertyList.OpenProperty
➥("Answer"+questionNumber+"b"));
                                AnswerCLabel.SetText(PropertyList.OpenProperty
➥("Answer"+questionNumber+"c"));
                                AnswerDLabel.SetText(PropertyList.OpenProperty
➥("Answer"+questionNumber+"d"));
                            }

                            function ShowElapsedTime()
                              {
                                 nowDate = new Date();
                                 nowTime = nowDate.getTime();
                                //Convert milliseconds to seconds
                                 elapsedTime = (nowTime - startTime)/1000;
                                //Penalize for more than 20 seconds
➥ for incorrect answer
                                if ( (elapsedTime > 20) | (correctFlag == 0))
                                   {
                                       elapsedTime = 20.0;
                                   }
                                //Set or add "GameTime" property
                                if (PropertyList.PropertyExists("GameTime"))
```

LISTING 9.3 Continued

```
                                        {
                                           newTime =
➥ PropertyList.OpenPropertyAsLong("GameTime");
                                           newTime = newTime + elapsedTime;
                                           PropertyList.SetProperty
➥("GameTime", newTime);
                                        } else {
                                         PropertyList.SetProperty
➥("GameTime", elapsedTime );
                                     }

                                PropertyList.SetPropertyAsString
➥("Time", elapsedTime);
                                ElapsedTimeListBoxControl.AddItem
➥(PropertyList.OpenProperty("Time"));
                            }

                       function UserGuess()
                       {
                           NextQuestionButton.Enabled = true;
                           ShowElapsedTime();
                           DisableQuestionButtons()
                       }

                       function DisableQuestionButtons ()
                       {
                           AnswerAButton.Enabled = false;
                           AnswerBButton.Enabled = false;
                           AnswerCButton.Enabled = false;
                           AnswerDButton.Enabled = false;
                       }

                       function EnableQuestionButtons ()
                       {
                           AnswerAButton.Enabled = true;
                           AnswerBButton.Enabled = true;
                           AnswerCButton.Enabled = true;
                           AnswerDButton.Enabled = true;
                       }


                       function AnswerAButton_OnCommand(i_pIUICommand)
                       {
                           if (PropertyList.OpenProperty
➥("CorrectAnswer"+questionNumber)== "a")
```

LISTING 9.3 Continued

```
                {
                    correctFlag = 1;
                }

            UserGuess()
        }

        function AnswerBButton_OnCommand(i_pIUICommand)
        {
            if (PropertyList.OpenProperty
➥("CorrectAnswer"+questionNumber)== "b")
                {
                    correctFlag = 1;
                }
            UserGuess()
        }

        function AnswerCButton_OnCommand(i_pIUICommand)
        {
            if (PropertyList.OpenProperty
➥("CorrectAnswer"+questionNumber)== "c")
                {
                    correctFlag = 1;
                }
            UserGuess()
        }

        function AnswerDButton_OnCommand(i_pIUICommand)
        {
            if (PropertyList.OpenProperty
➥("CorrectAnswer"+questionNumber)== "d")
                {
                    correctFlag = 1;
                }
            UserGuess()
        }

        function NextQuestionButton_OnCommand(i_pIUICommand)
        {
            thisDate = new Date();
            startTime = thisDate.getTime();
            correctFlag = 0;
```

LISTING 9.3 Continued

```
                        if (totalQuestions > questionNumber )
                        {
                            questionNumber = questionNumber + 1;
                            ChangeLabels();
                            EnableQuestionButtons();
                            NextQuestionButton.Enabled = false;
                        }
                    }


                    function OnPropertyChanged(
                            i_Key,
                            i_pValue,
                            i_LocallyGenerated
                            )
                    {

                    }

                ]]>

            </SCRIPT>
```

TriviaQuiz3

The first and easiest property to disseminate and persist is the time property that you display in your `ElapsedTimeListBoxControl`. You need to know what value should be in the box when you start playing, and you need to know when someone else changes the property. The first condition is taken care of in the initialization code, and the second is addressed in an `OnPropertyChanged` function. You'll work on the initialization code first.

> **NOTE**
>
> The finished glue code for `TriviaQuiz3.tpl` appears in Listing 9.4 at the end of this section. The code up to the glue code portion is identical to that for `TriviaQuiz1.tpl`, with the exception of the tool name. In Listing 9.4, new code appears in bold.

Initialization Code

After the `ChangeLabels();` line, you will open a transaction on the telespace. *Transactions* are special operations that process changes to data. The classic example is a financial transaction—a transfer from checking to savings. Transactions are atomic, which means that your checking account is debited and your savings account is credited only if both operations occur. If only one occurs, the transaction is aborted. Groove uses transactions to ensure that the underlying data in a tool's data model does not change while processing a delta or executing code that relies on the state of the data model at the time of execution. It does this by suspending the processing of any deltas targeted to the space containing the tool currently modifying the data model until the transaction is either committed or aborted.

To open a transaction on a telespace, you need to retrieve the current telespace object. A pointer to the current telespace is held as the value of a property in the tool's `PropertyList`, and can be retrieved through the use of a Groove constant called `PROPERTY_TELESPACE`. `PROPERTY_TELESPACE` is defined in the `GrooveGlobalHelperFunctions.gsl` file you included earlier.

The code that retrieves a telespace interface pointer is

```
var pITelespace = PropertyList.OpenProperty(PROPERTY_TELESPACE);
```

The `pI` in the variable name, `pITelespace`, is a pointer to the interface of the telespace object. You can use the `OpenTransaction` method in either a read or a write mode.

The syntax for an open transaction, from the Groove JavaScript API Reference, is `object.OpenTransaction (i_Read As Boolean)`. If the transaction is read-only, then the parameter `i_Read` is `true`. It is `false` for write transactions. You want to read-only, so your open transaction code looks like this:

```
var pITransaction = pITelespace.OpenTransaction(true);
```

`pITransaction` is now an open transaction, and you are going to hunt through the telespace to see whether anyone has a `Time` property in his or her property list.

Because transactions affect the synchronization of shared spaces, you must be extremely careful anytime you operate with an open transaction. Consequently, you will always use a `try/catch` block whenever a transaction is open.

Use a `PropertyExists` test to see whether there is one, and if there is, write it into your `ElapsedTimeListBoxControl`. Then commit your transaction with an `EndRead()` method.

If there is any problem with the transaction, code execution will go to the `catch` block, where you abort the transaction. Use `GrooveDebugFunctions.Assert(false, );` to trigger your debugger if you have debugging enabled. The finished `initialize` function looks like this:

```
function Initialize()
   {
      startTime = thisDate.getTime();
      ChangeLabels();
```

```
    // Open a transaction on the telespace to freeze properties
    var pITelespace = PropertyList.OpenProperty(PROPERTY_TELESPACE);
    var pITransaction = pITelespace.OpenTransaction(true);

    // Perform all operations inside of try/catch block so if an
    // error occurs, you can abort transaction (VERY IMPORTANT)
    try
    {
    // Search for already existing time property
    // and list it in Elapsed time box.
    if (PropertyList.PropertyExists("Time"))
       {
       var propertyValue = PropertyList.OpenProperty("Time");

       // Add the property to the listbox
       var Index = ElapsedTimeListBoxControl.AddItem(propertyValue);
       }

    // End the transaction (VERY IMPORTANT)
pITransaction.EndRead();
    }
    catch (e)
       {
    // An exception has occurred, so abort the transaction
    pITransaction.Abort();
    GrooveDebugFunctions.Assert(false, "");
    }
 }
```

With these changes in your `TriviaQuiz3` code, you can try out the tool. If you open this tool on two different computers in the shared space, which is best, or on two different accounts, you'll find that if one of the users answers a question and puts a time in the box, the other user will have that time in his display when he opens the tool. Additionally, if you answer one question, shut down Groove, and then reopen the tool, you'll find that the value in the box has persisted.

The `OnPropertyChanged` Function

Next, you'll use the second of your conditions. You need to know when someone else changes a property. You do that with an `OnPropertyChanged` function.

`OnPropertyChanged` has three parameters: `i_Key`, which is the property name; `I_pValue`, which is the property's value; and `I_LocallyGenerated`, which is a Boolean that tells you whether the change was made locally (on the current user's device) or remotely (on another user's device). You'll set a propertyName variable to i_Key, and then test to see whether the changed property is your Time property. If it is, you'll open a transaction as you did in the initialization code.

Then, in a try/catch block, check to see whether the Time property exists, and if it does, empty your list box. Then retrieve the telespace's time property, and put it into the list box. You'll then commit the transaction. The finished code should look like this:

```
function OnPropertyChanged
      (
      i_Key,
      i_pValue,
      i_LocallyGenerated
      )
   {

      var propertyName = i_Key;
      //  Use only "Time" or "QuestionNumber"

      if (i_Key == "Time")
         {
         // Open a transaction on the telespace to freeze properties
         var pITelespace = PropertyList.OpenProperty(PROPERTY_TELESPACE);
          var pITransaction = pITelespace.OpenTransaction(true);

         // Perform all operations inside of try/catch block so if an
         // error occurs, we can abort transaction (VERY IMPORTANT)
         try
            {
              if (PropertyName == "Time")
                {
                  if (PropertyList.PropertyExists("Time"))
                     {
                        //Show only one entry in
➥ listbox at a time, so clear before
                        ElapsedTimeListBoxControl.ResetContent();

                        var propertyValue =
➥ PropertyList.OpenProperty("Time");

                        // Add the property's value to the listbox
                        var Index =
➥ ElapsedTimeListBoxControl.AddItem(propertyValue);
                     }
                }
```

```
                // Commit the transaction (VERY IMPORTANT)
                pITransaction.EndRead();
             }

          catch (e)
             {
                // An exception has occurred, so abort the transaction
                pITransaction.Abort();
                GrooveDebugFunctions.Assert(false, "");
             }
          }
      }
  }
```

Delete the existing tool from your development space and add the new one. If you have two accounts or two different machines with the new tool, you can answer each question in the quiz on one machine and see the `Time` values change in the list box.

Remember that this is a group game. The time recorded will be that of whoever answers the question fastest. Once the question has been answered by any member, all the members move on to the next question. Therefore, the screens need to stay synchronized, putting both users on question 2 regardless of who answered question 1. You'll make that happen next.

Synchronizing Screens

A `QuestionNumber` variable changes the screens with your `ChangeLabels()` function. If that were a property rather than a variable, you could have all the users take action whenever that property changed. Let's rework your tool to make `QuestionNumber` a property:

1. Add a property to the `PropertyList` and give it a value of `1`:

   ```
   <g:Property Name="QuestionNumber" Value="1"/>
   ```

2. Remove the value from your global declaration near the top of your glue code but retain it as a global. It should read `var questionNumber;`.

3. Add this line to the `ChangeLabels()` function:

   ```
   questionNumber = PropertyList.OpenProperty("QuestionNumber");
   ```

4. Drop down to the `NextQuestionButton` code, and add these two lines below the `correctFlag` assignment:

   ```
   var propertyName = "QuestionNumber";
   var propertyValue = PropertyList.OpenProperty(PropertyName);
   ```

5. In the `if` block, use the following code to increment the `QuestionNumber` property:

   ```
   var newValue = parseInt(propertyValue) + 1;
   PropertyList.SetPropertyAsString(propertyName, newValue);
   ```

Your finished NextQuestionButton should now look like this:

```
function NextQuestionButton_OnCommand(i_pIUICommand)
   {
      thisDate = new Date();
      startTime = thisDate.getTime();
      correctFlag = 0;

      var propertyName = "QuestionNumber";
      var propertyValue = PropertyList.OpenProperty(propertyName);


      if (totalQuestions > propertyValue )
      {
         var newValue = parseInt(propertyValue) + 1;
         PropertyList.SetPropertyAsString(propertyName, newValue);
         EnableQuestionButtons();
         ChangeLabels();
         NextQuestionButton.Enabled = false;
      }
   }
```

Double-check your code, remove the old quiz, and install the new one. It should operate as it did before. This is just to check that you haven't inadvertently changed anything else.

Having changed the variable to a property, you can now listen for a change to that property, as you did for the Time property, and give your tool some code to react to the change.

Testing for Property Changes

Instead of testing i_Key for the Time property, you'll test for changes in either Time or QuestionNumber:

```
if (i_Key == "Time" | i_Key == "QuestionNumber")
```

Test to see whether the change is to Time or QuestionNumber inside the try/catch block, and if it is QuestionNumber, make sure that you have a QuestionNumber property. Then check to see whether the property change was locally generated. If the change was locally generated, you will have already dealt with it, so you are looking for QuestionNumber property changes where I_LocallyGenerated is false.

After you have identified the property as having been remotely generated, update your screen to the new label values using the ChangeLabels() function, and reset your startTime global variable. The OnPropertyChanged code should now look like this:

```
function OnPropertyChanged
      (
      i_Key,
```

```
      i_pValue,
      i_LocallyGenerated
      )
   {

      var propertyName = i_Key;
      //  Use only "Time" or "QuestionNumber"

      if (i_Key == "Time" | i_Key == "QuestionNumber")
         {
            // Open a transaction on the telespace to freeze properties
            var pITelespace = PropertyList.OpenProperty(PROPERTY_TELESPACE);
             var pITransaction = pITelespace.OpenTransaction(true);

            // Perform all operations inside of try/catch block so if an
            // error occurs, we can abort transaction (VERY IMPORTANT)
            try
               {
                 if (PropertyName == "Time")
                   {
                     if (PropertyList.PropertyExists("Time"))
                        {
                           //Show only one entry in
➥ listbox at a time, so clear before
                           ElapsedTimeListBoxControl.ResetContent();

                           var PropertyValue =
➥ PropertyList.OpenProperty("Time");

                           // Add the property's value to the listbox
                           var Index =
➥ ElapsedTimeListBoxControl.AddItem(PropertyValue);
                        }
                   }

                 if (i_Key == "QuestionNumber")
                   {

                     if (PropertyList.PropertyExists("QuestionNumber"))
                        {
                           if (!i_LocallyGenerated)
                              {
                                  ChangeLabels();
                                  thisDate = new Date();
                                  startTime = thisDate.getTime();
                               }
```

```
                        }
                    }

                    // Commit the transaction (VERY IMPORTANT)
                    pITransaction.EndRead();
                }

            catch (e)
               {
                    // An exception has occurred, so abort the transaction
                    pITransaction.Abort();
                    GrooveDebugFunctions.Assert(false, "");
               }
            }
        }
    }
```

If you delete your old tool from your development space and add this one, you'll find that the screens of the two computers now synchronize, no matter who answers the question.

A Few Tweaks

You can now play your game, but you end up on the last screen with no more questions to answer. To get back to the beginning, you have to delete the tool and reinstall it. This first version of your tool is not very elegant. You can improve it a little by returning to screen one, disabling all the buttons, and displaying the `GameTime` property, foreshadowing your scoring routines later.

In the `NextQuestionButton` code, you can add an `else` clause:

```
else
{
   //reset the "QuestionNumber"
   PropertyList.SetProperty("QuestionNumber", 1);
   ChangeLabels();
   NextQuestionButton.Enabled = false;
   ElapsedTimeListBoxControl.AddItem(PropertyList.OpenProperty("GameTime"));
}
```

Reset the `QuestionNumber` property to `1`, run your `ChangeLabels` routine, and disable the `NextQuestionButton`. Finally, put `GameTime` into the list box.

You can display `GameTime` and disable the buttons in your `OnPropertyChanged` routine by adding the following code to the end of the locally generated test:

```
if (PropertyList.OpenPropertyAsLong("QuestionNumber") < 2)

   {
      DisableQuestionButtons();
      ElapsedTimeListBoxControl.AddItem(PropertyList.OpenProperty("GameTime"));
   }
```

Make these changes (the finished glue code appears in Listing 9.4, with changes in bold) and run the tool.

LISTING 9.4 `TriviaQuiz3.tpl` Glue Code

```
            <!-- Glue code -->
            <g:Component Name="TriviaQuiz3Glue">

                <g:ComponentResource FingerprintID="Groove"
➥ URL="http://components.groove.net/Groove/Components/Root.osd?
➥Package=net.groove.Groove.ToolComponents.GrooveCommonComponents_DLL&amp;
➥Version=0&amp;Factory=ScriptHost3"/>
                <g:ComponentConnections>
                    <g:Connection ConnectionID="0" Name="QuestionLabel"/>
                    <g:Connection ConnectionID="1" Name="AnswerALabel"/>
                    <g:Connection ConnectionID="2" Name="AnswerAButton"/>
                    <g:Connection ConnectionID="3" Name="AnswerBLabel"/>
                    <g:Connection ConnectionID="4" Name="AnswerBButton"/>
                    <g:Connection ConnectionID="5" Name="AnswerCLabel"/>
                    <g:Connection ConnectionID="6" Name="AnswerCButton"/>
                    <g:Connection ConnectionID="7" Name="AnswerDLabel"/>
                    <g:Connection ConnectionID="8" Name="AnswerDButton"/>
                    <g:Connection ConnectionID="9"
➥Name="ElapsedTimeListBoxControl"/>
                    <g:Connection ConnectionID="10" Name="NextQuestionButton"/>
                </g:ComponentConnections>

                <g:PropertyList Version="1">
                    <g:Property Name="Question1"
➥Value="What animal has the heaviest brain?"/>
                    <g:Property Name="Answer1a" Value="Man"/>
                            <g:Property Name="Answer1b" Value="Sperm whale"/>
                    <g:Property Name="Answer1c" Value="Elephant"/>
                    <g:Property Name="Answer1d" Value="Grizzly bear"/>
                    <g:Property Name="CorrectAnswer1" Value="b"/>
                    <g:Property Name="Question2"
➥Value="What note do most US cars beep in?"/>
                    <g:Property Name="Answer2a" Value="A"/>
                            <g:Property Name="Answer2b" Value="B"/>
```

LISTING 9.4 Continued

```
                    <g:Property Name="Answer2c" Value="D"/>
                    <g:Property Name="Answer2d" Value="F"/>
                    <g:Property Name="CorrectAnswer2" Value="d"/>
                    <g:Property Name="Question3"
➥Value="How many people were killed at the Battle of Lexington?"/>
                    <g:Property Name="Answer3a" Value="4"/>
                            <g:Property Name="Answer3b" Value="8"/>
                    <g:Property Name="Answer3c" Value="16"/>
                    <g:Property Name="Answer3d" Value="32"/>
                    <g:Property Name="CorrectAnswer3" Value="a"/>
                    <g:Property Name="QuestionNumber" Value="1"/>
                </g:PropertyList>


                <TYPELIB LIBID="{FB1EBAB1-C159-11d3-80B6-00500487887B}"
➥ NAME="GrooveCollectionComponents" MAJORVER="1" MINORVER="0"/>
                <SCRIPT
➥ SRC="http://components.groove.net/Groove/Components/Root.osd?
➥Package=net.groove.Groove.ToolComponents.GrooveGlobalHelperFunctions_GSL&amp;
➥Version=0,1&amp;Factory=Open"/>
                <SCRIPT>

                    <![CDATA[
                            var totalQuestions = 3;
                            var questionNumber;
                            var thisDate = new Date();
                            var startTime;
                            var correctFlag = 0;

                            function Initialize()
                            {
                                startTime = thisDate.getTime();
                                ChangeLabels();

                                // Open a transaction on the telespace
➥ to freeze properties
                                var pITelespace =
➥ PropertyList.OpenProperty(PROPERTY_TELESPACE);
                                var pITransaction =
➥ pITelespace.OpenTransaction(true);

                                // Perform all operations inside of
➥ try/catch block so if an// error occurs, we can abort transaction
➥ (VERY IMPORTANT)
```

LISTING 9.4 Continued

```
                              try
                                  {
                                  // Search for already existing
➥ records and display
                                  // them in listbox
                                  if (PropertyList.PropertyExists("Time"))
                                      {
                                      var propertyValue =
➥ PropertyList.OpenProperty("Time");

                                      // Add the property to the listbox
                                      var Index =
➥ ElapsedTimeListBoxControl.AddItem(propertyValue);
                                      }
                                  if (PropertyList.PropertyExists
➥("QuestionNumber"))

                                      {
                                       ChangeLabels();
                                      }


                                  // Commit the transaction (VERY IMPORTANT)
                                  pITransaction.EndRead();
                                  }

                              catch (e)
                                  {
                                  // An exception has occurred,
➥ so abort the transaction

                                  pITransaction.Abort();
                                  GrooveDebugFunctions.Assert(false, "");
                                  }

                              }


                          function ChangeLabels()
                          {
                              questionNumber = PropertyList.OpenProperty
➥("QuestionNumber");
                              QuestionLabel.SetText(PropertyList.OpenProperty
➥("Question"+questionNumber));
                              AnswerALabel.SetText(PropertyList.OpenProperty
➥("Answer"+questionNumber+"a"));
```

LISTING 9.4 Continued

```
                                AnswerBLabel.SetText(PropertyList.OpenProperty
➥("Answer"+questionNumber+"b"));
                                AnswerCLabel.SetText(PropertyList.OpenProperty
➥("Answer"+questionNumber+"c"));
                                AnswerDLabel.SetText(PropertyList.OpenProperty
➥("Answer"+questionNumber+"d"));
                            }

                            function ShowElapsedTime()
                               {
                                  var nowDate = new Date();
                                  var nowTime = nowDate.getTime();
                                //Convert milliseconds to seconds
                                  var elapsedTime = (nowTime - startTime)/1000;
                                //Penalize for more than 20 seconds
➥ or incorrect answer
                                if ( (elapsedTime > 20) | (correctFlag == 0))
                                    {
                                        elapsedTime = 20.0;
                                    }
                                if (PropertyList.PropertyExists("GameTime"))
                                       {
                                          var newTime =
➥ PropertyList.OpenPropertyAsLong("GameTime");
                                          var propertyValue =
➥ newTime + elapsedTime;

                                          PropertyList.SetProperty
➥("GameTime", propertyValue);
                                       } else {
                                        propertyValue = elapsedTime;
                                        PropertyList.SetProperty
➥("GameTime", propertyValue );
                                    }

                                  PropertyList.SetPropertyAsString
➥("Time", elapsedTime);
                                  ElapsedTimeListBoxControl.AddItem
➥(PropertyList.OpenProperty("Time"));
                               }

                            function UserGuess()
                            {
                                NextQuestionButton.Enabled = true;
                                ShowElapsedTime();
                                DisableQuestionButtons()
                            }
```

LISTING 9.4 Continued

```
function DisableQuestionButtons ()
{
    AnswerAButton.Enabled = false;
    AnswerBButton.Enabled = false;
    AnswerCButton.Enabled = false;
    AnswerDButton.Enabled = false;
}

function EnableQuestionButtons ()
{
    AnswerAButton.Enabled = true;
    AnswerBButton.Enabled = true;
    AnswerCButton.Enabled = true;
    AnswerDButton.Enabled = true;
}


function AnswerAButton_OnCommand(i_pIUICommand)
{
    if (PropertyList.OpenProperty
➥("CorrectAnswer"+questionNumber)== "a")
        {
            correctFlag = 1;
        }

    UserGuess()
}

function AnswerBButton_OnCommand(i_pIUICommand)
{
    if (PropertyList.OpenProperty
➥("CorrectAnswer"+questionNumber)== "b")
        {
            correctFlag = 1;
        }
    UserGuess()
}

function AnswerCButton_OnCommand(i_pIUICommand)
{
    if (PropertyList.OpenProperty
➥("CorrectAnswer"+questionNumber)== "c")
        {
            correctFlag = 1;
        }
```

LISTING 9.4 Continued

```
                                UserGuess()
                            }

                            function AnswerDButton_OnCommand(i_pIUICommand)
                            {
                                if (PropertyList.OpenProperty
➥("CorrectAnswer"+questionNumber)== "d")
                                    {
                                        correctFlag = 1;
                                    }
                                UserGuess()
                            }

                            function
NextQuestionButton_OnCommand(i_pIUICommand)
                            {
                                thisDate = new Date();
                                startTime = thisDate.getTime();
                                correctFlag = 0;

                                var propertyName = "QuestionNumber";
                                var propertyValue =
➥ PropertyList.OpenProperty(propertyName);


                                if (totalQuestions > propertyValue )
                                {
                                    //Increment the question number
                                    var newValue = parseInt(propertyValue) + 1;
                                    PropertyList.SetPropertyAsString
➥(propertyName, newValue);

                                    EnableQuestionButtons();
                                    ChangeLabels();
                                    NextQuestionButton.Enabled = false;
                                }
                                else
                                {
                                    //reset the "QuestionNumber"
                                    PropertyList.SetProperty("QuestionNumber",
➥1);

                                    ChangeLabels();
                                    NextQuestionButton.Enabled = false;
                                    ElapsedTimeListBoxControl.AddItem
➥(PropertyList.OpenProperty("GameTime"));
```

LISTING 9.4 Continued

```
                }
            }

            function OnPropertyChanged
                (
                i_Key,
                i_pValue,
                i_LocallyGenerated
                )
            {

                var PropertyName = i_Key;
                //  Use only "Time" or "QuestionNumber"

                if (i_Key == "Time" | i_Key ==
"QuestionNumber")
                {

                    if (PropertyName == "Time")
                    {
                        //Show only one entry in listbox
➥ at a time, so clear before

ElapsedTimeListBoxControl.ResetContent();
                    }

                // Open a transaction on the telespace
➥ to freeze properties
                var pITelespace =
➥ PropertyList.OpenProperty(PROPERTY_TELESPACE);
                var pITransaction =
➥ pITelespace.OpenTransaction(true);

                // Perform all operations inside of
➥ try/catch block so if an
                // error occurs, we can abort
➥ transaction (VERY IMPORTANT)
                try
                    {
                    if (PropertyName == "Time")
                        {
                        if
(PropertyList.PropertyExists("Time"))
                        {
```

LISTING 9.4 Continued

```
                                        var PropertyValue =
➥ PropertyList.OpenProperty("Time");

                                        // Add the property's value
➥ to the listbox
                                        var Index =
➥ ElapsedTimeListBoxControl.AddItem(PropertyValue);
                                    }
                                }

                                if (i_Key == "QuestionNumber")
                                    {

                                    if (PropertyList.PropertyExists
➥("QuestionNumber"))
                                    {
                                    if (!i_LocallyGenerated)
                                        {
                                            ChangeLabels();
                                            thisDate = new Date();
                                            startTime = thisDate.getTime();

                                            if
(PropertyList.OpenPropertyAsLong
➥("QuestionNumber") < 2)

                                                {

ElapsedTimeListBoxControl.AddItem
➥(PropertyList.OpenProperty("GameTime"));
                                                 DisableQuestionButtons();
                                                }
                                        }
                                    }
                                }

                                // Commit the transaction (VERY IMPORTANT)
                                pITransaction.EndRead();
                                }

                            catch (e)
                                {
                                // An exception has occurred,
➥ so abort the transaction
```

LISTING 9.4 Continued

```
                                pITransaction.Abort();
                                GrooveDebugFunctions.Assert(false, "");
                                }
                            }
                        }
                ]]>

            </SCRIPT>
```

Summary

The final version of the sample code provides the foundation for your trivia-game application. The approach of developing a tool skeleton, and then populating it with components and code, was designed to teach you the basics of Groove programming.

Do not be discouraged if you found the exercise difficult. Groove has developed a tool that you'll look at later to make this whole process more efficient. You will probably not have to work as hard ever again to develop Groove tools. It is much easier to learn about the components and their properties, however, if you hand-code a few tools before using the helper applications.

In the next chapter, we'll take the same approach with publishing, but as with development, Groove has created a tool to make this process easier. After you really understand the basics, you can develop and publish tools without excessive typing.

Publishing a Basic Groove Tool

CHAPTER

10

IN THIS CHAPTER

In this chapter, we will look at the four files needed to publish a Groove tool: the tool template, the tool descriptor, the OSD, and the injector (`.GRV`) file. We'll talk about the preparation necessary to publish tools, and you'll set up a directory structure for publishing. Finally, you will go step-by-step through the actual publishing of your TrivaQuiz3 Tool.

Some of the challenges of installing software via the Internet are small package sizes for fast downloads, and informing the user in the process. As you saw in Chapter 6, "Essential OSD," changes are coming in Groove's tool publishing process. The procedures contained in this chapter are current at the time of this writing and will be supported even if some processes are changed later.

Besides what you learn in this chapter, you may want to study Groove OSD samples in the current GDK to keep current with those changes. The best sources of current OSD samples are the OSD of tools in the `Samples` folder of the GDK, and the OSD produced by the Tool Publisher Tool that you'll explore in Chapter 11, "Easier Groove: The Tool Creator and Tool Publisher."

Preparation

Before you can publish a tool, you need to create a directory structure in your `localhost` folder that will mirror your Web site's directory structure. The text assumes that you have a Web server. If you don't, you can still test the injection of your tool. Simply structure your `localhost` directory as you would want to structure a Web server.

You can test injection from your `localhost` directory because when you inject a tool, Groove first looks in your manifest to see whether you already have the components installed. If you do not, it checks to see whether the tool's components are available in your `localhost` directory. If the components are there, Groove installs the tool from that location. Consequently, you can test installation and operation of your tool before you make it available on your Web site simply by duplicating the directory structure in your `localhost` folder. As a result, you can thoroughly test your injection before staging your files to your Web server. So, in a way, `localhost` is to publishing what My Template is to development.

For this project, create a folder in your `localhost` directory named `MyGrooveTools`. Inside that folder, create another named `TriviaQuiz3`, and place a copy of your `TriviaQuiz3.tpl` file in that folder. Your `localhost` directory tree now looks like `\MyGrooveTools\TriviaQuiz3\TriviaQuiz3.tpl`. If your Web address is `http://www.MyCompany.com`, the Web address for your template file will be this:

```
http://www.MyCompany.com/MyGrooveTools/TriviaQuiz3/TriviaQuiz3.tpl
```

Writing the Files

Besides a proper file structure on your Web site and in your `localhost` folder, you are going to need your tool template and any supporting files for it in your `TriviaQuiz3` folder. Then you will need to write three files: the tool descriptor, the OSD, and the injector.

The tool descriptor file is an XML file that provides basic information about a tool and points to its OSD file. Upon injection, it is downloaded and copied into the account database and the `\Data\XML Files` directory. The tool's description then appears in the Add Tool dialog, and the tool can be added to the shared space.

The OSD file is an XML file that identifies all the various files and components needed by the tool, their locations, and how they are to be installed. The OSD establishes hierarchies of dependencies so that the tool arrives with everything it needs to function.

The injector (`.GRV` file) is associated with Groove in the registry. You can double-click it to download the tool descriptor.

Creating a Tool Descriptor

The first file you will write is the tool descriptor. Create `TriviaQuiz3Descriptor.xml` in your `localhost\MyGrooveTools\TriviaQuiz3\` directory.

A tool descriptor is an XML file, so you can start writing your file by placing opening and closing `Document` tags. You'll fill in the `Name` attribute and indicate the proper namespace for the document:

```
<g:Document Name: "TriviaQuiz3Descriptor.xml" xmlns:g="urn:groove.net">
</g:Document>
```

Inside the `Document` tags, you'll place a `TemplateDescriptorList`. The list will include one item, a `TemplateDescriptor`, which is an empty element that usually has 10 attributes:

```
<g:Document Name= "TriviaQuiz3Descriptor.xml" xmlns:g="urn:groove.net">
   <g:TemplateDescriptorList>
      <g:TemplateDescriptor/>
   </g:TemplateDescriptorList>
</g:Document>
```

The attributes are detailed here:

- The first attribute of the `TemplateDescriptor` is the `Name` attribute. In this case, the value will be `Trivia Quiz 3`. The `Name` attribute is used in the lists displayed in the Add Tool and Create Shared Space dialogs.

- The second attribute is Long Name, for which you'll also use Trivia Quiz 3. For the Category attribute you'll use \Groove\Starter. The Description attribute is also displayed in the Add Tool dialog, and you'll use a value of A tutorial tool.
- For the next attribute, Author, you can put your company name, and in the HelpAbout attribute you can add Created by My Company, Copyright 2002. Add a ReleaseDate attribute of January 1, 2002 and a Version of 0,0,0,0.

  The four version digits (0,0,0,0) represent, from left to right: major version, minor version, custom version, sequence version. We will cover versioning in more depth in Chapter 14, "Advanced Topics."
- Your Type attribute will have a Tool value. It is used to determine the proper icon in the Add Tool and Create Shared Space dialogs. The two choices are Tool and Toolset.
- The last attribute is a ResourceURL that points to the location of your OSD file on the Web. You'll use http://components.MyCompany.com/MyGrooveTools/TriviaQuiz3/TriviaQuiz3.osd?Package=com.MyCompany.MyGrooveTools.TriviaQuiz3.TriviaQuiz3_TPL&Version=0&Factory=Open.

Your completed tool descriptor file looks like this:

```
<g:Document Name= "TriviaQuiz3Descriptor.xml" xmlns:g="urn:groove.net">
   <g:TemplateDescriptorList>
      <g:TemplateDescriptor
         Name="Trivia Quiz 3"
         LongName="Trivia Quiz 3"
         Category="/groove/starter"
         Description="A tutorial tool"
         Author="My Company"
         HelpAbout="Created by My Company, Copyright 2002"
         Version="0,0,0,0"
         Type="Tool"
         ResourceURL=
➥"http://components.MyCompany.com/MyGrooveTools/TriviaQuiz3/TriviaQuiz3.osd?
➥Package=com.MyCompany.MyGrooveTools.TriviaQuiz3.TriviaQuiz3_TPL&amp;
➥Version=0&amp;Factory=Open"
   </g:TemplateDescriptorList>
</g:Document>
```

Save your changes to this file.

Creating Your OSD

Your tool descriptor (created in the preceding section) references an OSD file. You will now write the OSD file. To do so, first create a TriviaQuiz3.osd file in your localhost\MyGrooveTools\TriviaQuiz3\ directory.

Like the tool descriptor file, your OSD is an XML file, so begin with a `Document` tag pair:

```
<g:Document Name: "TriviaQuiz3.osd" xmlns:g="urn:groove.net">
</g:Document>
```

The first element within the pair is a `<g:ComponentSecurity>` element. Inside the `ComponentSecurity` component is the digital fingerprint. Because you have been using Groove-standard components within your own local spaces, and because you have component security turned off, you have not needed a digital fingerprint. You will need one, however, if others download your tools from your Web site.

Every component that is to be installed in Groove must be listed in an OSD file signed with a digital certificate that identifies the originator of the component. You will be generating a real digital fingerprint in the next chapter, but for now, you add the Groove digital fingerprint that is inside the OSD files of the sample applications in the GDK to your OSD file like this:

```
        <g:FingerprintTable>
            <g:Entry FingerprintID="Groove"
➥Fingerprint="4262-dcb1:4552-d303:123d-36a6:0a96-62e5:24a7-d7db"/>
        </g:FingerprintTable>
```

You are able to use Groove's fingerprint in this instance because you are going to have component authentication turned off. Although you do use Groove's fingerprint in tool template files to identify the source of the component, you couldn't use it to actually publish a tool.

Here is your OSD file so far:

```
<g:Document Name="TriviaQuiz3.osd" xmlns:g="urn:groove.net">

    <g:ComponentSecurity>
        <g:FingerprintTable>
            <g:Entry FingerprintID="Groove"
➥Fingerprint="4262-dcb1:4552-d303:123d-36a6:0a96-62e5:24a7-d7db"/>
        </g:FingerprintTable>
    </g:ComponentSecurity>
</g:Document>
```

Next, you'll include a `SOFTPKG`. The Groove manifest is a device-wide running registry of every component, dependency, and descriptor that has ever been installed by any account user on the computer. Components are represented in the manifest by `SOFTPKG`. `SOFTPKG`s list the name and version of the component; an `IMPLEMENTATION`, which includes the `CODEBASE HREF`; and a Groove OSD extension called `<g:install>` that tells where and how the component was installed. The `SOFTPKG` can also list the name and location of every component dependency. The first `SOFTPKG` element you will write will be for the tool descriptor file, `TriviaQuiz3Descriptor.xml`.

The SOFTPKG element requires a Name attribute. SOFTPKG names are arbitrary, but to minimize the possibility of duplicate names, Groove strongly recommends a convention that was first used to uniquely identify Java packages. The reverse domain name of the network location of the file is used. For your example, it would be this:

```
com.MyCompany.MyGrooveTools.TriviaQuiz3.TriviaQuiz3Descriptor_XML
```

SOFTPKG also requires a VERSION attribute that is a string value corresponding to the major, minor, custom, and sequence version numbers.

Here is how your empty SOFTPKG element looks:

```
<SOFTPKG NAME=
➥"com.MyCompany.MyGrooveTools.TriviaQuiz3.TriviaQuiz3Descriptor_XML"
➥ VERSION="0,0,0,0">
</SOFTPKG>
```

Within the SOFTPKG you will place an IMPLEMENTATION element. An IMPLEMENTATION element further describes SOFTPKG in terms of the environment of the tool. IMPLEMENTATIONs specify the language, hardware, operating system, and codebase the tool requires. Because IMPLEMENTATIONs are written in XML, they are extensible. A SOFTPKG can have multiple IMPLEMENTATIONs, each describing a different environment.

In future versions of Groove, it will be possible to have conditional installations. You will be able to tailor an IMPLEMENTATION to the entries a user makes to a Web form. If a user specifies an age of 45 to 50, for example, he or she might be directed to an implementation that downloads a different skin from one designed for 25- to 30-year-olds.

The IMPLEMENTATION element can include LANGUAGE, OS, PROCESSOR, and CODEBASE elements. The OS element specifies the operating system for which the implementation is designed. The attributes carry the values for various OS's. Like the OS element, the PROCESSOR element describes the processor the code requires. It is also an empty element with attributes describing the values. You will not be using LANGUAGE, OS, or PROCESSOR elements in this sample, but expect to see them and use them when they are appropriate.

The CODEBASE element specifies the location of the file to be used in the installation. An empty element, it has the attribute HREF. HREF points to the file's location on the network.

Add the following IMPLEMENTATION element to your TriviaQuiz3.OSD file:

```
<SOFTPKG NAME=
➥"com.MyCompany.MyGrooveTools.TriviaQuiz3.TriviaQuiz3Descriptor_XML"
➥ VERSION="0,0,0,0">
        <IMPLEMENTATION>
            <CODEBASE HREF="http://components.MyCompany.com/MyGrooveTools/
➥TriviaQuiz3/TriviaQuiz3Descriptor.xml"/>
        </IMPLEMENTATION>
</SOFTPKG>
```

Next, you will add two Groove extensions to the OSD standard: `<g:Install>` and `<g:Factory>`. As mentioned earlier, the `<g:Install>` element tells Groove how and where to install your template. Here is your sample `<g:Install>` element:

```
<g:Install TargetDir="$GROOVEDATA$\XML Files" Type="Copy"/>
```

With this line, you are telling Groove that you want `TriviaQuiz3Descriptor.xml` to be installed by copying it to the `XML Files` directory in Groove's `Data` directory—`/Groove/Data/XML Files`. `$GROOVEDATA$` is a Groove variable that identifies the current location of the Groove `Data` folder.

The next Groove extension to be added is the `<g:Factory>` element. You will tell Groove that `TriviaQuiz3Descriptor.xml` is a `Temporary XML Document` to be opened:

```
<g:Factory Filename="$GROOVEDATA$\XML Files\TriviaQuiz3Descriptor.xml"
➥ Name="Open" Type="Temporary XML Document"/>
```

Putting all this code together, here is your `SOFTPKG` so far:

```
<SOFTPKG NAME=
➥"com.MyCompany.MyCompanyTools.TriviaQuiz3.TriviaQuiz3Descriptor_XML"
➥ VERSION="0,0,0,0">
      <IMPLEMENTATION>
         <CODEBASE HREF="http://components.MyCompany.com/MyCompanyTools/
➥TriviaQuiz3/triviaquiz3Descriptor.xml"/>
         <g:Factory Filename="$GROOVEDATA$\XML Files\TriviaQuiz3Descriptor.xml"
➥ Name="Open" Type="Temporary XML Document"/>
      </IMPLEMENTATION>
</SOFTPKG>
```

At this point, add a dependency with a `DEPENDENCY` element. The `DEPENDENCY` makes the installation of the tool descriptor dependent on the installation of the tool template (installation of the tool descriptor will force the tool template to be installed).

By making the tool descriptor dependent on the tool template, you ensure that all components for the tool have been downloaded before the tool shows up in the Add Tool and Create Shared Space dialogs.

The `DEPENDENCY` element will hold the `SOFTPKG` for the template. The `SOFTPKG` name attribute for the tool template will be this:

```
<SOFTPKG NAME="com.MyCompany.MyGrooveTools.TriviaQuiz3.TriviaQuiz3_TPL"
➥ VERSION="0,0,0,0">
```

You'll add an `IMPLEMENTATION` to this element, and within the `IMPLEMENTATION` you'll have another `CODEBASE` element.

Your DEPENDENCY, so far, looks like this:

```
<DEPENDENCY>
   <SOFTPKG NAME="com.MyCompany.MyCompanyTools.TriviaQuiz3.TriviaQuiz3_TPL"
➥ VERSION="0,0,0,0">
      <IMPLEMENTATION>
         <CODEBASE HREF=
➥"http://components.MyCompany.com/MyCompanyTools/TriviaQuiz3/TriviaQuiz3.tpl"/>
</IMPLEMENTATION>
    </SOFTPKG>
</DEPENDENCY>
```

Next, you will add three Groove extensions to the OSD standard: the <g:Install> and <g:Factory> you saw previously, plus a <g:ComponentURIProvider>.

You'll use these attributes for your <g:Install> element:

```
<g:Install DatabaseURI="$TEMPLATESURI$" DocumentName="TriviaQuiz3.tpl"
➥ SchemaURI="$DEFAULTSCHEMA$" Type="Import To XSS"/>
```

And you'll use these for your <g:Factory> element:

```
<g:Factory DatabaseURI="$TEMPLATESURI$" DocumentName="TriviaQuiz3.tpl"
➥ Name="Open" Type="XML Document"/>
```

With the first line, you are telling Groove that you want TriviaQuiz3.tpl to be installed by importing it to your Templates.XSS file, and that the tool will use the default schema file if it requires one. The values in DatabaseURI and SchemaURI are Groove variables. $TEMPLATESURI$ is the current location of the Templates.xss file, and $DEFAULTSCHEMA$ is the current location of the schemas.xss schema database. The next line tells Groove that TriviaQuiz3.tpl is an XML document to be opened from the Templates.XSS database.

The last Groove extension to the OSD standard used here is the <g:ComponentURLProvider>. You will specify a ComponentURLProvider for the use of your template parser. The template parser scans your templates for Groove components and resolves OSD to point to Groove standard components. Inside the tag, you specify the database to which your template has been copied (DatabaseURI), as well as the document's name, the filename, and the type:

```
<g:ComponentURLProvider Argument="TriviaQuiz3.tpl"
➥ DatabaseURI="$TEMPLATESURI$" DocumentName="TriviaQuiz3.tpl"
➥ DocumentType="Template" ProgID="Groove.TemplateParser"/>
```

Here is your completed OSD. Check it against your file:

```
<g:Document Name="TriviaQuiz3.osd" xmlns:g="urn:groove.net">

   <g:ComponentSecurity>
       <g:FingerprintTable>
```

```
            <g:Entry FingerprintID="Groove"
➥ Fingerprint="4262-dcb1:4552-d303:123d-36a6:0a96-62e5:24a7-d7db"/>
         </g:FingerprintTable>
    </g:ComponentSecurity>

    <SOFTPKG NAME=
➥"com.MyCompany.MyGrooveTools.TriviaQuiz3.TriviaQuiz3Descriptor_XML"
➥ VERSION="0,0,0,0">
       <IMPLEMENTATION>
          <CODEBASE HREF="http://components.MyCompany.com/MyGrooveTools/
➥TriviaQuiz3/TriviaQuiz3Descriptor.xml"/>
          <g:Install TargetDir="$GROOVEDATA$\XML Files" Type="Copy"/>
          <g:Factory Filename="$GROOVEDATA$\XML Files\TriviaQuiz3Descriptor.xml"
➥ Name="Open" Type="Temporary XML Document"/>
       </IMPLEMENTATION>
       <DEPENDENCY>
          <SOFTPKG NAME=
➥"com.MyCompany.MyGrooveTools.TriviaQuiz3.TriviaQuiz3_TPL"
➥ VERSION="0,0,0,0">

             <IMPLEMENTATION>
                <CODEBASE HREF=
➥"http://components.MyCompany.com/MyGrooveTools/TriviaQuiz3/TriviaQuiz3.tpl"/>
                <g:Install DatabaseURI="$TEMPLATESURI$"
➥ DocumentName="TriviaQuiz3.tpl" SchemaURI="$DEFAULTSCHEMA$"
➥ Type="Import To XSS"/>
                <g:Factory DatabaseURI="$TEMPLATESURI$"
➥ DocumentName="TriviaQuiz3.tpl" Name="Open" Type="XML Document"/>
                <g:ComponentURLProvider Argument="TriviaQuiz3.tpl"
➥ DatabaseURI="$TEMPLATESURI$" DocumentName="TriviaQuiz3.tpl"
➥ DocumentType="Template" ProgID="Groove.TemplateParser"/>
             </IMPLEMENTATION>
          </SOFTPKG>
       </DEPENDENCY>
    </SOFTPKG>
</g:Document>
```

With your OSD completed, you can move on to the file that starts the whole installation process: the `.GRV` file.

Creating the .GRV

You already created one `.GRV` file in Chapter 8, "Customizing Groove." You created that `.GRV` by modifying the `ToolTemplateBoilerplate` file.

This time, you will use another approach, one that the Groove Tool Publisher Tool will use automatically in Chapter 11. To use this method, you will need to have Perl installed. If you did not install it before, you can download and install Perl from `http://aspn.activestate.com/ASPN/Downloads/ActivePerl/index/`.

After you have Perl installed, open your Notepad application. You will use it to write a batch file that will drive the Perl script `MakeGRV.pl`. In Notepad, type the following:

```
perl.exe MakeGRV.pl TriviaQuiz3.GRV ToolTemplateBoilerplate
➥ "http://components.MyCompany.com/MyGrooveTools/
➥TriviaQuiz3/TriviaQuiz3.osd?Package=com.MyCompany.MyGrooveTools.
➥TriviaQuiz3.TriviaQuiz3Descriptor_XML&amp;
➥Version=0&amp;Factory=Open"/
If errorlevel 1 goto ErrorOccurred
```

The `.bat` file says to use `perl.exe` to open the `MakeGRV.pl` script, using three parameters. The first parameter is the name you want assigned to your `.GRV` file. Normally, it will be the name of the tool. In your case, you will use `TriviaQuiz3`.

The second parameter is the proper boilerplate file for the type of `.GRV` you are building. `.GRV` files come in several types: `.GRV` files for User Account transfers, shared space invitations, `.GRV`s for injecting skins, `.GRV`s that add or update the Groove help files, `.GRV`s to create a new shared space from a template, and a `.GRV` that runs the `TransportUpdate.osd` from `Groove.net` to automatically update the base components that make up the Groove application. And, of course, there are `Tool` and `Toolset.GRV`s that are created by tool developers. You will use the `ToolTemplateBoilerplate` as your second parameter.

The third parameter is the value for the `TemplateDescriptorURL` that you edited in `ToolTemplateBoilerplate` when you created your skin `.GRV` file. It is the address of the OSD file on the Web, or, if you have the template in your `localhost` folder, the address on your hard disk. Here you'll put the following:

```
http://components.MyCompany.com/MyGrooveTools/TriviaQuiz3/TriviaQuiz3.osd?
➥Package=com.MyCompany.MyGrooveTools.TriviaQuiz3Descriptor_XML&amp;
➥Version=0&amp;Factory=Open"/
```

The last lines of the batch file cause the Perl script to display error information.

Save your file as `TriviaQuiz3.bat`. Running `TriviaQuiz3.bat` creates a `.GRV` file. Open it with WordPad, and it should read like this:

```
<?xml version='1.0'?><?groove.net version='1.0'?>
<g:fragment xmlns:g="urn:groove.net">
<g:InjectorWrapper AccountGUID="grooveIdentity:///DefaultIdentity"
➥ MessageID="d7g4v4pbmpqdu2wk6bs3hsvqsx4meamiwtk6s7c"
➥ ResourceURL="grooveIdentityMessage:///ToolMessage;Version=3,0,0,0"
➥ LocalDeviceURLs="Injector">
```

```
    <g:IdentityMessageHeader>
        <g:MessageHeader MessageType="ToolMessage"
➥ MessageID="d7g4v4pbmpqdu2wk6bs3hsvqsx4meamiwtk6s7c"
➥ Version="1,0,0,0" CreateTime="9/24/00 7:41 PM"
➥ CreatorDeviceURL="dpp://friends.groove.net/0sGnePZSnu-AY-fePpNqEqzwSOPo9910">
            <g:SenderContact/>
            <g:RecipientContact/>
        </g:MessageHeader>
        <g:MessageBody BodyName="MessageBody">
            <g:ToolMessage>
                <g:ToolMessageHeader ToolURL=
➥"grooveAccountTool:;CategoryName=grooveToolCategory:
➥//Account/ToolTemplateList,ComponentName=ToolTemplateList"/>
                <g:ToolMessageBody>
                    <g:TemplateDescriptorList>
                        <g:TemplateDescriptorURL URL=
➥"http://components.MyCompany.com/MyGrooveTools/TriviaQuiz3/TriviaQuiz3.osd?
➥Package=com.MyCompany.MyGrooveTools.TriviaQuiz3.TriviaQuiz3Descriptor_XML&amp;
➥Version=0&amp;Factory=Open"/>
                    </g:TemplateDescriptorList>
                </g:ToolMessageBody>
            </g:ToolMessage>
        </g:MessageBody>
    </g:IdentityMessageHeader>
</g:InjectorWrapper>

</g:fragment>
```

Testing and Troubleshooting

In this chapter you will test injection. You are not going to move these files to your Web server. In Chapter 12, “Easier Groove: Modifying the Basic Groove Tool with Tool Creator and Tool Publisher,” you will move files to your Web server and test injection of Groove tools over the Internet.

Before you can test your injection locally, you might have to change some of your registry settings. Follow these steps to ensure that you test your injection accurately:

1. Shut down Groove.
2. Navigate to Groove’s registry files in the GDK, and locate `DisableWebAccess.reg`.

   `DisableWebAccess` means that when Component Manager goes looking for components, it looks exclusively in `localhost` and doesn’t go out to the Web. If your injection succeeds, you know that you injected precisely what was in the `localhost` directory and that you didn’t download something unexpectedly from the Web.

Double-click the `.REG` file and you'll receive confirmation that your registry files have changed.

3. If you have ComponentAuthentication enabled, you'll have to disable it by running `DisableComponentSecurity.REG` because the TriviaQuiz3 OSD is not properly signed.
4. If you have enabled the My Templates registry setting, you should disable it by running the `DisableMyTemplates.reg` file. When you look in the Add Tool dialog, you want to be sure you are looking at the tool you just injected, not the file you used to prototype.
5. When you have finished, restart Groove.

Double–click your new `Trivia3.GRV` file and watch your wonderful application get installed in Groove. When it is installed, go to your Development Space and launch your tool. If it works, congratulate yourself and celebrate. If it doesn't, you'll need to debug it.

Injection problems occur because of downloading problems or because of faulty OSD. Download errors occur if you are not connected to the network, or if a file is not in the location specified by the OSD.

Faulty OSD is often the result of incorrect `ComponentURL` attributes. You'll need to check spelling and capitalization, make sure that no whitespace or carriage returns appear in quoted strings, and verify that the directory structure is accurate.

It is also possible that the XML is not well-formed in at least one of your three files. The best way to check that is to change the extensions of the files to `.XML` and open them in XML Notepad or Internet Explorer. Be sure to change the extensions back when you are finished.

Finally, Groove provides a tech note, "Using GrooveCSM Viewer to Troubleshoot Injection," that can help. By monitoring the Download Manager and Component Manager, you can usually determine which of your files is causing the problem.

Debugging OSD can be difficult. You should be extremely happy to see the Tool Publisher Tool that you'll work with in the next chapter.

Summary

It is important to know how these files work, but you probably won't have to write a lot of OSD. As you'll see in the next couple of chapters, Groove is making every effort through the use of tools and wizards to make tool publishing as easy and as automatic as possible.

Easier Groove: The Tool Creator and Tool Publisher

CHAPTER 11

IN THIS CHAPTER

In this chapter, we will look at two Groove-supplied tools that make the process of developing and publishing tools much easier. The two tools, Groove Tool Creator and Groove Tool Publisher, take a lot of the busy work out of the process and let you concentrate on tool design and glue code.

You can use the Groove Tool Creator Tool to create and modify tool templates and to update templates already in your account as you change them. As you use the tool to add Groove-supplied components, the Tool Creator builds an in-memory XML document that can be written to disk as a tool template file.

The Groove Tool Publisher Tool will help you create the files necessary to stage and publish your tool templates. The Tool Publisher creates the OSD, tool descriptor, and injector files that enable Groove users to install your tool template in their account.

You will learn how to install these two tools and how to use them to more easily create and publish tool templates.

Tool Creator

Let's look at the Tool Creator first. You'll learn how to install it into your shared space, how to use its wizard to set up the top-level elements of your design, and then how to use it to add components and configure their properties. You'll see how to create layouts and write glue code in the tool.

Installation

To install the Tool Creator, follow these steps:

1. If you have ComponentAuthentication enabled, disable it with the `DisableComponentAuthentication.REG` file.
2. Launch Groove and open the transceiver to your development account.
3. Find the `Groove ToolCreator Tool` directory in the GDK and locate the `ToolCreatorTool.GRV` file. Double-click the injector. Groove notifies you that ComponentAuthentication is disabled and asks whether you want to continue. Click Yes. If you are prompted for an account, select your development account.
4. Create a new space or open an existing one in which you would like to use the tool.
5. From the AddTool tab, add the newly injected Tool Creator to your space.
6. The first time you use the Tool Creator Tool after injection, it opens the Create Tool Wizard. After the first time, you can open the wizard by clicking the New Tool button.

Tool Creation

In this section you will re-create the tool skeleton you built by hand in the beginning of Chapter 9, "Building a Basic Groove Tool." You'll see how much quicker and easier it is to build a tool in Tool Creator. Follow these steps:

1. In the first panel of the wizard, name your tool ToolSkeleton2 and make sure that the check box is checked to include a view container component. The name you choose is used as the `Name` attribute for the XML document and, together with a `.TPL` extension, as the template's filename. You need a view container to hold your layout anytime your tool contains UI items. Click Next.
2. You included an HTML Table Layout layout manager in your original `ToolSkeleton.tpl`, so accept the default here and click Next.
3. You also included a form delegate written in JavaScript in `ToolSkeleton.tpl`. You should remember that the `Delegate` attribute identifies the glue code to be associated with the view. So, again, accept the defaults and click Next.
4. In this panel you can choose to include one of Groove's standard engines. If you want to persist and disseminate data with your tool, choose Yes. Change the option, though, from `PropertyListEngine` to `RecordSetEngine`. You will be working with a `RecordSetEngine` for the rest of the TriviaQuiz tutorial. Click Finish.

Take a minute to look at the Tool Creator. You'll see four tabs located at the bottom of the tool, labeled Tool Info, Components, Fingerprints, and Tool Source. The Tool Info panel shows the Tool Template Name, the Default Tool Display Name, and the Template Display Name filled in with the information you entered in the first panel of the wizard.

Click the Components tab, and you'll see that a view container, a layout, a delegate, and a `RecordSetEngine` have been added to the list of components. To the right of the Components Currently Added to Tool panel are the component panel tabs: Info, Properties, Connections, and Component Source. You can use the tools in these four tabs to add components, change component properties, establish connections between components, and edit or view the source code for each added component. You will now use these tools to flesh out your `ToolSkeleton` code:

1. Click on the `MyViewContainer` component in the added components list. Change its name to `ToolViewContainer`. Notice that the Component is the Default View check box is checked. This check box is used to add the `DefaultView` attribute to the `ComponentGroup`.
2. Change the name of the layout from `MyLayout` to `ToolLayout` and the delegate's name from `MyFormDelegate` to `ToolGlue`. Changing the name of the delegate changes the name of the `ComponentGroup` component's `Delegate` attribute.

3. Change the name of `MyRecordSetEngine` to `ToolRecordSetEngine`.
4. Click on the Properties tab. Highlight the `Background` property, and enter the following code in the Property Value window:

   ```
   <g:BackgroundStyle Style="SectionBackground"/>
   ```

   Click Set Element to add this code to your tool. You must click the Set Element button each time you enter a property. If you don't, and you go on to set another property, the code you entered is lost and you will have to re-enter it.

   With this operation, you have set the view container's background to the `SectionBackground` style defined in the skin resources file.
5. Reselect the `ToolViewContainer` and click on the Connections tab. You will need to provide for component connections to your layout and glue code, so in the first combo box to the right of the Choose a Component to Connect To label, choose `ToolCreatorTestLayout`; in the second combo box, choose `ToolCreatorTestGlue`. Then, click the Apply Connections to Component button. The Tool Creator Tool uses this information to write the `ComponentConnections` code for the view container. You'll make the component connections to your glue code later.

NOTE

Some components, such as your layout manager, `ToolLayout`, don't expect component connections. In that event, no combo box is displayed. Others, such as `RecordSetEngine`, may be able to accept component connections, but have no appropriate components in the tool to connect to. In that case, the combo box is present but has no choices.

6. Now select the `ToolLayout` component, go to the Properties tab, and select Layout from the properties list.
7. Open your copy of `ToolSkeleton.tpl` you created in Chapter 9, and copy the entire `<TABLE>` element. Paste the table code in the Property Value window and click the Set Element button. Tool Creator now adds your layout code to the tool code.
8. Return to the Info tab. Find the Choose a Component to Add to Your Tool combo box and click Button. Name the button `ToolButton`.
9. With `ToolButton` selected, go to the Properties tab. You'll see that there are several button properties you can set. Use the combo box to set the `Style` property to a value of `StandardButton`. You must click the Set Value button each time you make a property value change for the change to take effect. Set the `Label` property by entering **Press to &Initiate Action** in the space provided. Set the `Tooltip` property's value to **This is a tooltip**. Your button properties are now written to the tool's source code.

10. Return to the Info tab and select the `ToolRecordSetEngine`. Check the Component Added to Delegate Connections check box, and then go to the `ToolButton` component and do the same thing. You have now added connections to those two items in your glue code component.

11. Next, you'll add a function to your glue code. Select the `ToolGlue` component and click on the Properties tab, and then enter the following code:

```
function ToolButton_OnCommand(i_pIUICommand)
   {
   }
```

    This empty function and the component connection to it will activate the button. As a result, you will be able to see the button change state as you roll over it or press it. Because the function is empty, the button won't do anything but act like a button.

    Use the Validate Code button to validate the code, and then save it using the Save Code button. The validation button checks for syntax errors in your code, allowing you to catch them in tool development rather than in tool testing.

12. Next, go to the Fingerprints tab and click the Add Fingerprint button. Groove uses the fingerprint to verify the origin of components. Because you aren't developing any custom components, but instead are using standard Groove components, you'll put Groove's fingerprint value in the appropriate column. Click the Add Fingerprint button and enter **Groove** for the Fingerprint ID. Copy the value of the Fingerprint from your `ToolSkeleton.tpl` code and paste it into the Fingerprint Value field and click OK. When you close the dialog, you get a confirmation that the `ComponentSecurity` element was added to the code.

13. Now click the Tool Source tab. If you study the code, you'll find that it is functionally identical to the code you wrote for the `ToolSkeleton.tpl` Tool in Chapter 9. You might find that many of the elements are in different places, but you will see that the tool's look and behavior are nearly the same. And you wrote most of it by clicking buttons!

14. Tool Creator now has completed an in-memory version of the tool. Click the Save to File button on the toolbar, and navigate the file browser to your development directory. After you have saved the file, copy it into your `My Templates` folder. You will now be able to use the Add Tool tab in your development space to add `ToolSkeleton2.tpl`.

Look at your tool, play with the button, and compare it with `ToolSkeleton.tpl`.

You used the wizard to create `ToolSkeleton2.tpl`, but you can also create a new tool manually. To do so, follow these steps:

1. Click on the New Tool button in the Tool Creator Tool. Accept the Are You Sure You Want to Remove All Components? choice. When the wizard appears, cancel it and click on the Tool Info tab. You are now ready to create a tool manually.

2. Name your tool by filling in the Tool Template Name, the Default Tool Display Name, and the Template Display Name. As you have seen, the Tool Template Name is the name of the XML document and the filename, the Default Tool Display Name is the name displayed in the toolbar when the tool is active, and Template Display Name is used in the Add Tool dialog to identify the tool.
3. Add your components. You'll usually need a view and a layout, a delegate or glue code for your view, and an engine, as well as some UI components. You'll also need to add a `ComponentSecurity` component through the use of the Fingerprint tab. You can also make modifications on the Info tab.
4. Select one of the components in the Components tab and then click the Properties tab or Connections tab, as appropriate.

   How you modify a property will vary depending on the component. Some UI properties are modifiable with clicks to radio buttons or check boxes, whereas other components, such as the `Layout` property or the view's `Background` property, might require XML. In this case, your delegate's property is, of course, JavaScript.

   You can see the component's code and edit it directly, if you want, by clicking the Component Source tab. Script code is more easily modified in a text editor or in your IDE.

TIP

Using the properties shown for the UI components together with the `ComponentCatalog` help file is a great way to gain a better understanding of Groove-standard components. You can see what properties are available for each component and gain an understanding of what those properties do by reading the `ComponentCatalog`. The more you know about components, the easier your Groove tool development will become.

5. You can now make your component connections. You'll need to make connections to your layout and glue code in the view, and connections to your UI components in the glue code. Connections to the view are made by selecting from the drop-downs in the Connections tab, whereas connections to glue code are made by checking the Component Added to Delegate Connections check box in the Info tab for the component to be connected.

Tool Modification

You can also modify tools with Tool Creator. Click the Open Tool button on the toolbar. You are presented with a file browser. Locate the template you want to modify, and click Open to load the template file into the Tool Creator tool.

After the template file is loaded, save it under a different name. That way, you won't overwrite a functional tool. Be sure to change the tool's names in the Tool Info tab. Now, you can add or remove components, or change your components' properties or connections.

Overlay a Tool

You can also use the Tool Creator to modify an existing tool that you have previously injected. Injecting a tool installs its template into the template database maintained by Groove (`Templates.XSS`).

Like the Groove Database Navigator Tool, the Tool Creator Tool is capable of overlaying templates. Click the Overlay Template button and the Tool Creator searches `Templates.XSS` for tools that match the loaded tool's Tool Template Name. If it does not find a match, the tool alerts you with the message "You can only overlay templates if the templates have already been injected and installed." If the tool does find a match, it deletes the old template and replaces it with the template loaded in the tool's memory.

If you want to modify a template that you already injected, you can follow these steps:

1. Open the template's source code with Tool Creator.
2. Modify the tool.
3. Save the new file as another filename.
4. Click the Overlay Template button.

You can then test the tool. If it works as you want, great. If it doesn't, you can repeat the procedure.

View Source

You can also use the Tool Creator to view the source of any tool you can load. Click the Tool Source tab, and you will see a read-only listing of the tool's code.

Tool Creator is one of the two tools Groove provides to make the creation of tools an easier and more efficient process. The second is the Tool Publisher Tool.

Tool Publisher

The Tool Publisher Tool helps you easily create the files necessary to stage and publish your tools. The tool outputs the OSD, the tool descriptor file, and the `.GRV` file, files that allow Groove users to add your tool to their accounts. In addition, it also allows you to generate a unique certificate enabling you to sign your tools. After you have generated a certificate, you can use it to publish as many tools as you want.

Installation

To install the Tool Publisher Tool, follow these steps:

1. Disable ComponentAuthentication and make sure that you are in your development account. Now you are ready to install Groove's Tool Publisher Tool.
2. Create a new space or open an existing one where you would like to use the tool.
3. Navigate to the GDK and find the `GrooveToolPublisher` directory. Inside it, you'll find the `ToolPublisherTool.GRV`. Double-click the injector. Groove notifies you that ComponentAuthentication is disabled and asks whether you want to continue. Click Yes. If you are prompted for an account, select your development account.
4. From the AddTool tab, add the newly injected Tool Creator to your space.

Preparation

Before you can publish a tool, you need to create a directory structure in your `localhost` folder that will mirror the structure of the directory on your Web site:

1. Make sure that you have disabled Web access and MyTemplates. If you have not, shut down Groove and run the appropriate `.REG` files. When Groove installs a tool, it first looks to see whether the user has a `My Templates` folder and if MyTemplates is enabled in the registry. It then checks the `localhost` directory. If it finds the necessary files, it installs the tool from there.

   If your Web address was `http://www.MyCompany.com`, the Web address for your template file would be `http://www.MyCompany.com/MyCompanyTools/ToolSkeleton/ToolSkeleton/ToolSkeleton.tpl`. By duplicating the Web directory structure in your `localhost` folder, you can test installation and operation of your tool before you make it available on your Web site.
2. Create a `MyCompanyTools` folder in your `localhost` directory. Within that folder, create a `ToolSkeleton` folder; inside that, copy from `My Templates` the `ToolSkeleton2.tpl` file you just wrote with the Tool Creator. All the files associated with your project must be in this folder.

You have now created a structure on your hard drive that mirrors your Web structure. When you have completed your preparation phase, you are ready to start publishing your tool.

Publishing a Tool

Tool publishing with Groove's Tool Publisher involves four operations: creating a project, adding tool descriptor information and OSD information, generating a certificate, and publishing the project.

Creating a Project

To create a project, follow these steps:

1. If you already shut down Groove to run `.REG` files, relaunch it.
2. Navigate to your development space and to the Tool Publisher Tool. The Tool Publisher needs certain information about your Web site and your tool's location in order to publish it. You enter that information in the Project Information tab of the Tool Publisher. The tool should open to this tab.
3. Click the New button, and then enter the name of your project, **ToolSkeleton2**. This name will be used to name your tool descriptor, OSD, and injector files. Be consistent because your tool may be hosted on a UNIX Web site.
4. Enter the Root Package Name. The Root Package Name is used as a default base name for all the package names in your OSD file. The name itself is constructed from the location of your files on your Web site. It is the same reverse domain notation that was first used for Java packages and is used throughout Groove with Groove components. It works very well to uniquely define your tool and separate it from all others that might have the same name. In this example, the Root Package Name is `com.MyCompany.MyCompanyTools.ToolSkeleton2`.
5. Enter the Web Server URL. The Web Server URL is the address portion of the component URL. For this example, it is `http://components.MyCompany.com`.
6. Enter the Web Server Directory. The Web Server Directory is the directory path on your server that specifies the location of your components. It is exactly the portion of the Web site directory structure that you created in your `localhost` directory in the preparation phase, `MyCompanyTools/ToolSkeleton2`. Enter that in the Web Server Directory space. When you have finished, click Save.

   Notice that the information you just added is the decomposition of the reverse Java notation package name.

Adding Tool Descriptor Information and OSD Information

Enter the tool descriptor information as shown here:

1. Click on the Tool Descriptor tab.
2. Click the Add Templates button, and you are presented with a file browser. In the browser, you can locate the template file you want to install. If you have placed `ToolSkeleton2.tpl` in the `ToolSkeleton2` folder, find it now and click Open.

   The entries in the Name and Description fields will be written by the tool as the `Name` and `Description` attributes of the `TemplateDescriptor` element of the tool descriptor file. Both the name and the description are shown in the lists displayed in the Add Tool and Create Shared Space dialogs. The `Name` should be a descriptive name that will uniquely identify the tool, in this case, `ToolSkeleton2`. The `Description` should succinctly describe the tool, for example, `Simple tool created with Tool Creator`. Fill in those fields now, and list yourself as the author. When you have finished, continue to the Project Files tab.

Adding Additional Files

You'll see the template file and the tool descriptor file already listed in the Files panel. Click the template file, and you'll find that the Tool Publisher has entered the information in the fields to the right based on the information you have provided so far. Check the template file and the descriptor file to make sure that the information in both is correct.

If the information is not correct, you can edit every field except the file path. The file path is set when you add files. If you need to add additional files, you can add them now. After you have verified that the information is correct in the fields, click on the Install tab.

Verifying Installation Options

To verify the installation options, follow these steps:

1. Select the `ToolSkeleton.tpl` template file from the files list. Verify that the fields are properly filled in with the information for this file.
2. In the case of your template file, you want it to be installed by adding it to your `templates.xss` file, so you should see Import to XSS in the Type field. Take a second to pull down the drop-down menu, and you'll see the other install types currently supported. Install types were covered in Chapter 6, "Essential OSD."
3. The values in Database URI and Schema URI are Groove variables. `$TEMPLATESURI$` is the current location of the `Templates.xss` file, and `$DEFAULTSCHEMA$` is the current location of the `schemas.xss` schema database. Accept the defaults. No target directory is entered because the install type is Import to XSS.
4. Select the tool descriptor file. You'll see that the type is Copy, so a Target Directory is specified. Again, the field holds a Groove variable, `$GROOVEDATA$`, that represents the location of the Groove `Data` directory. The remaining three fields are unused with a Copy Type. If the tool required a schema, it would use `$DEFAULTSCHEMA$`, another Groove variable. This one represents the location of the `schemas.xss` database.
5. Click on the Factories tab. You will want to see Open as the factory name for both files. The template is opened from the location of `Templates.XSS`, and the descriptor is opened as a temporary XML document from the `XML Files` directory.

Adding a Dependency

You click the Dependencies tab to add a dependency. Let's use it to add a dependency on the `.tpl` file to the descriptor. Creating a dependency on the descriptor for the tool template ensures that the tool template is downloaded before the tool is available to add to a space. Here are the steps:

1. Click the descriptor filename in the Files list.
2. In the Choose Dependency Targets panel, select the `ToolSkeleton2.tpl` template file, and then click the Add button.
3. Save your values by returning to the Project Information tab and clicking the Save button.

Generating a Certificate

Every component that is to be installed in Groove must be listed in an OSD file signed with a digital certificate that identifies the originator of the component. OSD files include a `ComponentSecurity` component, within which is the digital fingerprint. You have not needed a digital fingerprint before, because you have been using Groove with component security turned off. If you expect to have others download your tools, you need to generate a certificate:

1. Click on the Generate Certificate tab. In the Common Name field, put either your name or your company's name. Under the Organization Unit (Dept.), enter information that is useful to you, for example, **MyCompany Groove tool development**.
2. Enter information in your Organization line to further qualify your department information, for example, **Tool Skeleton Developers section**.
3. Enter the Country information.
4. Enter your start and stop dates. In special circumstances, you could use the certificate's start and stop dates to restrict the lifetime of any component signed with it. If, however, you are doing normal development, you won't want to be dealing with certificate expiration issues, so give yourself a hundred years. The dates 1/1/2002 to 1/1/2102 might be appropriate, for example.
5. Next, you need to use a passphrase to create your unique digital certificate, so choose one, and then enter and confirm it. When you click the Generate Certificate button, you are prompted for a location to store your keystore and certificate files. It is a good idea to store this file outside of the Groove `Data` directory. If you need to replace your data directory, you could lose your certificate. After you have generated a certificate, you can reuse it for every tool you publish, so put it where you can find it easily and are not likely to accidentally delete it.

You can open both your keystore file, with WordPad, and your certificate file, by double-clicking on it. You should verify the information in your certificate file. The Thumbprint is equivalent to Groove's digital fingerprint. After you have completed your certificate, you can publish your project.

Publishing the Project

Publish the project as described here:

1. Click the Publish Project tab. You can edit the Tool Display Name and double-check the Output Directory. This is the directory where your descriptor, `.GRV`, and OSD files will be written. The Tool Display Name is the name displayed in the toolbar when the tool is active.
2. Click on the Create Files button, and Groove confirms the creation of those files and their location.
3. You are now ready to sign your OSD. All the fields except your passphrase should be filled in. Input your passphrase and click the Sign OSD button.

If you now take a look at your OSD file, you'll see something similar to this:

```
<g:ComponentSecurity Version="1,0,0,0">
   <g:FingerprintTable>
      <g:Entry Fingerprint="c424 d7e4 a8ed 2ba9 49c6 06af adb2 7854 312a 378c"
FingerprintID="com.MyCompany"/>
   </g:FingerprintTable>
   <g:Signatures>
      <g:Signature Certificate="MIIEsDCCA5qgAw..."UserTrust="True"
Value="nX4cmDW7/hzW..."/>
   </g:Signatures>
   <g:Certificate Value="MIIEsDCCA5qgAw..."/>
   <g:Signature Value="SczwvozxClWp..."/>
</g:ComponentSecurity>
```

And within the `IMPLEMENTATION` elements you'll see this:

```
<CODEBASE Digest="GD1o44lK8W8JgKkAH9pgCtHz3gM=" FileSize="418"
➥HREF="http://components.MyCompany.com/MyCompanyTools/..."/>
```

The values have been truncated in this code in the interest of space.

The `FingerprintTable` corresponds to the Thumbprint entry in your certificate. A private key was created with the thumbprint. The private key was used to generate the signature.

The `Digest` is a key generated by Groove at the time of OSD signing. Its function is to guarantee that no changes have been made to the downloaded files since they were signed. This ensures that no one has tampered with your files.

As a last step, use the registry files to disable Web access and enable component authentication. Remember to shut down Groove to make the new registry settings effective.

That's it. You're done. You can now double-click the `.GRV` file and test the injection of your tool from your `localhost` folder. Use the procedures in the preceding chapter to troubleshoot your injection. You will not test injection from the Web in this chapter. You'll do that in the next chapter with a "real" tool.

If you want, you can compare the OSD and tool descriptor files. You'll find that they are essentially the same as the files you created by hand in the preceding chapter, with the exception of the digests and fingerprint table.

Publishing Subsequent Tools

When you publish subsequent tools, you will not need to generate another certificate. You may find that when you return to the Tool Publisher Tool the Generate Certificate tab fields are blank. If they are, fill in the Private Keystore File Path field. Enter the path where you store your `ComponentSigningPrivateKeyStore.xml` file and your fields will be restored.

If you have already published a tool, you can use Tool Publisher's Import button to import the tool's tool descriptor, `.GRV`, and OSD files. Importing these files causes the tool to fill in all the appropriate fields of the Tool Publisher.

Summary

The Groove Tool Creator and Groove Tool Publisher tools are evolving rapidly, even as Groove evolves. With each generation of these tools, they become more wizard-like. As wizards, they shield the developer from the complexities of the underlying Groove structure, and that is good news from a productivity standpoint.

However, when something goes wrong, it is extremely useful to be able to understand the underlying technology. As a serious tool developer, you should try to keep up with the complexity these tools mask. Spend time reading the code the wizards produce, and you will learn Groove programming more quickly and will be able to debug more efficiently.

In the next chapter, you'll spend more time with these tools as you continue to develop your Trivia Quiz Tool.

Easier Groove: Modifying the Basic Groove Tool with Tool Creator and Tool Publisher

CHAPTER

12

IN THIS CHAPTER

In this chapter, you will use Tool Creator to extend and refine your trivia game. In `Trivia Quiz3.tpl` you stretched the limits of the `PropertyListEngine`. It should be clear that if you are going to substantially increase the number of questions in your quiz, you are going to need a better means of storing and retrieving them.

In this chapter, you will provide a Welcome screen and a method to enter new questions, rather than programming them directly into the tool. In the process, you'll explore some new components, learn new ways to use layouts, make some aesthetic enhancements, extensively study the `RecordSetEngine` and `DataViewer`, and make modifications to your menus. Finally, you'll use the Tool Publisher to construct more complex OSD files, descriptors, and `.GRV` files to publish your tool.

Your tool is about to change from a one-screen tool to a three-screen application. You'll have one screen to welcome users to your tool and let them choose to either play the trivia game or enter more trivia questions into your trivia database. Then you will provide a screen to enter those questions, and, finally, you'll make a few improvements to your game.

The Welcome Screen

The Welcome screen is going to be pretty basic. Let's take a look at the cocktail-napkin rendition, shown in Figure 12.1.

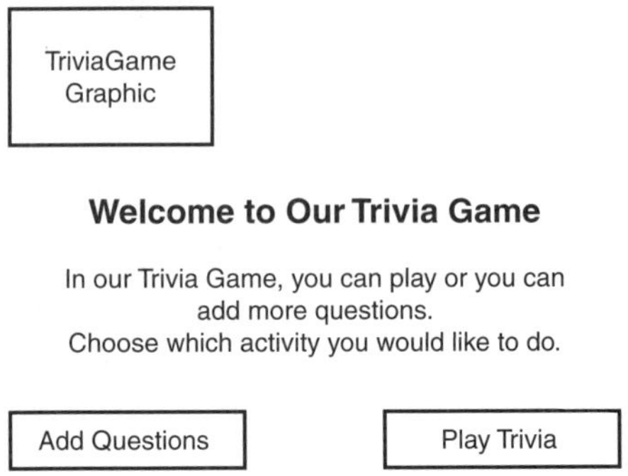

FIGURE 12.1
The Welcome screen.

You're going to need a graphic, a headline, some text, and two buttons. Because the layout here is so simple, it can be done with a `GrooveMultiCellLayout` component. You can put the graphic on the first row, the headline on the second, the text on the third, and the row of buttons on the fourth.

Let's translate your words into a `GrooveMultiCellLayout`:

1. You want a series of rows, so use a `<MULTIROW>` element rather than a `<MULTICOL>` one.
2. Establish some room around the border of your layout with values for your `<BORDER>` element.
3. Set up some default values for the padding of your cells. You can override these values if you want, by specifying a pad value within your `<CELL>` elements.
4. Lay out a series of rows with cells to hold your components. You will also use empty cells to provide spacing. Remember that each row does not have to have the same number of cells.

Your layout, based on what you said you wanted in your sketch, is shown here:

```
<MULTIROW>
      <BORDER BottomPad="10" RightPad="5" TopPad="5" LeftPad="5"/>
      <DEFAULTPAD BottomPad="2" RightPad="3" TopPad="2" LeftPad="3"/>
      <ROW>
         <CELL HEIGHT="100">
            TriviaGraphic
         </CELL>
         <CELL/>
         <CELL/>
</ROW>
      <ROW>
         <CELL HEIGHT="100">
            WelcomeTitle
         </CELL>
      </ROW>
      <ROW>
         <CELL HEIGHT="100">
            WelcomeText
         </CELL>
      </ROW>
      <ROW>
         <CELL/>
         <CELL HEIGHT="100">
            GoEnterButton
         </CELL>
         <CELL HEIGHT="100">
            GoPlayButton
         </CELL>
         <CELL/>
      </ROW>
</MULTIROW>
```

Cells in rows or columns will evenly split the space available if no height or width is specified. If multiple heights or widths are specified, the largest value for each cell is used. If you had a row with three cells, for example, that had cell heights of 20, 30, and 40, each cell in the row would have a height of 40. Consequently, it is good practice to specify as few height and width properties as possible. The remaining space will be divided evenly among the cells. In the first row, for example, you only need to specify a height in the first cell.

Adding a Layout

Before you begin, back up your `Groove\Data` directory. You'll get started in actually modifying your tool by opening your Development Space and loading your `TriviaQuiz3.tpl` into the Tool Creator. Then, you'll add a layout:

1. Fire up Tool Creator and click the Open Tool button. In the file browser, find `TriviaQuiz3.tpl` and click Open.
2. From the Tool Info tab, change the three name fields to `TriviaQuiz` and save as `TriviaQuiz` to your `My Templates` directory.

TIP

> If you want, you can develop in your `Groove Development` directory and copy into your `My Templates` directory for testing. There are a couple of problems associated with developing in the `My Templates` directory. First, if you have Groove running while you're doing developing, you will get an error message if you save the file and there's an error in it that you haven't addressed yet. If you save early and often, you may get these errors when you really don't yet care—in some ways it's like compiling your code when you know it won't compile. The second disadvantage is that you must copy your code from the `Groove Development` directory to the `My Templates` directory every time you want to test.
>
> Which method you use is a personal preference. There are successful developers who develop in the `My Templates` folder and there are also successful developers who copy into `My Templates`. Use whichever is most comfortable for you.

3. Click on the Components tab and be sure you are in the Info tab of the tool. You will change the name of some of these components to reflect the changes you will be making to them in this part of the tutorial.
4. Change the name of the glue component to `TriviaQuizGlue`. With `TriviaQuizGlue` selected, click the Component Is the Delegate check box. Change the name of the layout to `TriviaQuizLayout` because that will be the layout in which you will play the game.

You are going to be changing three layouts with glue code. Select the view container and change its name to TriviaQuizViewContainer, and then check the Component Added to Delegate Connections check box. With TriviaQuizViewContainer selected, click on the Connections tab. Select TriviaQuizLayout in the top drop-down menu and TriviaQuizGlue in the bottom one. Click the Apply Connections to Component button.

5. Select the QuestionLabel component and check the Component Added to Delegate Connections check box. In turn, select each of the answer button and answer label components and again check the Component Added to Delegate Connections check box. Do the same for the ElapsedTimeListBoxControl component and the NextQuestionButton.
6. Now you are ready to add your welcome layout. Go to the Components tab and, in the combo box marked Choose a Component to Add to Your Tool, select MultiCellLayout. Rename the component WelcomeLayout. In the Properties tab, select Layout and paste the layout code shown earlier into the Property Value panel, and then click the Set Element button.
7. Go back to the Info tab and select TriviaQuizViewContainer. Go to the Connections tab and, in the top Choose a Component to Connect To combo box, choose WelcomeLayout. Next, click the Apply Connections to Component button. This will establish a component connection for your new layout in the TriviaQuizViewContainer code.
8. Save the changes by clicking the Save to File button on the toolbar.

Adding a Graphic

Let's add your graphic. You can make one or use the TriviaGraphic.jpg and TriviaGraphic.BMP files on the CD/Web site. If you make your own, TriviaGraphic.jpg must be a 72-dpi .JPG file in 24-bit color. The mask, TriviaGraphicMask.BMP, will be a monochrome .BMP file. Store these files in Groove's ToolBMPs folder.

When the user injects your published tool, these files will be copied into the user's Groove\Data\ToolBMPs directory.

After you have created the files and placed them into the Groove\Data\ToolBMPs directory, you can add an image control to your quiz. Here are the steps:

1. In the Info tab, select ImageControl from the Choose a Component to Add to Your Tool combo box and click Add. Rename the newly added component TriviaGraphic.
2. Go to the Properties tab. Select AcceptedFileTypes and enter **bmp**, **.jpg**, **.jpeg** into the Properties field, and then click Set Value. This restricts the file types TriviaGraphic can accept.

3. Tool Creator is an evolving tool. If your version of the tool contains a method for locating the source of the graphic, use it. If it does not, use the following instructions. Go to the Component Source tab, and find the `PropertyList` element. Below the `AcceptedFileTypes` property you added, enter the following code:

   ```
   <g:Property Name="Image">
      <g:Image ImageURL="grooveFile:///ToolBMPs\TriviaGraphic.jpg"
   ➥ ImageMaskURL="grooveFile:///ToolBMPs\TriviaGraphicMask.bmp"
   ➥ Height="100" Width="200"/>
   </g:Property>
   ```

   Click the Save button to save these properties into the tool source.

Adding a Title Element

Next, you'll create a `WelcomeTitle` element:

1. Click the Info tab and select `StaticText` from the combo box marked Choose a Component to Add to Your Tool. Click Add, and then rename the component **WelcomeTitle**.
2. In the Properties tab, highlight the `Label` property, and in the Property Value field, type **Welcome to Our Trivia Game**. Then click Set Value.
3. Select the `Style` property and choose `Header` from the drop-down menu in the Property Value pane. Click Set Value; then choose the `HAlignment` property and add a value of `Center`. Click Set Value.
4. Return to the Info tab and add a `staticText` component. Title it **WelcomeText**. In the Properties tab, select the `Label` value and enter **In our trivia game, you can play, or you can add more questions. Choose which activity you would like to do.** Click Set Value.
5. Select the `BreakType` property, and from the drop-down menu select `WordBreak`. Click Set Value. Select `HAlignment` and choose `Center`. Again, click Set Value.
6. Open the Component Source tab and paste the following code into the source as a new property element below the `HAlignment` property:

   ```
   <g:Property Name="LabelFont">
      <g:FontDesc Color="#000000" Typeface="Tahoma" Height="18"/>
   </g:Property>
   ```

   Click Save.

Adding Two Buttons

Now you can add your two buttons, following these steps:

1. Go back to the Info tab, add a button component from the list of available components, and rename it `GoEnterButton`. Click the Component Added to Delegate Connections check box.
2. Go to the Properties tab, select `Label`, and type **Enter Questions**. Remember to click Set Value at this point and every time you set a new property.
3. Click on the Style tab and select `StandardButton` from the drop-down list.
4. Click the `Tooltip` property and type **Click here if you'd like to enter questions for others to guess**.
5. Add the `GoPlayButton` in the same way as the `GoEnterButton`. For the `Label` property's value type **Play Trivia**, and for the `Tooltip` property's value type **Click here if you'd like to play the trivia game**.

Save the tool using the Save to File button on the toolbar. If you are developing in your `Groove Development` directory, you will need to copy `TriviaQuiz` to your `My Templates` directory. You can now add the tool to your Development Space and preview the Welcome screen. Right-click on `TriviaQuiz`'s Tool tab and select Delete Tool to remove it when you are finished.

The Add Questions Screen

For your second layout, you will want a place to input your question and each of the four answers. In addition, you'll need to input which of the four answers is the correct one. You'll need two buttons: one for entering all the data, and another for editing records. In addition, you will want to see the records you have entered, so you will use a `DataViewer` control. Figure 12.2 shows a sketch of your second screen.

You will again use a `MultiCellLayout` using the same padding values as you did earlier:

```
<MULTIROW>
      <BORDER BottomPad="10" RightPad="5" TopPad="5" LeftPad="5"/>
      <DEFAULTPAD BottomPad="2" RightPad="3" TopPad="2" LeftPad="3"/>
<MULTIROW>
```

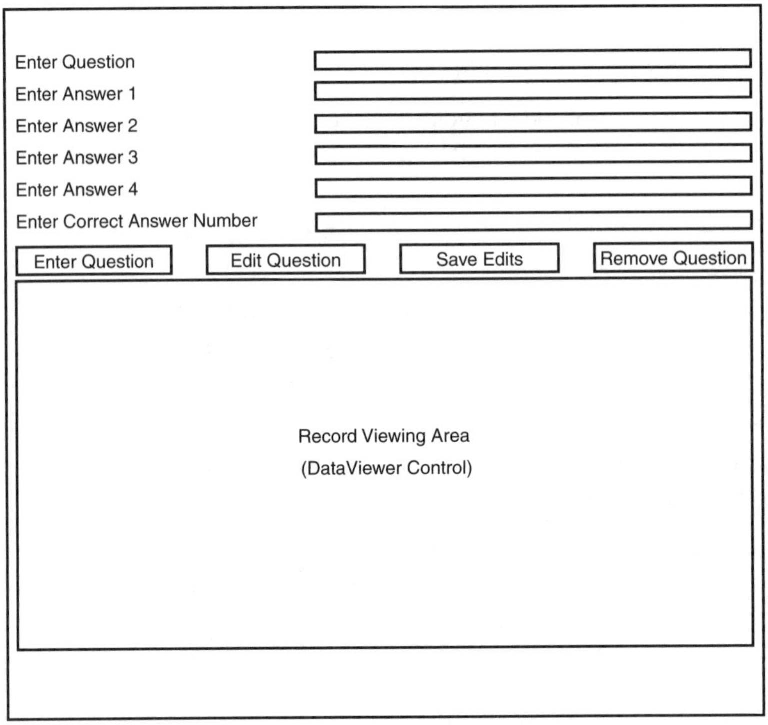

Enter Question
Enter Answer 1
Enter Answer 2
Enter Answer 3
Enter Answer 4
Enter Correct Answer Number
Enter Question | Edit Question | Save Edits | Remove Question
Record Viewing Area
(DataViewer Control)

FIGURE 12.2
The Add Questions screen.

Next, you'll add a `StaticText` component and an `EditControl` for the question and each of the four possible answers. You'll also need a `StaticText` component and an `EditControl` for the correct answer. You'll set the last cell's `WIDTH` property to `75%`. The code for one of these rows is shown here:

```
<ROW>
    <CELL>
        QuestionInputLabel
    </CELL>
    <CELL WIDTH="75%">
        QuestionInput
    </CELL>
</ROW>
```

You will handle the buttons somewhat differently. Currently, your first column is 25% of the available space. If you put in two buttons the same size as the first column, you'll need to include an empty cell with a `WIDTH` property value of `50%`. That row is shown here:

```
<ROW>
   <CELL>
      EnterQuestionButton
   </CELL>
   <CELL>
      EditQuestionButton
   </CELL>
   <CELL WIDTH="50%"/>
</ROW>
```

When you site the `DataViewer` control, you are going to want to see as many records as possible, so you'll set the height of that cell to 75%. The remaining seven rows above it will take up the remaining 25%:


```
<ROW>
   <CELL HEIGHT="75%">
      DataViewer
   </CELL>
</ROW>
```

Your entire layout for the Question Entry screen should look like this:

```
<MULTIROW>
    <BORDER BottomPad="10" RightPad="5" TopPad="5" LeftPad="5"/>
    <DEFAULTPAD BottomPad="2" RightPad="3" TopPad="2" LeftPad="3"/>
    <ROW>
        <CELL>
            QuestionInputLabel
        </CELL>
        <CELL WIDTH="75%">
            QuestionInput
        </CELL>
    </ROW>
    <ROW>
        <CELL>
            Answer1InputLabel
        </CELL>
        <CELL WIDTH="75%">
            Answer1Input
        </CELL>
    </ROW>
    <ROW>
        <CELL>
            Answer2InputLabel
        </CELL>
        <CELL WIDTH="75%">
            Answer2Input
```

```
        </CELL>
    </ROW>
    <ROW>
        <CELL>
            Answer3InputLabel
        </CELL>
        <CELL WIDTH="75%">
            Answer3Input
        </CELL>
    </ROW>
    <ROW>
        <CELL>
            Answer4InputLabel
        </CELL>
        <CELL WIDTH="75%">
            Answer4Input
        </CELL>
    </ROW>
    <ROW>
        <CELL>
            CorrectAnswerInputLabel
        </CELL>
        <CELL WIDTH="75%">
            CorrectAnswerInput
        </CELL>
    </ROW>
    <ROW>
        <CELL>
            EnterQuestionButton
        </CELL>
        <CELL>
            EditQuestionButton
        </CELL>
        <CELL>
            SaveEditsButton
        </CELL>
        <CELL>
            RemoveQuestionButton
        </CELL>
    </ROW>
    <ROW>
        <CELL HEIGHT="70%">
          QuestionDataViewer
        </CELL>
    </ROW>
    <ROW>
```

```
        <CELL/>
        <CELL/>
        <CELL/>
        <CELL/>
        <CELL>
            ReturnButton
        </CELL>
    </ROW>
</MULTIROW>
```

Let's add this layout to your tool:

1. In the Info tab of the Components tab of Tool Creator, choose a `MultCellLayout` component from the drop-down list, and click Add.
2. Change the name of this component to **QuestionInputLayout**.
3. Click on the Properties tab, and then select `Layout`. Add the code you wrote earlier and click the Set Element button.

With your layout in place, you can start creating the components you have sited.

Adding Components

Let's start with the `QuestionInputLabel`. Here are the steps for adding it:

1. The label is, of course, a `StaticText` control, so add a `StaticText` component from the list of available components in the Components tab as before.
2. Select the new component, and in the Info tab, rename it **QuestionInputLabel**.
3. In the Properties tab set the `Label` property to **Enter Question** and click the Set Value button.
4. Using the same procedure, create the remaining labels, renaming them **Answer1 InputLabel**, **Answer2InputLabel**, **Answer3InputLabel**, **Answer4InputLabel**, and **CorrectAnswerInputLabel**, with **Enter Answer 1**, **Enter Answer 2**, **Enter Answer 3**, **Enter Answer 4**, and **Enter Correct Answer Number** as the `Label` property values, respectively. In the Properties tab with `CorrectAnswerInputLabel` selected, click on the `Clip` property, choose `WordEllipsis`, and click Set Value. If the tool is resized, this property clips the label text and inserts an ellipsis if there is not enough room to display all the text.
5. Create the `EditControl` components. In the Info tab, select `EditControl` from the list and click the Add button. As you create them, rename them **QuestionInput**, **Answer1Input**, **Answer2Input**, **Answer3Input**, **Answer4Input**, and **CorrectAnswerInput**, and click the Component Added to Delegate Connections check box for each.

Next, create the buttons:

1. Select Button in the pull-down list and click Add. Rename the button **EnterQuestion Button** and click the Component Added to Delegate Connections check box.
2. In the Properties tab, select the `Style` property and choose `StandardButton`. Then click Set Value. Click the `Tooltip` property and enter **Add a question to the database**. Type **Enter Question** into the `Label` property value field. Remember to click Set Value every time you set or change a property.
3. Add the second button, naming it **EditQuestionButton**. Use `StandardButton` for the style, **Click to edit selected question.** for the value of the `Tooltip` property, and **Edit Selected Question** for the label. Remember to check the Component Added to Delegate Connections check box for each button.
4. Add the third and fourth buttons, naming them **SaveEditsButton** and **RemoveQuestion Button**. Use `StandardButton` for the style, and use **Click to save your edits.** and **Click to remove selected question.** for the values of the `Tooltip` properties. Use **Save Edits** and **Remove Selected Question** for the labels.
5. Add the Return button. The Return button is a `StandardIconButton`. The `Label` value should be **&Return**, and the `Tooltip` value should be **Return to Welcome Page**. The rest of the properties need to be added by hand in the Component Source tab until the property list looks like this:

   ```
   <g:PropertyList Version="1">
      <g:Property Name="Style" Value="StandardIconButton"/>
      <g:Property Name="OverrideLabelPosition" Value="InsideRight"/>
      <g:Property Name="ImageURL"
   ➥ Value="grooveFile:///ToolBMPs\Arrows16x16Images.jpg"/>
      <g:Property Name="ImageMaskURL"
   ➥ Value="grooveFile:///ToolBMPs\Arrows16x16ImagesMask.bmp"/>
      <g:Property Name="ImageOffset" Value="0"/>
      <g:Property Name="ImageHeight" Value="16"/>
      <g:Property Name="ImageWidth" Value="16"/>
      <g:Property Name="Label" Value="&amp;Return"/>
      <g:Property Name="Tooltip" Value="Return to Welcome Page"/>
      <g:Property Name="Mnemonic" Value="ALT+R"/>
   </g:PropertyList>
   ```

   Click the Component Added to Delegate Connections check box for the Return button, and then save your tool.

Before you add your `DataViewer` with Tool Creator, you will have to add a schema for your records. You need to add the schema in order to test your tool. You will delete it later when you test your publication. To add the schema, follow these steps:

1. Open the TriviaQuiz.tpl in My Templates with WordPad and add the following code between the ComponentGroup tag at the top of the file and the TriviaQuizViewContainer component:

```
<g:Schemas>
   <g:Schema URL="grooveDocument:///GrooveXSS/$PersistRoot/
➥ Schemas.xss/TriviaQuizSchema.xml"/>
</g:Schemas>
```

   This line identifies a schema in Schemas.xss that defines the records for your Trivia Quiz.

2. Type this code into a blank document and save it as TriviaQuizSchema.xml:

```
<g:Schema Version="1,0,0,0" URL="TriviaQuizSchema.xml"
xmlns:g="urn:groove.net">
    <g:IncludeSchemas>
        <g:AdditionalSchema URI="grooveDocument:///GrooveXSS/$PersistRoot/
➥ Schemas.xss/GrooveStandardRecordsSchema2.xml"/>
    </g:IncludeSchemas>
    <g:ElementDecl ElementTemplate="true"
➥ Name="urn:groove.net:TriviaQuizRecord">
        <g:ElementRef IsChildElement="0" Element="urn:groove.net:Record"/>
        <g:AttrGroup>
            <g:AttrDef Type="String" Name="Question"/>
            <g:AttrDef Type="String" Name="Answer1"/>
            <g:AttrDef Type="String" Name="Answer2"/>
            <g:AttrDef Type="String" Name="Answer3"/>
            <g:AttrDef Type="String" Name="Answer4"/>
            <g:AttrDef Type="String" Name="CorrectAnswer"/>
        </g:AttrGroup>
    </g:ElementDecl>
</g:Schema>
```

3. Switch to the Groove Database Navigator Tool that you installed in Chapter 7, “Creating a Groove Development Environment.” Use Groove Database Navigator to import this schema into the Schema.xss database. In the top pane, select Schemas.xss and click the Import Document into Database button. Accept the defaults by clicking OK on the Import Options dialog. Find the TriviaQuizSchema.xml file, and click Open. Now, TriviaQuizSchema.xml has been imported into Schemas.xss.

You are now ready to add your DataViewer component.

Adding the DataViewer

DataViewer is a complex component that provides a list control for Groove record-based data. It is used in conjunction with a RecordSetEngine component, a ToolCollectionsComponent, and a ModelGlue component. All these must be present and functioning properly for DataViewer to work.

In addition, the `DataViewer` component takes many elements, some of which are properties like you've see so far, some of which are `ComponentConnections`, and some of which are `ComponentGroups`, with their own individual components included. Some of these elements are available through Tool Creator, whereas others need to be hand-coded. Add the `DataViewer` with these steps:

1. Return to the Tool Creator Tool and the Info tab, choose `DataViewer` from the drop-down list, and click the Add button. Rename the `DataViewer` component **QuestionData Viewer**, and then click the Component Added to Delegate Connections check box.
2. Click on the Properties tab. `GridLineDescriptors`, `Sorts`, and `Views` are listed in the property panel. Let's enter the `Views` property first.
3. You'll use a view to set the information you would like to display in your `DataViewer` control. You will include a `<DataViewerView>` element to enclose your column definitions. While you're at it, you'll name your `DataViewerView` and set it as your default. You will have only one view in your `DataViewer` but you could have several. Begin your `Views` property by entering the following line in the Property Value panel:

```
<g:DataViewerView Default="True" Name="Main">
```

TIP

In addition to these attributes, you could have specified an initial sort of your data by including the name of one of your `Sort` properties, or you could have chosen to include a query of the underlying data, using the `@[field name]=[field value]` syntax.

4. Let's define one of the columns. For `DataType` you'll be using `String` values. You'll use this column for your question, so you'll name it **Question** and also use **Question** for the label. Finally, you'll assign the column a width that will let you get six columns across your screen. Add this line to the one in the Property Value panel:

```
<g:DataViewerColumn DataType="String" Name="Question"
➥ Label="Question" Width="18%"/>
```

TIP

In addition to these attributes, you could have specified that the data of a column be `ReadOnly`, and could have hidden the column with a `Visible` property. You can find the descriptions of other attributes and their values in the `Components Catalog` file you downloaded from the GDK page of the Groove DevZone.

5. Your completed `DataViewerView` block is as follows:

```
<g:DataViewerView Default="True" Name="Main">
   <g:DataViewerColumn Label="Question" DataType="String"
➥ Name="Question" Width="18%"/>
   <g:DataViewerColumn Label="Answer1" DataType="String"
➥ Name="Answer1" Width="16%"/>
   <g:DataViewerColumn Label="Answer2" DataType="String"
➥ Name="Answer2" Width="17%"/>
   <g:DataViewerColumn Label="Answer3" DataType="String"
➥ Name="Answer3" Width="16%"/>
   <g:DataViewerColumn Label="Answer4" DataType="String"
➥ Name="Answer4" Width="17%"/>
   <g:DataViewerColumn Label="CorrectAnswer" DataType="String"
➥ Name="CorrectAnswer" Width="16%"/>
</g:DataViewerView>
```

   Finish entering it into the Property Value space in Tool Creator and click Set Element.

6. Select the `Sorts` property. Sorting won't be too valuable for you in this application. You'll just create an ascending order sort for each of the columns. Enter this code into the Property Value space:

```
<g:DataViewerSort DataType="String" Column="Question"
➥ Order="Ascending" Name="ByQuestion"/>
<g:DataViewerSort DataType="String" Column="Answer1"
➥ Order="Ascending" Name="Answer1"/>
<g:DataViewerSort DataType="String" Column="Answer2"
➥ Order="Ascending" Name="Answer2"/>
<g:DataViewerSort DataType="String" Column="Answer3"
➥ Order="Ascending" Name="Answer3"/>
<g:DataViewerSort DataType="String" Column="Answer4"
➥ Order="Ascending" Name="Answer4"/>
<g:DataViewerSort DataType="String" Column="CorrectAnswer"
➥ Order="Ascending" Name="CorrectAnswer"/>
```

   Be sure to click the Set Element button when you have finished entering the code in order to write the code into the component source.

7. Click the last of the provided properties, `GridLineDescriptor`. As the name implies, the `GridLineDescriptor` property controls how the gridlines are displayed in the `DataViewer` component. Grid lines can be shown or hidden, can use different line colors and patterns, and can display horizontal or vertical grid lines, or both. We'll use this:

```
<g:DataViewerGridLineDescriptor Visible="0"
➥ Color="#DCDCDC" Style="Solid" Orientation="Both"/>
```

   Enter this code into the Property Value space with `GridLineDescriptor` chosen as the property, and click the Set Element button. `GridLineDescriptor` is the last of the properties you can add to your tool through the Properties tab. You will continue from here entering your properties directly into the source through the Component Source tab.

8. Your QuestionDataViewer will display text as RichText, so you are going to need to associate a RichTextPainter and a RichTextEditor with your DataViewer control. The properties you will enter, Painters and Editors, refer to RichTextPainter and RichTextEditor components that you will be instantiating in a ComponentGroup that you will construct a little later. Both take two attributes. The ElementTag attribute describes the type of content handled by the painter or editor, and the Handler attribute lists the name of the component defined in the DataViewer component group that handles the painting or editing of that type. For now, select the Component Source tab, and add the following code below the last property of the PropertyList:

```
<g:Property Name="Painters">
   <g:PropertyValue>
      <g:Painter ElementTag=
➥"urn:groove.net:RichText" Handler="RichTextPainter"/>
   </g:PropertyValue>
 </g:Property>

<g:Property Name="Editors">
   <g:PropertyValue>
      <g:Editor ElementTag=
➥"urn:groove.net:RichText" Handler="RichTextEditor"/>
   </g:PropertyValue>
</g:Property>
```

   Be sure to click the Save button.

9. In addition to the properties we've just discussed, DataViewer has four optional properties. It has properties for allowing single or multiple selection of records and for allowing in-place editing on non-read-only columns. DataViewer can also be set to move focus to the last record when the view is loaded, and can use bullets to indicate records that have no children. You will not be using any of the last three, but you will use SingleSelection; so paste the optional property below the last property of the PropertyList and click Save:

```
<g:Property Name="SingleSelection" Value="True"/>
```

10. The DataViewer needs component connections to two components, a ModelGlue component and a ColumnHeaders component, both of which you will instantiate later. A ModelGlue component consists of wrappers around the RecordSetEngine and ToolCollectionsComponent. The glue provides script access to methods to access and manipulate indexed, persistent record storage. ModelGlue provides the application logic for record storage access. ColumnHeaders is the name of a Header component you will be adding shortly. A Header component is used by DataViewer to display columns. Here is the code for your component connections. Replace the <g:ComponentConnections/> tag in the Component Source tab with this:

```
<g:ComponentConnections>
  <g:Connection ConnectionID="0" Name="ModelGlue"/>
  <g:Connection ConnectionID="1" Name="ColumnHeaders"/>
</g:ComponentConnections>
```

Be sure to save.

11. You'll include a component group to hold your RichTextPainter and RichTextEditor components. RichTextPainter is used to render rich text in Groove, and RichTextEditor is used to edit it. RichTextEditor has three properties to allow cell pasting, to provide different background styles, and to show or hide a border. Go to the Component Source tab of Tool Creator and enter this code after the component connections, and then save:

```
<g:ComponentGroup>
   <g:Component Name="RichTextPainter">
      <g:ComponentResource FingerprintID="Groove"
➥ URL="http://components.groove.net/Groove/Components/Root.osd?
➥Package=net.groove.Groove.ToolComponents.GrooveTextTools_DLL&amp;
➥Version=0&amp;Factory=TextPainter"/>
   </g:Component>

   <g:Component Name="RichTextEditor">
      <g:ComponentResource FingerprintID="Groove"
➥ URL="http://components.groove.net/Groove/Components/Root.osd?
➥Package=net.groove.Groove.ToolComponents.GrooveTextTools_DLL&amp;
➥Version=0,3&amp;Factory=TextView2"/>
      <g:PropertyList Version="1">
         <g:Property Value="true" Name="CellPaste"/>
         <g:Property Value="transparent" Name="BackStyle"/>
         <g:Property Value="false" Name="BorderVisible"/>
      </g:PropertyList>
   </g:Component>
</g:ComponentGroup>
```

This completes the creation of your DataViewer code, but you still need to do more before you can look at your new layout.

DataViewer components work in conjunction with three other components. All must be present for DataViewer to work. The three are ModelGlue, ToolCollectionsComponent, and a RecordSetEngine. You will also need the ColumnHeaders component you referenced in the DataViewer component connections.

The ModelGlue Component

You'll start with the ModelGlue component. ModelGlue is not included in the list of components to be added, so follow these steps:

1. Return to the Info tab and add a ComponentPlaceholder. Rename it **ModelGlue**. Click the Component Added to Delegate Connections check box.

2. In the Component Source tab, add **Groove** as the `ComponentResource Fingerprint ID` attribute value, and enter the following into the URL attribute:

```
"http://components.groove.net/Groove/Components/Root.osd?
➥Package=net.groove.Groove.ToolComponents.GrooveDataViewerTool_DLL&amp;
➥Version=0&amp;Factory=ModelGlue"
```

   Make sure that there is no whitespace in the quoted strings or extra returns in the code. Click Save.

3. The `ModelGlue` component takes two connections: one to the `Collection` component that you haven't created yet, and one to the `RecordSetEngine`:

```
<g:ComponentConnections>
   <g:Connection ConnectionID="0" Name="Collection"/>
   <g:Connection ConnectionID="1" Name="RecordSetEngine"/>
</g:ComponentConnections>
```

   Replace the `<g:ComponentConnections/>` tag in the Component Source tab of the Tool Creator with the preceding code and click Save. You have now created a `ModelGlue` component.

The `ColumnHeaders` Component

Next, you'll add your `ColumnHeaders` component. Return to the Info tab and find Header in the drop-down list; click Add. Rename the component **ColumnHeaders**. No changes need to be made to this component.

The `ToolCollectionsComponent` Component

The next component you will need is a `ToolCollectionsComponent`. The `ToolCollections Component` is used to control the lifetime of the collection of records that it wraps. It is used by the `RecordSetEngine` and `ModelGlue` components to display specific records. Find `ToolCollection` in the drop-down list and click Add. Rename the component **Collection**. The only property for this component is a required `EngineDesc` tag, and Tool Creator fills this in automatically.

The `RecordSetEngine` Component

You also need a `RecordSetEngine` to store your questions and answers. Here are the necessary steps:

1. Select `RecordSetEngine` from the drop-down list and click Add. Click the Component Added to Delegate Connections checkbox.

2. In the Properties tab, select `ClassInfoList`. It has already been filled in, but change the `Name` attribute to **Name="urn:groove.net:TriviaQuizRecord"** so that the `RecordSetEngine` knows that your records are defined in a custom schema. Be sure to click Set Element.

3. The RecordSetEngine needs to connect to the Collection component, so click on the Connections tab, find Collections in the drop-down list, and click the Apply Connections to Component button.

Viewing the Layout

You now have all the components sited and interconnected, so you can see your new layout. You'll need to switch the view container's default view to the QuestionInputLayout:

1. Select the TriviaQuizViewContainer and click the Connections tab.
2. Find QuestionInputLayout in the top pull-down list, and click the Apply Connections to Component button.
3. Save the changes by clicking the Save to File button on the toolbar.

When you add the tool to your Development Space, you can see the question input area, the buttons, and the data viewer area.

Changing Screens

Now you are ready to activate your buttons on the Welcome layout, but you first have to make sure that you have created connections from your layouts and buttons to the glue code:

1. Return to the Info tab of Tool Creator and make sure that the Component Added to Delegate Connections check box is checked for QuestionInput, Answer1Input, Answer2Input, Answer3Input, Answer4Input, CorrectAnswerInput, EnterQuestionButton, and ReturnButton.
2. Connect the ModelGlue, RecordSetEngine, and QuestionDataViewer components so that your database of questions, and your mechanism to view its records, is connected to your glue code.
3. Save this file as TriviaQuiz.tpl.

You are now finished with Tool Creator, so open TriviaQuiz.tpl in WordPad.

Check the ComponentConnections section of your code at the top of your delegate. The finished connections for the glue component should look like this:

```
<g:ComponentConnections>
   <g:Connection ConnectionID="0" Name="TriviaQuizViewContainer"/>
   <g:Connection ConnectionID="1" Name="QuestionLabel"/>
   <g:Connection ConnectionID="2" Name="AnswerAButton"/>
   <g:Connection ConnectionID="3" Name="AnswerALabel"/>
   <g:Connection ConnectionID="4" Name="AnswerBButton"/>
   <g:Connection ConnectionID="5" Name="AnswerBLabel"/>
```

```
    <g:Connection ConnectionID="6" Name="AnswerCButton"/>
    <g:Connection ConnectionID="7" Name="AnswerCLabel"/>
    <g:Connection ConnectionID="8" Name="AnswerDButton"/>
    <g:Connection ConnectionID="9" Name="AnswerDLabel"/>
    <g:Connection ConnectionID="10" Name="ElapsedTimeListBoxControl"/>
    <g:Connection ConnectionID="11" Name="NextQuestionButton"/>
    <g:Connection ConnectionID="12" Name="GoEnterButton"/>
    <g:Connection ConnectionID="13" Name="GoPlayButton"/>
    <g:Connection ConnectionID="14" Name="QuestionInput"/>
    <g:Connection ConnectionID="15" Name="Answer1Input"/>
    <g:Connection ConnectionID="16" Name="Answer2Input"/>
    <g:Connection ConnectionID="17" Name="Answer3Input"/>
    <g:Connection ConnectionID="18" Name="Answer4Input"/>
    <g:Connection ConnectionID="19" Name="CorrectAnswerInput"/>
    <g:Connection ConnectionID="20" Name="EnterQuestionButton"/>
    <g:Connection ConnectionID="21" Name="EditQuestionButton"/>
    <g:Connection ConnectionID="22" Name="SaveEditsButton"/>
    <g:Connection ConnectionID="23" Name="RemoveQuestionButton"/>
    <g:Connection ConnectionID="24" Name="ReturnButton"/>
    <g:Connection ConnectionID="25" Name="QuestionDataViewer"/>
    <g:Connection ConnectionID="26" Name="ModelGlue"/>
    <g:Connection ConnectionID="27" Name="RecordSetEngine"/>

</g:ComponentConnections>
```

If any connections are missing, add them so that your code matches the preceding code.

Now that your components are connected, you can write some glue code to change the layouts. Enter this function at the end of your glue code:

```
function GoPlayButton_OnCommand(i_pIUICommand)
    {
        try
        {
            TriviaQuizViewContainer.LayoutByName = "TriviaQuizLayout";
            ChangeLabels();
        }
        catch(objError)
        {
            showError(objError);
        }
    }
```

Your `showError` function displays the error. Here's the code:

```
function showError(objError)
{
    var strErrMsg;
```

```
    strErrMsg = "Error #" + objError.number + "\n";
    strErrMsg += objError.description;
    GrooveDebugFunctions.Assert(false, strErrMsg);
}
```

Put this utility code at the end of the glue code.

`LayoutByName` is a `ViewContainer` property. When you set its value to `TriviaQuizLayout`, the `ViewContainer` immediately uses that layout. You can have only one layout at a time.

Similarly, the `GoEnterButton` code should look like this:

```
function GoEnterButton_OnCommand(i_pIUICommand)
  {
     try
     {
        TriviaQuizViewContainer.LayoutByName = "QuestionInputLayout";
     }
     catch(objError)
     {
        showError(objError);
     }
  }
```

Put it below the `GoPlayButton` code.

`ReturnButton` code can take the same form, except that you should use `ReturnButton`, of course, and `WelcomeLayout` for the property value. Put the `ReturnButton` code below the `GoEnterButton`.

You will be modifying your HTML table layout for the Trivia screen a little later, but you can easily place your return button in the layout so that you can test your navigation buttons. Replace the last row of the `TriviaQuizLayout` with this code:

```
<TR>
   <TD COLSPAN="3" HEIGHT="60">
      NextQuestionButton
   </TD>
   <TD/>
   <TD COLSPAN="3" HEIGHT="60">
      ReturnButton
   </TD>
   <TD/>
</TR>
```

Save the file by clicking the Save to File button on the toolbar, and then add the tool to your Development Space. You can now navigate easily among the three screens.

Code for Entering Questions

Next, you are going to write some glue code to support your Enter Question button on the Question Input screen. Enter the code just below the return button function. First make sure that the `QuestionInput` edit control has text in it; if it doesn't, just return:

```
function EnterQuestionButton_OnCommand(i_pIUICommand)
   {
      if ("" == QuestionInput.Text)
         return;
```

You must remember that you are working on a database with multiple users. To prevent two or more users from trying to change a record simultaneously, you will perform any kind of record read/write operations inside a transaction:

```
// Begin the read/write transaction
      // Open a transaction on the telespace to freeze properties
      var pITelespace = PropertyList.OpenProperty(PROPERTY_TELESPACE);
      var pITransaction = pITelespace.OpenTransaction(false);
```

Next, you'll create a record to give to the `RecordSetEngine`. The parameter points to the `TriviaQuizRecord` that you defined in your schema, but to further protect your data, you need to do this inside a `try/catch` block:

```
try
{
   // Create a record to give to add to the RecordSetEngine
var pIRecord =
➥ ModelGlue.CreateRecord("urn:groove.net:TriviaQuizRecord");
   pITransaction.Commit();
}
catch (objError)
{
   pITransaction.Abort();
         showError(objError);
}
```

After you have a record, you can set each of the fields individually. Set each field in turn to the contents of the input controls. The changes to the code are in bold:

```
try
      {
         // Create a record to give to add to the RecordSetEngine
         var pIRecord =
ModelGlue.CreateRecord("urn:groove.net:TriviaQuizRecord");
         // Set the fields in the record
         pIRecord.SetField("Question", QuestionInput.Text);
         pIRecord.SetField("Answer1", Answer1Input.Text);
```

```
        pIRecord.SetField("Answer2", Answer2Input.Text);
        pIRecord.SetField("Answer3", Answer3Input.Text);
        pIRecord.SetField("Answer4", Answer4Input.Text);
        pIRecord.SetField("CorrectAnswer", CorrectAnswerInput.Text);

        pITransaction.Commit();
    }
catch (objError)
    {
        pITransaction.Abort();
        showError(objError);
    }
```


Having defined its fields, you can now add the record to the database inside the same `try/catch` block:

```
// Add the record
   ModelGlue.AddRecord(pIRecord);
```

After completing the transactions, reset your input controls:

```
// Reset the Question input text
   QuestionInput.Text = "";
   Answer1Input.Text = "";
   Answer2Input.Text = "";
   Answer3Input.Text = "";
   Answer4Input.Text = "";
   CorrectAnswerInput.Text = "";
```

Your completed `EnterQuestionButton` code should look like this:

```
function EnterQuestionButton_OnCommand(i_pIUICommand)
{
   if ("" == QuestionInput.Text)
   return;
   // Begin the write transaction
   // Open a transaction on the telespace to freeze properties
   var pITelespace = PropertyList.OpenProperty(PROPERTY_TELESPACE);
   var pITransaction = pITelespace.OpenTransaction(false);



   //Put the operation in a try/catch block
   try
   {
   // Create a record to give to add to the RecordSetEngine
   var pIRecord = ModelGlue.CreateRecord("urn:groove.net:TriviaQuizRecord");
      // Set the fields in the record
      pIRecord.SetField("Question", QuestionInput.Text);
```

```
        pIRecord.SetField("Answer1", Answer1Input.Text);
        pIRecord.SetField("Answer2", Answer2Input.Text);
        pIRecord.SetField("Answer3", Answer3Input.Text);
        pIRecord.SetField("Answer4", Answer4Input.Text);
        pIRecord.SetField("CorrectAnswer", CorrectAnswerInput.Text);
        // Add the record
        ModelGlue.AddRecord(pIRecord);
        pITransaction.Commit();
    }
        catch (objError)
    {
            pITransaction.Abort();
            showError(objError);
}
    // Reset the Question input text
    QuestionInput.Text = "";
    Answer1Input.Text = "";
    Answer2Input.Text = "";
    Answer3Input.Text = "";
    Answer4Input.Text = "";
    CorrectAnswerInput.Text = "";
}
```

Populating Edit Controls

Now, let's use your `EditQuestionButton` to populate those same edit controls with an existing record. Enter the code below the `EnterQuestionButton` function. When a user selects a record to edit, you would like to know which record ID he or she selected. Fortunately, `IGrooveDataViewer2` has an operation, `GetIDOfFocusRow()`, that will return the ID of the selected row. The `RecordSetEngine` has an operation that returns a record from a record ID.

When you have the record, you can use the `IGrooveRecord` operation `OpenField` to open each field. So when you know the ID of the record, you can put each field of the record into the appropriate edit control. Crashes and database corruption can occur if two people are trying to access the same record at the same time, so you'll need to open a transaction to protect the data and wrap your code in a `try/catch` block. You'll also need to add a global variable to the top of your glue code, `currentRecordID`, to keep track of the record you have in the editing fields. Your `EditQuestionButton` code should look like this:

```
function EditQuestionButton_OnCommand(i_pIUICommand)
    {
        // Begin the read transaction
// Open a transaction on the telespace to freeze properties
        var pITelespace = PropertyList.OpenProperty(PROPERTY_TELESPACE);
        var pITransaction = pITelespace.OpenTransaction(true);
```

```
      //Put the operation in a try/catch block
      try
      {
         var RecordID = QuestionDataViewer.GetIDOfFocusRow();
         if (RecordSetEngine.HasRecord(RecordID)) {
            var pIRecord = RecordSetEngine.OpenRecord(RecordID);
            var questionField = pIRecord.OpenField("Question");
            var answer1Field = pIRecord.OpenField("Answer1");
            var answer2Field = pIRecord.OpenField("Answer2");
            var answer3Field = pIRecord.OpenField("Answer3");
            var answer4Field = pIRecord.OpenField("Answer4");
           var correctAnswerField = pIRecord.OpenField("CorrectAnswer");
         }

         pITransaction.EndRead();
catch (objError)
   {
         pITransaction.Abort();
         showError(objError);
}

QuestionInput.Text = questionField;
      Answer1Input.text = answer1Field;
      Answer2Input.text = answer2Field;
      Answer3Input.text = answer3Field;
      Answer4Input.text = answer4Field;
      CorrectAnswerInpput.text = correctAnswerField;
      currentRecordID = RecordID;
   }
```

Now you can write the code for your `SaveEditsButton`. Put the `SaveEditsButton` code right after the `EditQuestionButton` function. You will use code similar to that for your `EnterQuestionsButton` code, except that after you have created the record and populated its fields with your data, you are going to replace the old record with the new one. You have stored the old record ID in your global, so your modified line looks like this:

```
ModelGlue.ReplaceRecord(currentRecordID, pIRecord);
```

Again, complete this operation in a transaction and within a `try/catch` block:

```
function SaveEditsButton_OnCommand(i_pIUICommand)
{
   if ("" == QuestionInput.Text)
   return;
   // Begin the read/write transaction
   // Open a transaction on the telespace to freeze properties
   var pITelespace = PropertyList.OpenProperty(PROPERTY_TELESPACE);
   var pITransaction = pITelespace.OpenTransaction(false);
```

```
   //Put the operation in a try/catch block
   try
   {
   // Create a record to give to add to the RecordSetEngine
   var pIRecord = ModelGlue.CreateRecord("urn:groove.net:TriviaQuizRecord");
      // Set the fields in the record
      pIRecord.SetField("Question", QuestionInput.Text);
      pIRecord.SetField("Answer1", Answer1Input.Text);
      pIRecord.SetField("Answer2", Answer2Input.Text);
      pIRecord.SetField("Answer3", Answer3Input.Text);
      pIRecord.SetField("Answer4", Answer4Input.Text);
      pIRecord.SetField("CorrectAnswer", CorrectAnswerInput.Text);
      // Replace the record
      ModelGlue.ReplaceRecord(currentRecordID, pIRecord);
      pITransaction.Commit();
}
      catch (objError)
   {
         pITransaction.Abort();
         showError(objError);
}

   // Reset the Question input text
   QuestionInput.Text = "";
   Answer1Input.Text = "";
   Answer2Input.Text = "";
   Answer3Input.Text = "";
   Answer4Input.Text = "";
   CorrectAnswerInput.Text = "";
   //Reset global
   currentRecordID = "";
}
```

Right now, you want to check to see whether `QuestionInput.Text` is blank, but you don't want any of the fields to be blank. You'll write a helper function called `FieldIsBlank()` and then call it from your button code. Enter the `FieldIsBlank` code below the `ShowError` function near the end of the glue code. `FieldIsBlank()` is just an extended `OR` test:

```
function FieldIsBlank()
{
   if(""==QuestionInput.Text|
      ""==Answer1Input.Text|
      ""==Answer2Input.Text|
      ""==Answer3Input.Text|
      ""==Answer4Input.Text|
```

```
      ""==CorrectAnswerInput.Text){
      return true;
      }
return false;
}
```

You can now replace

```
   if ("" == QuestionInput.Text)
   return;
```

with

```
if (FieldIsBlank()) return;.
```

in both the `EnterQuestionButton` and the `SaveEditsButton` functions.

You don't really want to just abort the operation without telling your user why, so you need to look at `GrooveMessageBox`. You'll develop a helper function to alert the user. You'll supply information on what happened and why in the form of two parameters: `ActionName` and `error`.

You need to know which account in the telespace you're talking to so that you can open a window there. Then you'll define a top-level window in that account for your message box component to open in.

After your concatenated message, you need to supply the title of the window, the message box style (in this case, a window with an OK button), and the icon you want displayed:

```
function DisplayError(actionName, error)
{
   var Account = OpenAccountFromPropertyList(PropertyList);
   var Window = UIPropertyList.OpenProperty(UIPROPERTY_TOP_LEVEL_WINDOW);
   App.GrooveMessageBox(Window, Account, "Unable to " + ActionName +
➥ " because of the following error: \n" +
➥ error, "Error", GrooveMessageBoxStyle_OK, GrooveMessageBoxIcon_Error);
}
```

Next you need to add two local string variables to your calling functions, `ActionName` and `error`. You can then call your function:

```
if (FieldIsBlank())
   {
   var actionName="enter this record";
   var error="one of the fields is blank";
   DisplayError(actionName, error);
   return;
}
```

Similarly you can check to make sure that your `CorrectAnswerNumber` is between 1 and 4:

```
//check correctAnswer range
//cast text to num
var answerNum=parseInt(CorrectAnswerInput.Text);
//if answerNum is not a number, make it one.
if(isNaN(answerNum)) answerNum=5;
if (answerNum < 1 |answerNum > 4)
{
var actionName="enter this record";
   var error="correct answer not 1 through 4";
   DisplayError(actionName, error);
   return;
  }
```

Also add this error-checking code to your `EnterQuestionButton` function right after the `FieldIsBlank` block.

Your finished `SaveEditsButton` function should look like this:

```
function SaveEditsButton_OnCommand(i_pIUICommand)
{
   if (FieldIsBlank())
   {
      var actionName="enter this record";
      var error="one of the fields is blank";
      DisplayError(actionName, error);
      return;
   }
//check correctAnswer range
   //cast text to num
   var answerNum=parseInt(CorrectAnswerInput.Text);
   //if answerNum is not a number, make it one.
if(isNaN(answerNum)) answerNum=5;
   if (answerNum < 1 |answerNum > 4)
   {
      var actionName="enter this record";
      var error="correct answer not 1 through 4";
      DisplayError(actionName, error);
      return;
     }
   // Begin the write transaction
   // Open a transaction on the telespace to freeze properties
   var pITelespace = PropertyList.OpenProperty(PROPERTY_TELESPACE);
   var pITransaction = pITelespace.OpenTransaction(false);
// Create a record to give to add to the RecordSetEngine
   var pIRecord = ModelGlue.CreateRecord("urn:groove.net:TriviaQuizRecord");
```

```
    //Put the operation in a try/catch block
    try
    {
         // Set the fields in the record
       pIRecord.SetField("Question", QuestionInput.Text);
       pIRecord.SetField("Answer1", Answer1Input.Text);
       pIRecord.SetField("Answer2", Answer2Input.Text);
       pIRecord.SetField("Answer3", Answer3Input.Text);
       pIRecord.SetField("Answer4", Answer4Input.Text);
       pIRecord.SetField("CorrectAnswer", CorrectAnswerInput.Text);
       // Add the record
ModelGlue.ReplaceRecord(currentRecordID, pIRecord);
       pITransaction.Commit();
    }
       catch (objError)
    {
          pITransaction.Abort();
          showError(objError);
}
    // Reset the Question input text
    QuestionInput.Text = "";
    Answer1Input.Text = "";
    Answer2Input.Text = "";
    Answer3Input.Text = "";
    Answer4Input.Text = "";
    CorrectAnswerInput.Text = "";
    currentRecordID = "";
}
```


Removing Records

Next, you'll need to write the code for your `RemoveRecordButton`. It is similar to that for your `EditQuestionButton`, and you'll use the same mechanism to identify the selected record. You will again protect the database with a transaction and do your business in a `try/catch` block. In this case, your business is to identify the record number, retrieve the record, and then remove it from the `RecordSetEngine`. Enter this code below the `SaveEditsButton` function:

```
function RemoveQuestionButton_OnCommand(i_pIUICommand)
{
   // Begin the read/write transaction
   // Open a transaction on the telespace to freeze properties
   var pITelespace = PropertyList.OpenProperty(PROPERTY_TELESPACE);
   var pITransaction = pITelespace.OpenTransaction(false);

   //Put the operation in a try/catch block
try
```

```
        {
            var RecordID = QuestionDataViewer.GetIDOfFocusRow();
            var pIRecord = RecordSetEngine.OpenRecord(RecordID);
            RecordSetEngine.RemoveRecord(RecordID);
            pITransaction.Commit();
        }
        catch (e)
        {
            pITransaction.Abort();
        }
}
```

This completes the code for your Enter Questions screen. Now you need to make some serious changes to your `TriviaQuiz` code on the Play Trivia side.

The Play Trivia Screen

Before you get too far into the coding of your `RecordSetEngine`, let's do some cosmetics on the Play Trivia screen itself.

A Sleeker Interface

First, you will be rewriting the `TriviaQuizLayout`. Let's remove the Our Trivia Game static text and replace it with the graphic you used on the Welcome screen. You can use the same `TriviaGraphic` component, but its height is 100, so you'll have to change the `HEIGHT` attribute of the `TD` tag to `110`. You will also add a `rightPad` value of `163` so that the graphic lines up with the graphic on the Welcome page. You need to change the code in `TriviaQuizLayout` from

```
<TD COLSPAN="4" HEIGHT="30">
   TitleLabel
</TD>
```

to

```
<TD COLSPAN="4" HEIGHT="110" RightPad="163">
   TriviaGraphic
</TD>
```

Next, you will combine the function of the button and static text components for the questions. Because buttons have label properties, you can just as easily manipulate the button labels as you can the static text labels. Doing so, and deleting the static text, will give you a much cleaner interface. To do this, you first need to combine the button space, the spacer area, and the static text space in the layout. Change your first answer row in `TriviaQuizLayout` from

```
<TR>
   <TD HEIGHT="60"/>
   <TD>
      AnswerAButton
   </TD>
   <TD/>
   <TD>
      AnswerALabel
   </TD>
   <TD/>
   <TD>
      AnswerCButton
   </TD>
   <TD/>
   <TD>
   AnswerCLabel
   </TD>
 </TR>
```

to

```
<TR>
   <TD HEIGHT="60"/>
   <TD COLSPAN="3">
      AnswerAButton
   </TD>
   <TD/>
   <TD COLSPAN="3">
      AnswerCButton
   </TD>
</TR>
```

Do the same for the second answer row.

Finally, you will be changing the type of control you use to display the elapsed time, so search and replace all instances of `ElapsedTimeListControl` to `ElapsedTimeDisplay` in the `TriviaGraphics.tpl` file, including the one in the layout. The altered layout should now match the following:

```
<g:Component Name="TriviaQuizLayout">
   <g:ComponentResource FingerprintID="Groove"
➥ URL="http://components.groove.net/Groove/Components/Root.osd?
➥ Package=
➥ net.groove.Groove.ToolComponents.GrooveCommonComponents_DLL&amp;
➥Version=0&amp;Factory=HTMLTableLayout"/>
 ➥Factory=HTMLTableLayout"/>
```

```
<!-- Layout Property List -->
<g:PropertyList Version="1">
   <g:Property Name="Layout">
      <g:PropertyValue>
       <TABLE CELLPADDING="2">
         <TR>
           <TD COLSPAN="4" HEIGHT="110" RightPad="163">
               TriviaGraphic
           </TD>
           <TD WIDTH="2%"/>
           <TD WIDTH="10%"/>
           <TD WIDTH="2%"/>
           <TD WIDTH="35%"/>
         </TR>
         <TR>
           <TD HEIGHT="30" WIDTH="6%"/>
          <TD WIDTH="10%"/>
           <TD WIDTH="2%"/>
           <TD WIDTH="35%"/>
           <TD/>
           <TD/>
           <TD/>
           <TD/>
         </TR>
         <TR>
           <TD/>
           <TD COLSPAN="7" HEIGHT="30">
               QuestionLabel
           </TD>
         </TR>
         <TR>
           <TD HEIGHT="30"/>
           <TD/>
           <TD/>
           <TD/>
           <TD/>
           <TD/>
           <TD/>
           <TD/>
         </TR>
         <TR>
           <TD HEIGHT="60"/>
           <TD COLSPAN="3">
               AnswerAButton
           </TD>
           <TD/>
```

```
  <TD COLSPAN="3">
      AnswerCButton
  </TD>
</TR>
<TR>
  <TD HEIGHT="30"/>
  <TD/>
  <TD/>
  <TD/>
  <TD/>
  <TD/>
  <TD/>
  <TD/>
</TR>
<TR>
  <TD HEIGHT="60"/>
  <TD COLSPAN="3">
AnswerBButton
  </TD>
  <TD/>
  <TD COLSPAN="3">
      AnswerDButton
  </TD>
</TR>
<TR>
  <TD HEIGHT="30"/>
  <TD/>
  <TD/>
  <TD/>
  <TD/>
  <TD/>
  <TD/>
  <TD/>
</TR>
<TR>
  <TD HEIGHT="60"/>
  <TD>
      ElapsedTimeLabel
  </TD>
  <TD/>
  <TD>
      ElapsedTimeDisplay
  </TD>
  <TD/>
  <TD/>
  <TD/>
```

```
                    <TD/>
                  </TR>
                  <TR>
                    <TD HEIGHT="30"/>
                    <TD/>
                    <TD/>
                    <TD/>
                    <TD/>
                    <TD/>
                   <TD/>
                    <TD/>
                  </TR>
                  <TR>
                    <TD COLSPAN="3" HEIGHT="60">
                        NextQuestionButton
                    </TD>
                    <TD/>
                    <TD COLSPAN="3" HEIGHT="60">
                        ReturnButton
                    </TD>
                    <TD/>
                  </TR>
                </TABLE>
            </g:PropertyValue>
        </g:Property>
    </g:PropertyList>
</g:Component>
```

Next, you need to change the type of the answer buttons to `StandardButton`, and the value of the label to an empty string, like this:

```
<g:Component Name="AnswerAButton">
    <g:ComponentResource FingerprintID="Groove"
➥  URL="http://components.groove.net/Groove/Root.osd?
➥Package=net.groove.Groove.ToolComponents.GrooveCommonComponents_DLL&amp;
➥Version=0&amp;Factory=Button"/>
        <g:PropertyList Version="1">
            <g:Property Name="Style" Value="StandardButton"/>
            <g:Property Name="OverrideLabelPosition" Value="Center"/>
            <g:Property Name="Label" Value=""/>
            <g:Property Name="Tooltip" Value=""/>
            <g:Property Name="Mnemonic" Value="ALT+A"/>
        </g:PropertyList>
</g:Component>
```

Do this for each answer button.

Next you'll change your elapsed time display. In `TriviaQuiz3.tpl` you displayed the time for each question and the total elapsed time in the same control. In `TriviaQuiz`, you will display only the time for each question, so you will display only one value. You could use an edit control, but because you really don't want the value to be editable, you'll change the list control to a static text component and make a few changes in how the static text appears on your screen. Locate the `ElapsedTimeDisplay` component now.

You need to change the factory from `ListBox` to `Static` and replace the properties. You should use `Header` for the style, which will bold the time, and use a white background. The component should now look like this:


```
<g:Component Name="ElapsedTimeDisplay">
   <g:ComponentResource FingerprintID="Groove"
➥ URL="http://components.groove.net/Groove/Components/Root.osd?
➥Package=net.groove.Groove.ToolComponents.GrooveCommonComponents_DLL&amp;
➥Version=0&amp;Factory=Static"/>
   <g:PropertyList Version="1">
      <g:Property Name="Label" Value=""/>
      <g:Property Name="Style" Value="Header"/>
      <g:Property Name="BackgroundColor" Value="#FFFFFF"/>
   </g:PropertyList>
</g:Component>
```

Now you need to go through your code and eliminate the unused components. Find and erase `AnswerALabel`, `AnswerBLabel`, `AnswerCLabel`, and `AnswerDLabel`. Continue on to the component connections in your glue code and eliminate their connections as well. Renumber the connections. Connection numbers and their order are not significant. These connections could be numbered 0, 2, 5, 3, but in the interest of clean code, you should number them consecutively. Your component connections element now should look like this:

```
<g:ComponentConnections>
   <g:Connection ConnectionID="0" Name="TriviaQuizViewContainer"/>
   <g:Connection ConnectionID="1" Name="QuestionLabel"/>
   <g:Connection ConnectionID="2" Name="AnswerAButton"/>
   <g:Connection ConnectionID="3" Name="AnswerBButton"/>
   <g:Connection ConnectionID="4" Name="AnswerCButton"/>
   <g:Connection ConnectionID="5" Name="AnswerDButton"/>
   <g:Connection ConnectionID="6" Name="ElapsedTimeDisplay"/>
   <g:Connection ConnectionID="7" Name="NextQuestionButton"/>
   <g:Connection ConnectionID="8" Name="GoEnterButton"/>
   <g:Connection ConnectionID="9" Name="GoPlayButton"/>
   <g:Connection ConnectionID="10" Name="QuestionInput"/>
   <g:Connection ConnectionID="11" Name="Answer1Input"/>
   <g:Connection ConnectionID="12" Name="Answer2Input"/>
   <g:Connection ConnectionID="13" Name="Answer3Input"/>
```

```
    <g:Connection ConnectionID="14" Name="Answer4Input"/>
    <g:Connection ConnectionID="15" Name="CorrectAnswerInput"/>
    <g:Connection ConnectionID="16" Name="EnterQuestionButton"/>
    <g:Connection ConnectionID="17" Name="EditQuestionButton"/>
    <g:Connection ConnectionID="18" Name="ReturnButton"/>
    <g:Connection ConnectionID="19" Name="ModelGlue"/>
    <g:Connection ConnectionID="20" Name="RecordSetEngine"/>
    <g:Connection ConnectionID="21" Name="QuestionDataViewer"/>
    <g:Connection ConnectionID="22" Name="SaveEditsButton"/>
    <g:Connection ConnectionID="23" Name="RemoveQuestionButton"/>
</g:ComponentConnections>
```

For your changes to work with your existing code, you need to change the `ChangeLabels` function in your glue code. Because buttons do not support the `SetText` operation, you have to rewrite your `ChangeLabels` function like this:

```
function ChangeLabels()
   {
      questionNumber = PropertyList.OpenProperty("QuestionNumber");

QuestionLabel.SetText(PropertyList.OpenProperty("Question"+questionNumber));

AnswerAButton.Label=(PropertyList.OpenProperty("Answer"+questionNumber+"a"));

AnswerBButton.Label=(PropertyList.OpenProperty("Answer"+questionNumber+"b"));

AnswerCButton.Label=(PropertyList.OpenProperty("Answer"+questionNumber+"c"));

AnswerDButton.Label=(PropertyList.OpenProperty("Answer"+questionNumber+"d"));
   }
```

In addition, because static components use a `SetText` rather than an `AddItem` operation, you need to change the `Initialize` function, the `ShowElapsedTime` function, the `OnPropertyChanged` function, and the code for the `NextQuestionButton`. Find each instance and change the line from

```
ElapsedTimeDisplay.AddItem( ... )
```

to

```
ElapsedTimeDisplay.SetText( ... ).
```

Find the line in the `OnPropertyChanged` function that reads

```
ElapsedTimeListBoxControl.ResetContent();
```

and replace it with

```
ElapsedTimeDisplay.SetText("");
```

Find the line in the ShowElapsedTime function that reads

```
ElapsedTimeListBoxControl.AddItem(PropertyList.OpenProperty("Time"))
```

and change it to

```
ElapsedTimeDisplay.SetText(PropertyList.OpenProperty("Time"))
```

Save your tool.

You can now replace your tool and it will continue to operate correctly, as it did in TriviaQuiz3, with your cosmetic changes incorporated. Of course, it is still working with the property list rather than the recordset engine, but that change is what you'll do next.

Using the RecordSetEngine to Number the Questions

You now need to associate the record IDs with question numbers. To make that association, you'll write a function that cycles through all the records in your RecordSetEngine and puts their RecordID numbers into an array. The question number will be the position in the array, and the RecordID will be returned.

You'll need to declare the array a global, so add

```
var recordIDArray;
```

to the end of your globals at the start of your glue code.

Let's call your function BuildRecordIDArray. You will create your array at the beginning of the function so that the array gets rebuilt every time the function is called. You'll open an enumeration of record IDs through an operation on the RecordSetEngine and assign it to a variable, RecordIDEnum. Then you will set up a while statement and use the IGroove RecordEnum interface's HasMore() and OpenNext operations. You use the OpenNext method to get the next record ID to add to the array. Enter this block after the last function of your glue code:

```
function BuildRecordIDArray()
{
//Make sure array gets rebuilt each time
recordIDArray = new Array();
var index = 0
var RecordIDEnum = RecordSetEngine.OpenRecordIDEnum();
   while (RecordIDEnum.HasMore()) {
      ARecordID = RecordIDEnum.OpenNext();
      recordIDArray[index] = ARecordID;
      index = index + 1;
   }
}
```

You will need to call the function from two different points in your code: when you first open the tool, and whenever there is a change in the RecordSetEngine. The first condition is covered by your Initialize() function. Before you call the function, though, make sure that there are questions in the RecordSetEngine. There is no use in initializing the array if there are no recordIDs. There is also no use in playing trivia if there are no questions, so you need to disable your GoPlayButton button.

Your Initialize() function now should look like this:

```
function Initialize()
{
   startTime = thisDate.getTime();
if (RecordSetEngine.NumRecords > 0) {
   BuildRecordIDArray()
   }
   else
   {
      GoPlayButton.Enabled="false";
   }
   // Open a read transaction on the telespace to freeze properties
   var pITelespace = PropertyList.OpenProperty(PROPERTY_TELESPACE);
   var pITransaction = pITelespace.OpenTransaction(true);

   // Perform all operations inside of try/catch block so if an
   // error occurs, we can abort transaction (VERY IMPORTANT)
   try
      {
      // Search for already existing records and display
      // them in listbox
      if (PropertyList.PropertyExists("Time"))
         {
         var propertyValue = PropertyList.OpenProperty("Time");

         // Add the property to the listbox
         var Index = ElapsedTimeDisplay.SetText(propertyValue);
         }
      if (PropertyList.PropertyExists("QuestionNumber"))
         {
          ChangeLabels();
         }

      // Commit the transaction (VERY IMPORTANT)
      pITransaction.EndRead();
      }

      catch (objError)
```

```
   {
         pITransaction.Abort();
         showError(objError);
}


}
```

You now need an `OnRecordsetChanged()` function. You will open a read transaction; then, in a `try/catch` block, you'll build or rebuild the `recordIDArray`. Then, you'll enable the play button, unless the change results in an empty `RecordSetEngine`, in which case, you'll disable it. Put this function above the `OnPropertyChanged` function in your glue code:


```
function RecordSetEngine_OnRecordSetChanged
   (
   i_pIRecordSetEngine,
   i_RecordSetChangeType,
   i_pIRecordIDEnum
   )
// Begin the read transaction
   // Open a transaction on the telespace to freeze properties
   var pITelespace = PropertyList.OpenProperty(PROPERTY_TELESPACE);
   var pITransaction = pITelespace.OpenTransaction(true);

{
      try
      {
         BuildRecordIDArray();
         if (RecordSetEngine.NumRecords > 0) {
               GoPlayButton.Enabled="true";
         }
         else
         {
               GoPlayButton.Enabled="false";
         }
      // Commit the transaction (VERY IMPORTANT)
      pITransaction.EndRead();
      }
      catch (objError)
      {
         showError(objError);
         // An exception has occurred, so abort the transaction
         pITransaction.Abort();

      }
}
```

Next, you have to modify your ChangeLabels function. Currently, you set the labels from the property list. You need to set them from the RecordSetEngine. You can leave the setting of the questionNumber global alone. You'll modify it and use it as the index to your array of RecordIDs. You can erase everything else in the function.

Because you are reading records from the record set, you will have to open a transaction on the telespace, and you'll do all of your RecordSetOperations in a try/catch block so that your data remains safe:

```
function ChangeLabels()
{
   questionNumber = PropertyList.OpenProperty("QuestionNumber");
// Open a transaction on the telespace to freeze properties
   var pITelespace = PropertyList.OpenProperty(PROPERTY_TELESPACE);
   var pITransaction = pITelespace.OpenTransaction(true);

   // Perform all operations inside of try/catch block so if an
   // error occurs, we can abort transaction (VERY IMPORTANT)
   try
   {

      //recordIDArray is 0 based
      var indexNumber = questionNumber - 1;

      // Commit the transaction (VERY IMPORTANT)
      pITransaction.EndRead();
   }
   catch (objError)
   {
      showError(objError)
      // An exception has occurred, so abort the transaction
      pITransaction.Abort();
   }

}
```

Then you define a variable called currentRecordID by extracting the recordID in the IndexNumber position of the array. You then use the currentRecordID to pull the record from the recordset engine and assign it to the variable currentRecord.

To help keep the code clean, you'll create a utility function, GetRecordByID, to pull up the right record. Here's that function:

```
function GetRecordByID(i_RecordID)
{
   var Record;
```

```
    if (RecordSetEngine.HasRecord(i_RecordID)) {
        Record = RecordSetEngine.OpenRecord(i_RecordID);
        return Record;
    }
}
```

Put the utility function after the last function in your glue code. Then make the following changes to the `ChangeLabels` code:

```
function ChangeLabels()
{
    questionNumber = PropertyList.OpenProperty("QuestionNumber");

    // Open a transaction on the telespace to freeze properties
    var pITelespace = PropertyList.OpenProperty(PROPERTY_TELESPACE);
    var pITransaction = pITelespace.OpenTransaction(true);

    // Perform all operations inside of try/catch block so if an
    // error occurs, we can abort transaction (VERY IMPORTANT)
    try
    {

        //recordIDArray is 0 based
        var indexNumber = questionNumber - 1;
        var currentRecordID = recordIDArray[indexNumber];
        var currentRecord = GetRecordByID(currentRecordID);

        // Commit the transaction (VERY IMPORTANT)
        pITransaction.EndRead();

    }
    catch (objError)
    {
    showError(objError)
    // An exception has occurred, so abort the transaction
    pITransaction.Abort();
    }

}
```

After you have the record, you can extract the fields and place them in separate variables. You shouldn't set the button labels directly, because you have the telespace locked.

After you've closed the telespace, you can assign your variables to the button labels. You'll also set a global called `currentCorrectAnswer` to hold the right answer for later. Remember to add currentCorrectAnswer to the end of the global variable declarations at the top of the glue code:

```
function ChangeLabels()
{
   questionNumber = PropertyList.OpenProperty("QuestionNumber");
   // Open a read transaction on the telespace to freeze properties
var pITelespace = PropertyList.OpenProperty(PROPERTY_TELESPACE);
   var pITransaction = pITelespace.OpenTransaction(true);

   var indexNumber;
   var currentRecordID;
   var currentRecord;

   var questionText;
   var answerAText;
   var answerBText;
   var answerCText;
   var answerDText;
   var correctAnswer;

   // Perform all operations inside of try/catch block so if an
   // error occurs, we can abort transaction (VERY IMPORTANT)
   try
   {
//recordIDArray is 0 based
      indexNumber = questionNumber - 1;
      currentRecordID = recordIDArray[indexNumber];
      currentRecord = GetRecordByID(currentRecordID);

      questionText=(currentRecord.OpenField("Question"));
      answerAText=(currentRecord.OpenField("Answer1"));
      answerBText=(currentRecord.OpenField("Answer2"));
      answerCText=(currentRecord.OpenField("Answer3"));
      answerDText=(currentRecord.OpenField("Answer4"));
      correctAnswer=(currentRecord.OpenField("CorrectAnswer"));

      // Commit the transaction (VERY IMPORTANT)
      pITransaction.EndRead();
   }
   catch (objError)
   {
   showError(objError)
   // An exception has occurred, so abort the transaction
   pITransaction.Abort();
   }
```

```
   QuestionLabel.SetText(questionText);
   AnswerAButton.Label="A:" + answerAText;
   AnswerBButton.Label="B:" + answerBText;
   AnswerCButton.Label="C:" + answerCText;
   AnswerDButton.Label="D:" + answerDText;
   currentCorrectAnswer=correctAnswer;
}
```

Your `ChangeLabels` code is now complete. Check your code against the preceding listing.

Providing for More Questions

You are currently stopping the game at three questions, because you have defined a global variable called `totalQuestions` and given it a value of `3`. Let's initialize it with no value (`var TotalQuestions;`) and then set it to the number of records in the recordset engine in the `BuildRecordIDArray()` function. That way, you will continue to cycle through questions as long as you have any:

```
function BuildRecordIDArray()
{
//Make sure array gets rebuilt each time
RecordIDArray = new Array();
var index = 0
var RecordIDEnum = RecordSetEngine.OpenRecordIDEnum();
   while (RecordIDEnum.HasMore()) {
      ARecordID = RecordIDEnum.OpenNext();
      recordIDArray[index] = ARecordID;
      index = index + 1;
   }
   totalQuestions = RecordSetEngine.NumRecords;
}
```

Transitioning the Answer Buttons

Now, you need to transition your correct answer mechanism from the `PropertyList` to the `RecordSetEngine`. You change that through the `if` statements in the answer buttons. Let's take `AnswerAButton` as an example. Currently you have

```
function AnswerAButton_OnCommand(i_pIUICommand)
{
if (PropertyList.OpenProperty("CorrectAnswer"+questionNumber)== "a")
   {
      correctFlag = 1;
   }

   UserGuess()
}
```

You gave a value to a currentCorrectAnswer global in ChangeLabels(). You can simply change the if statement:

```
function AnswerAButton_OnCommand(i_pIUICommand)
{
   if (currentCorrectAnswer == "1")
   {
      correctFlag = 1;
   }

   UserGuess()
}
```

You make this change to all the answer buttons, comparing currentCorrectAnswer to "2", "3", and "4".

Improving the Timing

When TriviaQuiz was a one-screen tool, you could start the game's clock in the Initialize() function; however, now your game opens to the Welcome screen, so you have to delete your time initialization from the Initialization function and add it to the GoPlayButton function:

```
function GoPlayButton_OnCommand(i_pIUICommand)
{
   try
   {
      TriviaQuizViewContainer.LayoutByName = "TriviaQuizLayout";
      ChangeLabels();
      var thisDate = new Date();
      startTime = thisDate.getTime();
   }
   catch(objError)
   {
      showError(objError);
   }
}
```

Remove the startTime from the Initialize() function, and the thisDate global variable.

Fixing the Scoring

Now it's time to fix your crummy scoring system. You want to advise the members of the space of the time it took them to finish the quiz, and then reset the game. You should drop the players off at the Welcome screen so that they can decide whether to play again or enter more questions. You'll replace the entire contents of the else statement with two functions—ShowScore() and ResetGame(). Place them after the BuildRecordIDArray() function:

```
function NextQuestionButton_OnCommand(i_pIUICommand)
{
   thisDate = new Date();
   startTime = thisDate.getTime();
   correctFlag = 0;

   var propertyName = "QuestionNumber";
// Open a write transaction on the telespace to freeze properties
   var pITelespace = PropertyList.OpenProperty(PROPERTY_TELESPACE);
   var pITransaction = pITelespace.OpenTransaction(false);

   // Perform all operations inside of try/catch block so if an
   // error occurs, we can abort transaction (VERY IMPORTANT)
   try
   {

      var propertyValue = PropertyList.OpenProperty(propertyName);
      //Increment the question number
      var newValue = parseInt(propertyValue) + 1;
      PropertyList.SetPropertyAsString(propertyName, newValue);

      // Commit the transaction (VERY IMPORTANT)
      pITransaction.Commit();
      }
      catch (objError)
      {
         pITransaction.Abort();
         showError(objError);
      }
      if (totalQuestions > questionNumber)
      {
         EnableQuestionButtons();
         ChangeLabels();
         NextQuestionButton.Enabled = false;
      }
      else
      {
         ShowScore();
         ResetGame();
     }
}
```

In `ShowScore()`, you'll put up a window to display the `GameTime` property. Enter the following code after your last function in the glue code:

```
function ShowScore()
{
   NextQuestionButton.Enabled = false;
   var scoreString =
➥ "You have completed all the questions with a total time of: ";
   var Account = OpenAccountFromPropertyList(PropertyList);
   var Window = UIPropertyList.OpenProperty(UIPROPERTY_TOP_LEVEL_WINDOW);
   App.GrooveMessageBox(Window, Account, scoreString +
➥ (PropertyList.OpenProperty("GameTime"))+ " seconds.",
➥ "Congratulations", GrooveMessageBoxStyle_OK,
➥ GrooveMessageBoxIcon_Exclamation);
}
```

In `ResetGame()`, you'll reset the `QuestionNumber` property and remove the `GameTime` property. You'll clear the `ElapsedTimeDisplay` and enable the buttons. Finally, you'll switch the display to the Welcome screen. Enter the following code after the `ShowScore()` function:

```
function ResetGame()
{
      // Open a write transaction on the telespace to freeze properties
      var pITelespace = PropertyList.OpenProperty(PROPERTY_TELESPACE);
      var pITransaction = pITelespace.OpenTransaction(false);
   var finishFlag=0;

      // Perform all operations inside of try/catch block so if an
      // error occurs, we can abort transaction (VERY IMPORTANT)
      try
      {
           PropertyList.SetProperty("QuestionNumber", 1);
            PropertyList.RemoveProperty("GameTime",
➥GroovePropertyFlag_Disseminate);
            finishFlag = 1;
      // Commit the transaction (VERY IMPORTANT)
            pITransaction.Commit();
      }
      catch(objError)
      {
         pITransaction.Abort();
          showError(objError);
      }
   if (finishFlag==1){
```

```
        ElapsedTimeDisplay.SetText("");
        EnableQuestionButtons ();
            TriviaQuizViewContainer.LayoutByName = "WelcomeLayout";
   }
}
```

Finally, you need to make some changes to your `OnPropertyChanged` function. You will put the `ShowScore` and `ResetGame` functions outside the transaction. To do that, you'll use a flag as you did in the reset game function. Here is the code with the changes in bold:


```
function OnPropertyChanged
   (
      i_Key,
      i_pValue,
      i_LocallyGenerated
      )
{

   var finishFlag=0;
   var PropertyName = i_Key;
   //  Use only "Time" or "QuestionNumber".

   if (i_Key == "Time" | i_Key == "QuestionNumber")
   {

      if (PropertyName == "Time")
      {
         //Show only one entry in listbox at a time, so clear before
         ElapsedTimeDisplay.SetText("");;
      }

   // Open a transaction on the telespace to freeze properties
   var pITelespace = PropertyList.OpenProperty(PROPERTY_TELESPACE);
   var pITransaction = pITelespace.OpenTransaction(true);

   // Perform all operations inside of try/catch block so if an
   // error occurs, we can abort transaction (VERY IMPORTANT)
   try
      {
         if (PropertyName == "Time")
         {
         if (PropertyList.PropertyExists("Time"))
         {
            var PropertyValue = PropertyList.OpenProperty("Time");
```

```
            // Add the property's value to the listbox
            var Index = ElapsedTimeDisplay.SetText(PropertyValue);
         }
      }

      if (i_Key == "QuestionNumber")
      {

         if (PropertyList.PropertyExists("QuestionNumber"))
         {
         if (!i_LocallyGenerated)
         {
            ChangeLabels();
            thisDate = new Date();
            startTime = thisDate.getTime();

            if (PropertyList.OpenPropertyAsLong
➥("QuestionNumber") < 2)

            {
               ElapsedTimeDisplay.SetText
➥(PropertyList.OpenProperty("GameTime"));
               DisableQuestionButtons();
            }
            if (totalQuestions < questionNumber)
               {
                  finishFlag = 1;
               }
            }
         }
      }

   // Commit the transaction (VERY IMPORTANT)
   pITransaction.EndRead();
   }

   catch (objError)
   {
     // An exception has occurred, so abort the transaction
      pITransaction.Abort();
      showError(objError);
   }
   if (finishFlag==1) {
      ShowScore();
      ResetGame();
   }
}
```

Hiding the Correct Answer

The last thing you'll do is make it marginally harder to cheat. In the Enter Questions screen, you'll display the correct answers. Go back up to the `Views` property of the `QuestionDataViewer`.

Set the `Visible` attribute of the column to `false` and change the layout to minimize the `correctAnswer` column. This does not affect your ability to edit the answer number, but it does keep the correct answer from being obviously exposed in the Enter Questions screen:

```
<g:Property Name="Views">
   <g:PropertyValue>
      <g:DataViewerView Default="True" Name="Main">
         <g:DataViewerColumn Label="Question"
➥ DataType="String" Width="20%" Name="Question"/>
         <g:DataViewerColumn Label="Answer1"
➥ DataType="String" Width="18%" Name="Answer1"/>
         <g:DataViewerColumn Label="Answer2"
➥ DataType="String" Width="20%" Name="Answer2"/>
         <g:DataViewerColumn Label="Answer3"
➥ DataType="String" Width="18%" Name="Answer3"/>
         <g:DataViewerColumn Label="Answer4"
➥ DataType="String" Width="20%" Name="Answer4"/>
         <g:DataViewerColumn Label="CorrectAnswer"
➥ DataType="Long" Width="4%" Name="CorrectAnswer" Visible = "false"/>
      </g:DataViewerView>
   </g:PropertyValue>
</g:Property>
```

Now you can go back into your property list and remove the properties for the questions and answers, leaving only `QuestionNumber`.

This concludes the development of your trivia game. After you have tested it thoroughly, you get to publish it.

Publishing `TriviaQuiz`

The first task in preparing to publish `TriviaQuiz` is to make a CAB archive of your graphics. No directory information needs to be retained because you will be copying these two files directly into Groove's `ToolBMPs` folder. Name the finished CAB `TriviaGraphics.CAB`.

Next, you need to establish a directory structure in `localhost` to hold your template and its support files:

1. Create or reuse the `MyCompanyTools` folder. Within that folder, set up a `TriviaQuiz` directory and put `TriviaQuiz.TPL` into it. Add the `TriviaGraphics.CAB` and `TriviaQuizSchema.XML` files to it.

2. Make sure you have disabled Web access and `My Templates`. If you have not done so already, shut down Groove and run the appropriate `.REG` files so that Groove will use the files in your `localhost` directory.
3. Use Database Navigator to remove `triviaquizschema.xml` from `schemas.xss` so that you can tell whether your installation is putting the schema into the database. Also, remove the two graphics from `Data\ToolBMPs`.

After you have prepared your files, you can switch to Groove's ToolPublisher Tool:

1. When ToolPublisher comes up at the Project Information screen, click New, and then enter **TriviaQuiz** as the New Project Name in the input box.
2. The Root Package Name should be the reverse notation of your Web site. In your example, that is `com.MyCompany.MyCompanyTools.TriviaQuiz`.
3. In the Web Server URL field, type the Web server address, for example **http://www.MyCompany.com**.
4. For this example, put **MyCompanyTools/TriviaQuiz** into the Web Server Directory input area.
5. Click Save to save your project, and click on the Tool Descriptor tab.
6. In the Tool Descriptor tab, click the AddTemplates button.
7. Navigate the files browser to the `localhost` directory and find the template file in `MyCompanyTools\TriviaQuiz`. Click Open.
8. In the Name and Long Name blocks, enter **TriviaQuiz** and put **A Trivia Quiz Tutorial** into the Description field.
9. List yourself as the author, and then click on the Project Files tab.
10. In the Project Files tab, you'll see the template and the descriptor file listed in a tool that contains four tabs: Info, Install, Factories, and Dependencies. Click on the template file, and the fields are filled in with the information provided earlier. Review this information now and edit as necessary.
11. Use the Add Files button to add `TriviaGraphics.cab` and `triviagraphicsschema.xml`.
12. Select `TriviaGraphics.cab` in the Files pane and click on the Install tab. Make sure that the Type is `UnpackCAB` and enter **$GROOVEDATA$\ToolBMPs** into the Target Directory field.
13. Click on the `triviaquizschema.xml` file. From the Type pull-down menu, select Import to XSS. In the Database URI field, enter **$SCHEMASURI$**, and then put **triviaquizschema.xml** into the Document Name field. Leave the Schema URI field blank for the `triviaquizschema.xml` file.

14. You are finished with the Install tab, so click on the Factories tab. Accept the defaults for `TriviaQuiz.tpl`, `TriviaQuizDescriptor.xml`, and `TriviaGraphics.cab`.
15. Select `triviaquizschema.xml` in the Files pane, and change the type to XML Document. The Name field changes to Open. In the Database URI field, enter **$SCHEMASURI$**, and enter **triviaquizschema.xml** in the Document Name field.
16. In the Dependencies tab, click the `TriviaQuiz.tpl` file, and add the schema and the graphics as dependencies. Then, click on the tool descriptor in the Files pane and add the tool template as a dependency. This establishes the tool template as being dependent on the graphics and the schema, and the descriptor as being dependent on the template.
17. Go back to the Product Information tab and click Save.

Before you publish your tool, you must have a certificate. If you created a certificate earlier, you may use it. If you didn't, you must generate a certificate. The steps are as listed here:

1. Click on the Generate Certificate tab, and in the Common Name field, put either your name or your company's name.
2. In the Organization Unit field, enter **Tool Development**, and enter **TriviaQuiz Development** under Organization.
3. Fill in your country of choice.
4. For Start Date and End Date, choose a 100-year period, such as **1/1/2002** to **1/1/2102**.
5. Add and confirm a passphrase, something you can remember because you will be using it each time you sign your OSD.
6. Click the Generate Certificate button.
7. After the certificate has been generated, a file browser opens to let you save the file to a specific location. Put it somewhere that is convenient, because you will be using a path to it whenever you publish subsequent tools.
8. Click on the Publish Project tab.
9. When you return to the Publish Project tab, the Generate Certificate tab fields may be blank. If they are, fill in the Private Keystore File Path field in the Publish Project tab. Enter the path where the `ComponentSigningPrivateKeyStore.xml` file is stored, and the fields will be restored.
10. Now, the moment you have been waiting for. Click the Create Files button. You should get a confirmation.
11. To sign the OSD, fill in the Private Keystore Passphrase field and click the Sign OSD button.

    You should receive confirmation that the OSD has been signed.
12. Click the `.GRV` file and inject the `TriviaQuiz` tool.

Taking It to the Web

You are now ready to follow these steps to test installation of `TriviaQuiz` from the Web:

1. Make sure that your Web directories match the directory structure of your `localhost` file. In this case, your structure should be `http://www.MyCompany.com/MyCompanyTools/TriviaQuiz`.
2. Move all the files in your `MyCompanyTools` directory to the corresponding directory on the Web.
3. Run the `EnableWebAccess` registry file.
4. Because the manifest is a device-wide registry, you cannot install `TriviaQuiz` on the same machine you used to test it. If you do not have a clean machine, restore the backup `Data` directory you made when you started this chapter.

You can now make `TriviaQuiz` available by emailing the `.GRV` file as an attachment, or by adding a link to a Web page, like this:

```
<a href=http://www.MyCompany.com/MyCompanyTools/TriviaQuiz/TriviaQuiz.GRV>
```

Summary

Although `TriviaQuiz` is a great improvement over `TriviaQuiz3`, it would be nice to be able to split out the database of questions into an external database and then link into it at runtime. Let's move to the next chapter and take a look at Groove's methods for doing that.

Data Integration and Groove Bots

CHAPTER

13

IN THIS CHAPTER

In this chapter, we will study data integration in Groove through connectors and Groove bots. Data integration extends the reach of Groove tools by allowing them to connect with external information and applications resources. After we look at the value data integration brings to Groove, we will study the use of connectors in Groove tools. Then, we will discuss Groove bots and the Groove Enterprise Integration Server (GEIS).

Bots can be used for data integration, but their capabilities go far beyond this single use. We'll look at some of the features and capabilities of bots and the GEIS and some of the advantages they present to both developers and administrators. We will examine the value that can be created by utilizing a combination of Groove tools and bots, and we'll look at some programming examples. Finally, we will discuss an approach to integrating our "Trivia Quiz" application with an external database of questions, and a possible use of connectors or bots as enhancements.

Data Integration and Groove

In several places in Groove's marketing literature, you'll see the phrase "Right People, Right Tools, Right Time." Groove brings together the right people, at the right time, with the right information and tools, to collaborate effectively in a secure space.

Bringing the right information to a space is a challenge. In most of corporate America, information resides in centralized, well-protected systems where access is tightly controlled. These are the benefits of accessing external information:

- People are able to work together more easily and effectively.
- Data from an external server can be seeded into a shared space even before the participants enter it.
- People within the shared space can then interact with that data in meaningful ways, and can return the manipulated data back to the server.
- Users within a shared space can access a Web service or application from inside Groove tools using data supplied by centralized information resources.

These kinds of connections can be especially valuable in certain environments. One is a situation in which Web services or applications need input from several people simultaneously. An example might be an auction, or a production optimization program that needs input from various suppliers and subcontractors. Another would be a shared space that needs to be continually synchronized with a central server to provide current data, perhaps providing commodity prices.

To support data integration, Groove provides connectors and bots.

Connectors

Connectors are tools responsible for connecting shared spaces to an external application or system. They have various interfaces for connecting external data to Groove tools.

Groove also provides Simple Object Access Protocol (SOAP) services to provide connections with Web services that use this protocol. In addition to SOAP, Groove tools can use Microsoft Transaction Server and Microsoft Message Queue to communicate with various external or internal resources. Microsoft Transaction Server runs under IIS and maintains OBDC connections, whereas Microsoft Message Queue can integrate with IBM MQ series. Groove tools and connectors can also use ActiveX controls.

The Connectors Sample

In the `Samples` folder of the GDK, there is a `Connectors` folder. You can find instructions for setting up this sample in the Groove Integration Guide located in the GDK. If you choose to set it up, you will find a fascinating demonstration of connnector capability.

The demonstration lets you navigate your browser to a `faq.asp` Web page, where you will see a list of FAQs. On the upper-right side of the page, you'll see a box that has two fields and a message that reads, "Didn't find an answer to your question? Login and Groove with Support." If you fill in the fields and click the Log In button, the page refreshes with a personalized message and a link that reads, "Instant Groove with Groove Support now!" That link launches a `.GRV` file that downloads and installs a shared space to your Groove account, and opens Groove.

The shared space contains five tools: Sketchpad, Notepad, Web Browser, Files, and FAQ. In the FAQ Tool, you will see the questions and answers seeded from the same database that the ASP uses. You will also see an Invite CSR button. Clicking that button results in your designated customer service representative being invited into your space.

You and your CSR can now work together to obtain an answer to your question. When your issue is resolved, your CSR can enter your question and its resolution back into the database, which will update both your FAQ tool's data and the information displayed in the Web page, because they are both drawn from the same database. It is a very interesting and useful demo.

Let's look at the code to see how the shared space is dynamically created.

Dynamic Creation of a Shared Space

To dynamically create a shared space, you need to write a `.GRV` file. A `.GRV` file, you will remember, is an XML file that contains messages that the transceiver reads, and then forwards to the target component. Here is a listing of the `.GRV` file you wrote for `TriviaQuiz4`:

```
<?xml version='1.0'?><?groove.net version='1.0'?>
<g:fragment xmlns:g="urn:groove.net">
   <g:InjectorWrapper
      AccountGUID="grooveIdentity:///DefaultIdentity"
      MessageID="d7g4v4pbmpqdu2wk6bs3hsvqsx4meamiwtk6s7c"
      ResourceURL="grooveIdentityMessage:///ToolMessage;Version=3,0,0,0"
      LocalDeviceURLs="Injector">

      <g:IdentityMessageHeader>
         <g:MessageHeader
            MessageType="ToolMessage"
            MessageID="d7g4v4pbmpqdu2wk6bs3hsvqsx4meamiwtk6s7c"
            Version="1,0,0,0"
            CreateTime="9/24/00 7:41 PM"
            CreatorDeviceURL=
➥"dpp://friends.groove.net/0sGnePZSnu-AY-fePpNqEqzwSOPo9910">

            <g:SenderContact/>
            <g:RecipientContact/>
         </g:MessageHeader>
         <g:MessageBody BodyName="MessageBody">
            <g:ToolMessage>
               <g:ToolMessageHeader ToolURL="grooveAccountTool:
➥;CategoryName=grooveToolCategory://Account/ToolTemplateList,ComponentName=
ToolTemplateList"/>
               <g:ToolMessageBody>
                  <g:TemplateDescriptorList>
                  <g:TemplateDescriptorURL URL=
➥"http://components.YourCompany.com/MyGrooveTools/TriviaQuiz/TriviaQuiz.osd?
➥Package=
➥com.YourCompany.MyGrooveTools.TriviaQuiz.TriviaQuizDescriptor_XML&amp;
 ➥Version=0&amp;Factory=Open"/>
                  </g:TemplateDescriptorList>
               </g:ToolMessageBody>
            </g:ToolMessage>
         </g:MessageBody>
      </g:IdentityMessageHeader>
   </g:InjectorWrapper>

</g:fragment>
```

To change this `.GRV` file into one that injects a custom space, you need to change a few lines of the message. First, send a message to inject a shared space by changing the tool message header from the `ToolTemplateList` to the `TelespaceProvider` and changing the `ComponentName` from `ToolTemplateList` to `injector`. Also put a `Telespace` element in the `ToolMessageBody`. The changes to the code are in bold type:

```
<?xml version='1.0'?><?groove.net version='1.0'?>
<g:fragment xmlns:g="urn:groove.net">
   <g:InjectorWrapper
      AccountGUID="grooveIdentity:///DefaultIdentity"
      MessageID="d7g4v4pbmpqdu2wk6bs3hsvqsx4meamiwtk6s7c"
      ResourceURL="grooveIdentityMessage:///ToolMessage;Version=3,0,0,0"
      LocalDeviceURLs="Injector">

      <g:IdentityMessageHeader>
         <g:MessageHeader
            MessageType="ToolMessage"
            MessageID="d7g4v4pbmpqdu2wk6bs3hsvqsx4meamiwtk6s7c"
            Version="1,0,0,0"
            CreateTime="9/24/00 7:41 PM"
            CreatorDeviceURL=
➥"dpp://friends.groove.net/0sGnePZSnu-AY-fePpNqEqzwSOPo9910">

            <g:SenderContact/>
            <g:RecipientContact/>
         </g:MessageHeader>
         <g:MessageBody BodyName="MessageBody">
            <g:ToolMessage>
               <g:ToolMessageHeader ToolURL=
➥"grooveAccountTool:;CategoryName=grooveToolCategory:
➥//Account/TelespaceProvider,ComponentName=Injector"/>
                <g:ToolMessageBody>
                  <g:Telespace
                  DisplayName="Enterprise Support"
                  Visible="1"
                  DeleteOnRelease="0"
                  Description="Support for the enterprise"
                 >
               </g:ToolMessageBody>
            </g:ToolMessage>
         </g:MessageBody>
      </g:IdentityMessageHeader>
   </g:InjectorWrapper>

</g:fragment>
```

Having told Groove that you want to inject a shared space, you now have to define a toolset and tell it what tools you want in that space. You do that with a `Tools` element, and then you define a `ToolSetTemplate` to hold all your tools:

```
<?xml version='1.0'?><?groove.net version='1.0'?>
<g:fragment xmlns:g="urn:groove.net">
```

```
   <g:InjectorWrapper
      AccountGUID="grooveIdentity:///DefaultIdentity"
      MessageID="d7g4v4pbmpqdu2wk6bs3hsvqsx4meamiwtk6s7c"
      ResourceURL="grooveIdentityMessage:///ToolMessage;Version=3,0,0,0"
      LocalDeviceURLs="Injector">

      <g:IdentityMessageHeader>
         <g:MessageHeader
            MessageType="ToolMessage"
            MessageID="d7g4v4pbmpqdu2wk6bs3hsvqsx4meamiwtk6s7c"
            Version="1,0,0,0"
            CreateTime="9/24/00 7:41 PM"
            CreatorDeviceURL=
➥"dpp://friends.groove.net/0sGnePZSnu-AY-fePpNqEqzwSOPo9910">

            <g:SenderContact/>
            <g:RecipientContact/>
         </g:MessageHeader>
         <g:MessageBody BodyName="MessageBody">
            <g:ToolMessage>
               <g:ToolMessageHeader ToolURL="grooveAccountTool:
➥;CategoryName=grooveToolCategory:
➥//Account/TelespaceProvider,ComponentName=Injector"/>
                <g:ToolMessageBody>
                  <g:Telespace
                  DisplayName="Enterprise Support"
                  Visible="1"
                  DeleteOnRelease="0"
                  Description="Support for the enterprise"
                 >
                 <g:Tools>
                     <g:ToolSetTemplate>
                        <g:Template Name="StockTools"
➥ URL="http://components.groove.net/Groove/Components/Root.osd?
➥Package=net.groove.Groove.Tools.System.NewTelespaceToolsActivity_TST&amp;
➥Version=0&amp;Factory=Open"/>
                  </g:Tools>
               </g:ToolMessageBody>
            </g:ToolMessage>
         </g:MessageBody>
      </g:IdentityMessageHeader>
   </g:InjectorWrapper>

</g:fragment>
```

You can now load your `StockTools` template with tools. Notice that you had to put in all the tools in the shared space, not just the ones on your tabs:

```
<?xml version='1.0'?><?groove.net version='1.0'?>
<g:fragment xmlns:g="urn:groove.net">
<g:InjectorWrapper
   AccountGUID="grooveIdentity:///DefaultIdentity"
   MessageID="BAADFOOD10"
   ResourceURL="grooveIdentityMessage:///ToolMessage;Version=4,0,0,0"
   LocalDeviceURLs="Injector"
>
    <g:IdentityMessageHeader>
        <g:MessageHeader
         MessageType="ToolMessage"
         MessageID="BAADFOOD10"
         Version="1,1,0,0"
         CreationTime="984351209942"
      >
            <g:SenderContact/>
            <g:RecipientContact/>
        </g:MessageHeader>
        <g:MessageBody
         BodyName="MessageBody">
            <g:ToolMessage>
                <g:ToolMessageHeader ToolURL="grooveAccountTool:
➥;CategoryName=grooveToolCategory:
➥//Account/TelespaceProvider,ComponentName=Injector"/>
                <g:ToolMessageBody>
                  <g:Telespace
                  DisplayName="Enterprise Support"
                  Visible="1"
                  DeleteOnRelease="0"
                  Description="Support for the enterprise"
                 >
                  <g:Tools>
                     <g:ToolSetTemplate>
                        <g:Template Name="StockTools"
➥ URL="http://components.groove.net/Groove/Components/Root.osd?
➥Package=net.groove.Groove.Tools.System.NewTelespaceToolsActivity_TST&amp;
 ➥Version=0&amp;Factory=Open"/>
                           <g:Template Name="DefaultConv.Tool"
➥ Category="Conversation" DisplayName="Chat" Display="Custom""
➥URL="http://components.groove.net/Groove/Components/Root.osd?
➥Package=net.groove.Groove.Tools.System.IntercomTemplate_TPL&amp;
➥Version=2&amp;Factory=Open" FingerprintID="Groove"/>
```

```
                            <g:Template Name="LiveAudio.Tool"
➥ Category="LiveAudio" DisplayName="LiveAudio Tool" Display="Custom"
➥URL="http://components.groove.net/Groove/Components/Root.osd?
➥Package=net.groove.Groove.Tools.System.LiveAudio_TPL&amp;
➥Version=0&amp;Factory=Open" FingerprintID="Groove"/>

                            <g:Template Name="FollowMode.Tool"
➥ Category="FollowMode" DisplayName="Navigating Together" Display="Custom"
➥ URL="http://components.groove.net/Groove/Components/Root.osd?
➥Package=net.groove.Groove.Tools.System.FollowMode_TPL&amp;
➥Version=0&amp;Factory=Open" FingerprintID="Groove"/>
                            <g:Template Name="RootDisplay.Tool"
➥ Category="RootDisplay" DisplayName="Conversation Tool Set"
➥URL="http://components.groove.net/Groove/Components/Root.osd?
➥Package=net.groove.Groove.Tools.System.TabToolSetTool_TPL&amp;
➥Version=0&amp;Factory=Open" FingerprintID="Groove">
                           <g:Template Name="ConversationSketchPadTemplate.Tool"
➥ DisplayName="Sketchpad"
➥URL="http://components.groove.net/Groove/Components/Root.osd?
➥Package=net.groove.Groove.Tools.General.SketchPad.SketchPadTemplate_TPL&amp;
➥Version=3&amp;Factory=Open" FingerprintID="Groove"/>
                            <g:Template Name="ConversationRichEdit.Tool"
 ➥ DisplayName="Notepad"
➥URL="http://components.groove.net/Groove/Components/Root.osd?
➥Package=net.groove.Groove.Tools.General.RichText.RichTextTemplate_TPL&amp;
➥Version=3&amp;Factory=Open" FingerprintID="Groove"/>
                            <g:Template Name="ConversationWebBrowser.Tool"
➥ DisplayName="Web Browser"
➥URL="http://components.groove.net/Groove/Components/Root.osd?
➥Package=net.groove.Groove.Tools.General.WebBrowser.WebBrowserTemplate_TPL&amp;
➥Version=2&amp;Factory=Open" FingerprintID="Groove"/>
                            <g:Template
➥ Name="ConversationDocumentShareTemplate.Tool" DisplayName="Files"
➥URL="http://components.groove.net/Groove/Components/Root.osd?Package=
➥net.groove.Groove.Tools.General.DocumentShare.DocumentShareTemplate_TPL&amp;
➥Version=2,1&amp;Factory=Open" FingerprintID="Groove"/>
                            <g:Template Name="GroovePRMFAQ.Tool"
DisplayName="FAQ"
➥ URL="http://components.yourcompany.com/Gdk/Samples/
➥Connectors/PRM/FAQTool/Javascript/GroovePRM.osd?
➥Package=com.yourcompany.GDK.Samples.Connectors.
➥PRM.FAQTool.Javascript.GroovePRMFAQ_TPL&amp;
➥Version=1,2&amp;Factory=Open" FingerprintID="Groove">
x"PRMDataModelDelegate">
                                  <g:PropertyList>
                                     <g:Property Name="CSRContactFullName">
```

```
                                    <g:PropertyValue>
                                       <![CDATA[Paula Liszt]]>
                                    </g:PropertyValue>
                                 </g:Property>
                                 <g:Property Name="CSRContactGrooveContent">
                                    <g:PropertyValue>
                                       <![CDATA[localhost\GDK\Samples\
➥Connectors\PRM\contacts\]]>
                                    </g:PropertyValue>
                                 </g:Property>
                              </g:PropertyList>
                           </g:InitializationComponent>
                        </g:Template>
                     </g:Template>
                  </g:ToolSetTemplate>
               </g:Tools>
            </g:Telespace>
             </g:ToolMessageBody>
         </g:ToolMessage>
      </g:MessageBody>
   </g:IdentityMessageHeader>
</g:InjectorWrapper>

</g:fragment>
```


You will notice that your FAQ tool has an `InitializationComponent` that is used to seed initial data into your shared space. The information items to be seeded are the values of two properties: `CSRContactFullName` and `CSRContactGrooveContent`. To seed data, you need to specify the component that performs the initialization. In this case, it is the `PRMDataModelDelegate` component.

The `PRMDataModelDelegate` component is declared in the `ComponentGroup` element of `GroovePRMFAQ.tpl`:

```
<g:Component Name="PRMDataModelDelegate" SingleInstance="True">
   <g:ComponentResource
➥ URL="http://components.groove.net/Groove/Components/Root.osd?
Package=net.groove.Groove.ToolComponents.GrooveCommonComponents_DLL&amp;
➥Version=0,3&amp;Factory=ScriptFreeThreadedComponent3" FingerprintID="Groove"/>
   <g:ComponentConnections>
      <g:Connection ConnectionID="0" Name="RecordSetEngine"/>
   </g:ComponentConnections>

   <SCRIPT SRC=
➥"http://components.yourcompany.com/GDK/Samples/Connectors/PRM/FAQTool/
➥Javascript/GroovePRM.osd?Package=com.yourcompany.GDK.Samples.Connectors.PRM.
```

```
➥FAQTool.Javascript.PRMDataModelDelegate_GSL&amp;
➥Version=1,2&amp;Factory=Open" FingerprintID="Groove"/>

</g:Component>
```

ScriptFreeThreadedComponent implements the script hosting mechanism that allows script code to be called from any thread in the system. This component needs to be thread-safe because the tool thread will not have been initialized when the code is run.

If you follow the script source, you'll find the PRMDataModelDelegate.gsl file. There you'll see the following code:

```
<g:Document Name="PRMDataModelDelegate.gsl" xmlns:g="urn:groove.net">

   <g:ComponentSecurity>
      <g:FingerprintTable>
         <g:Entry FingerprintID=
➥"Groove" Fingerprint="4262-dcb1:4552-d303:123d-36a6:0a96-62e5:24a7-d7db"/>
      </g:FingerprintTable>
   </g:ComponentSecurity>

   <IMPLEMENTS IID=
➥"{BD219585-8266-4ee7-A61C-4438BD96FDC2}"
➥ LIBID="{5AA916C7-BF12-11d3-80A0-00C04FA1100A}">
      <SCRIPT>
         <![CDATA[

            function Initialize(i_pInitializationPropertyList)
            {
               try
               {
                  // Create a record object.
                  var pIRecord =
➥ RecordSetEngine.RecordFactory.CreateRecord("urn:groove.net:Record");

                  // Populate fields with the seed data from the PropertyList.
                  var pIElement =
➥ i_pInitializationPropertyList.OpenProperty("CSRContactFullName");
                  SetData
➥(pIRecord, "CSRContactFullName", pIElement.OpenContentText(0));

                  var pIElement =
➥ i_pInitializationPropertyList. OpenProperty
➥ ("CSRContactGrooveContent");
                  SetData(pIRecord, "CSRContactGrooveContent",
➥ pIElement.OpenContentText(0));
```

```
                    RecordSetEngine.AddRecord(pIRecord);
                }
                catch(error){}
            }
        ]]>
    </SCRIPT>
</IMPLEMENTS>

<SCRIPT>
    <![CDATA[
        function SetData(i_pIRecord, i_DataName, i_DataValue)
        {
            try
            {
                i_pIRecord.SetFieldAsString(i_DataName, i_DataValue);
            }
            catch(error){}
        }
    ]]>
</SCRIPT>

</g:Document>
```


This code contains an `<IMPLEMENTS>` element that you have not seen before in tool code. The `<IMPLEMENTS>` element provides the information that a host component needs in order to implement its interface and to respond to your code.

The Interface ID (`IID`) attribute is the GUID of the particular interface to implement. The IID can be found at the bottom of the page of the *Groove JavaScript API Reference* that describes the interface. In this case, the interface is the `IGrooveOneTimeInitializableComponent`.

The `LIBID` attribute is the GUID of the registered type library that defines the interface, in this case, `GrooveComponents`.

The `PropertyList` of the `InitializationComponent` of the `.GRV` is passed to the code in `PRMDataModelDelegate.gsl` as a parameter to the `Initialize()` function. The initialization function populates the fields in a record that is then stored in the tool's `RecordSetEngine`.

Accessing the Data

Now that the shared space has been created, you need the data. Here's how the database is accessed in the Connectors example. This is code from `PRMGlue.gsl`:

```
function GetFAQ()
    {
        try
        {
```

```
        //This section makes it possible for visitors to sort
        //the data in the columns in ascending order.
var StrSort = "FAQID ASC";

        strQuery="SELECT * FROM FAQ ORDER BY " + StrSort;

        //Database path statement describing the driver to
        //use and the path to the desired database.
        var strProvider = "DSN=GroovePRM;";

        //Instantiate a Recordset object and open a
        //recordset using the Open method
        var objRS = new ActiveXObject("ADODB.recordset");
        objRS.Open(strQuery, strProvider);

        if(objRS.EOF)
      PropertyList.SetPropertyAsString("FAQText",
➥ "There are no entries in the FAQ database.");
        else
        {
          var strFAQ = "";

            while(!objRS.EOF)
            {
              // Skip the FAQ Category Description
              //for now and start with index 2.
              for(var i = 2; i < objRS.fields.count; i++)
              {
                if(i == 2)
                  strFAQ += objRS(i) + "\n";
                else
                  strFAQ += "\t" + objRS(i);
              }
              objRS.MoveNext
              strFAQ += "\n\n";
            }
            PropertyList.SetPropertyAsString("FAQText", strFAQ);
        }
        objRS.Close;
        objRS = "";
        }
          catch(exception)
          {
            var strErrMsg;
```

```
            if(objRS)
            {
            objRS.Close;
            objRS = "";
          }
        strErrMsg = "Error #" + exception.number + "\n";
        strErrMsg += exception.description;
        PropertyList.SetPropertyAsString("FAQText", strErrMsg);
    }
}
```

The code is wrapped in a `try/catch` block.

After a sort substring and a query string are set up as variables, a variable is declared to hold the value of a system DSN entry in the OBDC Data Sources (32-bit) control panel of the user's machine. The System DSN entry describes both the system and the path to the data.

An ActiveX object, a connector to an Access database, is then instantiated, and an ADODB recordset is opened on it, using the query string and the data source. If the first record opened is an end-of-file marker, an error message is displayed. If not, a variable is initialized as an empty string.

The function then cycles through the ADODB recordset until it finds an end-of-file marker. The first field contains the `categoryName` that is not going to be displayed at this time, so the function begins with the second field. The second field is the question field, so the code writes it and adds a linefeed to the `strFAQ` variable that will hold the entire FAQ display text. The third field is the answer field, so it is indented from the question. The index is moved to the next record and two linefeeds are placed between the records. This continues until all the records have been read.

A `FAQText` property is then created in the `propertyList`, and `strFAQ` is assigned its value. The `ActiveX` object is then closed and disposed of. If there are problems, the `catch` code cleans up and stuffs the error message into the `FAQText` property. Further into the glue, the property is displayed in the `FAQView` edit control.

Now look carefully at the PRM demo: For the PRM demo to work, every machine (every "client" machine and every "customer service rep" machine) must have an ODBC connection to one instance of the Access database; otherwise, the database would not be updated when anyone else added a FAQ.

Having all the members of the shared space access the database directly is an example of multi-point database access.

Bots

A *bot* can be described as a remote, unattended agent operating on a tool or a set of tools in a shared space. It executes as a single instance, although it can be replicated on a cluster in the 2.0 release. To understand why the latter point is important, see the following sidebar.

Centralized and Multipoint Integration

In multipoint integration, many individual users access the central resource. A Web site is a good example of a resource that is multipoint integrated.

If a user in a shared space is using Groove's Web Browser tool with the Browse Together check box checked, each user's tool shows the same page. This is accomplished by distributing the Web address to all the participants. They individually connect to the Web site and download the target page. Because Web sites are set up to handle many users simultaneously, there is not a serious performance hit for the Web site. It is more bandwidth friendly for Groove to propagate the address rather than the page. The Groove shared space uses multipoint integration to access the Web page.

When you're connecting to an information resource such as a database, multipoint integration is generally a bad idea. Queries from each user require the database to open and close transactions to lock and unlock the data. If all the queries were different, this would be an unavoidable performance hit, but because every user will have the same information in the shared space, this approach makes little sense in a peer-to-peer context. Also, each instance of the tool that used the information in the shared space would require a database API to be installed and configured. Consequently, Groove uses centralized integration when using bots to connect with databases.

In centralized integration, a dedicated machine within a peer-to-peer environment is responsible for acting as a gateway between the shared space and the centralized information resource. That dedicated machine within the peer-to-peer environment hosts the bot server.

When a user's tool in the shared space generates a database query, that query goes to the bot residing on the bot server. The bot, through the bot server, queries the database. The database responds to the bot's query through the bot server, and the bot is responsible for disseminating the server response to other members of the shared space. All members have the data, but the database has been queried only once.

Another great advantage of this system is administrative. There is one point of control for access to the database from the shared space: the bot server.

Note, too, that the database itself may not be available to some or any of the members of the shared space. If the users were remote and the database was protected behind a firewall, they could still access the information if the bot server had a database connection and they had a connection to the bot server.

Groove bots, then, limit resource use by channeling requests through a single point. Groove bots are automated, so they are available 24/7. After they've been configured, bots are always "on."

In addition to performing database lookups and updates as requested by shared space members, bots can restrict access to the data based on which member makes the request and the access limits on the external database. They can also perform automatic synchronization between data in a shared space and data on an external information resource. Bots can provide read-only snapshots of rapidly changing data in a centralized repository. Bots can also run tasks in the background such as automatically initiating time-sensitive operations or alerting members of critical changes in data.

Bots are much more than connections to data, though. Bots have a unique identity and run under a Groove account. A bot is, in all respects, a member of the shared space. Always available, bots interact with members, information, and activities in shared spaces. As a centralized point of integration behind a firewall, they are controllable by an enterprise's IT personnel who can assure secure access to enterprise data by parties who have a legitimate interest in that data—partners and customers, for example.

Bots can be invited to a shared space, or they can invite others. Like any other member, they are subject to access control, thereby protecting data. Bots have the capability to respond to events external or internal to the shared space. They can respond to account creation and deletion, to the opening and closing of shared spaces, and to the addition of a new tool or a change in membership, as well as Groove application and timer events.

Using Groove-enabled code on the external system to which it is connected, and Groove's Secure Messaging, Groove bots can receive and respond to events generated by the external system. This allows for rich conversation between a shared space, or multiple shared spaces, and an external resource.

Developing Bots

The creation of bots is primarily defined by the developer, with some input from the eventual administrator. These are the benefits of Groove's bot development framework to the developer:

- Groove provides a robust runtime environment for the operation of bots and bot code.
- Bots have flexible configuration options.

- Bots can be programmed in any language (C++, VB, VBScript, JavaScript, or any scripting language Groove supports), which allows the developer to develop in familiar tools and environments.

To develop and test bots, you must download and install the GEIS. At the time of this writing, you cannot run the bot server and Groove on the same machine. Consequently, we will not dig too deeply into bot development.

There are several types of bots, but we'll limit our discussion to tool bots. As with a tool, you need to write code in a template file and write an OSD file, but in place of a tool descriptor, you write a bot configuration description file.

The Bot Configuration File

The bot configuration XML file provides the server with the information it needs in order to install the bot on the cluster. It also specifies the bot's associated tool in the shared space.

Eliza

The Eliza program was first described by Joseph Weizenbaum of Massachusetts Institute of Technology in a January 1966 article in *Communications of the ACM*, titled "ELIZA—A Computer Program for the Study of Natural Language Communication Between Man and Machine."

Eliza uses basic heuristic programming and artificial intelligence to make it seem that you are conversing with a real person. Back when computers were considered magic anyway, Eliza attracted many users who claimed therapeutic experiences while using Eliza.

The program is actually pretty simple. The input to the program is read and checked to see whether it contains a keyword. If it does, the sentence is transformed according to a rule associated with that keyword.

The rules Weizenbaum used were adapted from the work of Zelig Harris and Noam Chomsky. Incorporating keywords into sentences using the Harris and Chomsky transformations resulted in a conversational style that happened to correspond with a style of therapy called non-directive interviewing, developed by Carl Rogers and published in a paper in *American Psychologist* in 1946.

Groove's implementation of Eliza as a bot makes it seem that Eliza is actually a real person and member of your shared space. If you install the GEIS software, make it a point to talk to Eliza. It will help you recognize some of the possibilities of Groove bots.

Here is the `BotInstallation` element from the `GrooveElizaBot.xml` from the Groove "Classic Eliza Chatter Bot" tool demo from the GEIS installation:

```
<BotInstallations>
   <BotInstallation
      Active="1"
      Class="1"
      SignatureType="0"
      Signature=
         "http://components.groove.net/Groove/Components/Root.osd?
➥Package=net.groove.Groove.Tools.General.Discussion.DiscussionTemplate_TPL&amp;
➥Version=2&amp;Factory=Open"

      AgentTemplateResourceURL=
➥"http://components.groove.net/Groove/Components/Root.osd?
➥Package=net.groove.Groove.Tools.Business.Bots. GrooveElizaBot_TPL&amp;
➥Version=1&amp;Factory=Open"

   Connection="0"
   DisplayName="Classic Eliza Chatter Bot"
   MinScope="2"
   MinTelespaceRole="1"
   ToolConnectionType="0"
   />
</BotInstallations>
```

The signature identifies the tool the bot will use, and the `AgentTemplateResource` identifies the bot.

If the bot works on additional tools, or there are different implementations of a bot, a `BotInstallation` element is needed for each one. `Class = "1"` indicates that the bot is a tool bot, and `SignatureType="0"` tells the component connector to find the tool by resource URL. `MinScope="2"` limits the scope of the bot to all components in its associated tool, and `ToolConnectionType="0"` specifies the kind of connection that the bot will make with the tool—in this case, it will connect to the tool's data model delegate.

The Bot Template File

At a minimum, the bot template needs to define the data model delegate. The `IGrooveBot Component` is implemented in the `GrooveBotComponentImpl.gsl` script library. You must overload the methods in `GrooveBotComponentImpl.gsl`, defining a function with the same name as the function you are overloading and prefacing the method name with the word *My*.

Here is some code from `GrooveElizaBot.tpl`:

```
function MyIsInstanceEnabled(i_BotInstanceGuid)
   {
   var pEliza = new ElizaBotInstance(i_BotInstanceGuid);
   return pEliza.Enabled();
   }
```

```
function MyProvidesConfigurationUI()
   {
   return true;
   }


function MyOpenConfigurationUIAsSubform(i_BotInstanceGuid)
   {
   var pTool = PropertyList.OpenProperty("_Tool");
   var pUITool = pTool.UITool;
   var pForm = pUITool.CreateForm();
   var pSubForm = pForm.CreateFormByName("ConfigurationSubform");

   //Now we can pass context up to the dlg...
   var pSubformGlue = pSubForm.OpenDelegateComponent();

   var pBotInstanceDescriptor =
➥ g_pBotImplementation.BotInstanceDescriptor(i_BotInstanceGuid);

   //We now QI for IgrooveBotContextProvider
   //and set its reference to the instance
   pSubformGlue.IGrooveBotContextProvider.Instance = pBotInstanceDescriptor;

   return pSubForm;
   }


function MyCreateBotInstance(i_BotInstanceDescriptor,  i_NewInstance)
   {
   //make sure we can cross-reference...
   var BotInstanceGuid = i_BotInstanceDescriptor.BotInstanceGuid;

   var pBotInstanceDescriptor =
➥ g_GlobalBotHelperFunctions.GetBotInstanceDescriptorByBotInstanceGuid
➥ (BotInstanceGuid);

   var pDelegateComponent = i_BotInstanceDescriptor.Component;

   ScriptHostComponent.Advise(pDelegateComponent,
➥  "{72C3A310-46F1-11D4-80BB-0050DA5F08E3}");
   ScriptHostComponent.Advise(pDelegateComponent,
➥  "{71FCE590-88E9-11D4-80C4-0050DA5F08E3}");
   }


function MyOnRemoveBotInstance(i_pDelegateComponent, i_BotInstanceGuid)
```

```
    {
    ScriptHostComponent.Unadvise(i_pDelegateComponent,
➥   "{72C3A310-46F1-11D4-80BB-0050DA5F08E3}");
    ScriptHostComponent.Unadvise(i_pDelegateComponent,
➥   "{71FCE590-88E9-11D4-80C4-0050DA5F08E3}");
    }


function MyEnableBotInstance(i_BotInstanceGuid)
    {
    var pEliza = new ElizaBotInstance(i_BotInstanceGuid);
    pEliza.Enabled(true);

    Fire_OnStatusChanged(
       g_GlobalBotHelperFunctions.GetComponentURLFromBotInstanceGuid
➥(i_BotInstanceGuid),
       g_GlobalBotHelperFunctions.GetBotGuidFromInstanceGuid
➥(i_BotInstanceGuid),
       i_BotInstanceGuid,
       GrooveBotInstanceStatus_READY
       );
    }

function MyDisableBotInstance(i_BotInstanceGuid)
    {
    var pEliza = new ElizaBotInstance(i_BotInstanceGuid);
    pEliza.Enabled(false);

    Fire_OnStatusChanged(
       g_GlobalBotHelperFunctions.GetComponentURLFromBotInstanceGuid
➥(i_BotInstanceGuid),
       g_GlobalBotHelperFunctions.GetBotGuidFromInstanceGuid
➥(i_BotInstanceGuid),
       i_BotInstanceGuid,
       GrooveBotInstanceStatus_PAUSED
       );
       }
```


MyIsInstanceEnabled returns the enabled state of the bot instance. MyProvidesConfigurationUI returns true if a bot configuration form is available for the bot administrator. If it is, a MyOpenConfigurationUIAsSubform method is needed to open the form.

MyCreateBotInstance creates the instance and initializes the bot. The code in GrooveBotComponentImpl.gsl is responsible for actually creating the instance. MyRemoveBotInstance deletes it. Again, GrooveBotComponentImpl.gsl is responsible for actually deleting the bot.

MyEnableBotInstance sets the Enabled property to true and uses the Fire_OnStatusChanged method to set GrooveBotInstanceStatus_READY. MyDisableBotInstance sets the Enabled property to false and uses the Fire_OnStatusChanged method to set GrooveBotInstance Status_PAUSED.

Your bot must source events on the DGrooveBotInstanceListener and the IGrooveBot InstanceListener interfaces, but the GSL provides the implementations; so you can access the OnStatusChanged and OnLogEvent methods.

You will notice in the earlier MyCreateBotInstance code that when the bot server calls MyCreateBotInstance, it passes i_BotInstanceDescriptor to the function as a parameter. The BotInstanceDescriptor is an object that describes the context for your bot's execution. Using properties on the object, you can retrieve values for all the following: the tool's data model delegate, the tool object, the shared space that contains the tool, the URL to the telespace, the URL to the bot service, the URL to the tool, the URL for a component within the tool, the resource URL for the bot instance, the GUID of the bot from which your bot is derived, a bot object created by CreateBotInstance, the bot's data model delegate, and the resource URL of the device on which the bot is running.

In the MyCreateBotInstance code, the ATL Advise is used to connect itself as a listener to the BotInstanceDescriptor's component connection point and the IGrooveAggregatedRecordListener interfaces so that it can respond to changes in its tool's recordset engine.

TIP

The use of a constructor to set the pEliza variable may be a technique that's not familiar to you. This constructor,

```
var pEliza = new ElizaBotInstance(i_BotInstanceGuid);
```

restores any state information that may have existed in this code. The technique is required because you cannot have global variables in a multithreaded script environment.

Groove Enterprise Integration Server

The Groove Enterprise Integration Server (GEIS) is an easily deployed, server-based application that enables Groove shared-space users to share information across firewalls while still respecting company security and access restrictions. GEIS provides a runtime environment for Groove bots and can provide an automated connection to databases through SQL.

The server also can automate the backup of shared spaces and can monitor multiple shared spaces for action items. It also provides a vehicle for secure bot-to-bot messaging. Most important, it provides an administrator with the ability to centrally control access to and operation of bots.

The GEIS is a software application that runs on a dedicated machine within the peer-to-peer space but resides on the enterprise behind the firewall. Because it is behind the firewall, the enterprise data is available, yet secure.

A specialized runtime server, the GEIS operates totally under control of enterprise IT personnel. The IT personnel decide who gets to connect to what data.

Configuration is integrated in the bot console through a bot-specific custom UI, parameters and operations, and a server console for control and administration of user access. The bot server controls access through access control lists, and it can be administered either locally or remotely.

The bot server hosts the bots and controls the operation. When a bot is connected, the bot server automatically logs system use and behavior, and provides runtime status and event monitoring.

The bot server can also control the acceptance of invitations. It can accept them automatically, based on the policies defined for each service, or it can wait for administrative confirmation.

Now that you have an understanding of the methods required for database connectivity using connectors and bots, let's look at how you could integrate this knowledge into `TriviaQuiz`.

Data Integration, Bots, and `TriviaQuiz`

Certainly, `TriviaQuiz` could benefit from data integration. Right now, you have question entering and question answering in the same tool. It is a benefit that you can recruit all the members of the shared space in the entering of trivia data for our database, but, of course, this has disadvantages too. Each player who enters trivia questions will probably retain some of the correct answers, giving them an advantage. It is also not difficult to edit each question and see the correct answer.

If you were to move the question-and-answer database out of the tool, your game would become a game system. You could probably find existing databases already filled with questions and answers. Certainly, you could develop question-and-answer suites that were of interest to a wide variety of people and had appropriate degrees of difficulty.

You could parse in questions and answers from a database one at a time as they were needed, or you could import a whole set into your existing `RecordSetEngine`. Here's how the database is accessed in the Connectors example. This is code from `PRMGlue.gsl`:

```
function GetFAQ()
   {
      try
      {
         //This section makes it possible for visitors
         //to sort the data in the columns in ascending order.
var StrSort = "FAQID ASC";

         strQuery="SELECT * FROM FAQ ORDER BY " + StrSort;

         //Database path statement describing the driver to
         //use and the path to the desired database.
         var strProvider = "DSN=GroovePRM;";

         //Instantiate a Recordset object and open
         //a recordset using the Open method
         var objRS = new ActiveXObject("ADODB.recordset");
         objRS.Open(strQuery, strProvider);

         if(objRS.EOF)
      PropertyList.SetPropertyAsString("FAQText",
➥ "There are no entries in the FAQ database.");
         else
         {
            var strFAQ = "";

             while(!objRS.EOF)
             {
                // Skip the FAQ Category Description for now
                //and start with index 2.
                for(var i = 2; i < objRS.fields.count; i++)
                {
                   if(i == 2)
                      strFAQ += objRS(i) + "\n";
                   else
                      strFAQ += "\t" + objRS(i);
                }
                objRS.MoveNext
                strFAQ += "\n\n";
             }
             PropertyList.SetPropertyAsString("FAQText", strFAQ);
          }
```

```
        objRS.Close;
        objRS = "";
       }
          catch(exception)
          {
             var strErrMsg;
             if(objRS)
             {
             objRS.Close;
             objRS = "";
           }
       strErrMsg = "Error #" + exception.number + "\n";
       strErrMsg += exception.description;
       PropertyList.SetPropertyAsString("FAQText", strErrMsg);
    }
}
```

The code is wrapped in a `try/catch` block.

Using a Bot with `TriviaQuiz`

Hopefully, as a result of getting this far in the book, you can see how this code could be modified to read individual questions and answers into your `RecordSetEngine` to provide our tool with new questions and answers from an OBDC database. The connector would connect to the database, and the questions and answers would be accessible to all players.

How could you use a bot?

Of course, you could use a bot to access the data using centralized integration, but what if you added a degree of difficulty rating to each question? You could modify the previous code and that of your `TriviaQuiz` to allow questions to be drawn from the database directly into your Play Trivia screen.

You could then build a bot that kept track of your elapsed time as your space answered a set number of questions. If you did well, the bot would change a variable that you used in the quiz to filter questions from the database by degree of difficulty. The better you did as a space, the harder the questions would become; the worse you did, the easier.

Summary

It is pretty easy to dream up uses for both data integration and bots. This technology will have profound effects on our computer interactions, not only in Groove, within a very short time.

If you have a machine you can dedicate to the GEIS, download and install it, and try modifying some of the sample bots. It is the best way to learn to build your own.

In the next chapter, we'll look at some advanced topics we haven't yet discussed or used in the `TriviaQuiz` tool. The system could be used when there is a need for secure documentation of the users' interactions with each other, in legal or contractual situations, or when automated backup and archiving of shared spaces is required.

Advanced Topics

CHAPTER

14

IN THIS CHAPTER

In this chapter, we will study OSD in more depth by discussing strategy. We will then explore Groove versioning and its implications for writing tools. We will talk about how to add roles and permissions to your tools, and how to provide overview and context-sensitive help. We'll finish by discussing subforms and how they can be used as complex reusable components and as content for modal windows.

More About OSD

If you develop lot of complex Groove tools, the hardest part about OSD isn't writing it. The most difficult piece is deciding where your templates, graphics, schemas, and custom components are going to reside. Very early in the development process, this might not seem like a problem, but unfortunately, the decisions you make now about your naming conventions and location of your files on the Web server are likely to come back and haunt you. Because component names and locations have long-term impact, you need to develop naming and structural conventions before you deploy your first tool.

The impacts and effects of naming and structure are many. For example, after you have named a component, you can never change its name if you expect Groove's component manager to properly version your component.

Groove defines a *component* as any file for which a description can be written in OSD, so your tool templates, graphics, DLLs, or even other OSD files are, to Groove, components. The component manager manages the download of all components required by Groove to run on any supported platform. When the component manager loads, it checks the version of loaded components against the version recorded in the shared space component descriptor. If it needs a different version from the one it has, it identifies the proper source, downloads it, and installs it.

The component manager keeps track of every component by name in a single XML document—the Groove manifest. Here is a portion of the manifest that references `TrivaiQuiz3.tpl`:

```
<SOFTPKG Normalized="True"
➥ NAME="com.MyCompany.MyCompanyTools.TriviaQuiz3.TriviaQuiz3_tpl"
➥ VERSION="0,0,0,0">
   <IMPLEMENTATION>
      <CODEBASE HREF="http://components.MyCompany.com/
➥MyCompanyTools/TriviaQuiz3/TriviaQuiz3.tpl"/>
         <g:Install DatabaseURI="$TEMPLATESURI$"
➥ DocumentName="TriviaQuiz3.tpl" SchemaURI="$DEFAULTSCHEMA$"
➥ Type="Import To XSS"/>
         <g:Factory DatabaseURI="$TEMPLATESURI$"
➥ DocumentName="TriviaQuiz3.tpl" Type="XML Document" Name="Open"/>
         <g:ComponentURLProvider Argument="TriviaQuiz3.tpl"
➥ DocumentName="TriviaQuiz3.tpl" DocumentType="Template"
➥ DatabaseURI="$TEMPLATESURI$" ProgID="Groove.TemplateParser"/>
```

```
    </IMPLEMENTATION>
    <g:DependentsList>
       <g:Dependent URL="System" Name="com.MyCompany.MyCompanyTools.
➥TriviaQuiz3.triviaquiz3Descriptor_xml"/>
    </g:DependentsList>
</SOFTPKG>
<SOFTPKG Normalized="True"
➥ NAME="com.MyCompany.MyCompanyTools.TriviaQuiz3.triviaquiz3Descriptor_xml"
➥ VERSION="0,0,0,0">
    <IMPLEMENTATION>
       <CODEBASE HREF="http://components.MyCompany.com/
➥MyCompanyTools/TriviaQuiz3/triviaquiz3Descriptor.xml"/>
          <g:Install TargetDir="$GROOVEDATA$\XML Files" Type="Copy"/>
          <g:Factory
➥ Filename="$GROOVEDATA$\XML Files\triviaquiz3Descriptor.xml"
➥ Type="Temporary XML Document" Name="Open"/>
    </IMPLEMENTATION>
    <g:DependentsList>
       <g:Dependent
➥ URL="grooveAccount://8ti59dduzjyy4s332k0964b2v6cq75pbakr"
➥ Name="Account Template List"/>
    </g:DependentsList>
</SOFTPKG>
```

With this information, Groove can find any components it might need in order to run version `0,0,0,0 TriviaQuiz3` on this machine.

NOTE

Although reverse domain name package names are not required, Groove recommends them. With every component—those from Groove, others from third parties, and components of your own—listed in the manifest, there is substantial possibility of namespace collisions.

14 ADVANCED TOPICS

Managing the Component Tree Structure

Often, and particularly at the beginning of development, components are arranged in a tree structure. If we at MyCompany.com wrote a trivia quiz, we could simply put it into a directory called `myTriviaGame`, and Groove would find it easily if the OSD were properly written. But let's say that we're not satisfied to write just one program. We write an app or two, and maybe several other kinds of games.

We might want to put all our Groove tools into a `MyCompanyTools` directory, and have separate directories for apps and games. In the `Games` folder, we might have directories for word games, card games, and board games. Inside the `Word Games` directory, we would have a `TriviaGame` subdirectory, and have that further divided into `TriviaGameGraphics` and `TriviaGameSchema`. `TriviaGame.tpl` would go in the `TriviaGame` directory; `OurTriviaGame.jpg` and `TriviaGameSchema` would go into `TriviaGameGraphics` and `TriviaGameSchema`, respectively.

That would be a nice neat directory structure, and we could refer to the graphic package by name as `com.MyCompany.MyCompanyTools.Games.WordGames.TriviaGame.TriviaGameGraphics.OurTriviaGame.JPG`. We would want to mirror this structure on the Web, so our Web site would look as shown in Figure 14.1.

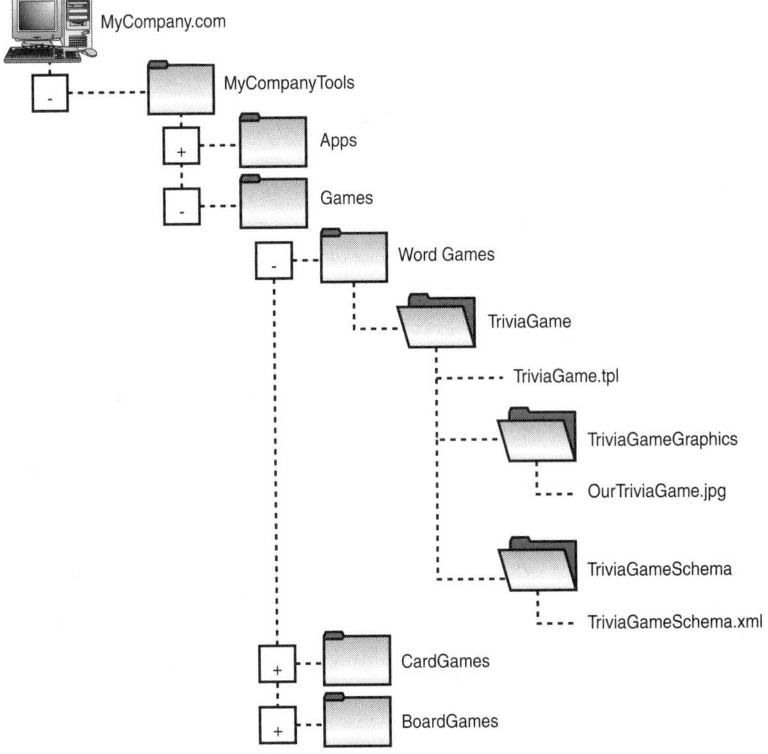

FIGURE 14.1
The MyCompany.com Web site.

So far, so good. Now we rewrite `TriviaQuiz` and develop a little custom component, `clock.dll`, which is a graphical clock component to show our elapsed time. It works great. We put it into the `TriviaGame` folder and write our OSD, and everything is dandy.

Then, we realize we could use that clock in the chess game that is in the `BoardGames` folder. Now what do we do?

We could rename the component `ChessGameClock.dll` and put it in with the chess game, but then we'd have two identical pieces of code that we would have to maintain separately, always trying to remember whether we updated all the instances. It would be better to recognize that we have a reusable component. Ideally, our component would go in the `Games` directory. That way, `Clock.dll` could be easily accessed by Trivia Quiz, chess, and any card game you wanted to play under pressure.

Now, to further complicate matters, we create a major version 2 Trivia Game Tool. It must continue to be named `TriviaGame.tpl` because we want component manager to help us update the existing spaces that have the earlier version. If the second version is named the same as the first, they can't both reside in the same folder on the Web site.

Because the new version of the component does not reside in the same folder as the old one, the component URLs may have to be changed. We certainly don't want to do this, because we want the component URLs to be as intuitive as possible to developers. The need to change component URLs could be eliminated by clever use of OSD and dependencies, but pretty soon you would have a huge maze of interconnected OSD. There are two techniques that can help keep these problems minimized: fanout OSD redirection and component manager OSD redirection.

Fanout OSD Redirection

Here is a typical Groove component resource URL:

```
<g:ComponentResource FingerprintID="Groove"
➥ URL="http://components.groove.net/Groove/Components/Root.osd?
➥Package=net.groove.Groove.ToolComponents.GrooveCommonComponents_DLL&amp;
➥Version=0&amp;Factory=ViewContainer"/>
```

The URL points to a `Root.osd` file that contains many `SOFTPKG` elements, including one whose name is `net.groove.Groove.ToolComponents.GrooveCommonComponents_DLL Version` and whose version is 0. The `Root.osd` file *fans out* to all the Groove components. In this particular case, the `SOFTPKG` contains an `IMPLEMENTATION` block. In that `IMPLEMENTATION` is a `CODEBASE` element with an `HREF` attribute that points to the current location of the `GrooveCommonComponents` DLL. The address of the DLL can change in the `HREF` attribute, but the component URL to `Root.osd` does not.

Component Manager OSD Redirection

The second technique is component manager OSD redirection. Here's how it works.

Groove's component manager searches for SOFTPKG names in an OSD file. It tries to find an exact match. If it doesn't find an exact match, it lops off all the text after the last period and repeats the search.

For example, if component manager were handed a component resource URL like

```
http://Mycompany.com/MyCompanyTools/Games/Games.osd?
➥Package=com.Mycompany.MyCompanyTools.Games.WordGames.
➥TriviaGame.TriviaGame_TPL&amp;Version=0&amp;Factory=Open/>
```

and Games.osd did not contain a SOFTPKG name that matched TriviaGame_TPL, component manager would lop off the TriviaGame_TPL part, like so:

```
com.Mycompany.MyCompanyTools.Games.WordGames.TriviaGame.
```

Component manager would then search the OSD again.

Now suppose we took advantage of this feature by writing a SOFTPKG in the Games.osd that looked like this:

```
<SOFTPKG Name="com.Mycompany.MyCompanyTools.Games.WordGames.TriviaGame.*"
➥ VERSION="0,0,0,0">
     <g:Redirect HREF="http://MyComponentFarm.Mycompany.com/Games/Games.osd>
</SOFTPKG>
```

The component manager would be redirected automatically from Mycompany.com/MyCompanyTools/Games/Games.osd to another server and to MyComponentFarm.Mycompany.com/Games/Games.osd. The latter file would contain a description of TriviaGame_TPL.

There is no reason, however, that /Games/Games.osd couldn't also contain a redirection. Redirections of multiple hops are possible.

These options give you a lot of flexibility in how you design both your component hierarchy and your Web server structure, but nothing will replace some serious forethought to prevent your component structure from becoming unmanageable.

Versioning

Versions are necessary because, after they've been published, SOFTPKG names can never change. Previous SOFTPKGs are retained so that users with older tools can continue to use them if they do not want to upgrade to the newer ones, and so that users invited to a space with the 1.0 tool can install the older version.

Each time the component manager initializes, it checks the version of the components that are loaded against the version numbers located in the descriptors of the components in the shared space. If it needs a different version from the one it has, it identifies the proper source from the descriptor and OSD, and downloads it.

There are four version numbers, separated by commas—for example, `VERSION="1,2,0,1096"`. These numbers are explained here:

- The first digit indicates the *major version*. A change in this number indicates a tool that is incompatible with previous major versions. A user in an existing shared space would need to upgrade in order to use data produced by the major versioned tool.
- The second number indicates a *minor version*. A minor version is one that includes changes that are all backward-compatible with all previous minor versions. A user would be able to access all data in an existing space without upgrading to the minor versioned tool.
- The third number is the *custom version*. Normally, the custom version would be used to identify a special-purpose version of the tool that did not affect the basic functionality of the tool. If we made a version of `TriviaQuiz` that was branded with a company's logo, we could version that with a custom version, because the change would have no effect on its capability to exist in a shared space with other non-custom version instances of the tool in a shared space. No changes in the other user's tools would be necessary to keep the shared space functioning properly. Groove uses custom version numbers with its utility tools, such as the Groove DBNavigator, Tool Creator, and Tool Publisher.
- The fourth digit is the *sequence version*. Groove uses the build number. The sequence number is frequently used to track bug fixes. Sequence versioning has no effect on shared space information access by users.

Major and Minor Versions

There are many differences between major and minor versions of components. Minor versions are used to make minor changes to components. The changes are considered minor because they are backward-compatible with respect to data model, interface, and command format. A shared space can function perfectly if some members have different minor versions of the same tool. All members can continue to access the same data in essentially the same way.

Making a Minor Version Change to a Tool

When you make a minor version change, you follow these steps:

1. Update the component, making sure not to change the data model, the interface, or the command format of the tool.
2. Update the OSD to add `SOFTPKG`s or dependencies for the new version. You should remove the `SOFTPKG`s of older versions. Be sure to sign your new OSD.
3. Update your server directory to include the new files.
4. Write and deploy a new `.GRV` file that specifies the new minor version of the tool descriptor.

If the user does not have the new version, it is found to be different in the manifest when the user clicks your `.GRV`. The old files get overwritten, the user instantiates the tool, and the new components are installed. After the new files are installed, re-injecting the tool will do nothing.

Making a Major Version Change

Major versions are very different. They can be thought of as entirely new tools, and they are backward-incompatible. Major revisions are made if the data model of the tool or the interface changes so that it is incompatible with older versions of the same tool. Major versions never replace older versions of a tool, and users can continue to use older versions whenever they want.

The process for major versioning goes like this:

1. Update the component. This time you are not concerned with compatibility, with respect to interface, data model, or command format.
2. Update the OSD to add new `SOFTPKG`s or dependencies for the component, being sure to increment the major version number.
3. If necessary, change a component's name so that it can coexist with older versions of the component on the user's machine.
4. Sign your OSD.
5. Set up a new Web server directory for your new version, making sure you have included all the necessary files.
6. Write and deploy a new `.GRV` file that specifies the correct version of the tool descriptor.

When a user runs the `.GRV` file, the new tool gets injected. Unlike with a minor revision, no files get overwritten.

Groove's versioning and component upgrade process ensures that users always have access to new tools, and have a pretty painless upgrade operation. This ease and transparency is a great benefit to the tool developer.

Roles and Permissions

There are some kinds of collaboration that benefit from a anarchic, free-for-all environment, such as brainstorming. However, other collaborative activities, such as conflict resolution, suffer in a no-controls atmosphere.

In a space without controls, any member can invite others, add and delete tools, and modify or delete important data. When any member makes a change to his or her local copy of data in a shared space, that change gets propagated to all other members' copies of that shared space. Consequently, in licensed versions, Groove introduced an access control framework to enforce some rules about who can change data in a shared space built around the concept of roles and permissions.

In Groove's scheme, a member can be assigned one of three roles: manager, participant, or guest:

- The Manager role is automatically assigned to the creator of the space. When the creator of the shared space invites other members, he or she assigns each invitee one of the three roles. As the creators of the space, managers have the greatest powers and abilities, or permissions. A *permission* is a right to make a change to a shared space or to its membership. By default, managers can invite other members, uninvite current members, use tools, change data, and add or delete tools.
- Participants can be thought of as active members of the shared space whose input is necessary to its functioning. Participants can, by default, invite other members, use tools, change data, and add tools.
- Guests are, as the name implies, nonparticipating members of the space. By default, guests can only view shared space tools.

Roles, however, are dynamic. A guest in a space may need to contribute in a more active way. In that case, the manager of the space can change the guest's role to that of a participant. Or, alternatively, the manager could allow all guests additional permissions, such as inviting new members or adding tools.

Roles are managed through a Roles dialog box available from the Roles selection in the Options menu. Shared space permissions are administered through the Permissions dialog box using the Shared Space Permissions selection.

As a developer, though, you may want a finer granularity than these top-level options allow. In `TriviaQuiz`, for example, you might not want all users to be able to edit the questions. You may decide to develop an access control scheme that allows only the creator of a question to edit it. Groove provides you with that ability through tool-level access control.

Tool-Level Access Control

Groove's Calendar Tool is a good example of the use of tool-level permissions. The manager of a shared space that includes the Calendar Tool can add a calendar entry, can edit any entry including his or her own, can delete any entry, and can even restrict other participants from viewing the tool. This functionality is available from the tool-specific permissions selection in the Options menu.

These permissions are also dynamic. Notice that the tool-specific permissions are linked to the shared space roles. This linking is accomplished through a role hierarchy. Code in `groovetelespacetemplate*.tpl` defines roles for shared spaces. Those roles are named `$Telespace.Manager`, `$Telespace.Member`, and `$Telespace.Guest`. As a developer, you can create tool permissions and assign the shared-space roles to them by listing these names as default parents to your tool's roles.

Creating Roles

Roles are created with Groove extensions to XML. For example, you can follow these steps to create code that assigns a permission to a user with either a manager or a participant shared space role:

1. Place the following code into a `componentGroup` element in your `.TPL` file. Begin with an `ObjectTypes` tag that holds an `ObjectType`. An `ObjectType` is an object to which access control applies, for example, a tool's component group:

```
<g:ObjectTypes>
   <g:ObjectType Name="$ComponentGroup">
</g:ObjectTypes>
```

2. An `AccessControl` tag holds the roles that apply to the `ObjectType`. The code in bold shows the additions:

```
<g:ObjectTypes>
   <g:ObjectType Name="$ComponentGroup">
      <g:AccessControl>
         <g:Roles>
         </g:Roles>
      <g:/AccessControl>
</g:ObjectTypes>
```

3. A `role` element contains several attributes. Like any other element, the `role` element has a `name` attribute. A `$ComponentGroup.AddEntry` name would indicate that the role was applied to an `AddEntry` operation in a component group.

   A `visible` attribute determines whether a role is displayed in the tool permissions dialog. If it is, a `category` and `displayName` are required.

   The `category` value is either `Role` or `Permission`, and the `DisplayName` value is the name of the `Role` as it appears in the dialog.

   The linking of the `role` element with a shared space role is accomplished with a `DefaultParentRoles` attribute. The value of the attribute is the name or names of the roles defined in `groovetelespacetemplate*.tpl`, or it can be set to the name of roles within the tool template, as you will soon see:

```
<g:ObjectTypes>
   <g:ObjectType Name="$ComponentGroup">
      <g:AccessControl>
         <g:Roles>
            <g:Role
               Name="$ComponentGroup.AddEntry"
```

```
                Visible="true"
                Category="Permission"
                DisplayName="Add Entry"
                DefaultParentRoles="$Telespace.Member $Telespace.Manager">
                >
            </g:Roles>
        <g:/AccessControl>
</g:ObjectTypes>
```

4. The particular operation for which the permission is granted needs to be specified. In this case, the operation is one to add a record to the `RecordSetEngine`:

```
<g:ObjectTypes>
    <g:ObjectType Name="$ComponentGroup">
        <g:AccessControl>
            <g:Roles>
                <g:Role
                    Name="$ComponentGroup.AddEntry"
                    Visible="true"
                    Category="Permission"
                    DisplayName="Add Entry"
                    DefaultParentRoles="$Telespace.Member $Telespace.Manager">
                    >
                    <g:Operations>
                        <g:Operation Name="AddRecord"
➥ TargetName="RecordSetEngine"/>
</g:Operations>
            </g:Roles>
        <g:/AccessControl>
</g:ObjectTypes>
```

This code is now a complete unit. The permission lets the user add an entry to the `RecordSetEngine`.

In some cases it could take two or more operations to achieve the result required by the role. For example,

```
<g:Role
    Name="$ComponentGroup.EditAnyEntry"
    Visible="true"
    Category="Permission"
    DisplayName="Edit Any Entry"
    DefaultParentRoles="$Telespace.Manager"
    >
    <g:Operations>
        <g:Operation Name="ReplaceRecord" TargetName="RecordSetEngine"/>
        <g:Operation Name="SetField"
➥ TargetName="urn:groove.net:TriviaQuizRecord"/>
```

```
    </g:Operations>
</g:Role>
```

Additionally, the permission may be constrained by some condition. For example, a permission to edit our own entries would need to constrain the user to only those entries the user created:

```
<g:Role
    Name="$ComponentGroup.EditOwnEntry"
    Visible="true"
    Category="Permission"
    DisplayName="Edit Own Entry"
    DefaultParentRoles="$Telespace.Member $Telespace.Manager"
    >
    <g:Operations>
        <g:Operation Name="ReplaceRecord" TargetName="RecordSetEngine">
            <g:Constraints IsCreator="true"/>
        </g:Operation>
        <g:Operation Name="RemoveRecord" TargetName="RecordSetEngine">
            <g:Constraints IsCreator="true"/>
        </g:Operation>
    </g:Operations>
</g:Role>
```

Continue to add role elements until you have described all the operations you want to include.

As mentioned earlier, the `DefaultParentRole` does not have to be a role defined in the `groovetelespacetemplate*.tpl`. The `DefaultParentRole` value can be the name of any role defined in the `AccessControl` element. This allows the creation of complex hierarchies of `roles`.

Adding Help

Groove Help takes two forms: the overview text that is shown when the user selects Show Overview in the View menu, and help files written in HTML that are displayed when the user chooses Help on [*custom tool name*] from the Help menu. The overview text is Rich Text Format (RTF) text that gives the user an overall view of the tool's purpose and operation. The text itself is pasted directly into the tool template in a `CDATA` block. The HTML Help file is referenced by URL in the template code, but is displayed in the user's default browser.

The Groove components that make the viewing of these files possible are called `RTFView` and `RTFHelpProvider`. `RTFHelpProvider` is designated as the help info provider in the `ComponentGroup` element attributes.

For example, let's write the necessary code to display both overview text and help files in our `TriviaQuiz` tool. Save a copy of `TriviaQuiz` into your development directory and make the following changes:

1. In the component group, add a `HelpInfoProvider` component like this:

```
<g:ComponentGroup Delegate="TriviaQuizGlue"
➥ DefaultView="TriviaQuizViewContainer"
➥ HelpInfoProvider="RTFHelpProvider">
```

2. Having designated a help provider, you now have to include in the component group the two components that make it possible: an `RTFHelpProvider` and an `RTFView` component. Like any other Groove component, `RTFView` takes a component URL. The package name for the component is `net.groove.Groove.ToolComponents.GrooveTextTools_DLL`, and the factory is `TextView`. Add the component with the following code:

```
<g:Component Name = "RTFView">
   <g:ComponentResource FingerprintID="Groove"
➥ URL="http://components.groove.net/Groove/Components/Root.osd?
➥Package=net.groove.Groove.ToolComponents.GrooveTextTools_DLL&amp;
➥Version=0&amp;Factory=TextView"/>
</g:Component>
```

3. The `RTFView` component takes four properties: `ReadOnly`, `BackStyle`, `MenuStyle`, and `BorderVisible`. As a general rule, you will want to keep your overview text identical to Groove's, so you should use the values the Groove tools use. These are `true`, `transparent`, `static`, and `false`, respectively:

```
<g:Component Name = "RTFView">
   <g:ComponentResource FingerprintID="Groove"
➥URL="http://components.groove.net/Groove/Components/Root.osd?
➥Package=net.groove.Groove.ToolComponents.GrooveTextTools_DLL&amp;
➥Version=0&amp;Factory=TextView"/>
   <g:PropertyList Version="1">
      <g:Property Name="ReadOnly" Value="true"/>
      <g:Property Name="BackStyle" Value="transparent"/>
      <g:Property Name="MenuStyle" Value="static"/>
      <g:Property Name="BorderVisible" Value="false"/>
   </g:PropertyList>
</g:Component>
```

4. The second necessary component is the `RTFHelpProvider`. Its package name is `net.groove.Groove.ToolComponents.GrooveCommonComponents_DLL`, and its factory is `RTFHelpProvider`. Add it with the following code:

```
<g:Component Name = "RTFHelpProvider">
   <g:ComponentResource FingerprintID="Groove"
➥ URL="http://components.groove.net/Groove/Components/Root.osd?
```

```
➥Package=net.groove.Groove.ToolComponents.GrooveCommonComponents_DLL&amp;
➥Version=0&amp;Factory=RTFHelpProvider"/>
</g:Component>
```

5. Like `RTFView`, it also takes a property list. The first property is named `ContextHelpURL` and its value is the URL to your help file. Use `Help\MyCompany.com\tools\TriviaQuiz\PlayingTrivia.htm`, which will look for the file in Groove's `Help` folder in the `Data` directory. We'll need to fill out the rest of the folders when we write our OSD. Add the properties to the component like this:

```
<g:Component Name = "RTFHelpProvider">
   <g:ComponentResource FingerprintID="Groove"
➥ URL="http://components.groove.net/Groove/Components/Root.osd?
➥Package=net.groove.Groove.ToolComponents.GrooveCommonComponents_DLL&amp;
➥Version=0&amp;Factory=RTFHelpProvider"/>
   <g:PropertyList Version="1">
      <g:Property Name="ContextHelpURL"
➥ Value="Help\MyCompany.com\tools\TriviaQuiz\PlayingTrivia.htm"/>
   </g:PropertyList>
</g:Component>
```

6. Next add a `ContextHelpDisplayType` property with a value of `0`. The `HelpDisplayName` property defines the name that will appear in the Help menu, and the `HeaderText` will show up as the first line in the Overview panel. Add these properties as follows:

```
<g:Component Name = "RTFHelpProvider">
   <g:ComponentResource FingerprintID="Groove"
➥ URL="http://components.groove.net/Groove/Components/Root.osd?
➥Package=net.groove.Groove.ToolComponents.GrooveCommonComponents_DLL&amp;
➥Version=0&amp;Factory=RTFHelpProvider"/>
   <g:PropertyList Version="1">
      <g:Property Name="ContextHelpURL"
➥ Value="Help\MyCompany.com\tools\TriviaQuiz\PlayingTrivia.htm"/>
      <g:Property Name="ContextHelpDisplayType" Value="0"/>
      <g:Property Name="HelpDisplayName" Value="TriviaQuiz"/>
      <g:Property Name="HeaderText" Value="TriviaQuiz"/>
   </g:PropertyList>
</g:Component>
```

7. Add a `Content` property and initially set its value to an empty string. Then use a `PropertyValue` element to enter your rich text as `CDATA`:

```
<g:Component Name = "RTFHelpProvider">
   <g:ComponentResource FingerprintID="Groove"
➥ URL="http://components.groove.net/Groove/Components/Root.osd?
➥Package=net.groove.Groove.ToolComponents.GrooveCommonComponents_DLL&amp;
➥Version=0&amp;Factory=RTFHelpProvider"/>
   <g:PropertyList Version="1">
```

```
        <g:Property Name="ContextHelpURL"
➥ Value="Help\MyCompany.com\tools\TriviaQuiz\PlayingTrivia.htm"/>
        <g:Property Name="ContextHelpDisplayType" Value="0"/>
        <g:Property Name="HelpDisplayName" Value="TriviaQuiz"/>
        <g:Property Name="HeaderText" Value="TriviaQuiz"/>
        <g:Property Value="" Name="Content">
            <g:PropertyValue>
                <![CDATA[]]>
            </g:PropertyValue>
        </g:Property>
    </g:PropertyList>
</g:Component>
```

8. You can now paste the rich text you want to display into the CDATA container. The easiest way to get raw rich text for this container is to write your overview text in WordPad, save it in Rich Text Format, and then open the saved document with Notepad. From Notepad, you can paste the code into the CDATA container as follows:

```
<g:Component Name = "RTFHelpProvider">
    <g:ComponentResource FingerprintID="Groove"
➥ URL="http://components.groove.net/Groove/Components/Root.osd?
➥Package=net.groove.Groove.ToolComponents.GrooveCommonComponents_DLL&amp;
➥Version=0&amp;Factory=RTFHelpProvider"/>
    <g:PropertyList Version="1">
        <g:Property Name="ContextHelpURL"
Value="Help\MyCompany.com\tools\TriviaQuiz\PlayingTrivia.htm"/>
<g:Property Name="ContextHelpDisplayType" Value="0"/>
        <g:Property Name="HelpDisplayName" Value="TriviaQuiz"/>
        <g:Property Name="HeaderText" Value="TriviaQuiz"/>
        <g:Property Value="" Name="Content">
            <g:PropertyValue>
                <![CDATA[{\rtf1\ansi\ansicpg1252\deff0\deflang1033{\fonttbl
➥{\f0\fswiss\fprq2\fcharset0 Verdana;}{\f1\fnil\fcharset0
➥ Times New Roman;}} \viewkind4\uc1\pard\b\f0\fs20 TriviaQuiz
➥\b0 lets you enter trivia questions in a database and then answer them
➥ as a group. \b TriviaQuiz \b0 checks your group\rquote s time to answer
➥ each question, and then computes your total time through the quiz.
➥ If you guess, \b TriviaQuiz\b0  will penalize you 20 seconds. \b You
➥ cannot do worse than 20 seconds for each question\b0 ,
➥ so if you\rquote re taking a long time, you might as well guess.\par
\par
When you first open the game, \b there are no questions
➥ \b0 in the database, \b so you must enter some \b0 before you can
play.\par
➥\f1\par
                }]]>
            </g:PropertyValue>
```

```
            </g:Property>
        </g:PropertyList>
    </g:Component>
```

9. Establish component connections between `RTFHelpProvider` and `RTFView`. The connection to `RTFView` requires an ID of `2`:

```
<g:Component Name = "RTFHelpProvider">
    <g:ComponentResource FingerprintID="Groove"
➥ URL="http://components.groove.net/Groove/Components/Root.osd?
➥Package=net.groove.Groove.ToolComponents.GrooveCommonComponents_DLL&amp;
➥Version=0&amp;Factory=RTFHelpProvider"/>
    <g:PropertyList Version="1">
        <g:Property Name="ContextHelpURL"
➥ Value="Help\YourCompnay.com\tools\TriviaQuiz\PlayingTrivia.htm"/>
        <g:Property Name="ContextHelpDisplayType" Value="0"/>
        <g:Property Name="HelpDisplayName" Value="TriviaQuiz"/>
        <g:Property Name="HeaderText" Value="TriviaQuiz"/>
        <g:Property Name="Content" Value="">
<g:PropertyValue>
                <![CDATA[{\rtf1\ansi\ansicpg1252\deff0\deflang1033{\fonttbl
➥{\f0\fswiss\fprq2\fcharset0 Verdana;}{\f1\fnil\fcharset0
➥ Times New Roman;}} \viewkind4\uc1\pard\b\f0\fs20 TriviaQuiz
➥\b0 lets you enter trivia questions in a database and then answer them
➥ as a group. \b TriviaQuiz \b0 checks your group\rquote s time to answer
➥ each question, and then computes your total time through the quiz.
➥ If you guess, \b TriviaQuiz\b0  will penalize you 20 seconds. \b You
➥ cannot do worse than 20 seconds for each question\b0 ,
➥ so if you\rquote re taking a long time, you might as well guess.\par
                }]]>
            </g:PropertyValue>
        </g:Property>
    </g:PropertyList>
    <g:ComponentConnections>
        <g:Connection Name="RTFView" ConnectionID="2"
    <g:ComponentConnections>
</g:Component>
```

10. Establish an external connection to `HelpHandler`. `HelpHandler` is an object that handles help requests. It requires a connection ID of `0`:

```
<g:Component Name = "RTFHelpProvider">
    <g:ComponentResource FingerprintID="Groove"
➥ URL="http://components.groove.net/Groove/Components/Root.osd?
➥Package=net.groove.Groove.ToolComponents.GrooveCommonComponents_DLL&amp;
➥Version=0&amp;Factory=RTFHelpProvider"/>
    <g:PropertyList Version="1">
        <g:Property Name="ContextHelpURL"
```

```
➥ Value="Help\YourCompnay.com\tools\TriviaQuiz\PlayingTrivia.htm"/>
        <g:Property Name="ContextHelpDisplayType" Value="0"/>
        <g:Property Name="HelpDisplayName" Value="TriviaQuiz"/>
        <g:Property Name="HeaderText" Value="TriviaQuiz"/>
        <g:Property Name="Content" Value="">
<g:PropertyValue>
            <![CDATA[{\rtf1\ansi\ansicpg1252\deff0\deflang1033{\fonttbl
➥{\f0\fswiss\fprq2\fcharset0 Verdana;}{\f1\fnil\fcharset0
➥ Times New Roman;}} \viewkind4\uc1\pard\b\f0\fs20 TriviaQuiz
➥\b0 lets you enter trivia questions in a database and then answer them
➥ as a group. \b TriviaQuiz \b0 checks your group\rquote s time to answer
➥ each question, and then computes your total time through the quiz.
➥ If you guess, \b TriviaQuiz\b0  will penalize you 20 seconds. \b You
➥ cannot do worse than 20 seconds for each question\b0 ,
➥ so if you\rquote re taking a long time, you might as well guess.\par
            }]]>
          </g:PropertyValue>
        </g:Property>
      </g:PropertyList>
      <g:ComponentConnections>
        <g:Connection Name="RTFView" ConnectionID="2"
      <g:ComponentConnections>
      <ExternalObjectConnections>
        <Connection Name="HelpHandler" ConnectionID="0">
      </ExternalObjectConnections>
</g:Component>
```

That completes the XML necessary to display help files in our `TriviaQuiz` tool. Of course, we still need to write our HTML file and install the help files.

To install help, we need to add a `SOFTPKG` for our help files to our tool's OSD. To make this somewhat easier, it is a good idea to put help files into a `.CAB` file. This is especially true if your HTML page has dependent graphics. Using a `.CAB` ensures that the files are as small as possible, and Groove is presented with a single file to install.

The directory structure necessary to nest your graphics or other support files can be implemented in the `.CAB`. The OSD needs only to unpack the `.CAB` to the designated directory. For example:

```
<SOFTPKG NAME="com.MyCompany.MyCompanyTools.TriviaQuiz.Help" VERSION="0,0,0,0">
   <IMPLEMENTATION>
      <CODEBASE
HREF="http://components.MyCompany.com/MyCompanyTools/TriviaQuiz/TriviaQuiz.CAB"/>
      <g:Install Type="Unpack CAB"
TargetDir="$GROOVEDATA$\Help\MyCompany.com\tools\TriviaQuiz"/>
   </IMPLEMENTATION>
```

```
</SOFTPKG>
```

You can see that it is relatively simple to provide help for your tools.

Subforms

Groove `SubForm` components provide a way to encapsulate a view and logic into a reusable unit. A `SubForm` contains a component group that includes a view container, a layout, and a delegate or glue code component. A subform can contain UI components, engines, or even other subforms, enabling component groups to be nested.

Let's create a sample subform and then put it into our tool skeleton code:

1. Begin with the component name and resource URL, using `SubForm` as the factory:

```
<g:Component Name="ASampleSubForm">
   <g:ComponentResource
➥ URL="http://components.groove.net/Groove/Components/Root.osd?
➥Package=net.groove.Groove.ToolComponents.GrooveCommonComponents_DLL&amp;
➥Version=0&amp;Factory=SubForm" FingerprintID="Groove"/>
```

2. Add a component group and specify `SubFormViewContainer` as the default view, and `SubFormGlue` as the delegate:

```
<g:ComponentGroup DefaultView="SubFormViewContainer"
Delegate="SubFormGlue">
```

3. Describe the `SubFormViewContainer` and include its layout:

```
<g:ComponentGroup DefaultView="SubFormViewContainer"
Delegate="SubFormGlue">
      <g:Component Name="SubFormViewContainer">
         <g:ComponentResource
➥ URL="http://components.groove.net/Groove/Components/Root.osd?
➥Package=net.groove.Groove.ToolComponents.GrooveCommonComponents_DLL&amp;
➥Version=0&amp;Factory=ViewContainer" FingerprintID="Groove"/>
         <g:PropertyList Version="1">
            <g:Property Name="PreferredWidth" Value="800"/>
            <g:Property Name="PreferredHeight" Value="200"/>
         </g:PropertyList>
         <g:ComponentConnections>
            <g:Connection Name="SubFormLayout" ConnectionID="0"/>
         </g:ComponentConnections>
         </g:Component>

      <g:Component Name="SubFormLayout">
         <g:ComponentResource
➥ URL="http://components.groove.net/Groove/Components/Root.osd?
➥Package=net.groove.Groove.ToolComponents.GrooveCommonComponents_DLL&amp;
```

```
➥Version=0&amp;Factory=MultiCellLayout" FingerprintID="Groove"/>
         <g:PropertyList Version="1">
            <g:Property Name="Layout">
               <g:PropertyValue>
                   <MULTIROW>
                      <ROW>
                        <CELL HEIGHT="35">SubFormTitle</CELL>
                     </ROW>
                     <ROW>
                        <CELL HEIGHT="55"/>
                        <CELL WIDTH="55" TopPad="10">SubFormButton</CELL>
                        <CELL WIDTH="8"/>
                     </ROW>
                   </MULTIROW>
               </g:PropertyValue>
            </g:Property>
         </g:PropertyList>
      </g:Component>
```

4. Add two UI components, some static text and a button, and just enough glue code to make the button respond:

```
      <g:Component Name="SubFormTitle">
         <g:ComponentResource
➥ URL="http://components.groove.net/Groove/Components/Root.osd?
➥Package=net.groove.Groove.ToolComponents.GrooveCommonComponents_DLL&amp;
➥Version=0&amp;Factory=Static" FingerprintID="Groove"/>
         <g:PropertyList Version="1">
            <g:Property Name="FontStyle" Value="DialogTitleText"/>
            <g:Property Name="Label" Value="The subform is in this pane."/>
            <g:Property Name="VAlignment" Value="Left"/>
         </g:PropertyList>
      </g:Component>

      <g:Component Name="SubFormButton">
         <g:ComponentResource
➥ URL="http://components.groove.net/Groove/Components/Root.osd?
➥Package=net.groove.Groove.ToolComponents.GrooveCommonComponents_DLL&amp;
➥Version=0&amp;Factory=Button" FingerprintID="Groove"/>
         <g:PropertyList Version="1">
            <g:Property Name="ImageHeight" Value="24"/>
            <g:Property Name="Label"
➥ Value="Press to &amp;Initiate Action in SubForm"/>
            <g:Property Name="Style" Value="StandardButton"/>
         </g:PropertyList>
      </g:Component>

      <g:Component Name="SubFormGlue">
```

```
          <g:ComponentResource
➥ URL="http://components.groove.net/Groove/Components/Root.osd?
➥Package=net.groove.Groove.ToolComponents.GrooveCommonComponents_DLL&amp;
➥Version=0&amp;Factory=ScriptHost2" FingerprintID="Groove"/>
          <g:ComponentConnections>
             <g:Connection Name="SubFormButton" ConnectionID="0"/>
          </g:ComponentConnections>
          <SCRIPT
➥SRC="http://components.groove.net/Groove/Components/Root.osd?
➥Package=net.groove.Groove.ToolComponents.GrooveGlobalHelperFunctions_GSL&
➥amp;Version=0,1&amp;Factory=Open" FingerprintID="Groove"/>

          <SCRIPT>
          <![CDATA[

          function Initialize()
          {

          }

          function Terminate()
          {

          }

          function SubFormButton_OnCommand(i_UICommand)
          {
          }
             ]]>
          </SCRIPT>
       </g:Component>
</g:ComponentGroup>
</g:Component>
```

5. Pull out the tool skeleton code created in Chapter 9, “Building a Basic Groove Tool,” and save the file in your `Groove Development` folder as `SubformDemo.tpl`. Change the document name to

   ```
   <g:Document Name="SubFormDemo.tpl" xmlns:g="urn:groove.net">
   ```

   and change the tool template names from

   ```
   <g:ToolTemplate
   ➥ Name=" ToolName.Tool" DefaultToolDisplayName="ToolName"
   ➥ TemplateDisplayName="ToolName">
   ```

   to

```
<g:ToolTemplate Name="SubFormDemo.Tool"
➥ DefaultToolDisplayName="SubFormDemo"
➥ TemplateDisplayName="SubFormDemo">
```

6. Paste the `MySubForm` component into the `SubFormDemo.tpl` file just above the first `UIComponent`, `ToolButton`.

7. Change the `ToolLayout` layout in the `SubFormDemo.tpl` file from

```
<g:Property Name="Layout">
   <g:PropertyValue>
      <TABLE>

         <TR>
            <TD>ToolButton</TD>
            <TD/>
         </TR>

         <TR>
            <TD/>
            <TD/>
         </TR>

         <TR>
            <TD/>
            <TD/>
         </TR>

      </TABLE>
   </g:PropertyValue>
</g:Property>
```

to

```
<g:Property Name="Layout">
   <g:PropertyValue>
      <TABLE>

         <TR>
            <TD>ToolButton</TD>
         </TR>

         <TR>
            <TD>MySubForm</TD>
         </TR>
      </TABLE>
   </g:PropertyValue>
</g:Property>
```

Now, copy the file from your `Groove Development` folder to the `My Templates` directory in your `Groove\Data` directory, and add the tool to your development space. You'll see two buttons. The top button is the button we put into the tool skeleton code, and it responds to the logic in the `ToolGlue` code. The bottom button is in the subform and responds to the logic in `SubFormGlue`.

Using Subforms

Subforms are used in the Groove tools in two ways. The first and most straightforward way is to combine functions into a single component, and then use that component in a layout. The `standardtransceiver.tpl` uses this approach for `StdMenuBarForm`, `QuickAccessSubForm`, `NavigationSubForm`, and `TitleBarSubForm2`, which means that everything on the screen with the exception of the tool area is in a subform.

The second way subforms are used in Groove tools is as content for complex modal windows. `PermissionsSubForm` of `groovetoolwindow.tpl` is a good example. Let's see how we could display the permissions dialog in its own window:

1. Open a `PROPERTY_FORM` property in the tool's property list.
2. Instantiate the `PermissionsSubForm` component and assign it to the variable `pPermissionsForm`:

   ```
   function OnPermissions()
      {
      // Create new instance of the assign roles subform
      var pForm = PropertyList.OpenProperty(PROPERTY_FORM);
      var pPermissionsForm = pForm.CreateFormByName("PermissionsSubForm");
   ```

3. Set a variable, `pScopeURL`, equal to the `ObjectTypesScopeURL` of the current tool. The `ObjectTypesScopeURL` is a relative URL to the component group that defines the object type `PermissionsSubForm`. `g_pTool` is a `global` that gets set when the local tool is initialized within the `groovetoolwindow` tool:

   ```
   // Get the scope URL
   var pScopeURL = g_pTool.ObjectTypesScopeURL;
   ```

4. Find the delegate component within the new instance of `PermissionsSubForm` and set the variable `pPermissionsHost` to its script host interface. Now it can call the `InitializePermissionScopeVariables` function of the instance and initialize the variables for the relative URL of the component group to which the role applies and the group's ID, the component group to which the permission applies and the group's ID, and the affected telespace:

   ```
   // Get the delegate
   var pPermissions = pPermissionsForm.OpenDelegateComponent();
   var pPermissionsHost = pPermissions.GetScriptDispatch();
   ```

```
pPermissionsHost
➥.InitializePermissionScopeVariables("", "$ComponentGroup",
➥ pScopeURL.String,"$ComponentGroup", g_pTelespace);
```

5. Preset the window properties of the dialog:

```
// Set up preferences for window to create
var pWindowProperties =
➥ GrooveScriptFunctions.CreateNewObject("Groove.WindowProperties");
pWindowProperties.Style = "PopupWindow";
pWindowProperties.Resizable = false;
pWindowProperties.CaptionVisible = true;
pWindowProperties.Visible = false;
pWindowProperties.VisibleInTaskbar = true;
pWindowProperties.Caption = "Permissions for " + g_pTool.DisplayName;
pWindowProperties.CloseButton = true;
pWindowProperties.HelpButton = true;
pWindowProperties.ParentWindow
➥ = UIPropertyList.OpenProperty(UIPROPERTY_TOP_LEVEL_WINDOW);
```

6. Create the window using `pWindowProperties` and containing `pPermissionsForm`:

```
// Create the window
var pWindowAccount =
UIPropertyList.OpenProperty(UIPROPERTY_WINDOW_ACCOUNT);
var pWindowManager =
GrooveScriptFunctions.CreateNewObject("Groove.WindowManager");
var pWindow =
➥ pWindowManager.CreateGrooveWindowForForm(pWindowAccount, "",
➥ pWindowProperties, pPermissionsForm);
```

7. Show the window:

```
// Show the window
pWindow.DoModal();
}
```

Here's the final result:

```
function OnPermissions()
   {
   // Create new instance of the assign roles subform
   var pForm = PropertyList.OpenProperty(PROPERTY_FORM);
   var pPermissionsForm = pForm.CreateFormByName("PermissionsSubForm");

   // Get the scope URL
   var pScopeURL = g_pTool.ObjectTypesScopeURL;

   // Get the delegate
   var pPermissions = pPermissionsForm.OpenDelegateComponent();
   var pPermissionsHost = pPermissions.GetScriptDispatch();
```

```
pPermissionsHost.InitializePermissionScopeVariables
➥("", "$ComponentGroup", pScopeURL.String,
➥ "$ComponentGroup", g_pTelespace);

   // Set up preferences for window to create
   var pWindowProperties =
➥ GrooveScriptFunctions.CreateNewObject("Groove.WindowProperties");
   pWindowProperties.Style = "PopupWindow";
   pWindowProperties.Resizable = false;
   pWindowProperties.CaptionVisible = true;
   pWindowProperties.Visible = false;
   pWindowProperties.VisibleInTaskbar = true;
   pWindowProperties.Caption = "Permissions for " + g_pTool.DisplayName;
   pWindowProperties.CloseButton = true;
   pWindowProperties.HelpButton = true;
   pWindowProperties.ParentWindow
➥ = UIPropertyList.OpenProperty(UIPROPERTY_TOP_LEVEL_WINDOW);

   // Create the window
   var pWindowAccount = UIPropertyList.OpenProperty(UIPROPERTY_WINDOW_ACCOUNT);
   var pWindowManager
➥ = GrooveScriptFunctions.CreateNewObject("Groove.WindowManager");
   var pWindow =
➥ pWindowManager.CreateGrooveWindowForForm(pWindowAccount, "",
➥ pWindowProperties, pPermissionsForm);

   // Show the window
   pWindow.DoModal();
   }
```

Summary

This concludes our survey of a few of the advanced topics in Groove and should serve as a springboard to further study. In Chapter 15, "The Future of Peer-to-Peer," we'll do some crystal-ball gazing. We will look at some of today's trends in peer-to-peer applications with respect to both peer-to-peer in general and Groove in particular.

The Future of Peer-to-Peer

CHAPTER

15

IN THIS CHAPTER

In this chapter, we will make some guesses about how peer-to-peer applications will develop in the years to come, and we will examine the opportunities that will arise for peer-to-peer application programmers.

The Killer App

Before the October 2000 preview release of Groove, there was a lot of talk around Groove about what the killer app for Groove would be. The first versions of the standard apps were finished, and the Personal Solutions Group had developed some custom applications, such as Family Groove. Everyone was excited and could think of numerous places where peer-to-peer eliminated many of the pain points of client-server architecture and the Web, but nobody could guess what the killer app would be.

Of course, there already was a killer peer-to-peer app: Napster. Napster was overwhelming the network systems of college campuses as students and others downloaded 3 billion songs a month, or somewhere in the neighborhood of 10 billion megabytes of data. But Napster had some real advantages over the killer apps we hope to build:

- Napster did not have to host the data itself, only an index of peer machines that contained the content.
- Napster did not have to distribute the content, so it didn't need massive bandwidth. The bandwidth was supplied, to a large extent, by college IT departments. From the point of view of Napster and college student users, the distribution bandwidth was nearly free.
- Other than a directory and the underlying software, Napster was not distributing a product. The product that was being distributed—the music that college students and others were downloading from each other—was, in effect, free.
- Napster didn't build the directory. Every time a user downloaded a song from a peer, that user's machine and song were automatically added to the index of hosts and music, so the index was built by volunteers—the music swappers themselves.

Still, in spite of its huge success, Napster had one problem: decentralization. The very strength of this peer-to-peer concept meant that there was no central point to collect money on transfers, and no means of enforcing collection if money could be collected. This is not to say that Napster was unsuccessful, but imagine a one-cent charge for each of 3 billion downloads per month.

Peer-to-Peer Challenges

The Napster experience points vividly to both the strengths and the weaknesses of peer-to-peer. There are two serious challenges any killer app needs to address, especially in a business or enterprise environment. The two challenges derive from the competing needs of two groups: managers and users.

The decentralization of peer-to-peer makes it difficult for managers to monitor usage. If all traffic goes through a central server, it is relatively easy to log activity and to determine what enterprise resources are being utilized and, by extension, how cost-effective those resources are with respect to organizational goals.

Peer connections can make it difficult to safeguard intellectual property, as we have seen so convincingly with Napster. The lack of usage information and exposure of enterprise data make it difficult for IT managers to allocate resources in an organization and to tune the network with respect to proper access, use validation, and local and enterprise data security. Addressing the needs of IT managers has been a continuing priority in the development of Groove.

Users, on the other hand, need access to information that is often found on central servers. This is particularly true in either intra- or inter-enterprise collaboration. What the participants are collaborating about is most often data or applications that reside in centralized proprietary systems.

Users also need the ability to quickly and easily locate others as either collaboration partners or information sources. They also want to be able to set up an ad hoc network without any ISP, network administrator, or IT management involvement. Finally, users need an application with an extremely easy and intuitive interface, particularly for collaboration.

Michael Schrage, author of the book *Serious Play,* has studied the effects of shared spaces on collaboration. He points out that we often use paper or napkins at lunch conversations to focus our dialogs. After a few drawings and revisions, the napkin becomes a capture device or reflector of the conversation. We begin talking through the napkin to the other person rather than to him. The nature of the shared space, then, whether it is a napkin, a whiteboard, a clay model, a slide projector, or a Groove shared space, fundamentally shapes and changes the conversation. A difficult or clumsy interface can therefore lead to poor collaboration and will certainly result in people not using the application.

Therefore, our killer app with its great interface, will have to meet the needs of both managers and users.

Potential Growth Areas for Peer-to-Peer

If we don't swap songs with our killer app, what do we do? What kinds of activities can we offer that are enhanced by peer-to-peer architecture?

Matchmaking

One of the most obvious, yet under-recognized activities that characterized Napster was matchmaking. We told Napster what song we wanted, and Napster told us who had it.

eBay has made an entire business out of matchmaking. eBay matches buyers with sellers, provides a payment mechanism, and extracts a transaction fee. Its matchmaking is quite large, public, and open, and so is better served by the traditional centralized server model.

The need, however, for matchmaking is very real, and there are applications for which the peer-to-peer model is particularly appropriate. Which of these scenarios would you prefer?

- Your sister-in-law sets up a secure Groove space and invites you and a potential blind date for you into it. You exchange photographs, plan a first meeting, and chat or talk to get to know each other.
- You make your name, picture, and contact information available to thousands of visitors a day on a public site.

Of course, with a hybrid peer-to-peer system, there is another choice. You could put your name and profile on a public server, generate responses, and then, after screening, individually invite those responders into a secure and private peer-to-peer space. This is a good illustration of the kind of hybrid systems now possible.

Blind auctions with suppliers might be an application ideally suited to peer-to-peer. For example, if Grant Washer Company needed .025-inch zinc sheets, the purchasing manager at Grant could use a shared space and invite suppliers into it. The space would list Grant Washer's expected use of zinc sheets for the year and lay out the specifications to which the company would hold suppliers. Each company could bid on the sheets. One tool of the application would show all the current bids, but not which company made them. Bidding could remain somewhat fluid until a particular date. On that date, Grant Washer would decide which of the suppliers would supply what amounts of zinc sheets. The information from the shared space could be exported into Grant Washer's purchasing system, and purchase orders for the year could be cut.

If we were dealing with a product more complex than washers, one in which the item being supplied was made from components supplied by subcontractors, the subcontractors could be invited into the space to create a collaborative bid.

Knowledge Portals

Another area of growth that can be an effective use of the peer-to-peer paradigm is the knowledge portal. Knowledge portals bring together the applications, content, and people necessary to solve problems and achieve goals.

For example, an internal knowledge portal might let people in the same company but in various geographical locations collaborate on product development. A prototypical use of an internal knowledge portal might be a space to develop a company newsletter. The budget and real-time expenditures against it might be one tool of the space.

In another tool, the production schedule might be maintained with deadlines assigned to each person for each task. File sharing could allow content production by authors, as well as editing. Picture tools could be used to assemble graphics and preview potential layouts. After the project was complete, a connection with the purchasing system could cause purchase orders to be issued for printing and distribution.

Most of this could, of course, be done with email, but doing it in a confidential peer-to-peer space allows easier file sharing and version control, a richer archive of discussions, and a more instant collaboration between members.

An external knowledge portal might allow customers to interact with support personnel in real-time, using custom tools, accessing enterprise data, and incorporating customer relationship management (CRM) functions through connection to back-end systems. The FAQ demo discussed in Chapter 13, "Data Integration and Groove Bots," is a perfect example of an external knowledge portal.

The alternative would be either email or telephone. The FAQs would still have to be updated by someone. The telephone solution is quite invasive, demanding immediate attention. Using a peer-to-peer shared space makes it possible for each participant to respond to the problem at his or her own convenience, and provides a context to the conversation that is much easier to follow than that which comes from reading multiple emails. The convergence of tools and data pointed at problem resolution can result only in higher productivity, and productivity increases sell applications.

Supply Chain Coordination

Supply chain coordination is another obvious area that is advantageous for peer-to-peer tools. With most day-to-day operations taken care of by client-server applications, there is an enormous need to deal effectively with exceptions—the 20% of all transactions that consumes 80% of worker effort. Bringing the right people into a space pre-seeded with server data can lead to rapid resolution of real-time concerns. The capability to transform the result of those interactions back into the enterprise information systems is also needed.

Groove's Web site provides an excellent example of supply chain coordination at

`http://www.groove.net/solutions/scenarios/distribution.html`

Distributing Clinical Information

CareScience's work with medical records reveals another area where peer-to-peer has an enormous advantage over the client-server model. CareScience's mission is to use peer-to-peer technology to manage and distribute clinical information immediately and securely at the point of care. That information can be located at numerous facilities and controlled by many different organizations, yet it can be needed at even different locations.

And, of course, confidentiality is important. The Health Insurance Portability and Accountability Act of 1996 (HIPAA) mandates a high degree of privacy for patient records. Patient records are protected not only by encryption, but also by access controls in the shared space.

CareScience accesses health organizations' medical record databases and makes some of those records available in a peer-to-peer space. As a result of peer-to-peer architecture, medical records can be maintained by the owning organizations while being accessed by others without compromising either confidentiality or integrity. Data ownership is managed by business policies and access rules that enable individual organizations to control their own data while making it available through the Care Data Exchange. Because CareScience doesn't have to reproduce or support an entire centralized computer infrastructure, its costs for providing the records are less.

For example, suppose that Dr. Wesley sees an automobile accident patient with a head injury in the emergency room of Farley General Hospital. He goes to the computer and looks up the patient's medical records. On the computer he sees records from several sources: the patient's primary care physician, a neurosurgeon who repaired a cervical disc three years ago, and a cardiac specialist who performed an angioplasty on the patient's arteries last year. Dr. Wesley reviews the X-rays of the neck surgery and treats his patient. After Dr. Wesley finishes administering to the patient, he enters his comments and observations into Farley General Hospital's medical records system, but they are immediately available to the other three organizations. This sample record has parts that are maintained by four different organizations but are securely available to all of them.

Many other situations, such as legal proceedings, mergers and acquisitions, financial transactions, and accounting activities, demand access and security that correlate with the medical records model.

Online Bill Payment

An offshoot of this idea is online bill payment. A company named Lightshare already enables e-commerce on peer-to-peer networks, and handles payment transfers between buyers and sellers at eBay. Through Lightshare, any individual consumer or business can sell products and information directly from their local computer, without the presence of a Web site or server.

Document Management

Another area that holds potential for peer-to-peer approaches is document management, an area that was a hot topic in the late 1980s and early 1990s. Today, companies still waste an enormous amount of time finding documents, and documents are still the lifeblood of organizations. But document creation and distribution in an organization seldom fit into the neat, logical, and controlled vision of database developers.

The thinking behind document management solutions was to standardize them. Documents should be standard-sized, have a standard look, be laid out in a standardized way, and be kept in a standard vault so that machine logic could control distribution and versioning. The result was a layer of bureaucracy involving forms and permissions, and work that had little immediate benefit to the document producer.

It seldom worked. But that doesn't mean that the problem went away.

If there were a shared space in an organization where content creators kept their documents, access and visibility could be controlled through a roles-and-permissions strategy. For example, author members of the shared space might have permission to change the documents, while a librarian might be the only person who could add or delete documents. A Human Resources member might not be able to see an Accounting document. The visibility of documents to other departments might be controlled by a high-level manager. In addition, a bot could be developed that, as a member of the document space, searched the space, created indexes of the documents, took note of new versions and announced them to users, noticed and logged similarities and duplication, and tracked access, all without intensive human involvement—and with little or no effort by the document producers themselves.

Another fruitful area for thinking about peer-to-peer tool development is the concept of backup. If you create a document on your PC, it is stored on your hard drive. At some point, depending on your comfort level, you will need to back up that file by copying it to removable media or to another machine on your network. If you leave it only on your hard drive and your hard drive crashes, you will lose your file because in your system there is a single point of failure: your hard drive.

If you put that document into a shared space, there are multiple points because the document is replicated in the space instances of your peers. If your peers are many and are separated by geography, your document is quite effectively "backed up." In fact, it doesn't take many geographically separate peers to make your document considerably more recoverable than it would be if you had copied it to removable media or to a network server. Obviously, security and access concerns would have to be addressed, but there is probably a good solution waiting to be discovered.

Real-Time Searching

Another area of peer-to-peer development is real-time searching. Sun Microsystems bought a small company named InfraSearch in March 2001 and renamed the product JXTA Search. It is set to compete with Internet search engines to provide more rapid searching through the use of distributed searches over peer networks.

On a smaller scale, though, there may be room for peer-to-peer development in search tools for smaller-scale projects. As shared spaces become larger and more complex, tools may be needed to search them.

Real-Time Collaborative Publishing

Another very interesting concept is real-time collaborative publishing. With more and more information bombarding us each day, people need to manage that information in a new way. Media providers are becoming more and more focused on specific niches, and consumers are responding by forming relationships with sources they trust.

Various information and media from widely separated contributors could be aggregated in a shared space and simultaneously published. The resulting document would update when any contributing member changed the information for which they were responsible.

It is not difficult to imagine an application that did HTML formatting of information supplied in real-time by shared space members and then disseminated that HTML either over the Internet or within the peer network. The result could be an always-current corporate communication, for example.

Personalization

One current emerging trend is the desire of consumers to have one-to-one consumer-to-business relationships. Peer-to-peer spaces can accomplish a degree of personalization that goes beyond today's "Hi, Joe" Web sites.

Suppose that you call your stockbroker to talk about stock allocation in your portfolio. He suggests that you go to the company's Web site; fill out a short form with your name, your account number, and a password; and click on the MySite link. You click on the link and your Groove application launches and opens a shared space.

Within the shared space are several tools, and a button to invite your broker. You click the Invite button and, while you wait for him to respond, you notice that the open tool lists your portfolio and that the prices of your stocks are being updated in real-time, and that the value of your portfolio is fluctuating with the stock prices. Your portfolio was seeded into the space from the brokerage's database when the shared space was created.

Now inside the space, your stockbroker asks what he can do for you today. You tell him you are concerned that you may be too concentrated in growth stocks and that you are worried about today's market conditions. He suggests that you click the Allocation Tool tab. To your surprise, when you do so, you see a pie chart that lists your stocks and bonds and their categories. "Here is how you are allocated now," your broker says. "Now take a look at the Plans and Goals tab."

You click that tab and see a timeline. You recognize it as the portfolio growth plan you and your stockbroker developed a year ago when you set up your account. It shows your portfolio value nearly the same as was expected. Your broker explains that you can use the What If tab to interactively change your allocation and see how the underlying assumptions of your plan can change some of your portfolio's metrics. You can see how your changes affect an overall risk index and a portfolio value goal. He then encourages you to play with the What If tab offline and call him in the morning.

This kind of collaboration and personalization is possible in a data-integrated peer-to-peer space.

Are any of these the killer app? Or is the killer app something entirely different? Could the killer app be a Microsoft .NET service?

The Microsoft/Groove Partnership

In October 2001, Microsoft took a 20% stake in Groove Networks. Concurrent with that news, Groove announced the results of a joint project that added support for products from its new industry partner, including the ability of Groove to exchange instant messages with Windows Messenger users. The two applications are more tightly integrated for `Windows` XP users, who can automatically jump from a `Windows` Messenger chat session into Groove collaboration. Ray Ozzie, Groove's founder, went on to say that the messaging effort was one of a dozen projects currently in joint development.

Microsoft's effort for the year has been spent on Windows XP and the .NET strategy. .NET is a software development platform designed with the Internet in mind. Eighty percent of Microsoft's research and development resources for 2001 were spent on .NET projects. Microsoft's .NET promises to have significant impact on the computing world in the next few years.

Today's Internet-enabled software is often difficult to produce and extremely proprietary and closed. Maybe you have had the experience of moving data from a database-driven Web application to an Excel spreadsheet to analyze it, or needed to associate personnel information from a PeopleSoft application running on Linux with accounting information from an Oracle database on Windows. If you have had any of these kinds of problems, you will understand that the variety of hardware, operating systems, programming languages, and competing standards makes distributed applications—applications that are created from components that may run on different servers and may be in different geographical locations—extremely difficult to produce.

The main reason distributed applications are difficult is the lack of standardization of interfaces among the application components, which could have been developed with incompatible languages, on incompatible platforms, with incompatible tools.

.NET is an effort to change the landscape by facilitating inter-application communication using standardized protocols such as SOAP and XML, and standardized interfaces. .NET encompasses many languages and execution platforms. Using extensive class libraries with well-defined interfaces, .NET manages rich communication between disparate components, which will allow and encourage highly distributed applications.

The .NET framework sits on top of the operating system. Immediately above the operating system is the Common Language Runtime, or CLR. The CLR is an execution engine that loads, executes, and manages code that has been compiled into an intermediate byte-code format. In a somewhat similar fashion to Java, .NET uses an intermediate language, called Microsoft Intermediate Language, or IL. IL code is compiled to native binary code for execution. CLR can handle compiled code from multiple languages. That capability allows for cross-language interoperability.

On top of that layer sits the .NET class framework. This framework has classes with routines that access and manipulate data, enable application security, allow configuration, provide access to metadata information, and send and receive data across the network using a wide variety of protocols.

At the top level are the user and program interfaces. Local users interact with .NET applications through Windows forms, whereas users on the Net interact through ASP. Devices with any hardware or OS connect with Web services over the Net using XML and SOAP.

This architecture makes it possible to deploy components over the Net and run them without complex installation, registration, or GUIDs. As a consequence, components can be accessed from several remote locations and be aggregated into distributed applications.

Over the past year, Microsoft has ported many of its products to .NET. One result of that port may be the addition of a service model to Microsoft applications. Instead of installing Microsoft Word on your desktop, you would access it over the Web and pay only for your use of the product. There may also be a service model for distributed applications, and even for components of those applications.

For example, early in the days of word processing, companies specialized in spell-checker components that were licensed to software developers for inclusion into their products. It is easy to imagine a sales-tax Web service that could be used in e-commerce. It would calculate the appropriate sales tax on a purchase, freeing the e-commerce developer from maintaining software code that frequently changed and required legal currency. Provided as a distributed service, the sales-tax component developer would derive revenue each time the component was run.

What kinds of opportunities will .NET and the Microsoft/Groove partnership produce for Groove tool developers? No one knows now, but it should open many avenues for the integration of Groove shared spaces with distributed Web applications.

Features of the Killer App

If we look at the possibilities previously mentioned, what do they tell us about peer-to-peer applications? What kind of features should a peer-to-peer application have? What should our killer app do?

First and foremost, our application must be focused on the user. Not only does it have to provide value for the user like any other application, but it also has to provide a means for the user to interact with others in a way that respects his or her importance and time. It has to be personal.

Next, the product must be dynamic, taking full advantage of the external connections. Regardless of whether those connections are people, or data, or even bots, the space's content needs to be fluid and relevant.

The application needs to be conversational. The flow of information needs to be interactive. The shared space needs to be something more than a view port.

If the application provides information, that information should be presented in real-time when the application is connected to an information source.

The Groove mantra of "bringing the right people together at the right time, with the right tools" is a good blueprint for Groove applications development. The best way to think about developing your killer Groove application is to ask four questions. Answer these questions accurately and you'll be on your way to, if not the killer app, at least a very good one:

- What problem should the application address?

  Shared space collaboration is about using shared information for problem solving. What organizational pain point are we trying to alleviate? What opportunities are we missing as a result of ineffective coordination?

- What people do we need to bring together in a space to solve this problem or exploit this opportunity?

  If you know the people, you can anticipate the resources they will need in order to be effective. You can determine what sorts of input they may need to bring to the solution.

- What information needs to be brought into the space from external resources?

  An important corollary to that question is: Should the external information be available to all members or to only a few? In a supply-chain coordination problem, it might be quite useful for an outside supplier to see your production schedule, but inappropriate for that same member to view labor costs. A balance must be achieved between a need to know and confidentiality. A tax attorney invited into an income-tax space would need to know the circumstances surrounding an income item, but might not need to know the amount.

- What tools does each person need?

  Each member of the space needs tools. Some of those tools, such as chat, will serve a general need for all members; some tools might present different members with different benefits; and other tools may present a benefit to only one of the members.

  Consider our earlier investment scenario. The Talk button fulfills a general need for both you and your broker. The allocation pie chart serves the broker's need to clearly illustrate your allocation and serves your need to understand it. The What If tool is designed to let you explore the allocation problem by yourself and make the decisions only you can make, so this tool serves your needs exclusively.

  Now let's say that the broker has a tool that captures the data you have altered in the space when you change your allocation, and exports that data to an application that actually makes changes to your portfolio. That tool would benefit the broker's needs.

Is There a Killer App?

It may be valid to ask whether there even is a killer app. Maybe we need to shift our thinking a little and stop thinking of Groove as an application. Instead, let's think of Groove, the computer, and the Internet as an appliance or utility.

Certainly, one of the big changes on the horizon for peer-to-peer will be ubiquity. You may be able to stop explaining what peer-to-peer is to your friends and family. As peer-to-peer becomes more common, it will begin to seem less a technology in itself and more a part of other processes. A good historical example is multimedia.

Multimedia is the use on a computer of sound, graphics, and animation in an application. The early multimedia products were games, tutorials, and presentations. But today Microsoft incorporates what would have been considered multimedia a few years ago into its trashcan-emptying routine.

Consider another ubiquitous utility, the telephone. Where is the killer app for the telephone? Or for email? Does the lack of a killer app make them any less attractive or useful?

If there is a killer app, it may not be apparent for some time. We have to remember how early we are in the technology development cycle. We began this book with a look at the history of the Internet, and we revisited Tim Berners-Lee's creation of the Web browser. For him, the killer app was what enabled physicists to share research in near real-time. He could not possibly have imagined that people would be using the Web and a browser to buy 50-year-old golf clubs from an individual in Utah, or to configure the features of a possible new car purchase.

Like Berners-Lee, none of us can guess where this is all going. So what do we do? A step in the right direction is to forget about the killer app. Instead, go find a problem to solve. Find a problem in your life, or in your department, or in your company, or in your community that can be solved by bringing the right people together at the right time, with the right tools.

You now have all the basic information you need in order to create Groove tools in shared spaces. You don't know everything, of course, but the rest will come to you as you find you need it. The most important step is to begin. As Nike says, "Just do it!"

APPENDIX A

Groove Template Component Reference

This section is a quick reference to Groove template components. See the Groove Component Catalog for up-to-date and detailed descriptions. It is available for download at `http://devzone.groove.net/gdk/`.

ViewContainer

Property	*Value*
`Background`	Standard descriptor
`PreferredHeight`	Height in pixels
`PreferredWidth`	Width in pixels

Connection	*Connection ID*
`Layout`	`0`
`CodeComponent`	`1`

HTMLTableLayout

Property	*Type*
`Layout`	HTML table definition

Table Elements	*Attributes*
`TABLE`	`HSPACE`—Padding applied to horizontal sides of table (pixels).
	`VSPACE`—Padding applied to vertical sides of table (pixels).
	`CELLPADDING`—Default padding applied to each side of table cells (pixels).
`TR`	None.
`TD`	`HEIGHT`—Cell height (pixels or percent).
	`WIDTH`—Cell width (pixels or percent).
	`COLSPAN`—Number of columns that the cell spans.
	`ROWSPAN`—Number of rows that the cell spans.
	`NAME`—String used to identify the cell for runtime manipulation.
	`LeftPad`—Padding applied to the left side of the cell (pixels or percent). If not specified, value in the `TABLE` element's `CELLPADDING` is used.

Table Elements	*Attributes*
	TopPad—Padding applied to the top of the cell (pixels or percent). If not specified, value in the TABLE element's CELLPADDING is used.
	RightPad—Padding applied to the right side of the cell (pixels or percent). If not specified, value in the TABLE element's CELLPADDING is used.
	BottomPad—Padding applied to the bottom of the cell (pixels or percent). If not specified, value in the TABLE element's CELLPADDING is used.

The HTMLLayout component has no connections.

MultiCellLayout

Property	*Type*
Layout	Element

Element	*Attributes*
MULTIROW	None.
MULTICOL	None.
BORDER	LeftPad—Padding to the left side of layout in pixels or percent.
	TopPad—Padding to the top of layout in pixels or percent.
	RightPad—Padding to the right side of layout in pixels or percent.
	BottomPad—Padding to the bottom of layout in pixels or percent.
DEFAULTPAD	LeftPad—Padding to the left side of each cell in the layout (pixels or percent).
	TopPad—Padding to the top of each cell in the layout (pixels or percent).
	RightPad—Padding to the right side of each cell in the layout (pixels or percent).
	BottomPad—Padding to the bottom of each cell in the layout (pixels or percent).
ROW	None.
COLUMN	None.

Element	*Attributes*
CELL	HEIGHT—Height of cell in pixels or percent. WIDTH—Width of cell in pixels or percent. NAME—String used to identify the cell for runtime manipulation. LeftPad—Padding to the left side of the cell in pixels or percent. If not specified, the value in any DEFAULTPAD element's LeftPad is used. TopPad—Padding to the top of the cell in pixels or percent. If not specified, the value in any DEFAULTPAD element's TopPad is used. RightPad—Padding to the right side of the cell in pixels or percent. If not specified, the value in any DEFAULTPAD element's RightPad is used. BottomPad—Padding to the bottom of the cell in pixels or percent. If not specified, the value in any DEFAULTPAD element's BottomPad is used.

The MultiCellLayout component has no connections.

XYLayout

Property	*Type*
Layout	Element

Attribute	*Description*
Name	Name of component to load and display in the control area.
Top	The Y coordinate of the top of the control. The origin is the top edge of the layout. If the coordinate starts with a minus sign (-), the origin is the bottom edge of the layout. (If this attribute is specified, either Bottom or Height must also be specified.)
Bottom	The Y coordinate of the bottom of the control. The origin is the top edge of the layout. If the coordinate starts with a minus sign (-), the origin is the top edge of the layout. (If this attribute is specified, either Top or Height must also be specified.)
Right	The X coordinate of the right edge of the control. The origin is the left edge of the layout. If the coordinate starts with a minus sign (-), the origin is the right edge of the layout. (If this attribute is specified, either Left or Width must also be specified.)

Attribute	*Description*
`Left`	The X coordinate of the left edge of the control. The origin is the left edge of the layout. If the coordinate starts with a minus sign (-), the origin is the right edge of the layout. (If this attribute is specified, either `Right` or `Width` must also be specified.)
`Width`	The width of the control. (If this attribute is specified, either `Left` or `Right` must also be specified.)
`Height`	The height of the control. (If this attribute is specified, either `Top` or `Bottom` must also be specified.)

The `XYLayout` component has no connections.

Splitter

Property	*Type*
`Orientation`	Vertical, Horizontal
`Size`	Small, Medium, Large, Zero
`UserResizable`	`True`, `False`
`Layout`	Element

Pane Attributes	*Value*
`NAME`	Text string
`LeftPad`, `RightPad`, `TopPad`, `BottomPad`	Value in pixels or percent
`Size`	Size in pixels or percent

The `Splitter` component has no connections.

SingleCellViewContainer

Property	*Type*
`Layout`	Element

Attribute	*Value*
`LeftPad`	Value in pixels or percent
`RightPad`	Value in pixels or percent
`TopPad`	Value in pixels or percent
`BottomPad`	Value in pixels or percent

The `SingleCellViewContainer` component has no connections.

ScriptHost

Property	*Value*
SourceCode	Element
EnforceInterfaces	0 or 1
AddInterfacesAsItems	0 or 1
EnableErrorSupport	0 or 1

The ScriptHost component has no connections.

GrooveEdit

Property	*Value*
Style	Password, Multiline, HorizontalScrollbar, VerticalScrollbar
Text	Text string
Enabled	True, False
Tooltip	Text string
TextLimit	Number of characters to limit the control to
Font	Standard descriptor
BackgroundColor	HTML-style RGB value #rrggbb; default is the skin background color

The GrooveEdit component has no connections.

GrooveComboBox

Property	*Value*
Tooltip	Text string
BackgroundColor	HTML-style RGB value #rrggbb; default is the skin background color
Font	Standard descriptor
DropDownSize	Height in pixels
Sort	True, False
InitialValues	Content element lists items
Editable	True, False

The GrooveCombobox component has no connections.

GrooveStatic

Property	*Value*
Style	Normal, Button, Header
Label	Text string
VAlignment	Top, Bottom, Center
HAlignment	Left, Right, Center
BreakType	WordBreak, SingleLine
Clip	WordEllipsis, EndEllipsis, PathEllipsis
Prefixing	NoPrefix—Does not convert "&" character into underscore
BackgroundColor	HTML-style RGB value #rrggbb or a skin color style; default is the skin background color
ToolTip	Text for tooltip
WantsEvents	True, False
Link	True, False
Font	Default is the skin EditText font; standard font descriptor
FontStyle	Skin font style; Font and FontStyle are mutually exclusive
BackgroundStyle	Skin background style

The GrooveStatic component has no connections.

ActiveXWrapper

Property	*Value*
ProgID	COM Program ID for the TreeView ActiveX control
GenerateEvents	True, False
Disseminate	True, False

The ActiveXWrapper component has no connections.

GrooveButton

Property	*Value*
Style	StandardButton, StandardIconButton, LargeButton, SmallTextButton, SmallIconButton, SmallIconTextButton, Checkbox, Radiobutton, LinkButton
Label	Text string
Tooltip	Text string
SingleLine	Bool
Default	True, False
Cancel	True, False
AutoSize	Bool
Enabled	True, False
IndicateFocus	True, False
Mnemonic	Text string
Menu	Component name within the same component group
IndicateMenu	True, False
CommandURL	Text string
AcceptFocus	True, False
Checkbox	True, False
Radiobutton	True, False
PushSoundURL	URL relative to persist root directory
LaunchURL	URL

The GrooveButton component has no connections.

GrooveImage

Property	*Value*
Image	Image to display
Background	Standard Descriptor
Scaling	ScaleDownOnly, ScaleToFit, NoScaling

Property	*Value*
`AcceptedFileTypes`	Comma-delimited list of file extensions
`DisplayTextWhenEmpty`	Text string
`LaunchURL`	URL to launch
`ToolTip`	Text string

The `GrooveImage` component has no connections.

GrooveListBox

Property	*Value*
`BackgroundColor`	HTML-style RGB value `#rrggbb`; default is the skin background color
`TextColor`	HTML-style RGB value `#rrggbb`; default is the skin text color
`ToolTip`	Text string
`Visible`	`True`, `False`
`Border`	`True`, `False`
`Sort`	`True`, `False`
`SelectionMode`	`Multiple` for multiselect; `Extended` for extended selection; `SingleSelection` for single selection
`InitialValues`	Content element lists items

The `GrooveListBox` component has no connections.

GrooveTabControl

Property	*Value*
`Enabled`	`True`, `False`
`ImageURL`	URL to image file
`ImageMaskURL`	`ImageMaskURL`
`ImageHeight`	Height of image in pixels
`ImageWidth`	Width of image in pixels
`EnableDragDrop`	`True`, `False`

The `GrooveTabControl` component has no connections.

RecordSetEngine

Property	*Type*
`ClassInfoList`	`ClassInfo` element

Attribute	*Description*
`Name`	Class of record that will be stored in the engine
`URL`	URL to associated COM class that implements the record type as an IGrooveRecord

Connection	*Connection ID*
`ToolCollections`	`0`

GrooveTimer

Property	*Value*
`Interval`	Time in milliseconds; default value is `0`
`Enable`	`True`, `False`

The `GrooveTimer` component has no connections.

GrooveMenu

Property	*Value*
`UICommands`	Element
`CommandURL`	Text string
`AlwaysEnabled`	`True`, `False`

`UICommands` Attribute	*Value*
`URL`	Text string
`ID`	ID
`Label`	Text string
`Mnemonic`	Ex: "Alt + B"
`Enabled`	`0`, `1`
`Default`	`0`, `1`

The `GrooveMenu` component has no connections.

GrooveListView

Property	*Value*
ViewStyle	Report, List, LargeIcon, SmallIcon
Enabled	True, False
TabStop	True, False
Visible	True, False
HasBorder	True, False
Has3DBorder	True, False
ShowSelectionAlways	True, False
SingleSelection	True, False
Sort	None, Ascending, Descending
Checkboxes	True, False
DisplayTextWhenEmpty	Text string
ColumnHeaders	True, False
FullRowSelect	True, False
HeaderClickable	True, False
FitLastColumnToWidth	True, False
ColumnsResizeable	True, False
NoLabelWrap	True, False
IconAlignmentLeft	True, False
IconAlignmentTop	True, False
IconAutoArrange	True, False
Columns	Initial set of columns

Column Attribute	*Value*
Name	Text string
Alignment	Left, Center, Right
HeaderAlignment	Left, Center, Right
AutoSize	True, False

Column Attribute	*Value*
`Width`	Width of column in pixels
`Resizable`	`True`, `False`

Connection	*Connection ID*
`ListDataModel`	`0`
`IconProvider`	`1`

The `GrooveListView` component has no connections.

GrooveTreeView

Property	*Value*
`EditLabels`	`True`, `False`
`Has3DBorder`	`True`, `False`
`HasButtons`	`True`, `False`
`HasLines`	`True`, `False`
`LinesAtRoot`	`True`, `False`

The `GrooveTreeView` component has no connections.

GrooveHeader

Property	*Value*
`Has3DBorder`	`True`, `False`
`Columns`	List of columns for the header control

The `GrooveHeader` component has no connections.

StandardDescriptors

Attribute	*Value*
`FontStyle`	See list below
`Typeface`	Ex: Helvetica
`Color`	Ex: `#rrggbb` value (see list below)
`Height`	Height of font in pixels

Attribute	*Value*
`Bold`	`True, False`
`Italic`	`True, False`
`Underline`	`True, False`

`FontStyle` *Values in a Skin*	*Description*
`TelespaceHeader`	Font of the telespace header
`ToolHeader`	Font of the tool header
`NoviceModeHeader`	Font of the novice mode header
`NoviceModeText`	Font of the text while in novice mode
`TransceiverPaneTitleText`	Title text of the transceiver
`DialogTitleText`	Title text for the dialog boxes
`LabelText`	Font of the labels
`DescriptionText`	Font of the description text
`EditText`	Font while editing
`ListText`	Font for lists
`LinkText`	Font for hyperlinks

`Color` *Values in a Skin*	*Description*
`TextColor`	General plain text color, usually darker value.
`BackgroundColor`	General plain background, usually lighter value.
`HighlightBackgroundColor`	Intended to be used like a highlight marker. This color usually works well with the `TextColor`.
`StrongTextColor`	Plain text with color. This text color usually draws user attention.
`StrongTextColor2`	Variation of plain `TextColor`.
`WeakTextColor`	Usually less saturated than the `TextColor`. Use this text color on text that should not attract much attention.
`DisabledTextColor`	Usually less saturated than the `TextColor`. Use this text color for disabled text.
`HeaderTextColor`	The text color used on the Static Header background.

`Color` *Values in a Skin*	*Description*
`SelectedTextColor`	Color used on selected texts. (Used in conjunction with `SelectedBackgroundColor`.)
`SelectedBackgroundColor`	Usually intended to attract user attention. (Used in conjunction with `SelectedTextColor`.)
`SectionBackgroundColor`	Similar to the `SectionBackground` Style. This color is usually very subtle. Like the `SectionBackground` Style (see the `Background` Style), this color is usually used to group a selection of controls. This color is a good substitute for `SectionBackground` Style.
`TooltipTextColor`	Text color for tooltip text. (Usually used in conjunction with `TooltipBackgroundColor`.)
`TooltipBackgroundColor`	Background color for tooltip text. (Usually used in conjunction with `TooltipTextColor`.)

Glossary

APPENDIX

B

This appendix provides definitions for most of the specialized terms used in this book and is reproduced from the Groove Developer's Reference Guide, available at `http://devzone.groove.net/gdk/`.

Account An account is a type of special-purpose shared space where information about the user is stored. This information includes a list of the user's identities, shared spaces (including a list of devices on which the shared spaces are instantiated), and contacts (which includes information about both client and relay devices).

Controller A controller is the top-level application utilizing Groove services. It is a wrapper or an application shell, and it can provide (but does not require) a user interface. It drives the work to be done. The controller could be `groove.exe`, an Internet Explorer ActiveX control, or some other type of solution.

Controlling code Tool code components are the controlling codes that make the engine, view, and rest of the tool fit together as a template and function as a tool, thus giving the tool its personality, behaviors, and functionality.

Delta A delta, which is a container that houses one or more commands created by an engine, represents changes to a shared space. It usually corresponds to a user-interface gesture (such as a keystroke). A delta can be local (created on your device) or external (created on the device of another member of your shared space). Each shared space member sends deltas corresponding to the changes they make to all other members. Examples of the type of data that is recorded and sent as a delta are a chat entry, a line drawn with a sketchpad, or the addition of a new tool to a shared space.

Device A device is the computer you use to run Groove. Although Groove runs only on desktop computers, in the future you might use your PC, your PIM, or some other type of computer. The device is what you are using to run Groove, but not necessarily where the device is located, or who you are. A device is specified by a globally unique device URL. Devices can be shared by more than one account (for example, you and your spouse may both use your computer at home).

DPP DPP is Groove's Device Presence Protocol, which provides a source client's Communications Subsystem sufficient information so that it can transmit information to a destination client along the best possible path. It can also notify the source client if a destination client is currently available for live SSTP service, whether directly or indirectly.

Endpoint An endpoint is a unique combination of an identity and a device (who and what). Endpoints referring to the same person could be *Development Manager on her PC at work* or *Mom on her PIM at home*. An endpoint allows Groove to identify a person among multiple users of the same device, and to identify a device among multiple devices used by one individual.

Engine A tool's engine is responsible for maintaining and changing the tool data model (the tool's persistence) in a shared space. An engine creates and executes deltas on behalf of the tool's view and acts on deltas received from other shared space member tools. An engine provides deltas asynchronously to the tool.

GUID A GUID is a Globally Unique Identifier. GUIDs are often used to identify unique objects.

Identity Every Groove account has at least one identity, and may have many identities. The default identity is the account name. An identity is a collection of data that corresponds to one persona for the user. This data includes a Groove identity URI, a vCard, and security information. An identity is the part of an endpoint that tells who is doing the interacting. Identity is specified by a globally unique computer-generated identity URL. A user's account contains a collection of a given user's identity data.

Member A shared space member is an entity who interacts with the other members of the shared space. This entity can be a person, a computer, a bot, or any other entity that can interact with other participants. Members interact through devices (usually computers) just as people on the phone interact through their telephones.

Relay A Groove relay is an intermediary device that stores and forwards or relays (hence the name) data between Groove members. Relay servers can store deltas for offline shared space members and provide fan-out delta distribution.

RVP RVP is Groove's peer-to-peer version of the Rendez-Vous protocol. This is a developing standard for locating and contacting people over networks.

Shared space A shared space is the private virtual location where Groove users (members) interact. A shared space usually contains one or more tools, and synchronizes the data for each tool. Examples of shared spaces would be *the Groove development team shared space* or *the Smith family shared space*. The persistent version of a shared space is a document database. Identical copies of this database are stored on each member's computer. All copies are constantly updated, so they always define the current state of the shared space. The documents in this database contain a list of every member of the shared space, which members are active, the tools that are being used, and the current state of all the shared space's data.

Skin A skin is a set of components that define the appearance and behavior of a Groove transceiver and tools.

SSTP SSTP (Groove's Simple Symmetrical Transmission Protocol) is a small application-layer protocol designed to allow two programs to engage in bidirectional, asynchronous communication over both TCP and UDP protocols.

Template A template is a static, persistent file that represents a tool, toolset, shared space, or skin. When you create an instance of a tool to use in a shared space, the shared space refers to the template for that type of tool.

Tool A tool is the program or shared application that shared space members use to interact. Each member of a shared space has access to the same tools and can use them to affect the shared space data. Examples of tools include a chat tool, a sketchpad, and a chess game. The Groove application consists of a top-level controller called a transceiver, and individual shared applications called tools. The transceiver provides local system-level functionality, such as communications, security, and account maintenance.

Toolset A toolset is a logical grouping of tools used for some purpose. The primary purpose of toolsets is to allow a group to work on more than one project within a single shared space. This means that a single group of people could use different sets of tools for different projects.

Transceiver The transceiver is Groove's top-level controller, which provides local system-level functionality such as account maintenance.

View A view displays the tool's data and provides a mechanism for capturing user input and gestures.

Complete Trivia Quiz Code

APPENDIX

C

Here is the complete code listing for TriviaQuiz. Be extremely careful of the continuation characters. The breaks are placed so that quoted strings are not broken. Notice that some lines have spaces after the continuation character and some don't. If you type parts of the program from this listing, make sure those spaces are in your final code.

LISTING C.1 TriviaQuiz.tpl

```
<g:Document xmlns:g="urn:groove.net" Name="TriviaQuiz.tpl">
    <!-- Component Security -->
    <g:ComponentSecurity>
        <g:FingerprintTable>
            <g:Entry
➥ Fingerprint="4262-dcb1:4552-d303:123d-36a6:0a96-62e5:24a7-d7db"
➥ FingerprintID="Groove"/>
        </g:FingerprintTable>
    </g:ComponentSecurity>
    <!-- Tool Template -->
    <g:ToolTemplate DefaultToolDisplayName="TriviaQuiz"
➥ TemplateDisplayName="TriviaQuiz" Name="TriviaQuiz.Tool">
        <!-- Tool View -->
        <g:ViewInfo Lifetime="Limited"/>
        <!-- Component Group -->
        <g:ComponentGroup Delegate="TriviaQuizGlue"
➥DefaultView="TriviaQuizViewContainer" HelpInfoProvider="">
            <!-- View -->
            <g:Component Name="TriviaQuizViewContainer">
                <g:ComponentResource FingerprintID="Groove"
➥ URL="http://components.groove.net/Groove/Components/Root.osd?
➥Package=net.groove.Groove.ToolComponents.GrooveCommonComponents_DLL&amp;
➥Version=0&amp;Factory=ViewContainer"/>
                <!-- View Property List -->
                <g:PropertyList Version="1">
                    <g:Property Name="Background">
                        <g:BackgroundStyle Style="SectionBackground"/>
                    </g:Property>
                </g:PropertyList>
                <!-- Connections -->
                <g:ComponentConnections>
                    <g:Connection ConnectionID="0" Name="WelcomeLayout"/>
                </g:ComponentConnections>
            </g:Component>
            <!-- Layout -->
            <g:Component Name="TriviaQuizLayout">
                <g:ComponentResource FingerprintID="Groove"
➥ URL="http://components.groove.net/Groove/Components/Root.osd?
➥Package=net.groove.Groove.ToolComponents.GrooveCommonComponents_DLL&amp;
➥Version=0&amp;Factory=HTMLTableLayout"/>
```

LISTING C.1 Continued

```
<!-- Layout Property List -->
<g:PropertyList Version="1">
    <g:Property Name="Layout">
        <g:PropertyValue>
                  <TABLE CELLPADDING="2">
                <TR>
                    <TD COLSPAN="4" HEIGHT="110" RightPad="163">
                        TriviaGraphic
                    </TD>
                    <TD WIDTH="2%"/>
                    <TD WIDTH="10%"/>
                    <TD WIDTH="2%"/>
                    <TD WIDTH="35%"/>
                </TR>
                <TR>
                    <TD HEIGHT="30" WIDTH="6%"/>
                    <TD WIDTH="10%"/>
                    <TD WIDTH="2%"/>
                    <TD WIDTH="35%"/>
                    <TD/>
                    <TD/>
                    <TD/>
                    <TD/>
                </TR>
                <TR>
                    <TD/>
                    <TD COLSPAN="7" HEIGHT="30">
                        QuestionLabel
                    </TD>
                </TR>
                <TR>
                    <TD HEIGHT="30"/>
                    <TD/>
                    <TD/>
                    <TD/>
                    <TD/>
                    <TD/>
                    <TD/>
                    <TD/>
                </TR>
                <TR>
                    <TD HEIGHT="60"/>
                    <TD COLSPAN="3">
                        AnswerAButton
```

LISTING C.1 Continued

```
            </TD>
            <TD/>
            <TD COLSPAN="3">
                AnswerCButton
            </TD>
        </TR>
        <TR>
            <TD HEIGHT="30"/>
            <TD/>
            <TD/>
            <TD/>
            <TD/>
            <TD/>
            <TD/>
            <TD/>
        </TR>
        <TR>
            <TD HEIGHT="60"/>
            <TD COLSPAN="3">
                AnswerBButton
            </TD>
            <TD/>
            <TD COLSPAN="3">
                AnswerDButton
            </TD>
        </TR>
        <TR>
            <TD HEIGHT="30"/>
            <TD/>
            <TD/>
            <TD/>
            <TD/>
            <TD/>
            <TD/>
            <TD/>
        </TR>
        <TR>
            <TD HEIGHT="30"/>
            <TD>
                ElapsedTimeLabel
            </TD>
            <TD/>
            <TD>
                ElapsedTimeDisplay
```

LISTING C.1 Continued

```
                                        </TD>
                                        <TD/>
                                        <TD/>
                                        <TD/>
                                        <TD/>
                                    </TR>
                                    <TR>
                                        <TD HEIGHT="30"/>
                                        <TD/>
                                        <TD/>
                                        <TD/>
                                        <TD/>
                                        <TD/>
                                        <TD/>
                                        <TD/>
                                    </TR>
                                    <TR>
                                        <TD COLSPAN="3" HEIGHT="60">
                                            NextQuestionButton
                                        </TD>
                                        <TD/>
                                        <TD COLSPAN="3" HEIGHT="60">
                                            ReturnButton
                                        </TD>
                                        <TD/>
                                    </TR>
                                </TABLE>
                            </g:PropertyValue>
                        </g:Property>
                    </g:PropertyList>
                </g:Component>
                <!-- TitleLabel -->
                <g:Component Name="TitleLabel">
                    <g:ComponentResource FingerprintID="Groove"
➥ URL="http://components.groove.net/Groove/Components/Root.osd?
➥Package=net.groove.Groove.ToolComponents.GrooveCommonComponents_DLL&amp;
➥Version=0&amp;Factory=Static"/>
                    <g:PropertyList Version="1">
                        <g:Property Name="Style" Value="Normal"/>
                        <g:Property Name="HAlignment" Value="Left"/>
                        <g:Property Name="BreakType" Value="WordBreak"/>
                        <g:Property Name="Label" Value="Our Trivia Game"/>
                        <g:Property Name="LabelFont">
                            <g:FontDesc Color="#000000"
➥Typeface="Tahoma" Height="18"/>
```

C

COMPLETE TRIVIA QUIZ CODE

LISTING C.1 Continued

```
                    </g:Property>
                </g:PropertyList>
            </g:Component>
            <!-- QuestionLabel -->
            <g:Component Name="QuestionLabel">
                <g:ComponentResource FingerprintID="Groove"
➥ URL="http://components.groove.net/Groove/Components/Root.osd?
➥Package=net.groove.Groove.ToolComponents.GrooveCommonComponents_DLL&amp;
➥Version=0&amp;Factory=Static"/>
                <g:PropertyList Version="1">
                    <g:Property Name="Style" Value="Normal"/>
                    <g:Property Name="HAlignment" Value="Left"/>
                    <g:Property Name="VAlignment" Value="Center"/>
                    <g:Property Name="BreakType" Value="WordBreak"/>
                    <g:Property Name="Label" Value=""/>
                    <g:Property Name="LabelFont">
                        <g:FontDesc Color="#000000"
➥Typeface="Tahoma" Height="14"/>
                    </g:Property>
                </g:PropertyList>
            </g:Component>
            <!-- Answer A Button -->
            <g:Component Name="AnswerAButton">
                <g:ComponentResource FingerprintID="Groove"
➥ URL="http://components.groove.net/Groove/Root.osd?
➥Package=net.groove.Groove.ToolComponents.GrooveCommonComponents_DLL&amp;
➥Version=0&amp;Factory=Button"/>
                <g:PropertyList Version="1">
                    <g:Property Name="Style" Value="StandardButton"/>
                    <g:Property Name="OverrideLabelPosition" Value="Center"/>
                    <g:Property Name="Label" Value="A:Man"/>
                    <g:Property Name="Tooltip" Value=""/>
                    <g:Property Name="Mnemonic" Value="ALT+A"/>
                </g:PropertyList>
            </g:Component>
            <!-- Answer B Button -->
            <g:Component Name="AnswerBButton">
                <g:ComponentResource FingerprintID="Groove"
➥ URL="http://components.groove.net/Groove/Root.osd?
➥Package=net.groove.Groove.ToolComponents.GrooveCommonComponents_DLL&amp;
➥Version=0&amp;Factory=Button"/>
                <g:PropertyList Version="1">
                    <g:Property Name="Style" Value="StandardButton"/>
                    <g:Property Name="OverrideLabelPosition" Value="Center"/>
```

LISTING C.1 Continued

```
                    <g:Property Name="Label" Value="B:Elephant"/>
                    <g:Property Name="Tooltip" Value=""/>
                    <g:Property Name="Mnemonic" Value="ALT+A"/>
                </g:PropertyList>
            </g:Component>
            <!-- Answer C Button -->
            <g:Component Name="AnswerCButton">
                <g:ComponentResource FingerprintID="Groove"
➥ URL="http://components.groove.net/Groove/Root.osd?
➥Package=net.groove.Groove.ToolComponents.GrooveCommonComponents_DLL&amp;
➥Version=0&amp;Factory=Button"/>
                <g:PropertyList Version="1">
                    <g:Property Name="Style" Value="StandardButton"/>
                    <g:Property Name="OverrideLabelPosition" Value="Center"/>
                    <g:Property Name="Label" Value="C:Sperm Whale"/>
                    <g:Property Name="Tooltip" Value=""/>
                    <g:Property Name="Mnemonic" Value="ALT+A"/>
                </g:PropertyList>
            </g:Component>
             <!-- Answer D Button -->
            <g:Component Name="AnswerDButton">
                <g:ComponentResource FingerprintID="Groove"
➥ URL="http://components.groove.net/Groove/Root.osd?
➥Package=net.groove.Groove.ToolComponents.GrooveCommonComponents_DLL&amp;
➥Version=0&amp;Factory=Button"/>
                <g:PropertyList Version="1">
                    <g:Property Name="Style" Value="StandardButton"/>
                    <g:Property Name="OverrideLabelPosition" Value="Center"/>
                    <g:Property Name="LabelFont">
                        <g:FontDesc Color="#000000"
➥Typeface="Tahoma" Height="14"/>
                    </g:Property>
                    <g:Property Name="Label" Value="D:Grizzly Bear"/>
                    <g:Property Name="Tooltip" Value=""/>
                    <g:Property Name="Mnemonic" Value="ALT+A"/>
                </g:PropertyList>
            </g:Component>
            <!-- Elapsed Time Label-->
            <g:Component Name="ElapsedTimeLabel">
                <g:ComponentResource FingerprintID="Groove"
➥ URL="http://components.groove.net/Groove/Components/Root.osd?
➥Package=net.groove.Groove.ToolComponents.GrooveCommonComponents_DLL&amp;
➥Version=0&amp;Factory=Static"/>
                <g:PropertyList Version="1">
```

LISTING C.1 Continued

```
                    <g:Property Name="Style" Value="Normal"/>
                    <g:Property Name="HAlignment" Value="Left"/>
                    <g:Property Name="VAlignment" Value="Center"/>
                    <g:Property Name="BreakType" Value="WordBreak"/>
                    <g:Property Name="Label" Value="Elapsed Time: "/>
                    <g:Property Name="FontStyle" Value="LabelText"/>
                </g:PropertyList>
            </g:Component>
            <!-- ElapsedTimeDisplay -->
            <g:Component Name="ElapsedTimeDisplay">
                <g:ComponentResource FingerprintID="Groove"
➥ URL="http://components.groove.net/Groove/Components/Root.osd?
➥Package=net.groove.Groove.ToolComponents.GrooveCommonComponents_DLL&amp;
➥Version=0&amp;Factory=Static"/>
                <g:PropertyList Version="1">
                    <g:Property Name="Label" Value=""/>
                    <g:Property Name="Style" Value="Header"/>
                    <g:Property Name="BackgroundColor" Value="#FFFFFF"/>
                </g:PropertyList>
            </g:Component>
            <!-- Next Question Button -->
            <g:Component Name="NextQuestionButton">
                <g:ComponentResource FingerprintID="Groove"
➥ URL="http://components.groove.net/Groove/Root.osd?
➥Package=net.groove.Groove.ToolComponents.GrooveCommonComponents_DLL&amp;
➥Version=0&amp;Factory=Button"/>
                <g:PropertyList Version="1">
                    <g:Property Name="Style" Value="StandardIconButton"/>
                    <g:Property Name="Enabled" Value="false"/>
                    <g:Property Name="OverrideLabelPosition"
➥ Value="InsideLeft"/>
                    <g:Property Name="ImageURL"
➥ Value="grooveFile:///ToolBMPs\Arrows16x16Images.jpg"/>
                    <g:Property Name="ImageMaskURL"
➥ Value="grooveFile:///ToolBMPs\Arrows16x16ImagesMask.bmp"/>
                    <g:Property Name="ImageOffset" Value="16"/>
                    <g:Property Name="ImageHeight" Value="16"/>
                    <g:Property Name="ImageWidth" Value="16"/>
                    <g:Property Name="Label"
➥ Value="Press for &amp;next question"/>
                    <g:Property Name="Tooltip" Value=""/>
                    <g:Property Name="Mnemonic" Value="ALT+A"/>
                </g:PropertyList>
            </g:Component>
```

LISTING C.1 Continued

```
            <!-- Glue code -->
            <g:Component Name="TriviaQuizGlue">
                <g:ComponentResource FingerprintID="Groove"
➥ URL="http://components.groove.net/Groove/Components/Root.osd?
➥Package=net.groove.Groove.ToolComponents.GrooveCommonComponents_DLL&amp;
➥Version=0&amp;Factory=ScriptHost3"/>
                <g:ComponentConnections>
                    <g:Connection ConnectionID="0"
➥ Name="TriviaQuizViewContainer"/>
                    <g:Connection ConnectionID="1" Name="QuestionLabel"/>
                    <g:Connection ConnectionID="2" Name="AnswerAButton"/>
                    <g:Connection ConnectionID="3" Name="AnswerBButton"/>
                    <g:Connection ConnectionID="4" Name="AnswerCButton"/>
                    <g:Connection ConnectionID="5" Name="AnswerDButton"/>
                    <g:Connection ConnectionID="6" Name="ElapsedTimeDisplay"/>
                    <g:Connection ConnectionID="7" Name="NextQuestionButton"/>
                    <g:Connection ConnectionID="8" Name="GoEnterButton"/>
                    <g:Connection ConnectionID="9" Name="GoPlayButton"/>
                    <g:Connection ConnectionID="10" Name="QuestionInput"/>
                    <g:Connection ConnectionID="11" Name="Answer1Input"/>
                    <g:Connection ConnectionID="12" Name="Answer2Input"/>
                    <g:Connection ConnectionID="13" Name="Answer3Input"/>
                    <g:Connection ConnectionID="14" Name="Answer4Input"/>
                    <g:Connection ConnectionID="15" Name="CorrectAnswerInput"/>
                    <g:Connection ConnectionID="16"
➥ Name="EnterQuestionButton"/>
                    <g:Connection ConnectionID="17" Name="EditQuestionButton"/>
                    <g:Connection ConnectionID="18" Name="SaveEditsButton"/>
                    <g:Connection ConnectionID="19"
➥ Name="RemoveQuestionButton"/>
                    <g:Connection ConnectionID="20" Name="ReturnButton"/>
                    <g:Connection ConnectionID="21" Name="QuestionDataViewer"/>
                    <g:Connection ConnectionID="22" Name="ModelGlue"/>
                    <g:Connection ConnectionID="23" Name="RecordSetEngine"/>
                </g:ComponentConnections>
                <g:PropertyList Version="1">
                    <g:Property Name="QuestionNumber" Value="1"/>
                </g:PropertyList>
                <TYPELIB MAJORVER="1"
➥ LIBID="{FB1EBAB1-C159-11d3-80B6-00500487887B}" MINORVER="0"
➥ NAME="GrooveCollectionComponents"/>
                <SCRIPT
➥ SRC="http://components.groove.net/Groove/Components/Root.osd?
➥Package=net.groove.Groove.ToolComponents.
➥GrooveGlobalHelperFunctions_GSL&amp;
➥Version=0,1&amp;Factory=Open"/>
```

C

COMPLETE TRIVIA QUIZ CODE

LISTING C.1 Continued

```
                <SCRIPT>
        <![CDATA[
           var totalQuestions;
           var questionNumber;
           var thisDate = new Date();
           var startTime;
           var correctFlag = 0;
           var recordIDArray;
           var currentCorrectAnswer;

           function Initialize()
           {

              if (RecordSetEngine.NumRecords > 0) {
                 BuildRecordIDArray();
              }
              else
              {
                 GoPlayButton.Enabled="false";
              }

              // Open a read transaction on the telespace to freeze properties
              var pITelespace = PropertyList.OpenProperty(PROPERTY_TELESPACE);
              var pITransaction = pITelespace.OpenTransaction(true);

              // Perform all operations inside of try/catch block so if an
              // error occurs, we can abort transaction (VERY IMPORTANT)
              try
                 {
                 // Search for already existing records and display
                 // them in listbox
                 if (PropertyList.PropertyExists("Time"))
                    {
                    var propertyValue = PropertyList.OpenProperty("Time");

                    // Add the property to the listbox
                    var Index = ElapsedTimeDisplay.SetText(propertyValue);
                    }
                 if (PropertyList.PropertyExists("QuestionNumber"))
                    {
                     ChangeLabels();
                    }
```

LISTING C.1 Continued

```
        // Commit the transaction (VERY IMPORTANT)
        pITransaction.EndRead();
        }

      catch (objError)
         {
              pITransaction.Abort();
              showError(objError);
          }

   }


function ChangeLabels()
{
   questionNumber = PropertyList.OpenProperty("QuestionNumber");


   // Open a transaction read on the telespace to freeze properties
   var pITelespace = PropertyList.OpenProperty(PROPERTY_TELESPACE);
   var pITransaction = pITelespace.OpenTransaction(true);

   var indexNumber;
   var currentRecordID;
   var currentRecord;

   var questionText;
   var answerAText;
   var answerBText;
   var answerCText;
   var answerDText;
   var correctAnswer;

   // Perform all operations inside of try/catch block so if an
   // error occurs, we can abort transaction (VERY IMPORTANT)
   try
   {
   //recordIDArray is 0 based
   indexNumber = questionNumber - 1;
   currentRecordID = recordIDArray[indexNumber];
   currentRecord = GetRecordByID(currentRecordID);

   questionText=(currentRecord.OpenField("Question"));
   answerAText=(currentRecord.OpenField("Answer1"));
```

LISTING C.1 Continued

```
        answerBText=(currentRecord.OpenField("Answer2"));
        answerCText=(currentRecord.OpenField("Answer3"));
        answerDText=(currentRecord.OpenField("Answer4"));
        correctAnswer=(currentRecord.OpenField("CorrectAnswer"));

        // Commit the transaction (VERY IMPORTANT)
        pITransaction.EndRead();

        }
        catch (e)
        {
           // An exception has occurred, so abort the transaction
           pITransaction.Abort();
           GrooveDebugFunctions.Assert(false, "");
        }

        QuestionLabel.SetText(questionText);
        AnswerAButton.Label="A:" + answerAText;
        AnswerBButton.Label="B:" + answerBText;
        AnswerCButton.Label="C:" + answerCText;
        AnswerDButton.Label="D:" + answerDText;
        currentCorrectAnswer=correctAnswer;
     }

     function ShowElapsedTime()
        {
           var nowDate = new Date();
           var nowTime = nowDate.getTime();
        //Convert milliseconds to seconds
           var elapsedTime = (nowTime - startTime)/1000;
        //Penalize for more than 20 seconds or incorrect answer
        if ( (elapsedTime > 20) | (correctFlag == 0))
           {
              elapsedTime = 20.0;
           }
        if (PropertyList.PropertyExists("GameTime"))
              {
                 var newTime =
➥ PropertyList.OpenPropertyAsString("GameTime");
                 var propertyValue = (newTime - 0) + elapsedTime;
                 PropertyList.SetPropertyAsString
➥("GameTime", propertyValue);
              } else {
              propertyValue = elapsedTime;
```

LISTING C.1 Continued

```
                    PropertyList.SetPropertyAsString
➥("GameTime", propertyValue );
                }

                PropertyList.SetPropertyAsString("Time", elapsedTime);
                ElapsedTimeDisplay.SetText
➥(PropertyList.OpenProperty("Time"));
            }

        function UserGuess()
        {
           NextQuestionButton.Enabled = true;
           ShowElapsedTime();
           DisableQuestionButtons()
        }

        function DisableQuestionButtons ()
        {
           AnswerAButton.Enabled = false;
           AnswerBButton.Enabled = false;
           AnswerCButton.Enabled = false;
           AnswerDButton.Enabled = false;
        }

        function EnableQuestionButtons ()
        {
           AnswerAButton.Enabled = true;
           AnswerBButton.Enabled = true;
           AnswerCButton.Enabled = true;
           AnswerDButton.Enabled = true;
        }


        function AnswerAButton_OnCommand(i_pIUICommand)
        {
           if (currentCorrectAnswer=="1")
              {
                 correctFlag = 1;
              }

           UserGuess()
        }

        function AnswerBButton_OnCommand(i_pIUICommand)
```

LISTING C.1 Continued

```
{
   if (currentCorrectAnswer=="2")
      {
         correctFlag = 1;
      }
   UserGuess()
}

function AnswerCButton_OnCommand(i_pIUICommand)
{
   if (currentCorrectAnswer=="3")
      {
         correctFlag = 1;
      }
   UserGuess()
}

function AnswerDButton_OnCommand(i_pIUICommand)
{
   if (currentCorrectAnswer=="4")
      {
         correctFlag = 1;
      }
   UserGuess()
}

function NextQuestionButton_OnCommand(i_pIUICommand)
{
   thisDate = new Date();
   startTime = thisDate.getTime();
   correctFlag = 0;

   var propertyName = "QuestionNumber";
   // Open a write transaction on the telespace to freeze properties
   var pITelespace = PropertyList.OpenProperty(PROPERTY_TELESPACE);
   var pITransaction = pITelespace.OpenTransaction(false);

   // Perform all operations inside of try/catch block so if an
   // error occurs, we can abort transaction (VERY IMPORTANT)
   try
   {
      var propertyValue = PropertyList.OpenProperty(propertyName);

      //Increment the question number
```

LISTING C.1 Continued

```
            var newValue = parseInt(propertyValue) + 1;
            PropertyList.SetPropertyAsString(propertyName, newValue);

            // Commit the transaction (VERY IMPORTANT)
            pITransaction.Commit();
         }
         catch (objError)
         {
            pITransaction.Abort();
            showError(objError);
         }




         if (totalQuestions > questionNumber)
         {
            EnableQuestionButtons();
            ChangeLabels();
            NextQuestionButton.Enabled = false;
         }
         else
         {
            ShowScore();
            ResetGame();
         }
      }



      function RecordSetEngine_OnRecordSetChanged
         (
         i_pIRecordSetEngine,
         i_RecordSetChangeType,
         i_pIRecordIDEnum
         )
      {
// Begin the read transaction
// Open a transaction on the telespace to freeze properties
var pITelespace = PropertyList.OpenProperty(PROPERTY_TELESPACE);
var pITransaction = pITelespace.OpenTransaction(true);

      try
         {
         BuildRecordIDArray();
```

LISTING C.1 Continued

```
            if (RecordSetEngine.NumRecords > 0) {
               GoPlayButton.Enabled="true";
               }
               else
               {
               GoPlayButton.Enabled="false";
               }

            }
            // Commit the transaction (VERY IMPORTANT)
            pITransaction.EndRead();
            catch (objError)
            {
               showError(objError)
               // An exception has occurred, so abort the transaction
               pITransaction.Abort();
            }
         }

         function OnPropertyChanged
            (
            i_Key,
            i_pValue,
            i_LocallyGenerated
            )
         {

            var finishFlag=0;
            var PropertyName = i_Key;
            //  Use only "Time" or "QuestionNumber".

            if (i_Key == "Time" | i_Key == "QuestionNumber")
            {

               if (PropertyName == "Time")
               {
                 //Show only one entry in listbox at a time, so clear before
                 ElapsedTimeDisplay.SetText("");;
               }

            // Open a transaction on the telespace to freeze properties
            var pITelespace = PropertyList.OpenProperty(PROPERTY_TELESPACE);
            var pITransaction = pITelespace.OpenTransaction(true);
```

LISTING C.1 Continued

```
// Perform all operations inside of try/catch block so if an
// error occurs, we can abort transaction (VERY IMPORTANT)
try
   {
   if (PropertyName == "Time")
      {
      if (PropertyList.PropertyExists("Time"))
         {
         var PropertyValue = PropertyList.OpenProperty("Time");

         // Add the property's value to the listbox
         var Index = ElapsedTimeDisplay.SetText(PropertyValue);
         }
      }

   if (i_Key == "QuestionNumber")
      {

      if (PropertyList.PropertyExists("QuestionNumber"))
         {
            if (!i_LocallyGenerated)
            {
            ChangeLabels();
            thisDate = new Date();
            startTime = thisDate.getTime();

            if (PropertyList.OpenPropertyAsLong
➥("QuestionNumber") < 2)

               {
                ElapsedTimeDisplay.SetText
➥(PropertyList.OpenProperty("GameTime"));
                DisableQuestionButtons();
               }
               if (totalQuestions < questionNumber)
                  {
                     finishFlag = 1;
                  }
            }
         }
      }

   // Commit the transaction (VERY IMPORTANT)
   pITransaction.EndRead();
   }
```

LISTING C.1 Continued

```
   catch (objError)
      {
      // An exception has occurred, so abort the transaction
      pITransaction.Abort();

      showError(objError);
      }
      if (finishFlag==1) {
         ShowScore();
         ResetGame();
      }
   }

}

function GoPlayButton_OnCommand(i_pIUICommand)
{
         try
         {

                  TriviaQuizViewContainer.LayoutByName
                  ➥"TriviaQuizLayout";
                  ChangeLabels();
                  var thisDate = new Date();
                  startTime = thisDate.getTime();
         }
         catch(objError)
         {
                  showError(objError);
         }
}


function GoEnterButton_OnCommand(i_pIUICommand)
{
   try
   {
      TriviaQuizViewContainer.LayoutByName = "QuestionInputLayout";
   }
   catch(objError)
   {
      showError(objError);
   }
}
```

LISTING C.1 Continued

```
function ReturnButton_OnCommand(i_pIUICommand)
{
   try
   {
      TriviaQuizViewContainer.LayoutByName = "WelcomeLayout";
   }
   catch(objError)
   {
      showError(objError);
   }
}


function EnterQuestionButton_OnCommand(i_pIUICommand)
{
   //check for blank field
   if (FieldIsBlank())
      {
         var actionName="enter this record";
         var error="one of the fields is blank";
         DisplayError(actionName, error);
         return;
   }
   // Begin the read/write transaction
   // Open a transaction on the telespace to freeze properties
   var pITelespace = PropertyList.OpenProperty(PROPERTY_TELESPACE);
   var pITransaction = pITelespace.OpenTransaction(false);


      //check correctAnswer range
   //cast text to num
   var answerNum=parseInt(CorrectAnswerInput.Text);
   //if anwerNum is not a number, make it one.
   if(isNaN(answerNum)) answerNum=5;
   if (answerNum < 1 |answerNum > 4)
   {
      var actionName="enter this record";
         var error="correct answer not 1 through 4";
         DisplayError(actionName, error);
         return;
     }
   // Create a record to give to add to the RecordSetEngine
    //Put the operation in a try/catch block
   try
```

LISTING C.1 Continued

```
            {
               var pIRecord =
➥ModelGlue.CreateRecord("urn:groove.net:TriviaQuizRecord");
                   // Set the fields in the record
               pIRecord.SetField("Question", QuestionInput.Text);
               pIRecord.SetField("Answer1", Answer1Input.Text);
               pIRecord.SetField("Answer2", Answer2Input.Text);
               pIRecord.SetField("Answer3", Answer3Input.Text);
               pIRecord.SetField("Answer4", Answer4Input.Text);
               pIRecord.SetField("CorrectAnswer", CorrectAnswerInput.Text);
               // Add the record
               ModelGlue.AddRecord(pIRecord);
               pITransaction.Commit();
            }
            catch (objError)
            {
               pITransaction.Abort();
               showError(objError);
            }

            // Reset the Question input text
            QuestionInput.Text = "";
            Answer1Input.Text = "";
            Answer2Input.Text = "";
            Answer3Input.Text = "";
            Answer4Input.Text = "";
            CorrectAnswerInput.Text = "";
         }


         function EditQuestionButton_OnCommand(i_pIUICommand)
         {
            // Begin the read transaction
            // Open a transaction on the telespace to freeze properties
            var pITelespace = PropertyList.OpenProperty(PROPERTY_TELESPACE);
            var pITransaction = pITelespace.OpenTransaction(true);

            //Put the operation in a try/catch block
            try
            {
            if (RecordSetEngine.HasRecord(RecordID)) {
                  var RecordID = QuestionDataViewer.GetIDOfFocusRow();
                  var pIRecord = RecordSetEngine.OpenRecord(RecordID);
                  var questionField = pIRecord.OpenField("Question");
```

LISTING C.1 Continued

```
                var answer1Field = pIRecord.OpenField("Answer1");
                var answer2Field = pIRecord.OpenField("Answer2");
                var answer3Field = pIRecord.OpenField("Answer3");
                var answer4Field = pIRecord.OpenField("Answer4");
                var correctAnswerField =
➥pIRecord.OpenField("CorrectAnswer");
            }

            pITransaction.EndRead();
        }
        catch (objError)
        {
            pITransaction.Abort();
            showError(objError);
        }
        QuestionInput.Text = questionField;
        Answer1Input.text = answer1Field;
        Answer2Input.text = answer2Field;
        Answer3Input.text = answer3Field;
        Answer4Input.text = answer4Field;
                CorrectAnswerInput.text = correctAnswerField;
        currentRecordID = RecordID;

        }

        function SaveEditsButton_OnCommand(i_pIUICommand)
        {
            if (FieldIsBlank())
                {
                    var actionName="enter this record";
                    var error="one of the fields is blank";
                    DisplayError(actionName, error);
                    return;
            }
                //check correctAnswer range
            //cast text to num
            var answerNum=parseInt(CorrectAnswerInput.Text);
            //if anwerNum is not a number, make it one.
            if(isNaN(answerNum)) answerNum=5;
            if (answerNum < 1 |answerNum > 4)
            {
                var actionName="enter this record";
                    var error="correct answer not 1 through 4";
                    DisplayError(actionName, error);
                    return;
              }
```

LISTING C.1 Continued

```
                  // Begin the read/write transaction
                  // Open a transaction on the telespace to freeze properties
                  var pITelespace = PropertyList.OpenProperty
➥(PROPERTY_TELESPACE);
                  var pITransaction = pITelespace.OpenTransaction(false);


                  //Put the operation in a try/catch block
                  try
                  {
                     // Create a record to give to add to the RecordSetEngine
var pIRecord = ModelGlue.CreateRecord
➥("urn:groove.net:TriviaQuizRecord");
                     // Set the fields in the record
                     pIRecord.SetField("Question", QuestionInput.Text);
                     pIRecord.SetField("Answer1", Answer1Input.Text);
                     pIRecord.SetField("Answer2", Answer2Input.Text);
                     pIRecord.SetField("Answer3", Answer3Input.Text);
                     pIRecord.SetField("Answer4", Answer4Input.Text);
                     pIRecord.SetField("CorrectAnswer",
➥ CorrectAnswerInput.Text);
                     // Add the record
                     ModelGlue.ReplaceRecord(currentRecordID, pIRecord);
                     pITransaction.Commit();
                  }
                  catch (objError)
                  {
                     pITransaction.Abort();
                     showError(objError);
                   }

                  // Reset the Question input text
                  QuestionInput.Text = "";
                  Answer1Input.Text = "";
                  Answer2Input.Text = "";
                  Answer3Input.Text = "";
                  Answer4Input.Text = "";
                  CorrectAnswerInput.Text = "";
                  currentRecordID = "";
               }

            function RemoveQuestionButton_OnCommand(i_pIUICommand)
            {
               // Begin the read/write transaction
```

LISTING C.1 Continued

```
        // Open a transaction on the telespace to freeze properties
        var pITelespace = PropertyList.OpenProperty(PROPERTY_TELESPACE);
        var pITransaction = pITelespace.OpenTransaction(false);

        //Put the operation in a try/catch block
        try
        {
           var RecordID = QuestionDataViewer.GetIDOfFocusRow();
           var pIRecord = RecordSetEngine.OpenRecord(RecordID);
           RecordSetEngine.RemoveRecord(RecordID);
           pITransaction.Commit();
        }
        catch (e)
        {
           pITransaction.Abort();
        }
        }


     function showError(objError)
     {
        var strErrMsg;
        strErrMsg = "Error #" + objError.number + "\n";
        strErrMsg += objError.description;
        GrooveDebugFunctions.Assert(false, strErrMsg);
     }

     function FieldIsBlank()
     {
        if(""==QuestionInput.Text|
              ""==Answer1Input.Text|
              ""==Answer2Input.Text|
              ""==Answer3Input.Text|
              ""==Answer4Input.Text|
              ""==CorrectAnswerInput.Text){
              return true;
              }
        return false;
     }

     function DisplayError(actionName, error)
     {
        var Account = OpenAccountFromPropertyList(PropertyList);
        var Window = UIPropertyList.OpenProperty
➥(UIPROPERTY_TOP_LEVEL_WINDOW);
```

LISTING C.1 Continued

```
            App.GrooveMessageBox(Window, Account,
➥ "Unable to " + actionName + " because of the following error: \n" +
➥error, "Error", GrooveMessageBoxStyle_OK, GrooveMessageBoxIcon_Error);
         }

         function BuildRecordIDArray()
         {
            //Make sure array gets rebuilt each time
            recordIDArray = new Array();

            var index = 0;
            var RecordIDEnum = RecordSetEngine.OpenRecordIDEnum();
               while (RecordIDEnum.HasMore()) {
                     ARecordID = RecordIDEnum.OpenNext();
                     recordIDArray[index]=ARecordID;
                     index = index + 1;
               }
            totalQuestions = RecordSetEngine.NumRecords;
         }


         function GetRecordByID(i_RecordID)
            {
            var Record;
            if (RecordSetEngine.HasRecord(i_RecordID))
            Record = RecordSetEngine.OpenRecord(i_RecordID);
            return Record;
         }


         function ShowScore()
         {
            NextQuestionButton.Enabled = false;
            var scoreString = "You have completed all the questions
➥ with a total time of: ";
            var Account = OpenAccountFromPropertyList(PropertyList);
            var Window = UIPropertyList.OpenProperty
➥(UIPROPERTY_TOP_LEVEL_WINDOW);
            App.GrooveMessageBox(Window, Account, scoreString +
➥ (PropertyList.OpenProperty("GameTime"))+
➥ " seconds.", "Congratulations",
➥ GrooveMessageBoxStyle_OK, GrooveMessageBoxIcon_Exclamation);
         }
```

LISTING C.1 Continued

```
            function ResetGame()
            {
                  // Open a write transaction on the telespace
                  //to freeze properties
                  var pITelespace =
➥PropertyList.OpenProperty(PROPERTY_TELESPACE);
                  var pITransaction = pITelespace.OpenTransaction(false);
               var finishFlag=0;

                  // Perform all operations inside of try/catch block so if an
                  // error occurs, we can abort transaction (VERY IMPORTANT)
                  try
                  {
                       PropertyList.SetProperty("QuestionNumber", 1);
                        PropertyList.RemoveProperty("GameTime",
➥ GroovePropertyFlag_Disseminate);
                        finishFlag = 1;
                  // Commit the transaction (VERY IMPORTANT)
                        pITransaction.Commit();
                  }
                  catch(objError)
                  {
                     pITransaction.Abort();
                      showError(objError);
                  }
               if (finishFlag==1){
                     ElapsedTimeDisplay.SetText("");
                     EnableQuestionButtons ();
                     TriviaQuizViewContainer.LayoutByName = "WelcomeLayout";
               }
            }

            function showError(objError)
            {
               var strErrMsg;
               strErrMsg = "Error #" + objError.number + "\n";
               strErrMsg += objError.description;
               GrooveDebugFunctions.Assert(false, strErrMsg);
            }


               ]]>
                </SCRIPT>
            </g:Component>
```

LISTING C.1 Continued

```
            <g:Component Name="TriviaGraphic">
                <g:ComponentResource FingerprintID="Groove"
➥ URL="http://components.groove.net/Groove/Components/Root.osd?
➥Package=net.groove.Groove.ToolComponents.GrooveCommonComponents_DLL&amp;
➥Version=0&amp;Factory=Image"/>
                <g:PropertyList Version="1">
                    <g:Property Value="bmp, jpg, jpeg"
➥Name="AcceptedFileTypes"/>
                    <g:Property Name="Image">
                        <g:Image
➥ ImageURL="grooveFile:///ToolBMPs\TriviaGraphic.jpg"
➥ ImageMaskURL="grooveFile:///ToolBMPs\TriviaGraphicMask.bmp"
➥ Width="200" Height="100"/>
                    </g:Property>
                </g:PropertyList>
            </g:Component>
            <g:Component Name="WelcomeLayout">
                <g:ComponentResource FingerprintID="Groove"
➥ URL="http://components.groove.net/Groove/Components/Root.osd?
➥Package=net.groove.Groove.ToolComponents.GrooveCommonComponents_DLL&amp;
➥Version=0&amp;Factory=MultiCellLayout"/>
                <g:PropertyList Version="1">
                    <g:Property Name=x"Layout">
                        <g:PropertyValue>
                            <MULTIROW>
                                <BORDER BottomPad="10" RightPad="5"
➥ TopPad="5" LeftPad="5"/>
                                <DEFAULTPAD BottomPad="2" RightPad="3"
➥ TopPad="2" LeftPad="3"/>
                                <ROW>
                                    <CELL HEIGHT="100">
                                        TriviaGraphic
                                    </CELL>
                                    <CELL/>
                                    <CELL/>
                                </ROW>
                                <ROW>
                                    <CELL HEIGHT="100">
                                        WelcomeTitle
                                    </CELL>
                                </ROW>
                                <ROW>
                                    <CELL HEIGHT="100">
                                        WelcomeText
```

LISTING C.1 Continued

```
                                        </CELL>
                                    </ROW>
                                    <ROW>
                                        <CELL/>
                                        <CELL HEIGHT="100">
                                            GoEnterButton
                                        </CELL>
                                        <CELL HEIGHT="100">
                                            GoPlayButton
                                        </CELL>
                                        <CELL/>
                                    </ROW>
                                </MULTIROW>
                            </g:PropertyValue>
                        </g:Property>
                    </g:PropertyList>
                </g:Component>
                <g:Component Name="WelcomeTitle">
                    <g:ComponentResource FingerprintID="Groove"
➥ URL="http://components.groove.net/Groove/Components/Root.osd?
➥Package=net.groove.Groove.ToolComponents.GrooveCommonComponents_DLL&amp;
➥Version=0&amp;Factory=Static"/>
                    <g:PropertyList Version="1">
                        <g:Property Name="Label"
➥ Value="Welcome to Our Trivia Game"/>
                        <g:Property Name="Style" Value="Header"/>
                        <g:Property Name="HAlignment" Value="Center"/>
                    </g:PropertyList>
                </g:Component>
                <g:Component Name="GoEnterButton">
                    <g:ComponentResource FingerprintID="Groove"
➥ URL="http://components.groove.net/Groove/Components/Root.osd?
➥Package=net.groove.Groove.ToolComponents.GrooveCommonComponents_DLL&amp;
➥Version=0&amp;Factory=Button"/>
                    <g:PropertyList Version="1">
                        <g:Property Name="Label" Value="Enter Questions"/>
                        <g:Property Name="Style" Value="StandardButton"/>
                        <g:Property Name="Tooltip"
➥ Value="Click here if you&apos;d like to enter questions
➥ for others to guess."/>
                    </g:PropertyList>
                </g:Component>
                <g:Component Name="WelcomeText">
```

LISTING C.1 Continued

```
                <g:ComponentResource FingerprintID="Groove"
➥ URL="http://components.groove.net/Groove/Components/Root.osd?
➥Package=net.groove.Groove.ToolComponents.GrooveCommonComponents_DLL&amp;
➥Version=0&amp;Factory=Static"/>
                <g:PropertyList Version="1">
                    <g:Property Name="LabelFont">
                        <g:FontDesc Color="#000000" Typeface="Tahoma"
➥ Height="18"/>
                    </g:Property>
                    <g:Property Name="Label" Value="In our trivia game you
➥ can play, or you can add more questions.
➥ Choose which activity you would like to do."/>
                    <g:Property Name="BreakType" Value="WordBreak"/>
                    <g:Property Name="HAlignment" Value="Center"/>
                    <g:Property Name="LabelFont">
                        <g:FontDesc Color="#000000"
➥ Typeface="Tahoma" Height="18"/>
                    </g:Property>
                </g:PropertyList>
            </g:Component>
            <g:Component Name="GoPlayButton">
                <g:ComponentResource FingerprintID="Groove"
➥ URL="http://components.groove.net/Groove/Components/Root.osd?
➥Package=net.groove.Groove.ToolComponents.GrooveCommonComponents_DLL&amp;
➥Version=0&amp;Factory=Button"/>
                <g:PropertyList Version="1">
                    <g:Property Name=x"Tooltip" Value="Click here if
➥ you&apos;d like to play the trivia game."/>
                    <g:Property Name="Label" Value="PlayTrivia"/>
                    <g:Property Name="Style" Value="StandardButton"/>
                </g:PropertyList>
            </g:Component>
            <g:Component Name="QuestionInputLayout">
                <g:ComponentResource FingerprintID="Groove"
➥ URL="http://components.groove.net/Groove/Components/Root.osd?
➥Package=net.groove.Groove.ToolComponents.GrooveCommonComponents_DLL&amp;
➥Version=0&amp;Factory=MultiCellLayout"/>
                <g:PropertyList Version="1">
                    <g:Property Name="Layout">
                        <g:PropertyValue>
                            <MULTIROW>
                                <BORDER BottomPad="10" RightPad="5"
➥ TopPad="5" LeftPad="5"/>
                                <DEFAULTPAD BottomPad="2" RightPad="3"
➥ TopPad="2" LeftPad="3"/>
```

LISTING C.1 Continued

```
<ROW>
    <CELL>
        QuestionInputLabel
    </CELL>
    <CELL WIDTH="75%">
        QuestionInput
    </CELL>
</ROW>
<ROW>
    <CELL>
        Answer1InputLabel
    </CELL>
    <CELL WIDTH="75%">
        Answer1Input
    </CELL>
</ROW>
<ROW>
    <CELL>
        Answer2InputLabel
    </CELL>
    <CELL WIDTH="75%">
        Answer2Input
    </CELL>
</ROW>
<ROW>
    <CELL>
        Answer3InputLabel
    </CELL>
    <CELL WIDTH="75%">
        Answer3Input
    </CELL>
</ROW>
<ROW>
    <CELL>
        Answer4InputLabel
    </CELL>
    <CELL WIDTH="75%">
        Answer4Input
    </CELL>
</ROW>
<ROW>
    <CELL>
        CorrectAnswerInputLabel
    </CELL>
```

LISTING C.1 Continued

```
                                        <CELL WIDTH="75%">
                                            CorrectAnswerInput
                                        </CELL>
                                    </ROW>
                                    <ROW>
                                        <CELL>
                                            EnterQuestionButton
                                        </CELL>
                                        <CELL>
                                            EditQuestionButton
                                        </CELL>
                                        <CELL>
                                            SaveEditsButton
                                        </CELL>
                                        <CELL>
                                            RemoveQuestionButton
                                        </CELL>
                                    </ROW>
                                    <ROW>
                                        <CELL HEIGHT="70%">
                                            QuestionDataViewer
                                        </CELL>
                                    </ROW>
                                    <ROW>
                                        <CELL/>
                                        <CELL/>
                                        <CELL/>
                                        <CELL/>
                                        <CELL>
                                            ReturnButton
                                        </CELL>
                                    </ROW>
                                </MULTIROW>
                            </g:PropertyValue>
                        </g:Property>
                    </g:PropertyList>
                </g:Component>
                <g:Component Name="QuestionInputLabel">
                    <g:ComponentResource FingerprintID="Groove"
➥ URL="http://components.groove.net/Groove/Components/Root.osd?
➥Package=net.groove.Groove.ToolComponents.GrooveCommonComponents_DLL&amp;
➥Version=0&amp;Factory=Static"/>
                    <g:PropertyList Version="1">
                        <g:Property Name="Label" Value="Enter Question"/>
```

LISTING C.1 Continued

```
                </g:PropertyList>
            </g:Component>
            <g:Component Name="Answer1InputLabel">
                <g:ComponentResource FingerprintID=xx"Groove"
➥ URL="http://components.groove.net/Groove/Components/Root.osd?
➥Package=net.groove.Groove.ToolComponents.GrooveCommonComponents_DLL&amp;
➥Version=0&amp;Factory=Static"/>
                <g:PropertyList Version="1">
                    <g:Property Name="Label" Value="Enter Answer 1"/>
                </g:PropertyList>
            </g:Component>
            <g:Component Name="Answer2InputLabel">
                <g:ComponentResource FingerprintID="Groove"
➥ URL="http://components.groove.net/Groove/Components/Root.osd?
➥Package=net.groove.Groove.ToolComponents.GrooveCommonComponents_DLL&amp;
➥Version=0&amp;Factory=Static"/>
                <g:PropertyList Version="1">
                    <g:Property Name="Label" Value="Enter Answer 2"/>
                </g:PropertyList>
            </g:Component>
            <g:Component Name="Answer3InputLabel">
                <g:ComponentResource FingerprintID="Groove"
➥ URL="http://components.groove.net/Groove/Components/Root.osd?
➥Package=net.groove.Groove.ToolComponents.GrooveCommonComponents_DLL&amp;
➥Version=0&amp;Factory=Static"/>
                <g:PropertyList Version="1">
                    <g:Property Name="Label" Value="Enter Answer 3"/>
                </g:PropertyList>
            </g:Component>
            <g:Component Name="Answer4InputLabel">
                <g:ComponentResource FingerprintID="Groove"
➥ URL="http://components.groove.net/Groove/Components/Root.osd?
➥Package=net.groove.Groove.ToolComponents.GrooveCommonComponents_DLL&amp;
➥Version=0&amp;Factory=Static"/>
                <g:PropertyList Version="1">
                    <g:Property Name="Label" Value="Enter Answer 4"/>
                </g:PropertyList>
            </g:Component>
            <g:Component Name="CorrectAnswerInputLabel">
                <g:ComponentResource FingerprintID="Groove"
➥ URL="http://components.groove.net/Groove/Components/Root.osd?
➥Package=net.groove.Groove.ToolComponents.GrooveCommonComponents_DLL&amp;
➥Version=0&amp;Factory=Static"/>
                <g:PropertyList Version="1">
```

LISTING C.1 Continued

```
                    <g:Property Name="Label"
➥ Value="Enter Correct Answer Number"/>
                    <g:Property Name="Clip" Value="WordEllipsis"/>
                </g:PropertyList>
            </g:Component>
            <g:Component Name="QuestionInput">
                <g:ComponentResource FingerprintID="Groove"
➥ URL="http://components.groove.net/Groove/Components/Root.osd?
➥Package=net.groove.Groove.ToolComponents.GrooveCommonComponents_DLL&amp;
➥Version=0&amp;Factory=Edit"/>
                <g:PropertyList Version="1"/>
            </g:Component>
            <g:Component Name="Answer1Input">
                <g:ComponentResource FingerprintID="Groove"
➥ URL="http://components.groove.net/Groove/Components/Root.osd?
➥Package=net.groove.Groove.ToolComponents.GrooveCommonComponents_DLL&amp;
➥Version=0&amp;Factory=Edit"/>
                <g:PropertyList Version="1"/>
            </g:Component>
            <g:Component Name="Answer2Input">
                <g:ComponentResource FingerprintID="Groove"
➥ URL="http://components.groove.net/Groove/Components/Root.osd?
➥Package=net.groove.Groove.ToolComponents.GrooveCommonComponents_DLL&amp;
➥Version=0&amp;Factory=Edit"/>
                <g:PropertyList Version="1"/>
            </g:Component>
            <g:Component Name="Answer3Input">
                <g:ComponentResource FingerprintID="Groove"
➥ URL="http://components.groove.net/Groove/Components/Root.osd?
➥Package=net.groove.Groove.ToolComponents.GrooveCommonComponents_DLL&amp;
➥Version=0&amp;Factory=Edit"/>
                <g:PropertyList Version="1"/>
            </g:Component>
            <g:Component Name="Answer4Input">
                <g:ComponentResource FingerprintID="Groove"
➥ URL="http://components.groove.net/Groove/Components/Root.osd?
➥Package=net.groove.Groove.ToolComponents.GrooveCommonComponents_DLL&amp;
➥Version=0&amp;Factory=Edit"/>
                <g:PropertyList Version="1"/>
            </g:Component>
            <g:Component Name="CorrectAnswerInput">
                <g:ComponentResource FingerprintID="Groove"
➥ URL="http://components.groove.net/Groove/Components/Root.osd?
➥Package=net.groove.Groove.ToolComponents.GrooveCommonComponents_DLL&amp;
➥Version=0&amp;Factory=Edit"/>
```

LISTING C.1 Continued

```
                <g:PropertyList Version="1"/>
            </g:Component>
            <g:Component Name="EnterQuestionButton">
                <g:ComponentResource FingerprintID="Groove"
➥  URL="http://components.groove.net/Groove/Components/Root.osd?
➥Package=net.groove.Groove.ToolComponents.GrooveCommonComponents_DLL&amp;
➥Version=0&amp;Factory=Button"/>
                <g:PropertyList Version="1">
                    <g:Property Name="Style" Value="StandardButton"/>
                    <g:Property Name="Tooltip"
➥ Value="Add a question to the database"/>
                    <g:Property Name="Label" Value="Enter Question"/>
                </g:PropertyList>
            </g:Component>
            <g:Component Name="EditQuestionButton">
                <g:ComponentResource FingerprintID="Groove"
➥ URL="http://components.groove.net/Groove/Components/Root.osd?
➥Package=net.groove.Groove.ToolComponents.GrooveCommonComponents_DLL&amp;
➥Version=0&amp;Factory=Button"/>
                <g:PropertyList Version="1">
                    <g:Property Name="Style" Value="StandardButton"/>
                    <g:Property Name="Tooltip"
➥ Value="Click to edit selected question"/>
                    <g:Property Name="Label" Value="Edit Selected Question"/>
                </g:PropertyList>
            </g:Component>
            <g:Component Name="SaveEditsButton">
                <g:ComponentResource FingerprintID="Groove"
➥ URL="http://components.groove.net/Groove/Components/Root.osd?
➥Package=net.groove.Groove.ToolComponents.GrooveCommonComponents_DLL&amp;
➥Version=0&amp;Factory=Button"/>
                <g:PropertyList Version="1">
                    <g:Property Name="Style" Value="StandardButton"/>
                    <g:Property Name="Tooltip"
➥ Value="Click to save yopur edits"/>
                    <g:Property Name="Label" Value="Save Edits"/>
                </g:PropertyList>
            </g:Component>
            <g:Component Name="RemoveQuestionButton">
                <g:ComponentResource FingerprintID="Groove"
➥ URL="http://components.groove.net/Groove/Components/Root.osd?
➥Package=net.groove.Groove.ToolComponents.GrooveCommonComponents_DLL&amp;
➥Version=0&amp;Factory=Button"/>
                <g:PropertyList Version="1">
```

LISTING C.1 Continued

```
                    <g:Property Name="Style" Value="StandardButton"/>
                    <g:Property Name="Tooltip"
➥ Value="Click to remove selected question"/>
                    <g:Property Value="Remove Selected Question" Name="Label"/>
                </g:PropertyList>
            </g:Component>
            <g:Component Name="ReturnButton">
                <g:ComponentResource FingerprintID="Groove"
➥ URL="http://components.groove.net/Groove/Components/Root.osd?
➥Package=net.groove.Groove.ToolComponents.GrooveCommonComponents_DLL&amp;
➥Version=0&amp;Factory=Button"/>
                <g:PropertyList Version="1">
                    <g:Property Name="Style" Value="StandardIconButton"/>
                    <g:Property Name="OverrideLabelPosition"
➥ Value="InsideRight"/>
                    <g:Property Name="ImageURL"
➥ Value="grooveFile:///ToolBMPs\Arrows16x16Images.jpg"/>
                    <g:Property Name="ImageMaskURL"
➥ Value="grooveFile:///ToolBMPs\Arrows16x16ImagesMask.bmp"/>
                    <g:Property Name="ImageOffset" Value="0"/>
                    <g:Property Name="ImageHeight" Value="16"/>
                    <g:Property Name="ImageWidth" Value="16"/>
                    <g:Property Name="Label" Value="&amp;Return"/>
                    <g:Property Name="Tooltip" Value="Return to Welcome Page"/>
                    <g:Property Name="Mnemonic" Value="ALT+R"/>
                </g:PropertyList>
            </g:Component>
            <g:Component Name="QuestionDataViewer">
                <g:ComponentResource FingerprintID="Groove"
➥ URL="http://components.groove.net/Groove/Components/Root.osd?
➥Package=net.groove.Groove.ToolComponents.GrooveDataViewerTool_DLL&amp;
➥Version=0&amp;Factory=DataViewer"/>
                <g:PropertyList Version="1">
                    <g:Property Name="Views">
                        <g:PropertyValue>
                            <g:DataViewerView Default="True" Name="Main">
                                <g:DataViewerColumn Label="Question"
➥ DataType="String" Width="20%" Name="Question"/>
                                <g:DataViewerColumn Label="Answer1"
➥ DataType="String" Width="18%" Name="Answer1"/>
                                <g:DataViewerColumn Label="Answer2"
➥ DataType="String" Width="20%" Name="Answer2"/>
                                <g:DataViewerColumn Label="Answer3"
➥ DataType="String" Width="18%" Name="Answer3"/>
```

LISTING C.1 Continued

```
                                <g:DataViewerColumn Label="Answer4"
➥ DataType="String" Width="20%" Name="Answer4"/>
                                <g:DataViewerColumn DataType="Long"
➥ Visible="false" Name="CorrectAnswer" Label="CorrectAnswer"/>
                            </g:DataViewerView>
                        </g:PropertyValue>
                    </g:Property>
                    <g:Property Name="Sorts">
                        <g:PropertyValue>
                            <g:DataViewerSort DataType="String"
➥ Column="Question" Order="Ascending" Name="ByQuestion"/>
                            <g:DataViewerSort DataType="String"
➥ Order="Ascending" Column="Answer1" Name="Answer1"/>
                            <g:DataViewerSort DataType="String"
➥ Column="Answer2" Order="Ascending" Name="Answer2"/>
                            <g:DataViewerSort DataType="String"
➥ Column="Answer3" Order="Ascending" Name="Answer3"/>
                            <g:DataViewerSort DataType="String"
➥ Column="Answer4" Order="Ascending" Name="Answer4"/>
                            <g:DataViewerSort DataType="Long"
➥ Column="CorrectAnswer" Order="Ascending" Name="CorrectAnswer"/>
                        </g:PropertyValue>
                    </g:Property>
                    <g:Property Name="GridLineDescriptor">
                        <g:PropertyValue>
                            <g:DataViewerGridLineDescriptor Visible="0"
➥ Color="#DCDCDC" Orientation="Both" Style="Solid"/>
                        </g:PropertyValue>
                    </g:Property>
                    <g:Property Name="Painters">
                        <g:PropertyValue>
                            <g:Painter Handler="RichTextPainter"
➥ ElementTag="urn:groove.net:RichText"/>
                        </g:PropertyValue>
                    </g:Property>
                    <g:Property Name="Editors">
                        <g:PropertyValue>
                            <g:Editor Handler="RichTextEditor"
➥ ElementTag="urn:groove.net:RichText"/>
                        </g:PropertyValue>
                        <g:Property Name="SingleSelection" Value="True"/>
                    </g:Property>
                </g:PropertyList>
                <g:ComponentConnections>
```

Listing C.1 Continued

```
                    <g:Connection ConnectionID="0" Name="ModelGlue"/>
                    <g:Connection ConnectionID="1" Name="ColumnHeaders"/>
                </g:ComponentConnections>
                <g:ComponentGroup>
                    <g:Component Name="RichTextPainter">
                        <g:ComponentResource FingerprintID="Groove"
➥ URL="http://components.groove.net/Groove/Components/Root.osd?
➥Package=net.groove.Groove.ToolComponents.GrooveTextTools_DLL&amp;
➥Version=0&amp;Factory=TextPainter"/>
                    </g:Component>
                    <g:Component Name="RichTextEditor">
                        <g:ComponentResource FingerprintID="Groove"
➥ URL="http://components.groove.net/Groove/Components/Root.osd?
➥Package=net.groove.Groove.ToolComponents.GrooveTextTools_DLL&amp;
➥Version=0,3&amp;Factory=TextView2"/>
                        <g:PropertyList Version="1">
                            <g:Property Value="true" Name="CellPaste"/>
                            <g:Property Value="transparent" Name="BackStyle"/>
                            <g:Property Value="false" Name="BorderVisible"/>
                        </g:PropertyList>
                    </g:Component>
                </g:ComponentGroup>
            </g:Component>
            <g:Component Name="ModelGlue">
                <g:ComponentResource FingerprintID="Groove"
➥ URL="http://components.groove.net/Groove/Components/Root.osd?
➥Package=net.groove.Groove.ToolComponents.GrooveDataViewerTool_DLL&amp;
➥Version=0&amp;Factory=ModelGlue"/>
                <g:ComponentConnections>
                    <g:Connection ConnectionID="0" Name="Collection"/>
                    <g:Connection ConnectionID="1" Name="RecordSetEngine"/>
                </g:ComponentConnections>
                <g:PropertyList Version="1"/>
            </g:Component>
            <g:Component Name="ColumnHeaders">
                <g:ComponentResource FingerprintID="Groove"
➥ URL="http://components.groove.net/Groove/Components/Root.osd?
➥Package=net.groove.Groove.ToolComponents.GrooveCommonComponents_DLL&amp;
➥Version=0&amp;Factory=Header"/>
                <g:ComponentConnections/>
                <g:PropertyList Version="1"/>
            </g:Component>
            <g:Component SingleInstance="True" Category="Engine"
➥ Name="Collection">
```

LISTING C.1 Continued

```
                <g:ComponentResource FingerprintID="Groove"
➥ URL="http://components.groove.net/Groove/Components/Root.osd?
➥Package=net.groove.Groove.ToolComponents.GrooveListComponents_DLL&amp;
➥Version=0&amp;Factory=ToolCollectionsComponent"/>
                <g:EngineDesc Tag="urn:groove.net:ToolCollectionsComponent"/>
                <g:PropertyList Version="1"/>
            </g:Component>
            <g:Component SingleInstance="True" Category="Engine"
➥ Name="RecordSetEngine">
                <g:ComponentResource FingerprintID="Groove"
➥ URL="http://components.groove.net/Groove/Components/Root.osd?
➥Package=net.groove.Groove.ToolComponents.GrooveListComponents_DLL&amp;
➥Version=0,6&amp;Factory=RecordSetEngine4"/>
                <g:EngineDesc Tag="urn:groove.net:RecordSetEngine"/>
                <g:ComponentConnections>
                    <g:Connection ConnectionID="0" Name="Collection"/>
                </g:ComponentConnections>
                <g:PropertyList Version="1">
                    <g:Property Name="ClassInfoList">
                        <g:PropertyValue>
                            <g:ClassInfo
➥ URL="http://components.groove.net/Groove/Components/Root.osd?
➥Package=net.groove.Groove.ToolComponents.GrooveListComponents_DLL&amp;
➥Version=0&amp;Factory=Record" Name="urn:groove.net:TriviaQuizRecord"/>
                        </g:PropertyValue>
                    </g:Property>
                </g:PropertyList>
            </g:Component>
        </g:ComponentGroup>
    </g:ToolTemplate>
</g:Document>
```

INDEX

SYMBOLS

*** (asterisk), 99**
@[field name]=[field value] syntax, 282
<!— comment, 91
| (pipe), 99
+ (plus sign), 99, 140
<? processing instruction, 91
? (question mark), 98

A

Accelerator Group (The), 11
AcceptedFileTypes property (GrooveImage), 391
AcceptFocus property (GrooveButton), 390
accessing
  data in Connectors example, code, 331-333
  external information, benefits, 322
Account Database, 72-73
Account Services, 72-73
Account Subsystem, 72
accounts
  creating, 36-37
  development, GDK (Groove Development Kit), 137-138
  passphrases, 36-37
  saving to files, 38
activating components, 74-75
activation, defined, 75

ActiveXWrapper, properties, 389

Add Contact button, 50, 161

Add Email Contact command (File menu), 50

Add Files button, 55

Add Pictures button, 58

Add Questions screen, 275-278

buttons, creating, 280

components, adding, 279-281

DataViewer

adding, 281-285

ColumnHeaders component, 286

ModelGlue component, 285-286

RecordSetEngine component, 286-287

ToolCollectionsComponent component, 286

layouts, viewing, 287

QuestionInputLabel, adding, 279

schemas, adding, 280-281

Add Templates button, 263

Add to My Contacts button, 51

Add Tool flowchart, 122

AddInterfacesAsItems property (ScriptHost), 388

American National Standards Institute (ANSI), 88

American Wooden Widgets (AWW), creating shared spaces, 32-33

Andreesen, Mark, 7

ANSI (American National Standards Institute), 88

answer buttons (trivia game)

changing, 302

transitioning, 311-312

answer labels (TriviaQuiz2), 214-215

AnswerAButton (TriviaQuiz1), 196-197

AnswerButton, OverrideLabelPosition property, 196-197

answers (trivia game)

currentCorrectAnswer, code, 310-311

hiding, 317

APIs, Groove JavaScript API Reference, 214

applications. *See also* peer-to-peer applications

client/server, 8-9

client/server and peer-to-peer, comparing, 10-11

Microsoft Visual Interdev, 138

Perl, downloading, 138

supplemental, 138

text editors, 138

XML Notepad, downloading, 138

architectures. *See also* Groove architecture

client/server, 8

hybrid peer-to-peer, 10

peer-to-peer, 9

ARPAnet, 6

Artifact engine, tools, 147

assembly files, OSD (Open Software Description), 132

asterisk (*), 99

attributes

Bold (StandardDescriptors), 395

Bottom (XYLayout), 386

BottomPad (SingleCellViewContainer), 387

CDATA, 99

CODEBASE (SOFTPKG), 248

Color, values in skins, 395-396

Columns property (GrooveListView), 393

declaring for DTDs (Document Type Definitions), 99-101

descriptions, 282

DTDs (Document Type Definitions), 96-98

ENTITIES, 100

ENTITY, 100

Enumerated, 99

FontStyle (StandardDescriptors), 394-395

Height

StandardDescriptors, 394

XYLayout, 387

ID, 99

IDREF, 100

IDREFS, 100

IMPLEMENTATION (SOFTPKG), 248

Italic (StandardDescriptors), 395

Left (XYLayout), 387
LeftPad (SingleCellViewContainer), 387
Name
Columns property, 393
RecordSetEngine, 392
SOFTPKG, 248
ToolGlueCode, 186
XYLayout, 386
names, qualified, 103
NMTOKEN, 100
NMTOKENS, 100
Right (XYLayout), 386
RightPad (SingleCellViewContainer), 387
StandardDescriptors, 394-396
<TABLE> tag, 183
<TD> tag, 183
Top (XYLayout), 386
TopPad (SingleCellViewContainer), 387
Typeface (StandardDescriptors), 394
Underline (StandardDescriptors), 395
URL (RecordSetEngine), 392
VERSION (SOFTPKG), 248
Width
Columns property, 394
XYLayout, 387

AttributeTypes, XML (eXtensible Markup Language) schema, 105-109

audio. *See* sounds

Audio Chat Tool, 29-30

Audio Tuning Wizard, 140, 161

authentication
of components, disabling, 139-140
data-origin, 82
end-entity, 82
shared spaces, 81-82

authenticators, deltas, 77

AutoSize property (GrooveButton), 390

AWW (American Wooden Widgets), creating shared spaces, 32-33

B

Background property
GrooveImage, 390
ViewContainer, 384

BackgroundColor (Color values in skins), 395

BackgroundColor property
GrooveComboBox, 388
GrooveEdit, 388
GrooveListBox, 391
GrooveStatic, 389

backgrounds
TransceiverWindowBackground.jpg, changing, 155-156
XML (eXtensible Markup Language) schema, 104-105

BackgroundStyle property (GrooveStatic), 389

backups, Data folder (GDK), 137

Berners-Lee, Tim, 6

Binary XML file, 54

.BMP file extension, 59, 62, 153

Body window, 53

Bold attribute (StandardDescriptors), 395

BORDER element (MultiCellLayout), 385

<BORDER> element, 271

borders
<BORDER> element, 271
of cells, .reg file extension, 192
DisableCellBorders.reg file, 142
EnableCellBorders.reg file, 142
Welcome screen, 271

Bosak, Jon, 89

BotInstallation element, code, 336-337

bots, 33
configuration XML file, 336-337
data integration, 334-335
developing, 335-336
Eliza program, 336
pEliza variable, setting with constructors, 340
template file, 337-340
TriviaQuiz, 341-343

Bottom attribute (XYLayout), 386

BottomPad attribute (SingleCellViewContainer), 387

Bricklin, Dan, 18
Browse Together button, 64
browsers, Web Browser Tool, 27-28, 63-65
browsing Web pages, 64
building
- tools in Tool Creator, 257-260
- XML (eXtensible Markup Language) schema, 105-109

BuildRecordIDArray function, 305
Business Month and Week views (Calendar Tool), 49
businesses, AWW (American Wooden Widgets), creating shared spaces, 32-33
buttons
- Add Contact, 50, 161
- Add Files, 55
- Add Pictures, 58
- Add Templates, 263
- Add to My Contacts, 51
- adding to Welcome screen, 275
- answer (trivia game)
  - *changing, 302*
  - *transitioning, 311-312*
- AnswerButton, OverrideLabelPosition property, 196-197
- appearances, changing, 156-162
- Browse Together, 64
- Change the Look of Groove, 152
- Checkbox, 161
- Create Shared Space, 40
- creating for Add Questions screen, 280
- disabling in GameTime, 232
- Down, 57
- Edit, 52
- EditQuestionButton
  - *code, 292-293*
  - *creating, 280*
- Enter Question (Question Input screen), 290-292
- EnterQuestionButton, creating, 280
- Export Document to File, 140
- Fill Color, 62
- GlobalGoTo, 162
- GoEnterButton, code, 289
- GoTo, properties, 158
- GoToButton, 157
- groovedefaultskinresources. tpl file, code, 157-158
- groovedefaultskinre-sources.xml file, 156
- GroovieTalkieLockButton, code, 160
- Individual Tools, 41
- Invite, 44
- Invite by Email, 44
- Invite CSR, 323
- Invite No One at This Time, 41
- Invite to Space, 51
- Label property, 184
- LargeButton, 161
- LaunchURL, 161
- link, 161
- Lock, 160
- Manually, Through a File, 38
- Mnemonic property, 185
- More, utilities, 51
- Multiple Computers, 38
- Navigate Together, 64
- NavigationSubForm component (standard-transceiver.tpl file), 170
- New Event, 48
- New Sketch, 63
- New Topic, 52
- NextQuestionButton
  - *code, 220*
  - *else clause, code to add, 232*
  - *functionality, building, 219-220*
- No Tools, 41
- Open Tool, 272
- Preview.jpg, 162
- QuickAccessSubForm component (standardtrans-ceiver.tpl file), 170
- RadioButton, 161
- Recipients, 43
- Record Voice Memo, 160
- Refresh icon, 64
- RemoveQuestionButton, creating, 280
- Respond, 53
- Return, creating, 280
- Right Arrow, 57
- Save, 52
- Save to File, 289
- SaveEditsButton, creating, 280

Send Message, 51
Set Element, 283
Show Picture List, 58
SmallIconButton, 160
SmallIconTextButton, 161
SmallTextButton, 161
Standard Tool Sets, 41
StandardButton, 161
StandardIconButton, 198, 280
StateImagesURL, 159
Stop Transmission, 64
Style property, 184
TitleBarSubForm2 component (standard-transceiver.tpl file), 170
tool template skeletons, 184-185
Tooltip property, 185
TransceiverBackButton, 161
TransceiverBackHistory-Button, 161
TransceiverButtonImages.jpg file, 156
TransceiverForthButton, 161
TransceiverForthHistory-Button, 161
TransceiverPushToTalk-Button, code, 159
Up, 57
XY layout, code, 172-173

Buttons component (UI), 178

C

.CAB (cabinet) files
creating, 163-164
utility to create, Web site, 153

CAB TriviaGraphics.CAB, 317

Calendar Tool, 21, 50
Business Month and Week views, 49
calendars, exporting and importing, 49
Day view, 48
links, creating, 49
Month view, 48
tool-level permissions, 353-356
Unread Marks, 49
Week view, 48

calendars
Calendar Tool, 21
exporting and importing, 49

Cancel property (GrooveButton), 390

cards, vCards, 50-51

CareScience
Care Data Exchange, 15
clinical information, distributing, 374

catalog.dtd file, code, 101

catalog.xml file, code, 108-109

catalogs
Component Catalog
downloading, 384
Web site, 156
data, code to load, 94-96
structure, 93-94

catalogSchema.xml file, code, 107-108

CDATA attribute, 99

<CELL> element, 271, 386

cells
borders, .reg file extension, 192
<CELL> element, 271
DisableCellBorders.reg file, 142
EnableCellBorders.reg file, 142
MultiCell layouts, 172
TELESPACE PANE TOOLS (standardtransceiver.tpl file), 170
Welcome screen, 271-272

Cellular Skin, 152, 171-172

cellularskintransceiver.tpl file, layout code, 171-172

centralized integration, 334

CERN (European Laboratory for Particle Physics), 6

certificates, 265, 319

Change the Look of Groove button, 152

ChangeLabels function
modifying, code, 308-309
rewriting, 304

chatting
audio (Audio Chat Tool), 29-30
text (Text Chat Tool), 29

Checkbox
button, 161
property (GrooveButton), 390

Clark, Jim, 7

ClassInfoList property (RecordSetEngine), 392

clauses, else, code to add to NextQuestionButton, 232

cleanups, deltas, 77

client/servers

- applications, 8-11
- architecture, 8

clinical information, distributing, 374

Clipboard files, dragging and dropping, 58

code

- attributes, DTDs (Document Type Definitions), 96-97
- BotInstallation element, 336-337
- catalog.dtd file, 101
- catalog.xml file, 108-109
- catalogSchema.xml file, 107-108
- cellularskintransceiver.tpl file, layout, 171-172
- ChangeLabels function
  - *modifying, 308-309*
  - *rewriting, 304*
- currentCorrectAnswer, 310-311
- data
  - *accessing in Connectors example, 331-333*
  - *loading, 94-96*
- descriptors, finding, 123-124
- DisableQuestionButtons( ) function, 219
- EditQuestionButton, 292-293
- ElapsedTimeDisplay property, clearing, 314
- else statement, replacing with ShowScore( ) and ResetGame( ) functions, 312-313
- factory element (OSD), 124-125
- FieldIsBlank( ) function, 294-295
- GameTime property, displaying or removing, 314
- GetRecordByID function, creating, 308
- glue, 70, 73
  - *component connections, 287-288*
  - *Enter Question button (Question Input screen), 290-292*
  - *Groove JavaScript API Reference, 214*
  - *ScriptHost component, 179*
  - *tool template skeletons, 186-189*
  - *tool templates, 179*
  - *for tools, 149*
  - *TriviaQuiz1, 199-211*
  - *TriviaQuiz2.tpl, 220-225*
  - *TriviaQuiz3.tpl, 233-241*
- GoEnterButton, 289
- groovedefaultskinresources.tpl file, buttons, 157-158
- GrooveElizaBot.tpl file, 337-339
- groovestandardrecord-schema.xml file schema, 148
- GroovieTalkieLockButton button, 160
- .GRV file extension
  - *custom spaces, injecting, 324-325*
  - *tool descriptor, 118*
  - *TriviaQuiz4, 323-324*
- help files, displaying, 357-362
- Initialize( ) function, 226-227, 304-307
- Layout component, 183-184
- MemberPaneBackground file, tracing, 154-155
- MySkin.GRV file, 167-168
- NextQuestionButton, 220
  - *else clause, adding, 232*
  - *function, rewriting, 304*
  - *TriviaQuiz3, 230*
- OnPropertyChanged
  - *function, 304, 315-316*
  - *TriviaQuiz3, 230-232*
- OnRecordsetChanged( ) function, 307
- OSD (Open Software Description) file, 116-117
- .OSD file extension
  - *tool descriptor file, 119*
  - *writing, 165-166*
- overview text, displaying, 357-362
- permissions dialog box, displaying, 366-368
- PRMDataModelDelegate component, declaring, 329-330
- PRMDataModelDelegate.gsl file, 330-331

PRMGlue.gsl file, 331-333, 342-343
Question Entry screen layout, 277-279
QuestionNumber property, resetting, 314
questions, entering, 290-292
ResetGame function, placing outside of transactions, 315-316
SaveEditsButton function, 296-298
ShowElapsedTime function, 218-219, 304
showError function, 288
ShowScore function, placing outside of transactions, 315-316
standardtransceiver.tpl file, layout component, 169-170
subforms, creating and placing in tool skeletons, 362-366
templates, installing, 124
time initialization, adding or deleting, 312
TitleLabel Static component, 195
tools
  components, installing, 125-130
  template skeletons, 189-192
ToolSkeleton, modifying, 257-259
TransceiverPushToTalkButton button, 159
TriviaQuiz1, 200-211
TriviaQuiz2.tpl, glue code, 220-225
TriviaQuiz3
  initializing, 225-227
  transactions, 228-229
TriviaQuiz3.tpl file, 233-241, 346-347
TriviaQuizLayout, changing, 298-299
UserGuess function, 219
XY layout, 172-173

CODEBASE
  attribute (SOFTPKG) 248
  element (OSD), 116

CodeComponent property (ViewContainer), 384

collaboration, decentralized (Unity), 15-16

collaborative publishing, real-time, 376

Color
  attribute, values in skins, 395-396
  command (Format menu), 61

colors of space names, changing, 163

COLUMN element (MultiCellLayout), 385

ColumnHeaders component (DataViewer), 286

columns
  data, ReadOnly, 282
  hiding, 282
  <MULTICOL> element, 271
  Welcome screen, 271

Columns property, 393-394

ComboBox component (UI), 178

Command Processor, 69

Command URL property (GrooveMenu), 392

commands
  Draw menu
    Fill Color, 62
    Line Color, 62
  Edit menu
    Copy Row as Link, 57
    Delete, 57
    Delete Sketch, 63
    Paste, 59
    Rename Sketch, 62
  File menu
    Add Email Contact, 50
    Create Shared Space, 40
    Delete Shared Space command, 42
    Export Rows as XML, 57
    Import, 54
    Remove Background Image, 62
    Selected Event, 49
  Format menu
    Color, 61
    More Colors, 61
    More Fonts, 61
    Size, 61
    Typeface, 61
  Help menu, Help, 356
  Options menu
    Roles, 353
    Send Message, 160
  View menu
    Detect URLs, 61
    Next Unread, 60, 63

Previous Unread, 60, 63

Show Overview, 356

Show/Hide Details, 57

CommandURL property (GrooveButton), 390

comments, <!--, 91

communications (multicasting, omnicasting, or unicasting), 78

Communications Manager, 77

delta communication, 78-79

devices (available and unavailable), 78

***Communications of the ACM*, "ELIZA—A Computer Program for the Study of Natural Language Communication Between Man and Machine," 336**

Communications Subsystem, 77

delta communication, 78-79

devices (available and unavailable), 78

comparing

Napster and killer apps, 370

peer-to-peer applications and client/server applications, 10-11

complex modal windows, subforms, 366-368

Component Catalog (Groove)

downloading, 384

Web site, 156

component connections, view containers, 182

Component Manager, 74-75, 119, 346

component manager

components, version checks, 350

OSD (Open Software Description) redirection, 349-350

component resource URL, 349

Component Services, 74, 120

Subsystem, 85

tool components, code to install, 125-130

component tree structures, managing, 347-348

component manager OSD (Open Software Description) redirection, 349-350

fanout OSD (Open Software Description) redirection, 349

ComponentGroups

DevaultView, 181

tool templates, 177

ViewContainer, 182-183

ComponentResourceURL, 120, 177

components

activating, 74-75

activation, defined, 75

adding to Add Questions screen, 279-281

authentication, disabling, 139-140

ColumnHeaders (DataViewer), 286

Component Services, 74

custom versions, numbers, 351

definition, 346

downloading, 74-75

functions, combining, 366

glue, connections, code, 287-288

Groove-standard, 260

installing, 74-75

Layout, code, 183-184

layout, standardtransceiver.tpl file, code, 169-170

major versions

numbers, 351

tools, changing, 352

manifest, 247

minor versions

numbers, 351

tools, changing, 351-352

ModelGlue (DataViewer), 285-286

PRMDataModelDelegate, code to declare, 329-330

PropertyList, tool template skeletons, 182

RecordSetEngine (DataViewer), 286-287

RTFHelpProvider, 356

RTFView, 356

ScriptFreeThreadedComponent, 330

ScriptHost, glue code, 179

sequence versions, numbers, 351

Static

properties, 195

text, changing, 214-215

SubForm, 362

TitleLabel Static, code, 195
tool templates
engines, 179
glue code, 179
UI, 178
view containers, 177-178
ToolCollectionsComponent (DataViewer), 286
TriviaQuiz1
AnswerAButton, 196-197
ElapsedTimeLabel, 197
ElapsedTimeListBox-Control, 197-198
NextQuestionButton, 198-199
QuestionLabel Static, 196
TitleLabel, 195-196
UI, 178-179
unused, deleting, 303
versions, 350
ViewInfo, 181

Components Catalog file, downloading, 282

ComponentSecurity element, 143
tool template skeletons, 180
tool templates, 177

ComponentURLProviders, OSD (Open Software Description), 131-132

***Computer Communication Review*, 7**

configurations, bot configuration XML file, 336-337

Conflict Resolution notification, 55

conflicts, Files Tool, 55-56

Connection property (ViewContainer), 384

connections
component, view containers, 182
glue component, code, 287-288
IconProvider (GrooveListView), 394
ListDataModel (GrooveListView), 394
ToolCollections (RecordSetEngine), 392

connectors
data access, 331-333
data integration, 323
samples, 323
shared spaces, dynamic creation, 323-331

Connectors example, data, code to access, 331-333

Connectors folder, 323

Connelly, Dan, 89

constructors, setting pEliza variable, 340

Contact Manager, 50-52

contacts
adding, 50
Known Groove Contacts, 43
managing, 51-52

containers
ContentViewContainer component (standardtransceiver.tpl file), 170
view
component connections, 182
tool templates, 177-178

ContentViewContainer component (standardtransceiver.tpl file), 170

controls
edit on screens, populating, 292-297
tool-level access, 353-356

conventions, naming, 187

Copy Row as Link command (Edit menu), 57

copying
GrooveDefault folder, 152
pictures, 59
vCards, 50

correct answers (trivia game), hiding, 317

CorrectAnswerNumber, checking numbers, 296

Create Account dialog box, 36

Create Shared Space button or command (File menu), 40

Create Space Wizard, 40-41

creating
accounts, 36-37
buttons for Add Questions screen, 280
.CAB files, 163-164
certificates, 319
descriptor files for skins, 164-167
EditQuestionButton button, 280
EnterQuestionButton button, 280
.GRV file, 167-168, 251-253
injector files for skins, 167-168
links
Calendar Tool, 49
to pictures, 59

My Templates folder, 142
OSD (Open Software Description) file, 246-251
projects for tool publishing, 263
RemoveQuestionButton button, 280
Return button, 280
roles, 354-356
SaveEditsButton button, 280
shared spaces, 40-41, 81
for AWW (American Wooden Widgets), 32-33
deleting, 42
dynamically, 323-331
for Great Schools Now, Inc., 30-32
tools, adding, 42
StandardIconButton button, 280
subforms and placing in tool skeletons, code, 362-366
tool template skeletons, 180, 192
buttons, 184-185
code, 189-192
ComponentGroups, 181-183
engines, 185-186
glue code, 186-189
HTMLTableLayout, 183-184
layouts, 183-184
RecordSetEngine, 185-186
ScriptHost, 187
ToolTemplate element, 180-181
TYPELIB, 188
ViewInfo component, 181
tools
descriptors, 245-246
dynamics of small group interaction, 33
manually, 259-260
skeletons, 257-260
TriviaQuiz1, layouts, 194-195
cryptography, public-key or secret-key technology, 80
Ctrl+V keyboard shortcut, 53
currentCorrectAnswer, code, 310-311
custom spaces, .GRV file, code to inject, 324-325
custom versions of components, numbers, 351
Customer Services Subsystem, 85
customizing Groove, 152

D

data
accessing in Connectors example, code, 331-333
disseminating in shared spaces, 82-83
loading, code, 94-96
querying, 282
ReadOnly, 282
recovering, 77
seeding into shared spaces, 329
sorting techniques, 282
writing in shared spaces, 82-83
Data folder (GDK), backing up, 137
data integration, 322
bots, 334
bot configuration XML file, 336-337
bot template file, 337-340
developing, 335-336
centralized, 334
connectors
data access, 331-333
samples, 323
shared spaces, dynamic creation, 323-331
Connectors example, code, 331-333
GEIS (Groove Enterprise Integration Server), 340-341
multipoint, 334
Database Navigator Tool
component authentication, disabling, 139-140
installing, 140
window panes, navigating, 140-141
databases
Account Database, 72-73
entries, expanding, 140
DataModeDelegate (ComponentGroups), 181
data-origin authentication, 82
DataViewer
adding to Add Questions screen, 281-287
component (UI), 179
<DataViewerView> element, 282

Day view (Calendar Tool), 48

DCD (Document Content Description), 104

debugging, EnableScriptDebugging.reg file, 141-142

decentralization, peer-to-peer applications, 371

decentralized collaboration (Unity), 15-16

declaring

- attributes for DTDs (Document Type Definitions), 99-101
- PRMDataModelDelegate component, code, 329-330

Default property (GrooveButton), 390

DEFAULTPAD element (MultiCellLayout), 385

DefaultToolBarBackground.jpg file, 155

DefaultView (ComponentGroups), 181

defining

- toolsets for shared spaces, 325-329
- ToolSetTemplate, 325

definitions

- activation, 75
- components, 346
- deltas, 71, 75
- durable transactions, 80
- Groove, 19

Delegate (ComponentGroups), 181

Delete Calendar Entry dialog box, 48

Delete command (Edit menu), 57

Delete Shared Space command (File menu), 42

Delete Sketch command (Edit menu), 63

deleting

- discussion topics, 54
- drawings, 62-63
- pictures, 59
- records, 297-298
- shared spaces, 42
- time initialization, code, 312
- tools, 42
- unused components, 303

deltas

- authenticators, 77
- cleanup, 77
- communicating, 78-79
- defined, 71, 75
- in shared spaces, 76-77, 83

dependencies, adding for tool publishing, 265

DEPENDENCY element, 115, 249-250

descriptions, attributes, 282

DescriptionText (FontStyle values in skins), 395

descriptors

- files for skins, creating, 164-167
- finding, code, 123-124
- tools, 149
  - *creating, 245-246*
  - *.GRV file extension, code, 118*
  - *information for, 263-265*
  - *.OSD file extension, code, 119*

designing OSD (Open Software Description), 132-133

Detect URLs command (View menu), 61

developing

- bots, 335-336
- tools, Groove Development and My Templates directories, 272

developing tools

- Artifact engine, 147
- descriptors, 149
- engines, 147-148
- files, writing, 143
- forms, 145
- glue code, 149
- .GRV file extension, 150
- layouts, 146
- OSD file, 149-150
- planning, 142-143
- PropertyList engine, 147-148
- publishing, 149-150
- RecordSetEngine engine, 148
- templates, 143-149
- viewing, 145-146

development accounts, GDK (Groove Development Kit), 137-138

development environments

- Data folder, backing up, 137
- Database Navigator Tool
  - *component authentication, disabling, 139-140*
  - *installing, 140*
  - *window panes, navigating, 140-141*

development accounts, 137-138
Development Space, 138
DevZone Web site, 136
GDK (Groove Development Kit), 136-137
Microsoft Visual Interdev, 138
Perl, downloading, 138
registry files, 141-142
specialized tools, 138
supplemental applications, 138
text editors, 138
Tool Creator Tool, 141
Tool Publisher Tool, 141
tools
Artifact engine, 147
descriptors, 149
developing, 143
development plans, 142-143
engines, 147-148
files, writing, 143
forms, 145
glue code, 149
.GRV file extension, 150
layouts, 146
OSD file, 149-150
PropertyList engine, 147-148
publishing, 149-150
RecordSetEngine engine, 148
templates, developing, 143-149
viewing, 145-146
XML Notepad, downloading, 138

Development Kit, 21

Development Space (GDK), 138, 192

device presence, 84-85

Device Presence Protocol (DPP), 78

devices, 38-40, 78

DevZone Web site
applications, supplemental, 138
GDK (Groove Development Kit), 136-137

dialog boxes
Create Account, 36
Delete Calendar Entry, 48
Groove Send Invitation, 43
Groove — Send Message, 51
Groove Login, 161
Import File, 54
New Calendar Event, 48
Permissions, 353
permissions, code to display, 366-368
Roles, 353
Save Picture As, 59
Select Contacts, 50
Select Recipients, 43
Windows Colors, 61-62
Windows Open With, 55

DigitalTitleText (FontStyle values in skins), 395

directories
Groove Development, developing tools, 272
Groove.net, 43
Local Network Directory, 43
localhost
mySkin folder, 153
structures for templates and files, 317-318
My Templates, developing tools, 272
structures, localhost folder, 244

DisableCellBorders.reg file, 142

DisableComponentAuthentication.reg file, 139

DisabledTextColor (Color values in skins), 395

DisableQuestionButtons( ) function, code, 219

disabling
buttons in GameTime, 232
component authentication, 139-140

Discussion Tool, 148
Body window, 53
discussions, 22, 54
engines, 179
tool templates, 179
Topics List window, 53
Unread Markers, 53

displaying
elapsed time, 299-302
GameTime property, code, 314
help files, code, 357-362
overview text, code, 357-362
permissions dialog box, code, 366-368
TriviaQuiz2 questions, 213

displays, changing elapsed time, 303

DisplayTextWhenEmpty property
GrooveImage, 391
GrooveListView, 393

distributed network services, 14-15

distributed processing

iPPPP (Intel Philanthropic Peer-to-Peer Project), 13

SETI@home, 12

distributed storage services, 13-14

.DLL file extension, 125

DNS (domain name server), 7

Document Content Description (DCD), 104

Document Type Definitions. *See* DTDs

documentation, GDK (Groove Development Kit), 136

documents

managing, 375

XML (eXtensible Markup Language)

attributes, code, 96-97

DTDs (Document Type Definitions), 91-102

namespaces, 102-103

prologs, 91

storage mediums, 90

tool templates, 177

well formed, 90-91

Documents (Root Folder) folder, 55

domain name server (DNS), 7

domains

reverse domain name package names, 347

reverse notations, 132

Down button, 57

Download Manager, 75

downloading

components, 74-75

Components Catalog file, 282

GDK (Groove Development Kit), 136

Groove Component Catalog, 384

.GRV file, 323

Microsoft Script Debugger, 141

Microsoft XML Notepad, 101

Perl, 138, 252

XML Notepad, 138

DPP (Device Presence Protocol), 78

dragging and dropping Clipboard files or pictures, 58

Draw menu commands

Fill Color, 62

Line Color, 62

drawings

deleting, 62-63

naming, 62-63

Sketchpad Tool, 27

DropDownSize property (GrooveComboBox), 388

DTDs (Document Type Definitions), 91

catalog.dtd file, code, 101

catalogs, code to load data, 94-96

CDATA attribute, 99

ENTITIES attribute, 100

ENTITY attribute, 100

Enumerated attribute, 99

ID attribute, 99

IDREF attribute, 100

IDREFS attribute, 100

Microsoft XML Notepad, downloading, 101

NMTOKEN attribute, 100

NMTOKENS attribute, 100

XML (eXtensible Markup Language) documents, 91

attributes, 96-101

elements, adding, 92-96

elements-only elements, 98-99

empty elements, 98

testing, 101-102

writing, 98-101

durable transactions, defined, 80

dynamic creations, shared spaces, 323-331

dynamic roles, members of shared spaces, 353

Dynamics Manager, 75

data, recovering, 77

deltas, 76-77

dynamics of small group interaction, creating tools, 33

E

eBay, matchmaking, 372

Edit button, 52

Edit component (UI), 178

edit controls on screens, populating, 292-297

Edit menu commands
- Copy Row as Link, 57
- Delete, 57
- Delete Sketch, 63
- Paste, 59
- Rename Sketch, 62

Editable property (GrooveComboBox), 388

editing
- groovedefaultskinresources.xml file, 162
- images, 154
- pictures, 59

editors, text, 26, 138

EditQuestionButton button
- code, 292-293
- creating, 280

EditText (FontStyle values in skins), 395

elapsed time
- displaying, 299-303
- TriviaQuiz2, 216-219

ElapsedTimeDisplay property, code to clear, 314

ElapsedTimeLabel (TriviaQuiz1), 197

ElapsedTimeListBoxControl, 197-198, 225

elements
- adding to DTDs (Document Type Definitions), 92-96
- BORDER (MultiCellLayout), 385
- <BORDER>, 271
- BotInstallation, code, 336-337
- CELL (MultiCellLayout), 386
- <CELL>, 271
- CODEBASE (OSD), 116
- COLUMN (MultiCellLayout), 385
- ComponentGroup, tool templates, 177
- ComponentSecurity, 143
  - *tool template skeletons, 180*
  - *tool templates, 177*
- <DataViewerView>, 282
- DEFAULTPAD (MultiCellLayout), 385
- DEPENDENCY (OSD), 115, 249-250
- elements-only, DTDs (Document Type Definitions), 98-99
- empty, DTDs (Document Type Definitions), 98
- factory (OSD), code, 124-125
- IMPLEMENTATION (OSD), 115
- LANGUAGE (OSD), 116
- MULTICOL (MultiCellLayout), 385
- <MULTICOL>, 271
- MULTIROW (MultiCellLayout), 385
- <MULTIROW>, 271
- names, qualified, 103
- OS (OSD), 116
- PROCESSOR (OSD), 116
- ROW (MultiCellLayout), 385
- Schema (XML), 105
- SOFTPKG (OSD), 115, 247-249
- TITLE (OSD), 116
- ToolTemplate, 143, 177, 180-181
- WelcomeTitle, adding to Welcome screen, 274
- XML documents, tool templates, 177

elements-only elements, DTDs (Document Type Definitions), 98-99

ElementTypes, XML (eXtensible Markup Language) schema, 105-109

Eliza program, 336-339

"ELIZA—A Computer Program for the Study of Natural Language Communication Between Man and Machine" (*Communications of the ACM*), 336

else clauses, code to add to NextQuestionButton, 232

else statement, replacing with ShowScore( ) or ResetGame( ) functions, 312-313

empty elements, DTDs (Document Type Definitions), 98

Enable property (GrooveTimer), 392

EnableCellBorders registry settings (TriviaQuiz1), 211

EnableCellBorders.reg file, 142

EnableComponentAuthentication.reg file, 139

Enabled property
- GrooveButton, 390
- GrooveMenu, 392
- NextQuestionButton, 198

EnableDragDrop property (GrooveTabControl), 391

EnableErrorSupport property (ScriptHost), 388

EnableMyTemplates.reg file, 142

EnableScriptDebugging.reg file, 141-142

end times, 216

end-entity authentication, 82

EnforceInterfaces property (ScriptHost), 388

Eng, Tony, 7

Engenia (Unity), 15

engines

- Artifact, tools, 147
- Discussion Tool, tool templates, 179
- GrooveDocumentShare-Engine, 56
- PropertyList, tools, 147-148
- RecordSetEngine (DataViewer), 286-287
  - *tool template skeletons, 185-186*
  - *tool templates, 179*
  - *tools, 147-148*
  - *trivia game questions, numbering, 305-311*

Enter Question button (Question Input screen), 290-292

Enter Questions screen, 298, 317

EnterQuestionButton button, creating, 280

ENTITIES attribute, 100

entity, XML (eXtensible Markup Language) documents, 90

ENTITY attribute, 100

entries in databases, expanding, 140

Enumerated attribute, 99

environments. *See* development environments

European Laboratory for Particle Physics (CERN), 6

Export Document to File button, 140

Export Rows as XML command (File menu), 57

exporting

- calendars, 49
- discussion topics, 54
- records, 57

eXtensible Markup Language. *See* XML

extensions

- <g:ComponentURLProvider>, 250
- <g:Factory>, 249-250
- <g:install>, 247
- <g:Install>, 249-250

extensions of files

- .bmp, 153
- .BMP, 59, 62
- .DLL, 125
- .GRV, 117, 137, 141, 150
- .GSL, 56
- .jpg, 153.
- JPG, 59, 62
- .reg, 142, 192
- .TPL, 139-141
- .VCF, 51
- .XML, 49, 123
- .XSS, 139

external information, access benefits, 322

F

factories, changing, 303

factory element (OSD), code, 124-125

fanout OSD (Open Software Description) redirection, 349

FAQ Tool, 323, 329

Favorites, saving, 63-64

features, killer app (peer-to-peer applications), 379-380

fetching shared spaces, 40

FieldIsBlank( ) function, code, 294-295

File menu commands

- Add Email Contact, 50
- Create Shared Space, 40
- Delete Shared Space command, 42
- Export Rows as XML, 57
- Import, 54
- Remove Background Image, 62
- Selected Event, 49

files

- accounts, saving to, 38
- assembly, OSD (Open Software Description), 132
- Binary XML, 54
- .BMP extension, 59, 62, 153

bot configuration XML, 336-337
bot template, 337-340
.CAB (cabinet)
creating, 163-164
utility to create, Web site, 153
catalog.dtd, code, 101
catalog.xml, code, 108-109
catalogSchema.xml, code, 107-108
cellularskintransceiver.tpl, layout, code, 171-172
certificate, opening, 265
Clipboard, dragging and dropping, 58
Components Catalog, downloading, 282
DefaultToolBarBackground.jpg, 155
descriptor, creating for skins, 164-167
DisableCellBorders.reg, 142
DisableComponent-Authentication.reg, 139
.DLL extension, 125
Documents (Root Folder) folder, 55
EnableCellBorders.reg, 142
EnableComponent-Authentication.reg, 139
EnableMyTemplates.reg, 142
EnableScriptDebugging.reg, 141-142
Files Tool, 22-24
Groove.net, 38
groovedefaultskinresources.tpl, buttons, code, 157-158
groovedefaultskinresources.xml, 152-156, 162
GrooveDefaultsSkinsTools.XML, 165
GrooveElizaBot.tpl, code, 337-339
GrooveGDK.exe, 136
groovestandardrecord-schema.xml schema, code, 148
.GRV extension, 117, 137, 141, 245
code for TriviaQuiz4, 323-324
code to inject custom spaces, 324-325
creating, 251-253
downloading, 323
for skins, creating, 167-168
tool descriptor, code, 118
tools, 150
writing, 150
.GSL extension, 56
handling, 55
HeaderBackground.jpg, 156
help, 356-362
injector, 167-168, 245
.JPG extension, 59, 62, 153
keystore, opening, 265
localhost directory structures, 317-318
MemberPaneBackground, tracing through code, 154-155
MemberPaneBackground.jpg, 154
mySkin folder, 168
MySkin.GRV, code, 167-168
mySkinDescriptor.xml, 164
NoviceModeBackground.jpg, 155
organizing, 55
OSD (Open Software Description), 245
code, 116-117
creating, 246-251
files, 74
tools, 149-150
writing, 121-130
.OSD file extension
code to write, 165-166
tool descriptor, code, 119
Preview.jpg, 162
PRMDataModelDelegate.gsl, code, 330-331
PRMGlue.gsl, code, 331-333, 342-343
redmondgrayskintransceiver.tpl, 152
.reg file extension, 142, 192
registry, 137, 141-142
Root.osd, location, 177
StandardTabs.jpg, 156
standardtransceiver.tpl, 152-154, 169-170
Templates.XSS, 261
tool descriptor, 245-246
tool publishing, 264
.TPL file extension, 139-141
TransceiverButtonImages.jpg, 156
TransceiverWindowBackground.jpg, changing, 155-156
Trivia3.GRV, 254

TriviaQuiz.tpl, opening in WordPad, 287
TriviaQuiz2.tpl, glue code, 220-225
TriviaQuiz3.bat, 252
TriviaQuiz3.tpl
code, 346-347
glue code, 233-241
.VCF file extension, 51
writing for tools
developing, 143
publishing, 245
.XML file extension, 49, 123
.XSS file extension, 139

Files Tool, 22-24, 54-56

Fill Color command (Draw menu), 62

finding descriptors, code, 123-124

flowcharts, Add Tool, 122

folders
Connectors, 323
Data (GDK), backing up, 137
Documents (Root Folder), 55
Groove Development, 153
groove.net, 152
GrooveDefault, copying, 152
Images, 153
localhost, directory structures, 244
My Templates, creating, 142
mySkin, 153, 168
RegistryFiles, 141-142
Skin, 152

Font property
GrooveComboBox, 388
GrooveEdit, 388
GrooveStatic, 389

FontStyle attribute
StandardDescriptors, 394
values in skins, 395

FontStyle property (GrooveStatic), 389

Format menu commands
Color, 61
More Colors, 61
More Fonts, 61
Size, 61
Typeface, 61

formats, discussion topics, 54

forms
subforms
complex modal windows, 366-368
creating and placing in tool skeletons, code, 362-366
functions, combining into single components, 366
permissions dialog box, code to display, 366-368
tools, 145

Francis, Paul, 7

functions
BuildRecordIDArray, 305
ChangeLabels
code to modify, 308-309
rewriting, 304
combining into single components, 366
DisableQuestionButtons( ), code, 219
FieldIsBlank( ), code, 294-295
GetRecordByID, code to create, 308
GoPlayButton, code to add time initialization, 312
Initialization, code to delete time initialization, 312
Initialize( )
code, 226-227, 306-307
rewriting, 304
TriviaQuiz2, 214
NextQuestionButton, rewriting, 304
OnPropertyChanged
code to change, 315-316
rewriting, 304
parameters, 227
TriviaQuiz3, 227-229
OnRecordsetChanged( ), code, 307
ResetGame( )
ElapsedTimeDisplay property, code to clear, 314
else statement, code to replace, 312-313
GameTime property, code to remove, 314
QuestionNumber property, code to reset, 314
transactions, code to place outside, 315-316
SaveEditsButton, code, 296-298
ShowElapsedTime
code, 218-219
rewriting, 304

showError, code, 288
ShowScore( )
else statement, code to replace, 312-313
GameTime property, code to display, 314
transactions, code to place outside, 315-316
UserGuess, code, 219

G

<g:ComponentURLProvider> extension, 250
<g:Factory> extension, 249-250
<g:Install> extension, 249-250
<g:install> extension, 247
games, Quake, 18. *See also* trivia games
GameTime
disabling buttons, 232
property, code to display or remove, 314
GDK (Groove Development Kit)
Data folder, backing up, 137
development accounts, 137-138
Development Space, 138
DisableComponentAuthentication.reg file, 139
documentation, 136
downloading, 136
EnableComponentAuthentication.reg file, 139
licenses, 137
registry files, 137
tools, 137-139
utilities, 137
Gedye, David, 11
GEIS (Groove Enterprise Integration Server), 322, 340-341
Generalized Markup Language (GML), 88
gestures of users, 75
GetRecordByID function, code to create, 308
GlobalGoTo button, 162
glue, ModelGlue (DataViewer), 58, 285-286
glue code, 70, 73
component connections, 287-288
Enter Question button (Question Input screen), 290-292
Groove JavaScript API Reference, 214
ScriptHost component, 179
tool template skeletons, 186-189
tool templates, 179
for tools, 149
TriviaQuiz1, 199-211
TriviaQuiz2.tpl, 220-225
TriviaQuiz3.tpl, 233-241
glue component, connections, code, 287-288
GML (Generalized Markup Language), 88
GoEnterButton code, 289
Goldfarb, Charles, 88
GoPlayButton function, code for adding time initialization, 312
GoTo button, properties, 158
GoToButton, 157
graphics, adding to Welcome screen, 273-274
Great Schools Now, Inc., creating shared spaces, 30-32
GridLineDescriptor property, 283
Groove
customizing, 152
definition, 19
ease of use, 19
history of, 18
installing, 36-40
instant, 71
launching, 153
Ozzie, Ray, 18
strategy spaces, 20
tools, 21
transceivers, 19-20
users, Local Network Directory, 43
Web site, 28, 36
Groove — Send Message dialog box, 51
Groove architecture, 68
Command Processor, 69
deltas, defined, 71
glue code, 70
Input-Processing-Output structure, 68
MVC (Model-View-Controller) structure, 68-69
platform services
Account Database, 72-73
Account Services, 72-73

Account Subsystem, 72
Communications Manager, 77-79
Communications Subsystem, 77-79
Component Manager, 74-75
Component Services, 74
Component Services Subsystem, 85
Customer Services Subsystem, 85
Download Manager, 75
Dynamics Manager, 75-77
Identity Services, 72-73
Idle Manager, 74
Install Manager, 75
My Groove Services, 85
OSD (Open Software Description) files, 74
Security Manager, 80-83
Shared Space Services, 75-76
Storage and XML Services, transactions, 79-80
Storage Manager, transactions, 79-80
UI Services, 73-75
Web Services, 84-8
Windows Manager, 73
shared spaces, 70-72
structures, 69-70
Virtual Message Queue, 69
Groove Component Catalog
downloading, 384
Web site, 156
Groove CSM Viewer Web site, 169
Groove Default skin, 152
images
changes, understanding, 154-155
editing, 154
modifying, 153
TransceiverWindow-Background.jpg, changing, 155-156
sounds, 162-163
standardtransceiver.tpl file, 152
Groove Development
directory, developing tools, 272
folder, 153
Groove Development Kit. *See* GDK
Groove Enterprise Integration Server (GEIS), 322, 340-341
***Groove JavaScript API Reference*, 214, 331**
Groove Login dialog box, 161
Groove Networks, 18
Groove Send Invitation dialog box, 43
Groove-standard components, 260
Groove.net
directory, 43
file, 38
groove.net folder, 152
GrooveButton, propertiees, 390
GrooveComboBox, properties, 388
GrooveDataViewerTool, 58
GrooveDefault folder, copying, 152
groovedefaultskinresources.tpl file, code for buttons, 157-158
groovedefaultskinresources.xml file, 152-156, 162
GrooveDefaultsSkinsTools.XML file, 165
GrooveDocumentShareEngine, 56
GrooveEdit, 388
GrooveElizaBot.tpl file, code, 337-339
GrooveGDK.exe file, 136
GrooveHeader, properties, 394
GrooveImage, properties, 390-391
GrooveListBox, properties, 391
GrooveListView, properties, 393-394
GrooveMenu, properties, 392
GrooveMultiCellLayout, Welcome screen, 271
groovestandardrecordschema.xml file schema, code, 148
GrooveStatic, properties, 389
GrooveTabControl, properties, 391
GrooveTimer, properties, 392
GrooveTreeView, properties, 394
GroovieTalkieLockButton button, code, 160

groups
ComponentGroups, 177, 181-182
dynamics of small group interaction, creating tools, 33
growth area potentials, peer-to-peer applications, 371
.GRV file extension, 117, 137, 141, 245
creating, 251-253
downloading, 323
injecting custom spaces, code, 324-325
for skins, creating, 167-168
tool descriptors, code, 118
tools, 150
TriviaQuiz4, code, 323-324
writing, 150
.GSL file extension, 56
guesses (TriviaQuiz2), handling, 219-220
guest role, members of shared spaces, 353

H

HAlignment property (Static), 195
hammer-and-pencil icons, 41
Has3DBorder property (GrooveHeader), 394
HasLines property (GrooveTreeView), 394
Header component (UI), 178
HeaderBackground.jpg file, 156
headers, ColumnHeaders component (DataViewer), 286
HeaderTextColor (Color values in skins), 395
Health Insurance Portability and Accountability Act of 1996 (HIPAA), 374
Height attribute
StandardDescriptors, 394
XYLayout, 387
Help
command (Help menu), 356
help files, 356-362
HelpInfoProvider (ComponentGroups), 181
hiding
columns, 282
trivia game answers, 317
HighlightBackgroundColor (Color values in skins), 395
HIPAA (Health Insurance Portability and Accountability Act of 1996), 374
histories
Groove, 18-19
OSD (Open Software Description), 114-115
peer-to-peer applications, 6-9
XML (eXtensible Markup Language), 88-90
HTML (Hypertext Markup Language), 89
<SCRIPT > tag, 188
<TABLE> tag, attributes, 183
Table, layout, 146
tables, tags, 183
<TD> tag, attributes, 183
HTMLTableLayout, 183-184
Layout property, 384
properties, 384-385
TABLE table element, 384
TD table element, 384-385
TR table element, 384
hybrid peer-to-peer architecture, 10
Hypertext Markup Language. *See* HTML

I

IconAlignmentTop property (GrooveListView), 393
IconListView component (UI), 179
IconProvider connection (GrooveListView), 394
icons, hammer-and-pencil or toolset, 41
ID
attribute, 99
property (GrooveMenu), 392
identities, 37-38
Identity Services, 72-73
Idle Manager, 74
IDREF attribute, 100
IDREFS attribute, 100
IGrooveVCardViewer, 52
IID (Interface ID), 331
Image component (UI), 178

Image Control, 60

Image property (GrooveImage), 390-391

ImageHeight property (GrooveTabControl), 391

ImageMaskURL property (GrooveTabControl), 391

images

- changes, understanding, 154-155
- DefaultToolBarBackground.jpg file, 155
- editing, 154
- groovedefaultskinresources.xml file, 154
- HeaderBackground.jpg file, 156
- MemberPaneBackground file, tracing through code, 154-155
- MemberPaneBackground.jpg file, 154
- modifying, 153
- NoviceModeBackground.jpg file, 155
- graphics, adding to Welcome screen, 273-274
- pictures, 25-27, 58-59
- Preview.jpg, 162
- StandardTabControlSelectedTab, 156
- StandardTabControlUnselectedTab, 156
- StandardTabs.jpg file, 156
- standardtransceiver.tpl file, 154
- TransceiverWindowBackground.jpg, changing, 155-156

Images folder, 153

ImageURL property (GrooveTabControl), 391

ImageWidth property (GrooveTabControl), 391

IMPLEMENTATION

- attribute (SOFTPKG), 248
- element (OSD), 115

Import command (File menu), 54

Import File dialog box, 54

importing

- calendars, 49
- discussion topics, 54
- records, 57
- vCards, 51

IndicateFocus property (GrooveButton), 390

IndicateMenu property (GrooveButton), 390

Individual Tools button, 41

information

- changes, tracking, 51
- clinical, distributing, 374
- external, access benefits, 322

InfraSearch (JXTA Search), 376

Initialization function, code to delete time initialization, 312

InitializationComponent (FAQ tool), seeding data into shared spaces, 329

Initialize( ) function

- code, 306-307
- rewriting, 304
- TriviaQuiz2, 214
- TriviaQuiz3, code, 226-227

Initialize method, 187

initializing TriviaQuiz3, code, 225-227

InitialValues property

- GrooveComboBox, 388
- GrooveListBox, 391

injected tools, overlaying templates, 261

injecting shared spaces, .GRV file, code, 324-325

injections

- testing, 168-169, 253-254
- troubleshooting, 253-254

injector files, 167-168, 245

Input-Processing-Output structure, 68

Install Manager, 75

installations

- options, verifying for tool publishing, 264
- TriviaQuiz, testing from Web sites, 320

installing

- components, 74-75
- Database Navigator Tool, 140
- Groove, 36-40
- templates, code, 124
- tool components, code, 125-130
- Tool Creator, 256
- Tool Publisher, 262

instant Groove, 71

instant messaging (Groove Instant Messaging Tool), 28-29

instructions, processing with <? processing instruction, 91
integration, centralized or multipoint, 334
Intel Philanthropic Peer-to-Peer Project (iPPPP), 13
Interface ID (IID), 331
interfaces
- IID (Interface ID), 331
- Play Trivia screen, 298-305
- UI, 178-179
- UI Services, 73-75

Internet service providers (ISPs), 7
Interval property (GrooveTimer), 392
invitations to shared spaces, handling 42-46, 81-83
Invite button, 44
Invite by Email button, 44
Invite CSR button, 323
Invite No One at This Time button, 41
Invite to Space button, 51
iPPPP (Intel Philanthropic Peer-to-Peer Project), 13
Iris Associates, 18
ISPs (Internet service providers), 7
issuing (sending) invitations to shared spaces, 42-45
Italic attribute (StandardDescriptors), 395

J

JavaScript API Reference, 214
.JPG file extension, 59, 62, 153
JXTA Search (InfraSearch), 376

K

Kapor, Mitch, 18
Kasnoff, Craig, 11
keyboard shortcuts
- Ctrl+V, 53
- Shift+down-arrow, 57
- Shift+Tab, 57
- Shift+up-arrow, 57

keys, public-key and secret-key technologies, 80
keystore files, opening, 265
keywords
- My, 337
- xmlns, 103

killer apps (peer-to-peer applications), 370
- existence of, 380-381
- features, 379-380
- Napster, comparing, 370

knowledge portals, peer-to-peer applications, 372-373
Known Groove Contacts, 43

L

Label property
- buttons, 184
- GrooveButton, 390
- GrooveMenu, 392
- GrooveStatic, 389
- Static component, 195

labels, TriviaQuiz2, 214-216
LabelText (FontStyle values in skins), 395
LANGUAGE element (OSD), 116
languages. *See also* XML
- GML (Generalized Markup Language), 88
- HTML (Hypertext Markup Language), 89
- meta-languages (XML), 90
- Perl, downloading, 138
- SGML (Standard Generalized Markup Language), 88-89

LargeButton, 161
LaunchURL
- button, 161
- property, 390-391

Layout component, code, 183-184
layout components, standardtransceiver.tpl file, code, 169-170
Layout property, 183
- HTMLTableLayout, 384
- MultiCellLayout, 385
- SingleCellViewContainer, 387
- Splitter, 387
- ViewContainer, 384
- XYLayout, 386

layouts
- Add Questions screen, viewing, 287
- adding to Welcome screen, 272-273
- cellularskintransceiver.tpl file, code, 171-172
- GrooveMultiCellLayout (Welcome screen), 271
- HTML Table, 146
- HTMLTableLayout, 183-184
- MultiCell, 146, 172
- Question Entry, code, 277-279
- SingleCell, 146
- Splitter, 146
- tool template skeletons, 183-184
- tools, 146
- TriviaQuiz1, creating, 194-195
- XY, 146, 172-173

Left attribute (XYLayout), 387

LeftPad attribute (SingleCellViewContainer), 387

licenses, GDK (Groove Development Kit), 137

lifetimes of shared spaces, 81-83

Line Color button or command (Draw menu), 62

lines (Sketchpad Tool), 62

link button, 161

links
- Calendar Tool, creating, 49
- to pictures, creating, 59

LinkText (FontStyle values in skins), 395

ListBox component (UI), 178

ListDataModel connection (GrooveListView), 394

listings. *See* code

ListText (FontStyle values in skins), 395

ListView component (UI), 178

loading tools into StockTools template, 327

Local Network Directory, 43

localhost directory
- mySkin folder, 153
- structures for templates and files, 317-318

localhost folder, directory structures, 244

Lock button, 160

Lotus Notes, 18

Lotus Symphony, 18

M

major versions of components, 351-352

Manager role, members of shared spaces, 353

managers
- Communications Manager, 77-79
- component, OSD (Open Software Description) redirection, 349-350
- Component Manager, 74-75, 119
- components, 346
- Download Manager, 75
- Dynamics Manager, 75-77
- Idle Manager, 74
- Install Manager, 75
- Security Manager, shared spaces, 80-83
- Storage Manager, transactions, 79-80
- Windows Manager, 73

managing
- component tree structures, 347-350
- contacts, 51-52
- documents, 375

manifests
- components, 247
- OSD (Open Software Description), 120-121, 130-131
- SOFTPKG, 120
- TriviaQuiz3.tpl file, code, 346-347

manually creating tools, 259-260

Manually, Through a File button, 38

markers, Unread Markers
- Discussion Tool, 53
- Outliner Tool, 58
- Pictures Tool, 60

marks, Unread Marks
- Calendar Tool, 49
- Sketchpad Tool, 63
- Web Browser Tool, 64

markup languages. *See also* XML
- GML (Generalized Markup Language), 88
- HTML (Hypertext Markup Language), 89

SGML (Standard Generalized Markup Language), 88-89

matchmaking

eBay, 372

peer-to-peer applications, 372

McAfee ASaP, 14-15

MemberPaneBackground file, tracing through code, 154-155

MemberPaneBackground.jpg file, 154

members of shared spaces, 46-47, 352-353

Menu

component (UI), 178

property (GrooveButton), 390

messages

Microsoft Message Queue, 323

Virtual Message Queue, 69

meta-languages, XML (eXtensible Markup Language), 90

methods, 187

Microsoft

and Groove partnership, peer-to-peer applications, 377-379

Message Queue, 323

OSD (Open Software Description), specifications, 115-117

Script Debugger, downloading, 141

Transaction Server, 323

Visual Interdev, 138

XML Notepad, downloading, 101

minor versions of components

numbers, 351

tools, changing, 351-352

Mnemonic property

buttons, 185

GrooveButton, 390

modal windows (complex), subforms, 366-368

Model-View-Controller (MVC) structure, 68-69

ModelGlue (DataViewer), 58, 285-286

models, OSD (Open Software Description), changes, 131-132

modes, stealth, 19

Month view (Calendar Tool), 48

More button, utilities, 51

More Colors command (Format menu), 61

More Fonts command (Format menu), 61

multicasting communications, 78

MultiCell layouts, 146, 172

MultiCellLayout

elements, 385

properties, 385-386

<MULTICOL> element, 271, 385

Multiple Computers

button, 38

Wizard, 38-39

multipoint integration, 334

<MULTIROW> element, 271, 385

MVC (Model-View-Controller) structure, 68-69

My Groove Services, 85

My keyword, 337

My Templates

directory, developing tools, 272

folder, creating, 142

MyCompany.com Web site, 348

mySkin folder, 153, 168

MySkin.GRV file, code, 167-168

mySkinDescriptor.xml file, 164

N

Name attribute

Columns property, 393

RecordSetEngine, 392

SOFTPKG, 248

ToolGlueCode, 186

XYLayout, 386

NAME pane attribute (Splitter), 387

names

of attributes, qualified, 103

drawings, 62-63

of elements, qualified, 103

reverse domain name packages, 347

SOFTPKG, 123, 350

spaces, colors, 163

of tools, changing, 42

namespaces
- attributes, qualified names, 103
- elements, qualified names, 103
- W3C recommendation, 102
- XML (eXtensible Markup Language) documents, 102-103

naming conventions, 187
Napster, 6, 15, 370
NAT (Network Address Translation), 7-8
Navigate Together button, 64
navigating Groove Database Navigator Tool window panes, 140-141
NavigationSubForm component (standardtransceiver.tpl file), 170
NCSA Mosaic, 7
.NET, peer-to-peer applications, 377-379
Netscape Communications, 7
Network Address Translation (NAT), 7-8
network services, distributed, 14-15
networks, Local Network Directory, 43
New Calendar Event dialog box, 48
New Event button, 48
New Sketch button, 63
New Topic button, 52
Next Unread command (View menu), 60, 63

NextQuestionButton
- code, 220
- else clause, code to add, 232
- functionality, building, 219-220
- TriviaQuiz1, 198-199
- TriviaQuiz3, code, 230

NextQuestionButton function, rewriting, 304
NMTOKEN attribute, 100
NMTOKENS attribute, 100
No Tools button, 41
Notepad (XML), downloading, 101, 138
Notepad Tool, 26, 60-61
notifications
- Conflict Resolution, 55
- of progress invitations to shared spaces, 44-45

NoviceModeBackground.jpg file, 155
NoviceModeHeader (FontStyle values in skins), 395
NoviceModeText (FontStyle values in skins), 395
numbers
- CorrectAnswerNumber, checking, 296
- versions (components), 351

O

OBJECT tag, 117
objects (XML), peer travel, 69
omnicasting communications, 78
OnCommand method, 187
online bill payment, 374
OnPropertyChanged
- code, 230-232
- function
  - *code to change, 315-316*
  - *parameters, 227*
  - *rewriting, 304*
  - *TriviaQuiz3, 227-229*
- method, 187

OnPropertyRemoved method, 187
OnRecordsetChanged( ) function, code, 307
OnViewContainerHide method, 187
OnViewContainerShow method, 187
Open Software Description. *See* OSD
Open Tool button, 272
open transactions, 226
OpenCola, 14
Options menu commands
- Roles, 353
- Send Message, 160

Orientation property (Splitter) 387
OS element (OSD), 116
OSD (Open Software Description)
- CODEBASE element, 116
- component manager, 346, 349-350
- Component Services, tool components, code to install, 125-130
- component tree structures, managing, 347-350

ComponentResourceURL, 120
components, definition, 346
DEPENDENCY element, 115
descriptors, code to find, 123-124
designing, 132-133
factory element, code, 124-125
fanout redirection, 349
files, 74, 245
code, 116-117
creating, 246-251
tools, 149-150
writing, 121-130
Groove, 117-119
assembly files, 132
ComponentURLProviders, 131-132
manifest, 120-121, 130-131, 346-347
SOFTPKG, 120
.GRV file extension, tool descriptors, code, 118
history of, 114-115
IMPLEMENTATION element, 115
LANGUAGE element, 116
Microsoft specifications, 115-117
model changes, 131-132
OS element, 116
.OSD file extension
tool descriptors, code, 119
writing, code, 165-166
PROCESSOR element, 116
samples, 244
SOFTPKG, 115, 123
templates, code to install, 124
TITLE element, 116
tool publishing, 263-265
Outliner Tool, 24, 56-58
records, importing and exporting, 57
Unread Markers, 58
outlines, Outliner Tool, 24
overlaying tool templates, 261
OverrideLabelPosition property (AnswerButton), 196-197
overview text (Help), 356-362
Ozzie, Ray, 18, 377

P

packages, reverse domain name package names, 347
pane attributes (Splitter), 387
parameters, OnPropertyChanged function, 227
parsers, TemplateParser, 120-121
participant role, members of shared spaces, 353
partnerships (Microsoft/Groove), peer-to-peer applications, 377-379
passphrases, 36-37, 81
Paste command (Edit menu), 59
pasting vCards, 50
paying bills online, 374
peer-to-peer (hybrid) architecture, 10
peer-to-peer applications
architecture, 9
challenges, 370-371
client/server applications, 8-11
clinical information, distributing, 374
connections, 371
decentralization, 371
decentralized collaboration (Unity), 15-16
distributed network services, 14-15
distributed processing, 12-13
distributed storage services, 13-14
document management, 375
future of
challenges, 370-371
clinical information, distributing, 374
decentralization, 371
document management, 375
growth area potentials, 371
killer app, 370, 379-381
knowledge portals, 372-373
matchmaking, 372
Microsoft/Groove partnership, 377-379
online bill payment, 374

peer connections, 371
personalization, 376-377
real-time collaborative publishing or searching, 376
shared spaces, 371
supply chain coordination, 373
user access, 371
growth area potentials, 371
history of, 6-7
ISPs (Internet service providers), 7
killer app, 370, 379-381
knowledge portals, 372-373
matchmaking, 372
Microsoft/Groove partnership, 377-379
NAT (Network Address Translation), 7-8
.NET, 377-379
online bill payment, 374
peer connections, 371
personalization, 376-377
real-time collaborative publishing or searching, 376
real-time searching, 376
shared spaces, 371
supply chain coordination, 373
user access, 371

peers, XML objects, 69

pEliza variable, setting with constructors, 340

Perl, downloading, 138, 252

permissions
members of shared spaces, 353
tool-level access control, 353-356

Permissions dialog box, 353, 366-368

personalization, peer-to-peer applications, 376-377

pictures, 25-27, 58-59

Pictures Tool, 25, 58-60

pipe (|), 99

planning tool development, 142-143

platform services (Groove)
Account Database, 72-73
Account Services, 72-73
Account Subsystem, 72
Communications Manager, 77-79
Communications Subsystem, 77-79
Component Manager, 74-75
Component Services, 74
Component Services Subsystem, 85
Customer Services Subsystem, 85
Download Manager, 75
Dynamics Manager, 75-77
Identity Services, 72-73
Idle Manager, 74
Install Manager, 75
My Groove Services, 85
OSD (Open Software Description) files, 74
Security Manager, shared spaces, 80-83
Shared Space Services, 75-76
Storage and XML Services, transactions, 79-80
Storage Manager, transactions, 79-80
UI Services, 73-75
Web Services
device presence, 84-85
Relay Server, 84
Windows Manager, 73

PLATO (Programmed Logic for Automated Teaching Operations), 18

Play Trivia screen
answer buttons, transitioning, 311-312
correct answers, hiding, 317
interfaces, 298-305
questions
adding, 311
numbering with RecordSetEngine, 305-311
scoring improvements, 312-316
timing improvements, 312

plus sign (+), 99, 140

populating edit controls on screens, 292-297

portals, knowledge for peer-to-peer applications, 372-373

PreferredHeight property, 182, 384

PreferredWidth property, 182, 384

Prefixing property (GrooveStatic), 389

presence, device presence, 84-85

presence servers, 78

Preview.jpg file, 162

Previous Unread command (View menu), 60, 63
PRMDataModelDelegate component, code to declare, 329-330
PRMDataModelDelegate.gsl file, code, 330-331
PRMGlue.gsl file, code, 331-333, 342-343
processing
- instructions with <?, 91
- iPPPP (Intel Philanthropic Peer-to-Peer Project), 13
- SETI@home, 12

Processor (XML), 90
PROCESSOR element (OSD), 116
ProgID property (ActiveXWrapper), 389
Programmed Logic for Automated Teaching Operations (PLATO), 18
programs, Eliza, 336-339
progress notifications, invitations to shared spaces, 44-45
Project Information screen, 318
projects
- creating, 263
- publishing, 266-267

prologs, XML (eXtensible Markup Language) documents, 91
properties
- AcceptedFileTypes (GrooveImage), 391
- AcceptFocus (GrooveButton), 390
- ActiveXWrapper, 389
- AddInterfacesAsItems (ScriptHost), 388
- AutoSize (GrooveButton), 390
- Background
  - *GrooveImage, 390*
  - *ViewContainer, 384*
- BackgroundColor
  - *GrooveComboBox, 388*
  - *GrooveEdit, 388*
  - *GrooveListBox, 391*
  - *GrooveStatic, 389*
- BackgroundStyle (GrooveStatic), 389
- Cancel (GrooveButton), 390
- Checkbox (GrooveButton), 390
- ClassInfoList (RecordSetEngine), 392
- CodeComponent (ViewContainer), 384
- Columns
  - *attributes, 393*
  - *GrooveHeader, 394*
  - *GrooveListView, 393*
  - *Name attribute, 393*
  - *Width attribute, 394*
- CommandURL
  - *GrooveButton, 390*
  - *GrooveMenu, 392*
- Connection (ViewContainer), 384
- Default (GrooveButton), 390
- DisplayTextWhenEmpty
  - *GrooveImage, 391*
  - *GrooveListView, 393*
- DropDownSize (GrooveComboBox), 388
- Editable (GrooveComboBox), 388
- ElapsedTimeDisplay, code to clear, 314
- Enable (GrooveTimer), 392
- Enabled
  - *GrooveButton, 390*
  - *GrooveMenu, 392*
  - *NextQuestionButton, 198*
- EnableDragDrop (GrooveTabControl), 391
- EnableErrorSupport (ScriptHost), 388
- EnforceInterfaces (ScriptHost), 388
- Font
  - *GrooveComboBox, 388*
  - *GrooveEdit, 388*
  - *GrooveStatic, 389*
- FontStyle (GrooveStatic), 389
- GameTime, code to display or remove, 314
- GoTo button, 158
- GridLineDescriptor, 283
- GrooveButton, 390
- GrooveComboBox, 388
- GrooveEdit, 388
- GrooveHeader, 394
- GrooveImage, 390-391
- GrooveListBox, 391
- GrooveListView, 393-394
- GrooveMenu, 392
- GrooveStatic, 389
- GrooveTabControl, 391
- GrooveTimer, 392
- GrooveTreeView, 394

Halignment (Static component), 195
Has3Dborder (GrooveHeader), 394
HasLines (GrooveTreeView), 394
HTMLTableLayout, 384-385
IconAlignmentTop (GrooveListView), 393
ID (GrooveMenu), 392
Image (GrooveImage), 390-391
ImageHeight (GrooveTabControl), 391
ImageMaskURL (GrooveTabControl), 391
ImageURL (GrooveTabControl), 391
ImageWidth (GrooveTabControl), 391
IndicateFocus (GrooveButton), 390
IndicateMenu (GrooveButton), 390
InitialValues
  GrooveComboBox, 388
  GrooveListBox, 391
Interval (GrooveTimer), 392
Label
  buttons, 184
  GrooveButton, 390
  GrooveMenu, 392
  GrooveStatic, 389
  Static component, 195
LaunchURL
  GrooveButton, 390
  GrooveImage, 391
Layout, 183
  HTMLTableLayout, 384
  MultiCellLayout, 385
  SingleCellViewContainer, 387
  Splitter, 387
  ViewContainer, 384
  XYLayout, 386
Menu (GrooveButton), 390
Mnemonic
  buttons, 185
  GrooveButton, 390
MultiCellLayout, 385-386
OnPropertyChanged, code, 230-232
Orientation (Splitter), 387
OverrideLabelPosition (AnswerButton), 196-197
PreferredHeight, 182, 384
PreferredWidth, 182, 384
Prefixing (GrooveStatic), 389
ProgID (ActiveXWrapper), 389
PushSoundURL (GrooveButton), 390
QuestionNumber
  changes, testing, 230
  code to reset, 314
  making into a property, 229
Radiobutton (GrooveButton), 390
RecordSetEngine, 392
ScriptHost, 388
SectionBackground, 182
SelectionMode (GrooveListBox), 391
SingleCellViewContainer, 387
SingleLine (GrooveButton), 390
Size (Splitter), 387
Sorts, 282-283
SourceCode (ScriptHost), 388
Splitter, 387
Static component, 195
Style
  buttons, 184
  GrooveButton, 390
  GrooveStatic, 389
  NextQuestionButton, 198
  Static component, 195
Text (GrooveEdit), 388
TextColor (GrooveListBox), 391
TextLimit (GrooveEdit), 388
Time, testing changes, 230
Tooltip
  buttons, 185
  GrooveButton, 390
  GrooveComboBox, 388
  GrooveEdit, 388
  GrooveImage, 391
ToolTip
  GrooveListBox, 391
  GrooveStatic, 389
UICommands (GrooveMenu), 392
UICommands Attribute (GrooveMenu), 392
URL (GrooveMenu), 392
Valignment (Static component), 195
ViewContainer, 384
Visible, 282, 393

WordBreak, Static component, 195
XYLayout, 386-387

property changes (TriviaQuiz3 screens), testing, 230-232

PropertyList
engine, tools, 147-148
questions, adding, 216
tool template skeletons, 182
TriviaQuiz2, 213

protocols
DPP (Device Presence Protocol), 78
RDV (Rendez-Vous), 78
SOAP (Simple Object Access Protocol), 323
SSTP (Simple Symmetrical Transport Protocol), 84
TCP/IP (Transmission Control Protocol/Internet Protocol), 7

public-key technology, 80

publishing
projects for tool publishing, 266-267
real-time collaborative, 376
skins, 163
descriptor files, creating, 164-167
.GRV files, creating, 167-168
injection, testing, 168-169
injector files, creating, 167-168
tools, 149-150, 244, 262
certificates, generating, 265
dependencies, adding, 265
descriptors, 149
files, adding, 264
.GRV file extension, 150, 245, 251-253
injection, testing, 253-254
injector file, 245
installation options, verifying, 264
OSD (Open Software Description) file, 149-150, 245-251, 263-265
preparing, 244, 262
projects, managing, 263, 266-267
tool descriptors, 245-246, 263-265
writing files, 245
TriviaQuiz, 317
certificates, creating, 319
with ToolPublisher Tool, 318-319

PushSoundURL property (GrooveButton), 390

Q

Quake, 18

qualified names of attributes or elements, 103

queries, data, 282

Question Entry screen, layout, code, 277-279

Question Input screen, Enter Question button, 290-292

question labels (TriviaQuiz2), 214-215

question mark (?), 98

QuestionInputLabel, adding to Add Questions screen, 279

QuestionLabel Static (TriviaQuiz1), 196

QuestionNumber property, 229
changes, testing, 230
resetting, code, 314

questions (trivia game)
adding, 216, 311
button functions and static components, combining, 298
entering, code, 290-292
numbering with RecordSetEngine, 305-311
totalQuestions variable, 311
TriviaQuiz2, displaying, 213

queues
Microsoft Message Queue, 323
Virtual Message Queue, 69

QuickAccessSubForm component (standardtransceiver.tpl file), 170

quizzes. *See* TriviaQuiz; TriviaQuiz1; TriviaQuiz2; TriviaQuiz3; TriviaQuiz4

R

RadioButton
button, 161
property (GrooveButton), 390

RDV (Rendez-Vous) protocol, 78

ReadOnly data, 282

real-time searching or collaborative publishing, 376
Recipients button, 43
Record Voice Memo button, 160
records
- Outliner Tool, importing and exporting, 57
- removing, 297-298

RecordSetEngine (DataViewer), 286-287
- ClassInfoList property, 392
- Name attribute, 392
- properties, 392
- tool template skeletons, 185-186
- tool templates, 179
- ToolCollections connection, 392
- tools, 148
- trivia game questions, numbering, 305-311
- URL attribute, 392

recovering data, 77
redirection, OSD (Open Software Description)
- component manager 349-350
- fanout, 349

redmondgrayskintransceiver.tpl file, 152
refined catalog structures, 94
Refresh icon button, 64
refreshing Web pages, 64
.reg file extension, 142, 192
registries, EnableCellBorders settings (TriviaQuiz1), 211
registry files, 137, 141-142
RegistryFiles folder, 141-142
Relay Server, 84
Remond Gray skin, redmondgrayskintransceiver.tpl file, 152
Remove Background Image command (File menu), 62
RemoveQuestionButton button, creating, 280
removing. *See* deleting
Rename Sketch command (Edit menu), 62
renaming, Sketchpad Tool, 42
Rendez-Vous (RDV) protocol, 78
ResetGame( ) function
- ElapsedTimeDisplay property, code to clear, 314
- else statement, code to replace, 312-313
- GameTime property, code to remove, 314
- QuestionNumber property, code to reset, 314
- transactions, code to place outside, 315-316

Respond button, 53
Return button, creating, 280
reverse domains
- name package names, 347
- notations, 132

Right Arrow button, 57
Right attribute (XYLayout), 386
RightPad attribute (SingleCellViewContainer), 387
roles
- creating, 354-356
- members of shared spaces, 353

Roles command (Options menu) or dialog box, 353
Root.osd file, location, 177
ROW element (MultiCellLayout), 385
rows
- <MULTIROW> element, 271
- Welcome screen, 271

RTFHelpProvider component, 356
RTFView component, 356
Rumor (VirusScan AsaP), 14

S

samples
- connectors, 323
- OSD (Open Software Description), 244

Save button, 52
Save Picture As dialog box, 59
Save to File button, 289
SaveEditsButton button
- creating, 280
- function, code, 296-298

saving
- accounts to files, 38
- Favorites, 63-64

Scale Eight, 14

Schema element (XML), 105

schemas

adding to Add Questions screen, 280-281

groovestandardrecord-schema.xml file, code, 148

XML (eXtensible Markup Language), 110-111

AttributeTypes, 105-109

background, 104-105

building, 105-109

catalog.xml file, code, 108-109

catalogSchema.xml file, code, 107-108

ElementTypes, 105-109

schools, Great Schools Now, Inc., creating shared spaces, 30-32

Schrage, Michael, 371

scoring (trivia game), improving, 312-316

screens

Add Questions, 275-278

buttons, creating, 280

components, adding, 279-281

DataViewer, 281-287

layouts, viewing, 287

QuestionInputLabel, adding, 279

schemas, adding, 280-281

changing, 287-289

edit controls, populating, 292-297

Enter Questions, 298, 317

Play Trivia

answer buttons, transitioning, 311-312

correct answers, hiding, 317

interfaces, 298-305

questions, 305-311

scoring improvements, 312-316

timing improvements, 312

Project Information, 318

Question Entry layout, code, 277-279

Question Input, Enter Question button, 290-292

questions, code for entering, 290-292

records, deleting, 297-298

TriviaQuiz1, 212

TriviaQuiz3

property changes, testing, 230-232

synchronizing, 229-232

Welcome, 270

borders, 271

buttons, adding, 275

cells, 271-272

columns, 271

graphics, adding, 273-274

GrooveMultiCellLayout, 271

layout, adding, 272-273

rows, 271

WelcomeTitle element, adding, 274

Script Debugger (Microsoft), downloading, 141

<SCRIPT> tag, 188

ScriptFreeThreaded-Component, 330

ScriptHost

glue code, 179

properties, 388

tool template skeletons, 187

scripting languages, Perl, downloading, 138

scripts, EnableScriptDebugging.reg file, 141-142

Search for Extraterrestrial Intelligence (SETI), 6

searching real-time, 376

secret-key technology, 80

SectionBackground property, 182

SectionBackgroundColor (Color values in skins), 396

security

ComponentSecurity element, tool templates, 177

identities, 37-38

public-key technology, 80

secret-key technology, 80

Security Manager, shared spaces, 80-83

Web Browser Tool, 64

Security Manager, shared spaces, 80-83

seeding data into shared spaces, 329

Select Contacts dialog box, 50

Select Recipients dialog box, 43

Selected Event command (File menu), 49

SelectedBackgroundColor (Color values in skins), 396

SelectedTextColor (Color values in skins), 396

SelectionMode property (GrooveListBox), 391

Send Message

- button, 51
- command (Options menu), 160

sending invitations to shared spaces, 42-45

sequence versions of components, numbers, 351

***Serious Play*, 371**

servers

- client/servers
  - *applications, 8-9*
  - *applications and peer-to-peer applications, comparing, 10-11*
  - *architecture, 8*
- GEIS (Groove Enterprise Integration Server), 322, 340-341
- Microsoft Transaction Server, 323
- Relay Server, 84

services

- Account Database, 72-73
- Account Services, 72-73
- Account Subsystem, 72
- Communications Manager, 77-79
- Communications Subsystem, 77-79
- Component Manager, 74-75
- Component Services, 74, 120
- Component Services Subsystem, 85
- Customer Services Subsystem, 85
- distributed network, 14-15
- distributed storage, 13-14
- Download Manager, 75
- Dynamics Manager, 75-77
- Identity Services, 72-73
- Idle Manager, 74
- Install Manager, 75
- My Groove Services, 85
- OSD (Open Software Description) files, 74
- Security Manager, 80-83
- Shared Space Services, 75-76
- Storage and XML Services, transactions, 79-80
- Storage Manager, transactions, 79-80
- UI Services, 73-75
- Web Services
  - *device presence, 84-85*
  - *Relay Server, 84*
- Windows Manager, 73

Set Element button, 283

SETI (Search for Extraterrestrial Intelligence), 6

SETI@home Project, 6, 11-12

SGML (Standard Generalized Markup Language), 88-89

shapes, Sketchpad Tool, 62

Shared Space Services, 75-76

shared spaces, 70-71

- authenticating, 81-82
- AWW (American Wooden Widgets), 32-33
- bots, 334
  - *bot configuration XML file, 336-337*
  - *bot template file, 337-340*
  - *developing, 335-336*
- creating, 40-41, 81
- data
  - *disseminating and writing, 82-83*
  - *seeding, 329*
- data integration, 322
  - *connectors, 323*
  - *data access, 331-333*
- deleting, 42
- deltas, 76, 83
  - *authenticators, 77*
  - *cleanup, 77*
  - *communicating, 78-79*
  - *defined, 71, 75*
- Development Space (GDK), 138
- dynamic creation, 323-331
- fetching, 40
- GEIS (Groove Enterprise Integration Server), 340-341
- Great Schools Now, Inc., 30-32
- Groove, 19
- .GRV file, code to inject, 324-325
- instant Groove, 71
- invitations
  - *progress notifications, 44-45*
  - *receiving, 45-46*
  - *sending, 42-45*
- inviting, 81-82

- lifetime, 81-83
- members, 46-47, 352-353
- passphrases, 81
- peer-to-peer applications, 371
- tools, 42, 72
- toolsets, defining, 325-329
- transceivers, 71-72
- uninviting, 83

Shift+down-arrow keyboard shortcut, 57

Shift+Tab keyboard shortcut, 57

Shift+up-arrow keyboard shortcut, 57

Shirky, Clay, 11-12

Show Overview command (View menu), 356

Show Picture List button, 58

Show/Hide Details command (View menu), 57

ShowElapsedTime function
- code, 218-219
- rewriting, 304

showError function, code, 288

ShowScore( ) function
- else statement, code to replace, 312-313
- GameTime property, code to display, 314
- transactions, code to place outside, 315-316

Simple Object Access Protocol (SOAP), 323

Simple Symmetrical Transport Protocol (SSTP), 84

SingleCell layout, 146

SingleCellViewContainer, properties, 387

SingleLine property (GrooveButton), 390

Size command (Format menu), 61

Size pane attribute (Splitter), 387

Size property (Splitter), 387

skeletons of tool templates
- buttons, properties, 184-185
- code, 189-192
- ComponentGroups, 181-183
- ComponentSecurity element, 180
- creating, 180
- Development Space, tools, 192
- engines, 185-186
- glue code, 186-189
- HTMLTableLayout, 183-184
- Layout component, code, 183-184
- layouts, 183-184
- PropertyList component, 182
- RecordSetEngine, 185-186
- <SCRIPT> tag, 188
- ScriptHost, 187
- ToolTemplate element, 180-181
- TYPELIB, 188
- view containers, component connections, 182
- ViewInfo component, 181
- windows, specifying heights and widths, 182

skeletons of tools
- creating, 257-260
- subforms, code to create and place, 362-366
- ToolSkeleton, code to modify, 257-259

Sketchpad Tool, 27, 42, 61-63

skins, 73
- .CAB files, creating, 163-164
- Cellular, 152
- cellularskintransceiver.tpl file, code to layout, 171-172
- change preparations, 152-153
- Color attribute (StandardDescriptors), values in, 395-396
- ContentViewContainer component (standardtransceiver.tpl file), 170
- DefaultToolBarBackground.jpg file, 155
- descriptor files, creating, 164-167
- FontStyle attribute (StandardDescriptors), values in, 395
- Groove, launching, 153
- Groove Default, 152
- Groove Development folder, 153
- groove.net folder, 152
- GrooveDefault folder, copying, 152
- groovedefaultskinresources.tpl file, code for buttons, 157-158

groovedefaultskinresources.xml file, 152-156, 162
GrooveDefaultsSkinsTools.XML file, 165
GroovieTalkieLockButton button, code, 160
.GRV files, creating, 167-168
HeaderBackground.jpg file, 156
images
changes, understanding, 154-155
editing, 154
modifying, 153
TransceiverWindowBackground.jpg, changing, 155-156
Images folder, 153
injection, testing, 168-169
injector files, creating, 167-168
MemberPaneBackground file, tracing through code, 154-155
MemberPaneBackground.jpg file, 154
MultiCell layouts, 172
mySkin folder, files, 168
MySkin.GRV file, code, 167-168
mySkinDescriptor.xml file, 164
NavigationSubForm component (standardtransceiver.tpl file), 170
NoviceModeBackground.jpg file, 155
.OSD files, code to write, 165-166
Preview.jpg, 162
publishing, 163-164
QuickAccessSubForm component (standardtransceiver.tpl file), 170
redmondgrayskintransceiver.tpl file, 152
sounds, 162-163
space names, changing, 163
StandardTabControlSelectedTab, 156
StandardTabControlUnselectedTab, 156
StandardTabs.jpg file, 156
standardtransceiver.tpl file, 152-154, 169-170
StdMenuBarForm component (standardtransceiver.tpl file), 170
TELESPACE PANE TOOLS cell (standardtransceiver.tpl file), 170
templates, changing, 162
TitleBarSubForm2 component (standardtransceiver.tpl file), 170
transceiver templates, 169-173
TransceiverButtonImages.jpg file, 156
TransceiverPushToTalkButton button, code, 159
transceivers, 152
XY layout, code, 172-173
Skins folder, 152
SmallIconButton, 160
SmallIconTextButton, 161
SmallTextButton, 161
SOAP (Simple Object Access Protocol), 323
SOFTPKG (OSD), 115
CODEBASE attribute, 248
component versions, names, 350
Groove manifest, 120
IMPLEMENTATION attribute, 248
Name attribute, 248
names, 123
VERSION attribute, 248
software. *See* OSD
sorting data techniques, 282
Sorts property, 282-283
sounds
audio chats, Audio Chat Tool, 29-30
Groove Default skin, 162-163
groovedefaultskinresources.xml file, editing, 162
space names, changing, 163
templates, changing, 162
SourceCode property (ScriptHost), 388
sources of tools, viewing, 261
space names, changing colors, 163
spaces. *See also* shared spaces
Development Space, tools, 192
Shared Space Services, 75-76
strategy (Groove), 20

specialized tools, 138
Database Navigator Tool
component authentication, disabling, 139-140
installing, 140
window panes, navigating, 140-141
Tool Creator Tool, 141
Tool Publisher Tool, 141
specifications, Microsoft OSD (Open Software Description), 115-117
Splitter, 146, 387
SSTP (Simple Symmetrical Transport Protocol), 84
Standard Generalized Markup Language (SGML), 88-89
Standard Tool Sets button, 41
StandardButton, 161
StandardDescriptors, attributes, 394-396
StandardIconButton button, 198, 280
StandardTabControl-SelectedTab, 156
StandardTabControl-UnselectedTab, 156
StandardTabs.jpg file, 156
standardtransceiver.tpl file, 152-154, 169-170
start times, 216
StateImagesURL button, 159
statements, else, replacing with ShowScore( ) or ResetGame( ) functions, 312-313
Static component
properties, 195
text, changing, 214-215
Static component (UI), 178
StdMenuBarForm component (standardtransceiver.tpl file), 170
stealth mode (Groove), 19
StockTools template, loading tools, 327
Stop Transmission button, 64
Storage and XML Services, transactions, 79-80
Storage Manager, transactions, 79-80
storage mediums, XML (eXtensible Markup Language) documents, 90
storage services, distributed, 13-14
strategy spaces (Groove), 20
StrongText2Color (Color values in skins), 395
StrongTextColor (Color values in skins), 395
Structured Text format, discussion topics, 54
structures
catalogs, 93-94
component trees, managing, 347-350
directory, localhost folder, 244
Groove architecture, shared spaces, 69-72
Input-Processing-Output, 68
localhost directory for templates and files, 317-318
MVC (Model-View-Controller), 68-69
tool templates, 143, 176
Style property
buttons, 184
GrooveButton, 390
GrooveStatic, 389
NextQuestionButton, 198
Static component, 195
SubForm components, 362
subforms
complex modal windows, 366-368
creating and placing in tool skeletons, code, 362-366
functions, combining into single components, 366
permissions dialog box, code to display, 366-368
Sun Microsystems, JXTA Search, 376
supplemental applications, 138
supply chain coordination, peer-to-peer applications, 373
Swarmcast (OpenCola), 14
synchronizing TriviaQuiz3 screens, 229-232
syntax, @[field name]=[field value], 282
systems
Account Subsystem, 72
Communications Subsystem, 77-79
Component Services Subsystem, 85
Customer Services Subsystem, 85

T

Tab component (UI), 178
table elements (HTMLTableLayout)
TABLE, 384
TD, 384-385
TR, 384
<TABLE> tag, attributes, 183
tables, HTML tags, 183
Tabular Text format, discussion topics, 54
tags
HTML tables, 183
OBJECT, 117
<SCRIPT > tag, 188
<TABLE> tag, attributes, 183
Table, layout, 146
<TD> tag, attributes, 183
TCP/IP (Transmission Control Protocol/Internet Protocol), 7
TD table element (HTMLTableLayout), 384-385
<TD> tag, attributes, 183
technologies, public-key or secret-key, 80
TELESPACE PANE TOOLS cell (standardtransceiver.tpl file), 170
TelespaceHeader (FontStyle values in skins), 395
telespaces, transactions, 225-226
TemplateParser, 120-121
templates
ActiveXWrapper, properties, 389
bot configuration XML file, 337
EnableMyTemplates.reg file, 142
GrooveButton, properties, 390
GrooveComboBox, properties, 388
GrooveEdit, properties, 388
GrooveElizaBot.tpl file, code, 337-339
GrooveHeader, properties, 394
GrooveImage, properties, 390-391
GrooveListBox, properties, 391
GrooveListView, properties, 393-394
GrooveMenu, properties, 392
GrooveStatic, properties, 389
GrooveTabControl, properties, 391
GrooveTimer, properties, 392
GrooveTreeView, properties, 394
HTMLTableLayout, properties, 384-385
installing, code, 124
localhost directory structures, 317-318
MultiCellLayout, properties, 385-386
RecordSetEngine, properties, 392
ScriptHost, properties, 388
SingleCellViewContainer, properties, 387
Splitter, properties, 387
StandardDescriptors, attributes, 394-396
StockTools, loading tools, 327
for sounds, changing, 162
tool, 143-149, 176-179, 261
ToolSetTemplate, defining, 325
for transceivers, 169-173
ViewContainer, properties, 384
XYLayout, properties, 386-387
Templates.XSS file, 261
Terminate method, 187
testing
DTDs (Document Type Definitions), 101-102
injections, 168-169, 253-254
TriviaQuiz from Web sites, 320
TriviaQuiz3 screen property changes, 230-232
text
chats (Text Chat Tool), 29
editors, 26, 138
overview
code to display, 357-362
Help, 356
Static component
changing, 214-215
properties, 195

Text property (GrooveEdit), 388

TextColor

Color values in skins, 395

property (GrooveListBox), 391

TextLimit property (GrooveEdit), 388

The Accelerator Group, 11

Thumbprint, 265

time

elapsed

DisableQuestionButtons( ) function, code, 219

displaying, 299-302

displays, changing, 303

ShowElapsedTime function, code, 218-219

TriviaQuiz2, 216-220

UserGuess function, code, 219

ElapsedTimeLabel, 197

ElapsedTimeListBoxControl, 197-198, 225

end or start times, 216

initialization, code to add or delete, code, 312

Time property, testing changes, 230

timing (trivia game), improving, 312

TITLE element (OSD), 116

TitleBarSubForm2 component (standardtransceiver.tpl file), 170

TitleLabel (TriviaQuiz1), 195-196

TitleLabel Static component, code, 195

Tool Creator Tool, 141

ColumnHeaders component, 286

DataViewer, adding to Add Questions screen, 281-285

installing, 256

ModelGlue component, 285-286

RecordSetEngine component, 286-287

screens, changing, 287

ToolCollectionsComponent component, 286

tools

building, 257-260

modifying, 260-261

sources, viewing, 261

templates, overlaying, 261

Welcome screen

buttons, adding, 275

graphics, adding, 273-274

layout, adding, 272-273

WelcomeTitle element, creating, 274

tool descriptors

creating, 245-246

.GRV file extension, code, 118

.OSD file extension, code, 119

Tool Publisher, 141, 256, 261

installing, 262

tools

certificates, generating, 265

dependencies, adding, 265

files, adding, 264

installation options, verifying, 264

OSD (Open Software Description) information, 263-265

projects, handling, 266-267

publishing, 262, 267

tool descriptor information, 263-265

tool skeletons

creating, 257-260

subforms, code to create and place, 362-366

ToolSkeleton, code to modify, 257-259

tool template skeletons

buttons, properties, 184-185

code, 189-192

ComponentGroups, 181-183

ComponentSecurity element, 180

creating, 180

Development Space, tools, 192

engines, 185-186

glue code, 186-189

HTMLTableLayout, 183-184

Layout component, code, 183-184

layouts, 183-184

PropertyList component, 182

RecordSetEngine, 185-186

<SCRIPT> tag, 188

ScriptHost, 187

ToolTemplate element, 180-181

TYPELIB, 188

view containers, component connections, 182
ViewInfo component, 181
windows, specifying heights and widths, 182

tool templates, 143-149, 176-179, 261

tool-level access control, 353-356

Toolbar component (UI), 178

ToolCollections connection (RecordSetEngine), 392

ToolCollectionsComponent component (DataViewer), 286

ToolGlueCode, Name attribute, 186

ToolHeader (FontStyle values in skins), 395

ToolPublisher Tool, publishing TriviaQuiz, 318-319

tools, 47. *See also* TriviaQuiz1; TriviaQuiz2; TriviaQuiz3; TriviaQuiz4

Add Questions screen, 275-278
buttons, creating, 280
components, adding, 279-281
DataViewer, 281-287
layouts, viewing, 287
QuestionInputLabel, adding, 279
schemas, adding, 280-281
adding, 42
Artifact engine, 147
Audio Chat Tool, 29-30
building in Tool Creator, 257-260
Calendar Tool, 21, 48-50
changing
in major versions, 352
in minor versions, 351-352
components, code to install, 125-130
Connectors example, code, 331-333
connectors, shared spaces (dynamic creation), 323-331
Contact Manager, 50-52
creating
dynamics of small group interaction, 33
manually, 259-260
data integration, 322
bots, 334-340
centralized, 334
connectors, 323
Database Navigator Tool
component authentication, disabling, 139-140
installing, 140
window panes, navigating, 140-141
DataViewer Tool, 58
deleting, 42
dependencies, adding, 265
descriptors, 149, 263-265
developing, 142-143, 272
Development Space, 192
DisableComponentAuthentication.reg file, 139
Discussion Tool, 21, 52, 148
Body window, 53
discussion topics, 54
tool templates, 179
Topics List window, 53
Unread Markers, 53
EnableComponentAuthentication.reg file, 139
engines, 147-148
FAQ
InitializationComponent, seeding data into shared spaces, 329
Tool, 323
files
adding, 264
writing, 143
Files Tool, 22-24, 54-56
forms, 145
GDK (Groove Development Kit), developing, 21, 137
GEIS (Groove Enterprise Integration Server), 340-341
glue code, 73, 149
Groove-standard components, 260
groovestandardrecord-schema.xml file schema, code, 148
.GRV file extension, writing, 150
injected, overlaying templates, 261
installation options, verifying, 264
Instant Messaging Tool, 28-29
layouts, 146
loading into StockTools template, 327

modifying in Tool Creator, 260-261
multipoint, 334
names, changing, 42
Notepad Tool, 26, 60-61
OSD file, 149-150
Outliner Tool, 24, 56-58
Pictures Tool, 25, 58-60
Play Trivia screen
answer buttons, transitioning, 311-312
correct answers, hiding, 317
interfaces, 298-305
questions, numbering with RecordSetEngine, 305-311
scoring improvements, 312-316
timing improvements, 312
PropertyList engine, 147-148
publishing, 149-150, 244, 262, 267
certificates, generating, 265
dependencies, adding, 265
files, adding, 264
.GRV file, 245, 251-253
injection, testing, 253-254
injector file, 245
installation options, verifying, 264
OSD (Open Software Description) file, 245-251, 263-265
preparing, 244, 262
projects, managing, 263, 266-267
tool descriptors, 245-246, 263-265
writing files, 245
RecordSetEngine engine, 148
screens
changing, 287-289
edit controls, populating, 292-297
questions, code for entering, 290-292
records, removing, 297-298
shared spaces, 72
skeletons, creating, 257-260
Sketchpad Tool, 27, 61
drawings, naming and deleting, 62-63
renaming, 42
sources, viewing, 261
specialized, 138
templates
ComponentSecurity element, 143
developing, 143-149
HTML Table layout, 146
MultiCell layout, 146
overlaying, 261
SingleCell layout, 146
Splitter layout, 146
structure, 143
ToolTemplate element, 143
XY layout, 146
Text Chat Tool, 29
Tool Creator Tool, 141
ToolPublisher Tool, 141, 318-319
ToolSkeleton, code to modify, 257-259
TriviaQuiz, 341-343
installations, testing from Web sites, 320
publishing, 317-319
unsigned, 139
viewing, 145-146
Web Browser Tool, 27-28, 63-65
Welcome screen, 270
buttons, adding, 275
graphics, adding, 273-274
layout, adding, 272-273
WelcomeTitle element, adding, 274

toolsets
defining for shared spaces, 325-329
icons, 41

ToolSetTemplate, defining, 325

ToolSkeleton, code to modify, 257-259

ToolTemplate element, 143, 177, 180-181

Tooltip property
buttons, 185
GrooveButton, 390
GrooveComboBox, 388
GrooveEdit, 388
GrooveImage, 391
GrooveListBox, 391
GrooveStatic, 389

TooltipBackgoundColor (Color values in skins), 396

TooltipTextColor (Color values in skins), 396

Top attribute (XYLayout), 386
topics of discussion, handling, 54
Topics List window, 53
TopPad attribute (SingleCellViewContainer), 387
totalQuestions variable, 311
.TPL file extension, 139-141
TR table element (HTMLTableLayout), 384
tracking information changes, 51
transactions
- durable, defined, 80
- open, 226
- ResetGame function, code to place outside, 315-316
- ShowScore function, code to place outside, 315-316
- Storage and XML Services, 79-80
- telespaces, 225-226
- TrivialQuiz3, code, 228-229

TransceiverBackButton, 161
TransceiverBackHistoryButton, 161
TransceiverButtonImages.jpg file, 156
TransceiverForthButton, 161
TransceiverForthHistoryButton, 161
TransceiverPaneTitleText (FontStyle values in skins), 395
TransceiverPushToTalkButton button, code, 159
transceivers, 71-72. *See also* buttons
- Groove, 19-20
- groovedefaultskinresources.xml file, 156
- skins, change preparations, 152-153
- standardtransceiver.tpl file, layout component, code, 169-170
- StdMenuBarForm component (standardtransceiver.tpl file), 170
- templates, 169-173
- TransceiverButtonImages.jpg file, 156

TransceiverWindowBackground.jpg, changing, 155-156
transitioning, answer buttons (trivia game), 311-312
trees, managing component tree structures, 347-348
- *component manager OSD (Open Software Description) redirection, 349-350*
- *fanout OSD (Open Software Description) redirection, 349*

TreeView component (UI), 178
trivia games
- Add Questions screen, 275-278
  - *buttons, creating, 280*
  - *components, adding, 279-281*
  - *DataViewer, 281-287*
  - *layouts, viewing, 287*
  - *QuestionInputLabel, adding, 279*
  - *schemas, adding, 280-281*
- Play Trivia screen
  - *answer buttons, transitioning, 311-312*
  - *correct answers, hiding, 317*
  - *interfaces, 298-305*
  - *questions, numbering with RecordSetEngine, 305-311*
  - *scoring improvements, 312-316*
  - *timing improvements, 312*
- questions, code for entering, 290-292
- screens
  - *changing, 287-289*
  - *edit controls, populating, 292-297*
  - *records, removing, 297-298*
- TriviaQuiz
  - *installations, testing from Web sites, 320*
  - *publishing, 317-319*
- Welcome screen, 270
  - *buttons, adding, 275*
  - *graphics, adding, 273-274*
  - *layout, adding, 272-273*
  - *WelcomeTitle element, adding, 274*

Trivia3.GRV file, 254
TriviaQuiz
- bots, 341-343
- CAB TriviaGraphics.CAB, 317

data integration, 341-343
help files, code to display, 357-362
installation, testing from Web sites, 320
localhost directory, structures for templates and files, 317-318
overview text, code to display, 357-362
publishing, 317
certificates, creating, 319
with ToolPublisher Tool, 318-319

TriviaQuiz.tpl file, opening in WordPad, 287

TriviaQuiz1, 192-194
AnswerAButton, 196-197
code, 200-211
ElapsedTimeLabel, 197
ElapsedTimeListBoxControl, 197-198
EnableCellBorders registry settings, 211
Enabled property, NextQuestionButton, 198
finished tool, 211-212
glue code, 199-211
layouts, creating, 194-195
NextQuestionButton, 198-199
QuestionLabel Static, 196
screen, 212
StandardIconButton, 198
Style property (NextQuestionButton), 198
TitleLabel, 195-196
TitleLabel Static component, code, 195

TriviaQuiz2, 212
answer labels, setting, 214-215
DisableQuestionButtons( ) function, code, 219
elapsed time, 216-219
Groove JavaScript API Reference, 214
guesses, handling, 219-220
Initialize function, 214
labels, changing, 215-216
NextQuestionButton, building functionality, 219-220
PropertyList, 213
propertyList, adding questions, 216
question labels, setting, 214-215
questions, displaying, 213
revised tool, 220-225
ShowElapsedTime function, code, 218-219
Static component, changing text, 214-215
UserGuess function, code, 219

TriviaQuiz2.tpl, glue code, 220-225

TriviaQuiz3
ElapsedTimeListBoxControl, 225
GameTime, disabling buttons, 232
Initialize function, code, 226-227
initializing, code, 225-227
NextQuestionButton
code, 230
else clause, code to add, 232
OnPropertyChanged
code, 230-232
function, 227-229
open transactions, 226
QuestionNumber property, 229-230
screens
property changes, testing, 230-232
synchronizing, 229-232
telespaces, transactions, 225-226
Time property, testing changes, 230
transactions code, 228-229
tweaking, 232-241

TriviaQuiz3.bat file, 252

TriviaQuiz3.tpl file
code, 346-347
glue code, 233-241

TriviaQuiz4, .GRV file, code, 323-324

TriviaQuizLayout
answer buttons, changing, 302
ChangeLabels function, rewriting, 304
code, changing, 298-299
components, deleting unused, 303
elapsed time, displaying, 299-303
factories, changing, 303
Initialize function, rewriting, 304
NextQuestionButton function, rewriting, 304
OnPropertyChanged function, rewriting, 304

questions, combining button functions and static components, 298
ShowElapsedTime function, rewriting, 304
troubleshooting injection, 253-254
Typeface attribute (StandardDescriptors), 394
Typeface command (Format menu), 61
TYPELIB, tool template skeletons, 188

U

UI
buttons
Label property, 184
Mnemonic property, 185
Style property, 184
tool template skeletons, 184-185
Tooltip property, 185
components, 178-179
Services, 73-75
tool templates, 178
UICommands Attribute property (GrooveMenu), 392
UICommands property (GrooveMenu), 392
Underline attribute (StandardDescriptors), 395
unicasting communications, 78
uninviting shared spaces, 83
Unity, 15-16
Unread Markers
Discussion Tool, 53
Outliner Tool, 58
Pictures Tool, 60
Unread Marks
Calendar Tool, 49
Sketchpad Tool, 63
Web Browser Tool, 64
unsigned tools, 139
unused components, deleting, 303
Up button, 57
URLs (uniform resource locators)
attribute (RecordSetEngine), 392
component resource, 349
ComponentResourceURL, 120, 177
ComponentURLProviders, OSD (Open Software Description), 131-132
property (GrooveMenu), 392
Root.osd file, location, 177
user access, peer-to-peer applications, 371
UserGuess function, code, 219
users, gestures, 75
utilities
CAB (cabinet) files, creatingWeb site, 153
GDK (Groove Development Kit), 137
More button, 51

V

VAlignment property (Static), 195
values in skins (StandardDescriptors)
Color attribute, 395-396
FontStyle attribute, 395
variables
pEliza, setting with constructors, 340
totalQuestions, 311
vCards, handling, 50-51
.VCF file extension, 51
VERSION attribute (SOFTPKG), 248
versioning components, numbers, 350-352
view containers
component connections, 182
tool templates, 177-178
View menu commands
Detect URLs, 61
Next Unread, 60, 63
Previous Unread, 60, 63
Show Overview, 356
Show/Hide Details, 57
ViewContainer, 182-183, 384
viewers, IGrooveVCardViewer, 52
ViewInfo component, 181
viewing
tools, 145-146, 261
Calendar Tool, 48-49
Virtual Message Queue, 69
VirusScan AsaP, Rumor, 14
Visible property, 282, 393

VisiCalc, 18

Visual Interdev (Microsoft), 138

W

W3C, namespace recommendation, 102

WeakTextColor (Color values in skins), 395

Web Browser Tool, 27-28, 63-65

Web pages, browsing or refreshing, 64

Web Services, device presence, 84-85

Web sites

- CAB (cabinet) files, utility to create, 153
- DevZone
  - *applications, supplemental, 138*
  - *GDK (Groove Development Kit), 136-137*
- Groove, 28, 36
  - *Component Catalog, 156, 384*
  - *CSM Viewer, 169*
- Microsoft
  - *Script Debugger, downloading, 141*
  - *XML Notepad, downloading, 101*
- MyCompany.com, 348
- Perl, downloading, 252
- SETI@home, 12
- TriviaQuiz, testing, 320

Week view (Calendar Tool), 48

Weizenbaum, Joseph (Eliza program), 336

Welcome screen, 270

- borders, 271
- buttons, adding, 275
- cells, 271-272
- columns, 271
- graphics, adding, 273-274
- GrooveMultiCellLayout, 271
- layout, adding, 272-273
- rows, 271
- WelcomeTitle element, adding, 274

WelcomeTitle element, adding to Welcome screen, 274

well formed XML (eXtensible Markup Language) documents, 90-91

Width attribute

- Columns property, 394
- XYLayout, 387

window panes (Groove Database Navigator Tool), navigating, 140-141

windows

- Body, 53
- complex modal, subforms, 366-368
- heights and widths, specifying, 182
- Topics List, 53
- TransceiverWindowBackground.jpg, changing, 155-156

Windows Color dialog box, 61-62

Windows Manager, 73

Windows Open With dialog box, 55

wizards

- Audio Tuning Wizard, 140, 161
- Create Space Wizard, 40-41
- Multiple Computers Wizard, 38-39

WordBreak property (Static), 195

WordPad, opening TriviaQuiz.tpl file, 287

writing

- data in shared spaces, 82-83
- DTDs (Document Type Definitions)
  - *attributes, declaring, 99-101*
  - *elements-only elements, 98-99*
  - *empty elements, 98*
- files for tools
  - *developing, 143*
  - *publishing, 245*
- .GRV file extension, 150
- OSD (Open Software Description) files, 121-130, 165-166

X-Z

XML (eXtensible Markup Language), 70, 88

- attributes, qualified names, 103
- Binary XML file, 54

bot configuration XML file, 336-337
catalogs, code to load data, 94-96
DCD (Document Content Description), 104
documents
attributes, code, 96-97
DTDs (Document Type Definitions), 91-102
elements, tool templates, 177
namespaces, 102-103
prologs, 91
storage mediums, 90
well formed, 90-91
elements, qualified names, 103
entity, 90
format, discussion topics, 54
GML (Generalized Markup Language), 88
Groove, 109-111
groovedefaultskinresources.xml file, 152
.GRV file extension, writing, 150
history of, 88-90
HTML (Hypertext Markup Language), 89
meta-language, 90
Notepad, downloading, 101, 138
objects, peer travel, 69
Processor, 90
redmondgrayskintransceiver.tpl file, 152
schema
AttributeTypes, 105-109
background, 104-105
building, 105-109
catalog.xml file, code, 108-109
catalogSchema.xml file, code, 107-108
ElementTypes, 105-109
Schema element, 105
SGML (Standard Generalized Markup Language), 88-89
standardtransceiver.tpl file, 152
Storage and XML Services, transactions, 79-80
W3C namespace recommendation, 102
.XML file extension, 49, 123

xmlns keyword, 103

.XSS file extension, 139

XY layout, 146, 172-173

XYLayout, properties, 386-387

Other Related Titles

ebXML
0-672-32367-2
Scott Neiman, Ron Schmelzer, et al.
$49.99 US/$74.95 CAN

An in-depth technical treatment written expressly for developers by several of the working group committee members and a team of managers with Oasis.

Building Web Services with Java: Making Sense of XML, SOAP, WSDL, and UDDI
0-672-32181-5
Steven Graham, Simeon Simeonov, et al.
$49.99 US/$74.95 CAN

Look for other Groove related programming and design titles during 2002!

SAMS
www.samspublishing.com

JXTA: Java P2P Programming
0-672-32366-4
Daniel Brookshier, N. Borwankar, D. Govoni, N. Krishnan, J. Soto
$39.99 US/$59.95 CAN

Focused on JXTA, developed by members of the Project JXTA Community.

XML and Web Services Unleashed
0-672-32341-9
Ron Schmelzer, Travis Vandersypen, Jason Bloomberg, Maddhu Siddalingaiah, et al.
$49.99 US/$74.95 CAN

Covers XML Fundamentals and applications as well as Web services.

Integrating XML and Web Services in a JSP Application
0-672-32354-0
Casey Kochmer and Erica Frandsen
$49.99 US/$74.95 CAN

JSP experts teach developers how to integrate XML and Web services.

All prices are subject to change.

What's On the CD-ROM?

The CD-ROM includes the Groove Development Kit, version 1.3; the Groove Preview Edition, version 1.3; and the Groove API Reference Guide.

Installation Instructions

Windows

1. Insert the disc into your CD-ROM drive.
2. From the Windows desktop, double-click the My Computer icon.
3. Double-click the icon representing your CD-ROM drive.
4. Double-click on `start.exe`. Follow the on-screen prompts to finish the installation.

NOTE

If you have the AutoPlay feature enabled, `start.exe` will be launched automatically whenever you insert the disc into your CD-ROM drive.

NOTE

This CD-ROM uses long and mixed-case filenames requiring the use of a protected-mode CD-ROM Driver.